The Church and Disability: The weblog disabledChristianity

by
Jeff McNair, Ph.D.

**To Kathi, my partner in ministry, and
Terry, Barb, Paula, Johnnie, Bert and Earnest**

Introduction

In April of 2004, I decided to put down in the form of a weblog, lessons I had learned and was in the process of learning about my experience with people with disabilities and the Christian church. I chose the title disabledChristianity because it was both about people with disabilities and the church, and how the church has been disabled by the lack of the presence of persons with disabilities.

Many of the experiences I shared there are positive and many were negative. I felt someone had to in some way confront the church about its lack of caring and at times outright negativity towards people with disabilities. You will find that the entries listed here are very confrontive. But they are written out of love for the church and a desire that it become what God intended it to be.

Let me be very clear in saying that I believe that the Christian church is God's answer to community integration and support for persons with disabilities and their families.

I say that because it is the answer to the community integration and support for persons without disabilities, and the Bible applies to all people equally.

It has been unfortunate, however, that the church has not recognized its role in the lives of persons with disabilities. In the many years that my wife Kathi and I have been involved in disability ministry, we have seen some growth, but there needs to be a place for people with disabilities in every church. Every church needs to be seeking to serve its whole community. Having a child born to me who has a disability, should not mean that I can no longer go to church or have to go to a different church.

As you read through the entries listed here, you will understand why this is important for the life of the local church and the Body of Christ around the world. You will learn about the negative attitudes within and outside of the church that need to be addressed today. You will learn about God's plan for people with disabilities. You will learn about who people with disabilities are. You will learn about ministry principles that the church should adopt to facilitate the spiritual growth of persons with and without disabilities.

It is my prayer, that the publication of the ideas developed in the disabledChristianity weblog in book form, might help to wake the church up to its responsibility towards persons with disabilities and their families. You will be encouraged by this book. You will be angered by this book whatever side of the issues you are on. I promise you it will make you think. Perhaps it will call you to action. Perhaps it will cause church leaders to repent. Perhaps it will provide "ammunition" for people with disabilities and their families. Perhaps it will challenge Christian schools, high schools, colleges and seminaries to open their eyes to the presence of nearly 20% of the population of the United States who experience some form of disability, and consider how the presence of these people impacts, program delivery. Maybe someday, I will not have the experience of asking the director of a seminary, "Do you discuss people with disabilities anywhere in your classes?" and being given the unapologetic response, "No." Perhaps someday, Christian colleges will be seeking to serve students with disabilities, rather than deliberately not offering programs that disabled students might be drawn to, out of fear of the Americans with Disabilities Act. Perhaps someday, Christian high schools will serve children with disabilities from Christian families, the siblings of their other students. Perhaps those who set themselves up as the Christian alternative to public school education, Christian schools, will be as interested in educating the disabled children of Christian families, as they are in their football program.

We as the church and its agents are the face of Jesus to the community, and by and large at the moment, the face we present indicates that we do not care about people with disabilities and this must change. If for no other reason than our desire to be obedient, this has to change. In order to be the complete body of Christ this has to change.

In the process of compiling this volume, the postings were significantly edited. My spelling is atrocious. If you go to the actual weblog at <http://www.disabledchristianity.blogspot.com>, you will see living proof. This is mostly because I just sit down with an idea and type off the top of my head. In this volume, very little if any content editing was done. Most of the essays here are as they originally appeared. The essays selected were the ones I felt were most relevant. You will find many others at the website that were not included in this volume. Additionally, this book only covers the first five years, so all entries beginning in 2009 are not present here.

Give this book to friends with disabilities having the ability to comprehend it (my experience is largely with persons with intellectual disabilities). Give this book to parents of children with disabilities. Give this book to your child's special education teacher or social worker or counselor. Parents of children with disabilities, and those with disabilities yourself, *please give this to your pastor* and ask him or her about it and what it implies needs to be done at the church. May God grant you favor with your leaders.

May the words provided here empower you the reader, and assist you in facilitating the change of loving people with disabilities, as that is what is needed in the Christian church.

Jeff McNair

The Church and Disability

Attitudes

Perfection and imperfection

As I have stated elsewhere in this blog, Kathi and I have adopted the practice of bringing friends of ours with intellectual disabilities to the Introduction to Special Education class when we teach it. We will bring 3 or 4 friends, interview them briefly, and then just allow our students to have the chance to sit down with the folks, grab a bite to eat and talk about whatever they want. The guest speakers know that they are there to help students understand the lives of people with disabilities, and are prepared to answer any question. At the end of the evening, students write a brief statement of reflection on the evening. Kathi is going through these reflection statements (hundreds of them) and looking at common themes.

In one of the papers, a student wrote, "why else would something perfect create imperfection but to set an example for us to follow." This is the type of thing students will often write, it is interesting from a variety of perspectives, some correct but mostly it is wrong. It is a platitude about disability and who God is.

First, the assumption is that those of us who do not have some recognizable, some diagnosable disability are somehow perfect and that those who do have a disability are somehow imperfect. That is the type of perspective that too many people have about who they are. They see themselves too much as "God's gift" even though they are drowning in their own sin, or trapped in their own vices, or just self impressed people. People with these characteristics are the "perfect" ones and those with some form of disability are the "imperfect" ones. In reality, we are all "imperfect" ones.

Second, God did and does create imperfect people and we all have the opportunity to observe it, from the example of imperfection in each and all of us. Perhaps we who are intellectually at a particular level deny our imperfection and those who are below that number do not have the ability to deny their imperfection. Even if they do, we intelligent ones find it cute or refreshing. We, however, are in more ways than not, identical to those with measured disability though we deny our imperfection.

So, third, in that way, those with disabilities are an example to us of us.

People with disabilities are not an example of imperfection to the perfect. They are an example of imperfection to the imperfect who think themselves perfect.

In that way, they are the example in a refreshing, nonthreatening manner. They do not come to us in their imperfection and say, look at me, follow my example. They come to us in their imperfection, and as we grow to know them and love them and in many ways become like them,

13

we say, "We are all the same." I am imperfect as you are imperfect. But you are also a creation in the Image of God as I am a creation in his image.

Fourth, people with disabilities are just people. This is the profound lesson that I have learned after 30+ years of interaction mostly with people with intellectual disabilities. They are not here to teach me lessons any more that I am here to teach them lessons. They are just people living their lives, and through the living of their lives I have the ability to benefit and learn from them in the same manner that I have the ability to benefit and learn from anyone else. However, to say that they are placed on the earth solely to help me learn something, is once again the result of my prideful self-impressed nature where I see the world revolving around me, and I see myself as perfect and they as something other. I have said elsewhere in this blog, people with disabilities are indispensable (ala 1 Corinthians 12:22), however, their lives have total value in themselves, not because of what they bring to me.

The notion of God creating imperfection is also very subjective. Is intellectual disability, for example, imperfection? It is certainly different. People with intellectual disability cannot do many of the things that people who do not have such a disability can. I am not one of those who denies that intellectual disability is disability. However, I am increasingly understanding intellectual disability more as difference. People can be successful in life with a wide range of ability levels. People also define success in a wide variety of ways. As a Christian, success is very antithetical to society's definition. Increasingly, I am understanding success from a Christian perspective, and I find that intellectual disability often becomes simply a difference relative to that success. It occurs to me that in his wisdom and his kindness, God sets the "success bar" at a level that is accessible to the majority of people, and simply says that to whom much is given much is expected (Luke 12:48). With that in mind, one must reexamine the notion of imperfection. If I haven't been given the intellect or opportunity to be a university professor, for example, am I imperfect? If I haven't the ability to build a wall straight, am I imperfect? If I haven't the ability to hold a family together because I cannot set the emotional tone, am I imperfect? If I haven't the ability to love others like a person with intellectual disabilities will often do, am I imperfect? I can choose a standard for perfection that I will succeed at and then use that as my plumb line, or I can use the plumb line that God provides for success and align myself with that. The notion of perfect and imperfect looks quite different when I align myself with God's notion of success or perfect.

It is funny that when I do the interviews I mentioned at the beginning, I ask one friend if he has a disability. He typically says, "I

14

don't think so." I then ask what would a person be like if he had a disability? My intellectually disabled friend doesn't talk about wheelchairs, or blindness, or inability to do something. He says "They can't get along with other people, swear a lot and get in fights." You could put a team of experts in disability in a room for a month and they probably would never come up with those criteria as the definition of disability. But I would have to say that my intellectually disabled friend's definition is probably much closer to what God would hold out as disability, as imperfection.

Monday, October 27, 2008

Scary questions and frightening answers

I have to admit that I like Quentin Tarantino movies. They are quirky and they make me think. In the film Pulp Fiction the dialogue between Vincent (John Travolta) and Jules (Samuel L. Jackson) is interesting. There is one point in the film where the following exchange occurs. Vincent says something to the effect "You are scaring me Jules." Jules responds,

> **"If my answers frighten you Vincent,
> then you should cease asking scary questions."**

That is the problem often, isn't it. We don't ask the hard, the scary questions because the answers will frighten us. You know I also think we have actually gotten to the point as a church where we have stopped asking some of the scary questions, perhaps because we have a good idea of what the answers would be.

Should my church make room for people with mental illness?
Should the Sunday school include children with autism?
Are worship services too knowledge oriented?
Do we love our neighbor as Jesus would have us love our neighbor?

The rich young ruler asked Jesus a question, for example, and he got a frightening answer (Luke 18:18). He didn't realize that his question was scary but it sure was. "What must I do to inherit eternal life?" I think he expected Jesus to say, "You know you are doing great. Just keep on doing what you are doing." But Jesus didn't say that. He said, "You lack one thing: go, sell what you own and give the money to the poor." Jesus' answer made the young man's question become a very scary question. It demanded him to change, to eschew his comforts, to step out in faith, to do something he had never done before, to take his commitment to God

15

seriously. You see if we ask the right questions, we may get frightening answers, but it they are from God, they are the best answers, the answers that will guide us to growth in our faith and in our likeness of Jesus.

But we first need to ask the questions and the questions are very basic, very very basic to what the Christian life is all about. Imagine asking questions like,

"Good teacher, should there be a place for everyone in the church, be they mentally ill, or physically disabled, or emotionally disturbed or mentally handicapped, or profoundly disabled, or are there some people who by their nature can be excluded from the church?"

"Jesus, am I loving my neighbor as a church if I pick and choose those in the community whom I will care about, particularly if I don't choose those who have been devalued, or are disabled, or are disenfranchised?"

"Lord, if the ways we do church from Sunday School to worship service, to social gatherings, to small group Bible studies are exclusive of particular people, are those programs worth retaining in their current form or should they be scrapped in their entirety and re-imagined with say, disabled people being present in mind?"

"Good teacher, if people with disabilities do not fit within the current structures of the church, should we exclude the people or change the structures?"

I suspect Jesus would look on us with love as he did to the man in the story because, hopefully we are asking out of a desire to be obedient. But I suspect his answers would rock our world.

But we must continue to ask these scary questions even though the answers truly do frighten me as well. As God reveals the answers to these questions to me, I pray that I will not "be shocked and go away grieving" because I was unprepared and unwilling to act in obedience to what I was told. I am asking the questions and I am beginning to understand some of the answers as they are revealed to me. May God give me, give us all the faith to do what we should do in spite of how the requisite changes will shock us and show us our disobedience.

Friday, January 04, 2008

"Missing Christ"

Tony Woodlief starts off his brief article "Missing Christ" (World Magazine, Nov.24, 2007) like this...

"I saw Christ on a street corner in Washington, D.C., disguised as an alcoholic felon. I don't often notice Christ. I can sit through entire church services and not see Him. I'll notice which worship songs are individualistic pabulum; I'll remember if the sermon is more about what the Bible doesn't say, or if the pastor is bent on setting people straight. But I'll miss Jesus, occupied as I am with criticizing on His behalf. So it was unexpected, this Christ-sighting."
(visit http://www.worldmag.com/articles/13529 for more)

That is the case with many churches, many Christians I believe. We come to church hoping to see Christ, and pass him on the way. Over time, we get so used to not seeing Christ at church that we think that is the way it is supposed to be. But getting used to things the way they are not supposed to be, is much different from enjoying things the way they are supposed to be. Both can bring a level of comfort and relaxation. Its just that one is not the truth and the other is. Woodlief goes on to say,

"For I was hungry and you gave Me food, Christ called out to me as I passed. It was late; I just wanted a meal and my comfortable hotel bed. But I made the mistake of eye contact. "They spit on me!" he shouted. It was so unusual that I stopped. He was crying with frustration. Someone had given him spittle instead of money. "

We do that in the church although hopefully not with actual spittle. But people wait in need, families wait in need, and we pass them by on our way to church and in the process of "doing church." We have been doing church in a way that is different from the way it is supposed to be and even though we know there are hurting people in the world, relative to this blog people with various disabilities, we get used to our comfortable yet wrong way of doing things. **The least of these, those who Christ says are his embodiment in the world right now are passed by. So we walk by the real Christ to worship a fictional Christ; a Christ of comfort and wealth and plenty and safety.**

Woodlief ends his article like this: "I wondered who blessed whom on that street corner, and if Christ will ever tire of coming to me in these ways, given how unfaithful I am in coming to Him."

Tough words which should give us pause. Jesus said that whatever you did **not** do for the least of these, you did **not** do for **me** (Matthew 25:45). No symbolism, no beating around the bush here. How much clearer, how much more direct could he have been?

Tuesday, December 04, 2007

From Sunday School to Seminary

I have been doing some writing lately related to the topic of inclusive religious education. I will keep you posted as the publication I am working on with a wonderful group of experts is made available.

Anyway in working through some of the ideas, I thought about religious education "from Sunday School to seminary" in relation to people with disabilities. Rarely are children with disabilities included in Sunday school to the degree such children are present in the community. In interactions with Christian kids at church, I have asked them where they have had experience with children with disabilities, and most often they will say in their class at public school. Some will relate experiences with children at church, but most experiences are not had at church. The same would be characteristic of Bible study groups of young people in Junior High School, High School or College. Few if any contacts with persons with disabilities as members of those groups, as the focus of ministry in those groups, or as a topic for discussion in those groups. They are ignored. In college, students study the Bible, or church ministry. Once again, it is as if people with disabilities have never existed. Even in Bible classes, where you would think people might be impressed by the text of the Bible (particularly the Gospels) that they are studying, little if any mention of disability or people affected by disabilities. In Christian ministry programs (I have personally spoken with directors of several) when asked if disability is mentioned in any of the classes, the response is either "No" or as a point of discussion in some ethics, or bioethics class. Finally, in seminary, perhaps the highest level of training of people preparing for leadership in the church and in ministry, once again there is little if any discussion of people with disabilities.

I have stated this elsewhere in this blog, but the US census says that nearly 20% of the population are people with disabilities. But to those in education in and around the church it is once again as if people with disabilities do not exist.

As I have thought through this, it tells me something about Christian religious education. To me at all levels, Christian education has a serious flaw. That people with disabilities would be overlooked on every level tells me that all levels of Christian education are wrong. They are wrong because they overlook some of the most needy, the poorest, the most disenfranchised people in the world. How could any group that claims to be Christian be so blind as to miss this group? To miss such a group in the light of the Gospels and the example of Christ is so wrong. Have those who do Christian education never met a person with a disability, never met the family of a person with a disability and recognized the socially imposed travails those people face? I don't know which would be more disconcerting...that churches have met such people and have ignored them, or that they don't know about such people. In either case, the response evidences a lack of caring. It causes me great concern to witness such blindness at every level. My concern is that this oversight is symptomatic of a pervasive lack of caring. This lack of caring is evidenced at **every** level of Christian education and that is disgraceful.

I have heard dozens of excuses from money, to training, to "I just didn't know" and all them are inexcusable. So God would tell us that those are all good reasons and would excuse us from caring? No, do something and find out what it would cost. Do something and learn in the process if you don't have training. Do something and find out how the life experience of people impacted with disability is the same or different as those not affected. Once again, if you really "just didn't know" what does that tell you about the religious education you have received at every level...I should probably include sermons in this discussion.

Additionally, every day we visit bathrooms that are handicapped accessible, or walk past handicapped parking spaces. Who are all these handicapped parking spaces and bathrooms for? Are they for figments of our imagination? Has the government lost its mind, or is it actually true that 20% of the population is disabled? No, things have to change in the Christian church. Christian education needs to become caring and particularly aware of the needs of the devalued members of the community.

May God forgive us for our practices at every level of so called "Christian" Education, from Sunday School to Seminary. No excuses. Just start doing what is right and teach about the caring that is or at least should be a critical aspect of the Christian faith. Otherwise we perpetuate a system that reproduces numb Christians with a significant flaw.

Sunday, November 18, 2007

Being shrewd

The pastor of my church gave a very interesting sermon last week about being shrewd (based upon Luke Chapter 16). I must admit that it was probably the first one I have ever heard on the topic, but it is something that more people should think about. One thing I have noted about Jesus himself is that he was shrewd in that he was never predictable. Just when someone thought they had him, he would come up with an answer or response that would totally surprise them. But he was not just clever in his answers, he was also shrewd.

We occasionally see Christians being shrewd. I remember when there was to be a huge Promise Keepers meeting in Washington D.C. one of the organizers was asked by an interviewer why Christian men should be trusted by women, be they Christian or not. His response was

19

something to the effect, "You shouldn't trust us." The interviewers were surprised. "You should test what we say by what we do, by our actions." They were expecting some self righteous justification, he agreed with them and as a result, he scored points with them and the audience listening.

As I listened to the sermon, though, I must admit I got caught up in verse 15 of the passage. It says, "You are the ones who justify yourselves in the eyes of men, but God knows your hearts. What is highly valued among men is detestable in God's sight."

Its true. We justify ourselves in the eyes of people, we look to the community for our approval too often, and at the very least, we look to the community for the methods we use in churches. There are too many business principles being applied to churches for my liking. Church growth can become a formula. Finance campaigns can be slick. People are judged and valued on the basis of what they can contribute to the church. Jesus says that what is valued among men is detestable in God's sight.

So I should step back and look at my church to see the things that are valued by men as they might actually be detestable things. I might also reverse the proposition and step back and look at the things which we think are "detestable" or at least less desirable, or problem causing, or whatever our negative feelings are, and ask whether they might be something that God delights in.

Is the exclusion of people with minor social skill deficits (or major ones for that matter) something that is valued by men? Is it something that people typically do? Do churches, and pastors, and adults, and teens, and children reject people on the basis of social skills? Is this accepted practice in the church setting? It is definitely accepted practice in the world of business or women's groups, or colleges, or high schools, or junior high schools, or elementary schools, or any other group. Social skills are definitely something that is highly valued by people in the world.

But I want to be shrewd, by God's standards.

You know I have related this before in this blog, but I often wonder why I see the things that I do relative to people with disabilities and the church. I am not the sharpest tool in the shed as the saying goes, and I also guarantee you that I am not a particularly shrewd person. I amaze myself quite often with how clueless I often am. But I feel like I am an investor in the 1970's who has heard about this thing called Microsoft (I might have my years wrong, but stick with me). So I see this amazing opportunity. In this case it is not an opportunity to make money. It is an amazing opportunity to correct the course of a Christian church which has not been going in the right direction. It has been "off course" in many ways. I see this opportunity to be obedient to God in ways that the Church perceives as entirely new ways. I see this opportunity to really learn what love means through loving people who some consider difficult to love. I see this opportunity to serve people who haven't been served, and provide wonderful opportunities for service.

If you are shrewd perhaps you will see it too.

Friday, September 21, 2007

"Do handicapped people go to hell?" One perspective...

Mike Hoggatt is a friend of mine. He is a friend for a lot of reasons, but for sure one of them is the way he sees the world. He has lived the whole group home scene, has worked with people with a variety of differences and disabilities of a variety of ages. He is a special educator, and an expert in adoption. Mike challenges me when we are together. We can get very excited when we get on issues of mutual interest. The last time we had the chance just to relax and talk was with another friend, Marvin Miller (Rayne ministries) at a burger place in Washington DC. It was great time, which will affect the direction of the National Association of Christians in Special Education (NACSPED) in its future development I suspect.

Mike hosts his own blog.. One recent entry is called, "Do handicapped people go to hell?" In it, he is wondering about people with intellectual or other disabilities that do not allow them to respond to the Gospel message in traditional ways. But the part of the entry that really touched me, was the following section that I quote from Mike's entry...

"Let's go back to the town of South Park for a moment. The children (vulgar, profane, etc) have been told by the priest that they are going to Hell...Rightly scared, they begin attending Sunday school. There they are taught about communion (which most have trouble understanding), confession and baptism. The boys take their eight year old understanding and attempt to get into Heaven. That is until one of the boys (Butters) runs up to the other boys full of concern. He tells the other boys that based on the rules they were taught (confession, communion and baptism), their friend Timmy will go to Hell because he can't confess (Timmy, if you remember, can only says his own name). Ultimately, the boys baptize Timmy themselves, but get little in the way of answers when they approach both the priest and the nun about Timmy (this led to the sequel of this episode to be titled- "Probably"). Unfortunately the real Church does little more to answer this meaningful question."

So a vulgar and profane television cartoon takes on the big issues of the Christian faith. What can we expect in the absence or more direction from the church itself? There may actually be some biblical truth in what the boys did, by the way. Look at the story of the paraplegic who was lowered through the roof to Jesus (Mark 2:2-12). The passage says, "When he saw their faith, he said to the disabled man, 'Your sins are forgiven.'" The South Park episode is obviously just a television story, but the baptism of Timmy by his 8 year old friends might be a perfect parallel to that passage. They believed what they were told about the importance of confession and became very concerned about their friend. Through God seeing their faith in baptizing Timmy, perhaps Timmy's sins were forgiven. When will we, the church, become concerned about the confession of our equally loved and valued by God, brothers and sisters with various disabilities to the point that we engage in acts of faith that will make a difference in the life of another?

I sometimes feel like the boys, particularly Butters concerned about friends of mine like Timmy and the lack of interest that the church has in them. Does it ever occur to you as you read this blog that I am a special education professor not a theologian? It concerns me if it doesn't concern you. Where are the theologians who are writing about issues of Christianity and disability? There are a few, but there are only a few. The South Park boys baptize Timmy because they believe what they were told, and think they understand the ramifications to their friend. The church leaders who were over them had no answers for them. Although once again just a story, it is not far from the truth that a bunch of vulgar 8 year olds in a profane television cartoon are concerned about their intellectually disabled friend's salvation when the priest and the nun are not (and I am in no way only challenging the Catholic Church, I am challenging the WHOLE Christian church). Theologians and pastors might be quick to criticize and dismiss their act on theological or other grounds, and I am in NO WAY advocating watching this television program, but what ARE the leaders doing? Criticize me, correct my perspective please, because if you did, that would imply that you are thinking about the issues, at least for the moment you are criticizing.

And when asked about the ramifications of disability on a person's relationship with God, church leaders are at best unable to figure it out, but at worst don't give a damn. Where is the theological discussion to try to flesh out these issues? Whenever I meet someone who is trained as a pastor, or in theology, who has even the remotest of interest in disability, I literally beg them to write about the issues for uninformed rank and file Christians, an uninformed clergy, uninformed seminary faculty, uninformed Christian leadership and so on.

The fact that many of these questions are unclear could be due to the issue itself, but I would doubt that the average church pastor could

22

explain the nuances of salvation for intellectually disabled people because THEY HAVE NEVER THOUGHT ABOUT IT!

As a result, you have people like me, some better, some worse who are out there trying to make sense of disability from a Christian perspective because those who should be doing the heavy theological lifting are not.

Wednesday, October 22, 2008

A real life metaphor

This past week in church, my pastor related the story of a man who saved his son who had fallen into a septic tank. The story might not typically get someone's notice except for the fact that the adult son who fell into the septic tank was a man with Down's syndrome and the man who saved his son, sacrificed his own life so that his son could live.
Thomas Vander Woude apparently held his son's head above the sewage water by somehow holding him on his shoulders or in some other way holding him up, while sacrificing his own life in the process.

My pastor used this story as a beautiful illustration of Christ coming to Earth (diving into a septic tank) in order to save those who were there, and ultimately sacrificing His own life to save ours. I will allow you to fill in the blanks relative to other aspects of the metaphor. But I was thinking more about the value this father put on the life of his son with Down's syndrome.

At the moment it is reported that 90% of children who are prenatally diagnosed as having Down's syndrome are aborted. Without getting political, that is one reason that Gov. Sarah Palin's decision to give birth to her son with Down's syndrome is actually quite remarkable. By that act, she places herself among the 10% of other women who were in that position and chose life.

But even more interesting, more worthy of consideration is that here is a man who after 20 years with a son with Down's syndrome saw his son's life as important enough that he would sacrifice his own life so that his son could live. It is a very powerful example to people who would make "decisions" about the lives of others, when they know little or nothing about those lives. I am not just talking about parents, but more those in the medical profession and those in pro-choice organizations both of whom probably have never had a cup of coffee with a person with Down's syndrome, or watched a ball game with someone to get to know them as persons. However, doctors may be quick to advocate for the prevention of their lives through abortion. If people really want to understand what disability is, they need to get with people with disabilities themselves as well as with people like parents and friends who really know them well.

Monday, September 22, 2008

Compartmentalizing disability

I am a person who became interested in persons with disabilities, particularly intellectual disabilities because of the way they drew me in, accepted and loved me when I was a college freshman. As a result of that group of adults back in 1974 with whom I just played basketball, or soccer or whatever else they wanted to do when we met on Friday nights, I have now spent over 30 years working to educate people with similar disabilities, working to educate those who educate them, and working to see they are full members of the community including the local Christian church. I have no family members who are disabled so that my involvement with people with disabilities has been a choice on my part. In contrast, many people that I know have had the life experience of disability thrust upon them by virtue of having a disability themselves or being the family member of a person with a disability.

But even in the best of situations, because my involvement is a choice, it can result in a kind of compartmentalizing of disability. I have the luxury of compartmentalizing my life, such that I am able to include or not include with people with disabilities in my life. In that regard, I am probably a part of the majority of people. I started to think about that idea of compartmentalizing disability.

For myself, I visit friends at a group home once per week. I involve myself with people at church every Sunday and at times when there are other events (which is pretty often). But it occurred to me that my "disabled life" occurs largely on Wednesdays and Sundays for about 7 hours a week. Often I talk with friends on the phone and other times we meet together just as friends do. With effort I get together for coffee once a month with friends, sometimes initiated by me and sometimes initiated by my friends, and I try to help people with problems as they arise. I understand that many people, particularly parents and people with disabilities themselves cannot compartmentalize which is a huge difference between them and myself. I can become unavailable if I want to for some reason, they must always be available. Groups attempt to provide respite care for parents such that they can explore other aspects of their lives, but even when they are benefiting from respite, they are still "on call" such that they are only physically absent for a brief while.

The question I have for myself is, how can I reduce the compartmentalization of my life in relation to people with disability? I have tried to make myself available in the midst of a busy work schedule and phone calls help to blend aspects of my life together. But I struggle with how, short of adopting a person with a disability, or having some with disability living in my home, I can live a more integrated life. I am not foolish enough to think or imply that life with disability is in any way easy, although I have learned that people do become accustomed, become used to their lives as they are lived.

I also wonder, at times, whether life with people who are intellectually disabled, when it is a choice because they are disabled, is little more than philanthropy? That implies a one way street in the definition of inclusiveness. I think that perception is the reason why many efforts to facilitate inclusive programs fail. Those without disability may see it as all giving on their part. They don't see the involvement as mutually beneficial. Until they do, efforts at inclusion are destined to live or die on the basis of philanthropy.

For myself, my efforts to break down the compartmentalization of disability in my own life are in part based upon philanthropy, I must admit, however I also have other motivations. I meet with my friends because they are truly my friends. I laugh with all of my friends, I am interested in what they are doing, I enjoy being with them, they enjoy being with me. When I am away from all of my friends I think about them. When I am away from friends I worry about issues I know they are facing in their lives. I try to defend them when I perceive them being threatened. I guess I recognize the impact all of my friends have made on my life and that is the reason why I don't want to compartmentalize them, but want our lives to blend. I freely commit myself to relationship like I do to any relationship and that commitment makes demands on me which I also freely embrace. At least that is what I hope to attain. It results in a blurring of the lines between characteristics of people. I see this blurring through the eyes of my intellectually disabled friends in the way they see people with and without disabilities and it is a very refreshing characteristic that I hope to learn.

Wednesday, September 10, 2008

Unencumbered by knowledge...

Kathi and I have been getting lots of emails about the new movie regarding comments made in the movie that demean persons with intellectual disabilities. I suspect that the movie is easily missed, however, it is important to note that the jokes are jokes and comments that many people routinely make. I don't think that the movie is leading the culture in this area, but more likely is reflecting the culture. I am confident that many people have either heard or hear others referring to someone as a "retard" or "retarded" but perhaps have not given it much thought.

Although I too am angered by the jokes, they are reflective of a larger problem of speaking about things about which they have no knowledge. Back in May of 2004, I related on this blog the story of David Hyde Pierce, who played Niles on Cheers and Frazier the Cheers spin-off. He was back then a spokesperson for Alzheimer's disease. Back then I wrote the following.

By contrast, David Hyde Pierce (Niles Crane on the television program Frazier) has been a strong advocate for persons with Alzheimer's disease. Recently, on the occasion of his birthday, there had been attacks on President Reagan by comedians regarding his Alzheimer's disease. Once again, without entering into the political fray (I have no idea what Mr. Pierce's political affiliation is) he stated that there are two types of people who make jokes about others with Alzheimer's. First, there are those who have never experienced the disease. Wisely he says he hopes they will continue to be able to make such unkind jokes as that would imply they have never experienced the disease. May they live on without ever having to face the ongoing debilitation and humiliation of one you deeply love. Second, are those who make jokes to try to ease their own pain or the pain of their loved ones who do have the disease.

Now, I wouldn't compare life with a person with Alzheimer's disease with a life with a person with intellectual disability/intellectual disabilities. But the principle illustrated by Mr. Hyde Pierce's comments fits perfectly. We will often make jokes about things that we don't understand.

We will also make pronouncements, at times about things we know nothing about. Recently the radio talk show host, Michael Savage, made ridiculous comments about autism and children with autism. Savage is know for his inflammatory rhetoric about political matters, however, at least in this case, he ventured into areas about which he knows nothing. I have had my heart broken by the insensitive people in grocery stores with their comments about controlling one's child as a parent struggles with their screaming child with autism. They have no idea of the courage it sometimes takes for a parent to even take a child with autism to a grocery store, only to be criticized by onlookers, potentially empowered by comments from some radio personality who literally has no idea what he is talking about. I have even heard the respected commentator, Michael Medved make comments about homeless mentally ill people and how they need to be in institutions. I would easily embrace nearly any inconvenience they could cause me if it meant keeping them out of institutions that can be so horrible. Are there people who could benefit

26

from increased supervision of one kind or another? Of course there are. However, I might advocate for such supervision, not so they would be gotten out of my face, but more because of the manner in which the quality of their lives would be improved.

But as a friend of mine, Dr. Bob Henderson once related to me, "Unencumbered by knowledge, they speak with great authority."

Once we do see the life of a person with intellectual disabilities or experience the love they give to others, we change our perspective. Once we see the way in which they are discriminated against by society, we should change our perspective. We begin to see these things as issues of social justice. That is, jokes that perpetuate negative stereotypes about innocents are working against social justice for those who are the butt of such jokes. So I think the issues are worthy of attending to and are worthy of bringing to the attention of those who make comments in the name of making someone laugh that demean others who are largely defenseless. We literally demean people and support negative attitudes about people in the name of "fun".

I will not be seeing this movie or any movie that demeans persons with intellectual disabilities. I will not be viewing any television program that demeans persons with intellectual disabilities.

I will not be viewing any "entertainment" which uses the demeaning of persons with intellectual disabilities as a vehicle for laughter at their expense.

Tuesday, August 12, 2008

Choosing to be "smart"

I just finished reading the book *Just Courage* by Gary Haugen, founder of International Justice Mission. He makes the following comments (pp. 118-119).

"The fact is, when people choose to be brave instead of smart, their courage is generally so threatening to those who are smart rather than brave that they end up being maligned, not congratulated. This is what the Bible says we can expect... So sometimes we have to decide: Are we going to love, or are we going to look smart? Because loving the needy doesn't look smart. And, sadly, in much of our culture this is one of our deepest fears: looking like a fool, naive, unsophisticated, a little too earnest, a loser... Generally, there is no wealth and very little regard in helping the needy... Sometimes the will of God is scary because he is asking us to choose between a life that looks successful and a life that is actually significant, between a life that wins the applause of our peers and a life that actually transforms lives through love."

That is often the issue with ministry to people with disabilities, particularly people with intellectual disabilities, the ones that I believe God has called me to serve. How is it smart to be in ministry to people with intellectual disability? But Haugen asks the real question that is behind a lot of the disinterest in devalued people. He says, "Are we going to love, or are we going to look smart?" Is it smart to minister to people who aren't going to "get better." What will people think of me if many of my friends are mentally handicapped? Will I be the victim of some form of sympathy stigma? I do run that risk. It is true that "Generally, there is no wealth and very little regard in helping the needy." To quote A League of Their Own, "It's supposed to be hard! If it wasn't hard, everyone would do it."

But there is the potential that a life will be transformed through love. The change to bet on is the change in your own life. The love learned is the love you learn. But they are not always easy lessons, so be prepared to be maligned.

It is also interesting how people will dismiss themselves from work with the needy, particularly those who are needy with intellectual disabilities. It is funny to most special educators, because the typical line you hear when you tell someone that you are a special ed teacher is that they say, "I don't have the patience for that." Not, "I would like to learn the patience for that because I hear patience is involved" or even, "I have heard that you need to be patient. Is that true?"

Significance of a life can be defined in a variety of ways. But I think most often significance is determined on the basis of what you did for others. And others, is a pretty open ended criteria. People respect a person who gave their life for the needy. So why aren't we doing more of that if that is what is remembered. People will sometimes lament the time others spent trying to make money, but rarely the time spent with people.

Saturday, August 09, 2008

A spiritual disconnect

Rec'd this link from a student of mine, Geoff.
http://www.ragamuffinsoul.com/?p=4757
The link depicts a man holding up his adult son with cerebral palsy while they are worshipping together. Check it out...you will have to scroll down the page a bit.

After the picture and the brief story, there are many comments. Listen to a few of them...

"What an awesome example of what it really is all about."
"beautiful… Jesus hands and feet "

28

"THIS is worship"

"I'm humbled"

"Your post really touched my heart. May we all take lessons from Matt and Jefferson"

"True worship sacrifice! Amazing! Thanks for hitting us over the head again"

"Wow. That is beautiful"

"speechless..."

"Amazing... Grace... Compassion... Authenticity..."

"Unreal man. Completely amazing"

"absolutely beautiful"

"I think the entire Church can learn true authenticity from this picture"

"... tears in my eyes ..."

"This is the best thing I've ever seen. this is the best thing I've ever seen. this is the best..."

"Sometimes God sends people like that along for us to wake us up"

"Wow! That is precious! THAT is what it's all about! Sacrifice - Worship - Praise - Hope! Yes. And so the question is almost. Was he real? Was he an angel?"

There is a disconnect here for me as I see the picture and read the comments. Yes it is wonderful that a father would love his son and assist him to participate in worship. But there are thousands of people who have no "father" to assist them in worship. The comments almost feel like posing sometimes because if people really felt it was so wonderful, why wouldn't they do it as well? The comments should read, "I think the entire Church can learn true authenticity from this picture and I am going to find a disabled person that I can help too." or "This is the best thing I have ever seen and I am going to be a part of it by helping a disabled person." or "THIS is worship and I want to be a part of facilitating worship for someone else." Is it only if you have a son with a disability that you facilitate a worship experience for someone? Would you ever facilitate worship for someone with a disability if you didn't have that person as a son or daughter?

If we are "Real" we will not just recognize the beauty of the situation, we will be a part of the beauty. If I tell you that your service to the poor is beautiful but never help with my giving or my time, I am a poser. If I am "Real" I will do something.

Another side of me that is disconnected is that a man assists his son who is disabled at a church and this is amazing. Why is it amazing rather than commonplace? It would be commonplace if it is happening all the time. Is it amazing that a father is helping his son? No, fathers help their sons all the time. I am confident that the father himself would say it is no big deal and in many ways, he is right.

Well, then...
Is it amazing because it is too infrequently observed at a church?
It is infrequent that disabled people are worshipping at church in community numbers.
Is it amazing because a disabled man's worship is being facilitated by someone else?
It is infrequent that someone assists another in worship.
Is it amazing because one man is having his worship "interrupted" in order to facilitate the worship of another?
It is infrequent that a disabled person's worship is a priority for someone else such that worship becomes something other than an uninterruptible individual experience.

Is it amazing because worship becomes transformed into something that it typically cannot be because we have been taught that worship is something that I do by myself and if someone for whatever reason imposes himself on me (through noise, or activity, or functional disability, or whatever) he should be removed so that I can worship?
It is amazing because it is worship in a different form. It is two men who are achieving an apparently nontraditional form of worship which entails one loving, being patient with, and facilitating the worship of another. However, in that service, the one being served also transforms the worship of the servant.
Probably to most people at church, the presence of a person with disability "imposing" themselves upon them, "interrupting" their worship is a cause for complaint. "How am I supposed to worship when so and so makes me have to hold him up so he can sing and dance along with everyone else?" "How am I supposed to worship in song when so and so sings and mostly is just making a loud, off tune noise?" "How am I supposed to worship during the sermon when so and so will not sit quietly and listen?" "How am I supposed to worship when so and so bothers me continuously with their inappropriate social skills?" I mean people complain if the music is not the right genre for goodness sake. You see these things are linked. It is supposedly so beautiful to see a father be imposed upon by his son and DELIGHT in that and use it as a means of service to his son. It is supposedly so beautiful that a son would not be ashamed of his need for assistance but would DELIGHT in the assistance he needs in order to participate in worship.
Let's not be posers, Christian. If service is beautiful when I see it in someone else, it is also beautiful for me. If "interrupted" worship is

beautiful for someone else, because it displays love in a kinda way it is supposed to be, then I should be more open to interruption. Worship needs to adapt to the impositions of imperfect people who are socially more imperfect than I due to their disabilities. My level of imperfection is acceptable, theirs causes me to reject them.

Let's be truly "Real," Christian, and do the thing we celebrate without excuses. Let's make the beautiful, the amazing acts of love commonplace such that when we see them, we still appreciate them but we are not amazed by them because they are not the rarities that they presently are. If it is beautiful to be loving and patient with people, let's make that the mundane within the Church.

Wednesday, May 07, 2008

Alarmed by numbers

I have been preparing a portion of a class for a certificate program that is being offered by the Joni and Friends organization. Should be good. I am talking about "intro to disability" Steve Bundy (their Christian Institute on Disability director) is talking about "the church and disability" and Kathy McReynolds (the CID policy person) is teaching about "bioethics and disability". Taken together is should be interesting. If you are interested in the certificate program, you should go to the Joni and Friends website to find out more.

Anyway, in the process of preparing, I have been looking through some historical issues related to disability in general, in the US. It is interesting that around the turn of the century, the early 1900's, that people became alarmed at what appeared to be a sudden rise in the numbers of people with disabilities. This apparent sudden rise was at least in part due to the fact that IQ tests had just been developed and used on large groups of people, institutions had been started promising rehabilitation and even cures for persons with severe disabilities so that people were coming forward in large numbers to receive services, as well as the urbanization of American society, such that people who had been doing fine in a rural setting, were not faring as well in an urban setting. Anyway, those and other factors, led to an apparent sudden rise in the number of people with disabilities who were coming to the attention of the general public. It was not a real rise in the actual numbers of people with disabilities, it was just that those who had been hidden in the past were coming out of the shadows and being seen for the first time.

As I think through this historical reaction to people with disabilities, I wonder whether there might be a similar reaction within the church. That is, people with various disabilities have largely been excluded from the church, or the church has not made the effort to reach out to them.

Imagine if the numbers of people with disabilities in the community suddenly came forward to take their place in the average local church. If a church of 1,000 suddenly had 90 people with severe disabilities, and 200 people with disabilities overall, would they react thinking that either they were singled out as the place where people with disabilities choose to go, or would they think there was a sudden epidemic in their area in disability as indicated by the numbers who were coming to their church. I doubt they would recognize the fact that 9% of our population has severe disabilities, and the fact that 20% overall of our population have a disability is just a reflection of US census figures for our country.

I cannot tell you how many times I have heard from people, "I just didn't know" when told about people with disabilities in the community. "I didn't know they were there." "I never thought about it."

So imagine if those who have never thought or didn't know were suddenly faced with a church of which 20% of the congregation was disabled in some way. How might they react? I suspect they would in fact react, and probably in a negative way.

One of the things we who are in the know a bit about disability can start to do, is to share with congregational leaders, to share with people we know, to share with anyone who will listen at church that 20% of our population is disabled, and 9% are severely disabled in order to prepare them for the coming of people with disabilities to church. In this way when they do, LORD WILLING, arrive, we will not be alarmed, but will rather be thinking, we knew they would be here eventually. We had heard that they were out there, but just hadn't come to church yet.

Monday, March 17, 2008

No accommodations

As I often do, I received an email from a parent today who spoke about how his daughter with a learning disability had been in Christian schools, unidentified but supported, throughout elementary school with pretty good success. However, as she entered Junior High, also at the Christian school, she began to have difficulty keeping up. She had to stop involvement in extracurricular activities as homework would consume her after school hours. The man contacted the school and asked for help for his daughter. He wondered whether she could perhaps be given a little more time on assignments or tests and quizzes, or whether perhaps less homework could be assigned. He indicated that the school replied in the following manner...

"One teacher, the supervisor for 3 others, stated that the school does not have a certificate of completion program there and so will not be able to accommodate or reduce what is required of her. I don't even know what that means."

He was not asking about a "certificate of completion" only extra help so his daughter could complete the work. No wonder he didn't know what they were talking about. But I am dismayed by the response and the lack of desire to help this parent and his daughter. In the public schools, a 504 plan might be the solution, however, because the school is private, many of the same regulations do not apply. **Literally, after years of participation in the Christian school, this family can be dismissed with a wave of a hand when a child begins to fall behind academically.** Elsewhere in the email it was implied by teachers that the child was not struggling academically (the implication being that the parent was not seeing the child struggle with homework every night) or that she just needed to work harder (denying the fact that the girl did indeed have a mild disability).

It would bother me much less if this were just some secular private school with who knows what set of standards they are reflecting. But this is a school that has identified itself with the Lord, Jesus Christ. As His agent, there is a different level of responsibility for service. This parent is being told that Christians do not understand, do not have compassion, do not want to help and are unwilling to change to assist a young girl with a **mild** disability. I wish this were not typical. I pray that God will not allow this to happen in the future. These who set themselves apart from the secular world of education and call themselves Christian are acting in a far from Christian manner. In reality, in the sphere of education, the secular world is acting much more Christian than probably 95% of the Christian schools in the United States are. But the saddest part is that they read a posting like this...

...and they don't care.

Thursday, January 17, 2008

Putting disabled people on display

As I was doing some work on my computer last night, I had the first night of the new American Idol season running in the background. As I watched something bothered me.

With such a program you have the typical people who are entering a singing contest who cannot sing. You have people who act crazy just in the hopes that they can be on TV, particularly on a show that is watched by a lot of people. You have people who think they can sing, and can to some extent but just not to the level of being selected to move on in the competition. But I saw something very different last night.

There were at least two people in the competition who struck me as being either mildly intellectually disabled, people who had perhaps high functioning asperger's syndrome, or were perhaps even mentally ill or emotionally disturbed. At times it seemed that these people provided the "comic relief" for the program. No doubt they provided "entertainment" value. Put a person with mentally illness in front of a camera and upset them (whether or not it is justified) and they will do things that are very different than what people might typically see in the community. But the "entertainment" they provided was comparable to watching someone with a physical disability in some sort of sideshow display. They draw our interest in a prurient kind of way (although not sexual in this context). It is an interest in seeing someone self-destruct, watching the mentally ill person act mentally ill. The individuals portrayed did not draw our compassion as did one of the scenes where an African-American woman was actually comforted by the evaluators. We were drawn to look because people were acting crazy due to a disability, all the while knowing that they were in some way aberrant which was the actual reason for their acting the way they did. Yet the camera did not turn away. It forced us to look and was actually a catalyst for the inciting of further irrational behavior.

I was very uncomfortable with the whole presentation for this reason. The program in some ways incites devalued people to aberrant behavior and then watches. It hopes for, aches for the crazy person to act crazy.

If I were to present myself before the judges thinking that I had a singing voice worthy of even moving to the next level, you would do me a favor by telling me that I should pursue some other area in my life as my singing voice will not take me most anywhere. However, if I am intellectually or emotionally disabled in some way, to use my display of irrationality due to my disability as a point of entertainment is not appropriate.

Wednesday, January 16, 2008

Understanding your experience

The following excerpt is from the book *Adam* by Henri Nouwen.

"How did I come to realize all that was happening to me?

One day a few months after I had arrived at Daybreak a minister friend who had taught pastoral theology to many students for many years came to visit me. He arrived after I had completely shifted and forgotten my initial, narrow vision of Adam. Now I no longer thought of him as a stranger or even disabled. We were living together, and life for me with Adam and the others in the home was very "normal." I felt so privileged to be caring for Adam, and I was eager to introduce him to my guest.

When my friend came to the New House and saw me with Adam, he looked at me and asked, "Henri, is this where you are spending your time?" I saw that he was not only disturbed but even angry. "Did you leave the university, where you were such an inspiration to so many people, to give your time and energy to Adam? You aren't even trained for this! Why do you not leave this work to those who are trained for it? Surely you have better things to do with your time."

I was shocked. My mind was racing, and I thought but did not say, "Are you telling me that I am wasting my time with Adam? You, an experienced minister and a pastoral guide! Don't you see that Adam is my friend, my teacher, my spiritual director, my counselor, my minister?" I quickly realized that he was not seeing the same Adam I was seeing. What my friend was saying made sense to him because he didn't really "see" Adam, and he certainly wasn't prepared to get to know him.

My friend had a lot more questions about Adam and the people who lived with me in my home: "Why spend so much time and money on people with severe disabilities while so many capable people can hardly survive?" And, "Why should such people be allowed to take time and energy which should be given to solving the real problems humanity is facing?"

I didn't answer my friend's questions. I didn't argue or discuss his "issues." I felt deeply that I had nothing very intelligent to say that would change my friend's mind. My daily two hours with Adam were transforming me. In being present to him I was hearing an inner voice of love beyond all the activities of care. Those two hours were pure gift, a time of contemplation, during which we, together, were touching something of God. With Adam I knew a sacred presence and I "saw" the face of God." (p. 52-53)

Nouwen gets so many things perfectly right in this section and illustrates how others can get things so wrong at the same time. The Bible teaches about how all people have equal value in God's eyes. It teaches how interactions with the "least of these" are interactions with Jesus himself. It teaches how love is the greatest commandment. It teaches that we should pour ourselves out in service, in the same manner Jesus did. Surely Jesus had better things to do than wash his disciples feet. Surely there were smarter people he could have given his time to than a bunch of fishermen.

Nouwen relates that his friend was a teacher of pastoral theology as a point, I think, of saying how the "experts" have gotten things all wrong.

They may think themselves experts in pastoral theology but they have not done pastoral theology to the point of understanding it. In the church, we have knowledge but not love. I wonder how many professors, how many experts, how many church leaders, how many university programs have anything to say about disability? I met recently with a dean of a pastoral program (training leaders in Christian ministry at a respected university) who indicated that they don't talk about disability anywhere in their curriculum. Do we need to list the times that Jesus interacts with disabled people and stick it under their noses before they realize that these people were a priority for him? It is an example of what I have spoken of elsewhere regarding how Christian religious education, from Sunday school to seminary has gotten it all wrong. Ignoring people with disabilities when you claim to be an agent of Jesus Christ speaks volumes about your lack of understanding of what is really important. It is about loving people independent of their personal characteristics. At the moment, we appear to love people or not love people, care for people or not care for people, prioritize or not prioritize people on the basis of their characteristics and that implies a very basic misunderstanding of the Christian faith at its most basic point, love.

I had the experience once of being asked by a pastor to head up the men's ministry at church because "working with those disabled people is just a black hole for service." This church leader compared people with and without disabilities and not only indicated that one group was better than the other, he even ridiculed those who would work with persons with disabilities as if they are wasting their time.

Teachers of students with severe disabilities, whether Christian or not, have also had the same experience. If you were to ask a teacher of students with severe disabilities, "Has anyone ever told you that you were wasting your time, wasting your professional life because of the students you are working with?" they will no doubt respond, "Yes." Students have told me how friends, family, parents, other teachers have all made such comments. I don't expect those who have not yet committed themselves to Christ to understand these issues from a Biblical perspective, but surely we might expect enlightenment from those within the church, within the Christian academic community, from those in Christian leadership, but unfortunately it is too often **not** the case. And as Nouwen states, "I didn't answer my friend's questions...I felt deeply that I had nothing very intelligent to say that would change my friend's mind." Do you catch that point? It is once again the notion of knowledge. I need something intelligent to say change someone's mind. Paul says, "The man without the Sprit does not accept the things that come from the Spirit of God, for they are **foolishness** to him and he cannot understand them, because they are spiritually discerned" (1 Corinthians 2:14). How foolish to waste your life with persons with severe disabilities. How very foolish. I will not say that people who do not understand these issues are "without the Spirit," however, I will say that if you, particularly as a Christian leader do not understand these issues, there is much room for spiritual growth. I continue to hammer on these issues, as did Nouwen through his life of writing, but I understand his feeling of not even being able to respond. You feel like the person who criticizes ministry to persons with severe disabilities doesn't understand the most basic of Biblical principles. It is a breathtaking lack of understanding.

Monday, January 14, 2008

Saving people in groups

I have talked elsewhere about the John 9 story of Jesus healing the blind man (see April 26, 2004 blog entry for one). However, I was touched recently by a passage further on in chapter 9. The blind man who was healed was being questioned by the church leaders.

A second time they summoned the man who had been blind. "Give glory to God, " they said. "We know this man is a sinner." He replied, "Whether he is a sinner or not, I don't know. One thing I do know. I was blind but now I see!"

This is really powerful to me. The blind man apparently did not know who Jesus was, but he is ready to come to his defense. Not because he had come to faith, or because he was convinced by some spiritual argument, but because he was blind and now could see. It strikes me that we as the church have missed a lot of such opportunities in the lives of disabled people. Not that they will necessarily be healed, but that we can be loving and caring to them. I can hear the following conversation...

"You know those Christians are judgmental and intolerant. They are religious zealots and dangerous. They believe in a nonexistent god." He replied, "Whether they are what you say or not, I don't know. One thing I do know is that I was alone and now I have friends. I was excluded and now I am included. No one loved me and now people love me."

That is the type of opportunity we are missing. Like my posting in 2004, the Glory of God is seen in what we do. "I don't know who their God is, but I am willing to find out because of what they have done for me."

Later, Jesus finds the man. Look at his response to Jesus in verses 35-38.

Jesus heard that they had thrown him out, and when he found him, he said, "Do you believe in the Son of Man?"

"Who is he, sir?" the man asked. "Tell me so that I may believe in him."

Jesus said, "You have now seen him; in fact, he is the one speaking with you."

Then the man said, "Lord, I believe," and he worshiped him."

I have known people with disabilities who have been accepted instead of being rejected. They have actually responded something to the effect, "Who is he so that I may believe in him?" That is the power of what we do when we reach out to rejected people. We help them to see the Glory of God in the way they are loved and accepted.

One other thing I note about this story is some of the things mentioned about the parents. It doesn't say that the blind man was begging. It just says that Jesus saw a blind man. Jesus says that the parents' sin was not the reason for the man's blindness. The parents tell the leaders, "Ask him. He is of age; he will speak for himself." His parents said this because they were afraid of the Jews.

I find these three facts/quotations interesting. At least according to this account, the man must have been cared for somehow if he wasn't begging. Perhaps it was his parents. They were not the reason for his blindness due to sin, perhaps in the form of lack of attending to him as a boy, or abuse, or something else they may have done. Also, they say that he can speak for himself. Actually, he speaks very well for himself. I suspect this blind man when he was a blind boy was well cared for and taught well to be able to interact with the church leaders in the way he did. I also note, however, he knows what a prophet is (that's what he says Jesus is), and his response to the church leaders is very telling about his upbringing. Verse 27 and following,

"He answered, 'I have told you already and you did not listen. Why do youwant to hear it again? Do you want to become his disciples, too?'

Then they hurled insults at him and said, "You are this fellow's disciple! We are disciples of Moses! We know that God spoke to Moses, but as for this fellow, we don't even know where he comes from."

The man answered, "Now that is remarkable! You don't know where he comes from, yet he opened my eyes. We know that God does not listen to sinners. He listens to the godly man who does his will. Nobody has ever heard of opening the eyes of a man born blind. If this man were not from God, he could do nothing."

38

The church leaders didn't believe he had been born blind so apparently for whatever reason he was not really known to them. But he knows how to exactly hit their buttons by asking if they want to be his disciple and by the statements he makes about who God is. His confidence as a blind man must be from his upbringing. The limited knowledge he has about God must have come from his family. When confronted about their son, the parents are scared, however, it appears they did a pretty good job in taking care of their disabled son. He is cared for, intelligent, and self-confident.

Additionally, he was waiting, on some level, to be told who the Son of Man is so that he might believe in him. First, someone needed to get his attention by addressing the thing that had separated him from the rest of the community, his disability. Jesus heals him, but we can at the least, accept people and refuse to make disability their defining characteristic. We can love and accept people. One other thing, what do you want to bet that as a result of Jesus' intervention into the man's life that his parents who appeared to care for him also became his followers. That is something that we must remember. It could be that when you love and accept people with disabilities, people get saved in groups, as families who are desperate for acceptance for their children and themselves.

Thursday, September 27, 2007

"I don't pass to girls"

When my daughter was younger, she played basketball, and me being a father who wanted her to play and enjoyed her playing, would often coach her teams. I remember when she was maybe 9, I was coaching her team at the YMCA. It was the first game of the league. Amy was the only girl on the team. I remember that at the start of the game, she would often be open, waving her hands, but the boy playing guard on the team would not throw the ball to her. This happened several times, Amy open, but no pass. I finally called a time out, and brought the team over. I asked the little guy playing guard,

"Did you see that Amy was open under the basket?"
He said, "Yeah."
I asked, "Then why didn't you throw the ball to her?"
He replied very matter-of-factly, "I don't pass to girls."
"You don't pass to girls?"
"No, I don't pass to girls."
I responded, "Well we have a place for players who don't pass to girls. It's called the bench."

Shortly after that interaction, probably before the end of the first half, he went back in the game and started to pass to the one girl on our team.

I believe there is a lesson here for us. In the game of YMCA basketball, you can pass to girls, or you can sit on the bench.

Fast forward 10 years. I had a conversation with a pastor who related that some of the people in leadership in the church, particularly people in leadership of small Bible study groups felt uncomfortable with people in their Bible study groups who were disabled, or didn't have perfect social skills. He wondered what he should do? I think the question was perhaps related to how he might limit the numbers of disabled people in a group, or change disabled person involvement in such a way that the leader didn't feel so uncomfortable. My response was that basically if you are a leader who can't handle disabled people, you probably shouldn't be a leader. You don't pass to girls, you get benched from the basketball game. You don't accept people with disabilities, you are disqualified from the leadership, you are benched.

Here is a further example.

OK, pick an ethnic/racial group, any ethnic/racial group. Imagine your leader coming to you and saying, "I don't like people from this particular ethnic/racial group in my Bible study." Your response would be:

a. "Yeah, I don't like those kinds of people either"

b. "You are benched"

Sure we could add another potential answer, like, we will provide you training before we put you in a position of leadership, or help you to get to know people, or whatever. That could be another option. But basically, the only responses are "a" or "b."

You might say, "But it is different if the people are disabled." I might even agree somewhat. There is no reason for people with profound intellectual disability to be in the Bible study group. But anyone who has the potential to understand even minimal levels of the content should be there. Anyone who would benefit from the social aspects of the interactions could be there as well. But social skill deficits are not a reason for excluding involvement. Particularly if they are minor.

Unfortunately, the Christian church's response has too often been "a." Look at the involvement of people with disabilities in churches, look at the involvement of people with disabilities in Christian schools, look at the lack of information shared about disability on Christian colleges, in departments of Christian ministry, in seminaries, look at the lack of sermons on disability that have been shared from the pulpit, look at the number of ministries to persons with disabilities at churches.

Matthew 23:23 says, "Woe to you, teachers of the law and Pharisees, you hypocrites! You give a tenth of your spices—mint, dill and cumin. **But you have neglected the more important matters of the law— justice, mercy and faithfulness**. You should have practiced the latter, without neglecting the former."

"Yeah, I don't like those kinds of people either"

Apparently, that is a statement some church leaders would attribute to Jesus Christ...

I think he would tell the leaders,

"Well, we have a place for leaders like you. It's called the bench."

Monday, September 24, 2007

Making their cry my own

Jean Vanier makes the following comment in his book, *Community & Growth: Our Pilgrimage Together* :

"Often a community stops crying out to God when it has itself stopped hearing the cry of the poor, when it has become well satisfied and found a way of life which is not too insecure. It is when we are aware of the distress and misery of our people and of their oppression and suffering, when we see them starving and sense our own inability to do anything about it that we will cry loudly to God: "Lord, you cannot turn a deaf ear to the cry of your people; listen then to our prayer." When the community makes a covenant with poor people, their cry becomes its own." (1979, Paulist Press, p. 124)

Obviously all people have problems of a greater or lesser degree. I find, however, that the problems of persons with disabilities are at times very difficult to solve. They can be difficult to solve for me personally, because to solve their problems implies a time commitment on my part. I have to change my priorities to include them when I would rather take my ease, watch TV, or read a book. But I don't think I am called to take my ease as much as I would like when my brother or sister is in need. It truly is not about me. At least it is not about me, or should NOT be all about me, if I am a Christian.

But another aspect of this is that when I see human need, I also see the insolvable nature of human need. Don't believe what the politicians or anyone else tells you...we will not be able to solve the problems of a fallen world because it is well, fallen. Sure I can help and I can lessen the pain of those around me by God's grace, however, I have come to believe that one of the reasons that there are people in need in the world is so that we will cry out to God. That we will seek God's wisdom, God's help for seemingly unsolvable problems. In my own little perfect life, with a good marriage, good children, good job, good income, good place to live and

41

so on, I may loose the desperation of my need for God. I have become intoxicated by my blessings, and rather than look to the source of my blessings, or look to see if others have blessings or need blessings, I go home and watch the football game on TV. But bringing myself into contact with those in need, those who are alone, those who may even be suffering, reconnects me to my helplessness without God in this world.

This is yet another reason why the church needs people with disabilities. They have challenges in their lives and the lives of their families which can only be addressed by a cry out to God. We truly do "sense our own inability to do anything about it that we will cry loudly to God" if we are aware at all. We are brought to a point where we sit without the answers, in deep distress, calling out together to God. I think that is a place God wants to take me, to take us. He wants to challenge our securities with insecurities so that we will be forced to rely on Him rather than our own resources. He wants us to step back and look at our resources, be they emotional, intellectual or monetary and physical, and be a part of the solution for others.

When I am in an uncomfortable situation with a person with a disability because I don't have the answers, or can't communicate clearly, or am reduced to simply praying because I don't know what to do, I inwardly smile a bit as I recognize God is challenging me to cry out to him on behalf of this person. God is wanting to grow MY faith and the faith of the person I am attempting to support. Once again God has connected me to a hurting person and given me the honor to share in that person's frustrations.

But remember, the solution is not to reject those who make us feel uncomfortable. The solution is to get in there with them and share their experience, share their struggles, and perhaps make others uncomfortable through our alignment with a disenfranchised person. The typical response is to reject, to exclude because involvement requires change on my part or the part of the institutions I am a part of. The answer, however, is to work through the uncomfortable feelings, to reflect on them and understand them and to change with them as appropriate.

Tuesday, September 11, 2007

Sin and social skills

So, a person with a intellectual or emotional or mental disability approaches you. He stands too close to your face. He asks you questions that you think are inappropriate. He touches you too much. He doesn't get your hint that you are feeling uncomfortable. He doesn't understand your language indicating that you want to end the conversation. He will not let the conversation end. Finally you break away. When you get with a friend, you comment, "That guy is weird. He's a mess. He doesn't get it at all, he was like standing too close and touching me and couldn't take a hint."

The question is...who just committed the sin?

He doesn't get it, you do.
He is kinda flailing around in attempting to be loving and friendly. You aren't nor do you want to be loving or friendly.
He will talk about you as his friend. You talk about him as weird and how he doesn't get it.
He will look forward to a chance to talk with you again. You will avoid him in the future.
He will give you all the time he has. You will give time only out of some feeling of guilt.

So who is committing the sin?

It is amazing what we, what I will do or think about a person just because their social skills are not all they should be. The person is not being evil, the person is not doing wrong, the person just doesn't understand many of what are truly the subtleties of social skills. My response is to reject him and 90% of my friends and 90% of the church would probably agree with my rejection of him. We as the Church of the Lord Jesus Christ, condone, understand, accept, advocate, discuss, follow through on rejection of people with various disabilities because of their social skills.

May God forgive us.

Yet as I approach the Lord, of course *my* behavior is obviously perfect and *my* social skills are flawless. I have nothing to hide, and to the Lord, interacting with me is no doubt "a day at the beach!" How fortunate for him that he is able to be in my presence (being the Lord, and being omnipresent, he kinda doesn't have a choice but to be in my presence). I am confident that the three persons of the trinity do not huddle together and say to each other, "McNair is weird." Surely they talk about how fortunate they are to have McNair on their side. But you know, in reality God's interactions with me, and my prayers to Him are "a day at the beach" because the Lord loves me. He loves me not because I **am** "a day at the beach" but because out of his love **he has chosen** to make interactions with me "a day at the beach." He has chosen to make me feel like I am "a day at the beach!" In spite of all my problems, my sins, my poor social skills, my pride, the crap that is in me and circles me like flies because of the choices I have made, HE LOVES ME! You see that is the example he provides. **He shows me, ME, as the example of loving someone who is difficult to love, and then He loves me**.

Do you think he cares about the social skills of the person who bothers you? Please! No, he treats him like he is "a day at the beach" just as much as he does to me.

So do you get it? Social skills deficits are not sin. If I reject another on the basis of social skills, that is sin and I am the sinner. We, I, need to learn about love. True love is not easy. It is messy and inconvenient. It makes you feel uncomfortable. It makes demands on you. I pray that when I am put to the test, when God asks me to show real love to another human being, I will not be worrying about that person's social skills. I hope my concern will be whether I am reflecting the kind of Love that God shows to me. I pray that I will be worried about the sin I am tempted to commit by rejecting another person who God truly loves.

Tuesday, August 21, 2007

People with Down's syndrome and Arthur Miller

A friend of mine sent me a fascinating link to an article in the Vanity Fair magazine. It is about the famous playwright, Arthur Miller (*Death of a Salesman, The Crucible*) and his inability to accept, come to grips with, the birth of a son named Daniel who had Down's syndrome. This was apparently a particular surprise to many because of Miller's voice of morality. As Vanity Fair states,

"The Denver Post called him "the moralist of the past American century," and The New York Times extolled his "fierce belief in man's responsibility to his fellow man—and [in] the self-destruction that followed on his betrayal of that responsibility."

Yet, he struggled with the acceptance of his son."

The article is excellent reading. It is fair to Miller, I felt, yet still wonders at the decisions he made about his son and the relationship he had with his son. Clearly we are looking at the situation through 2007 eyes which are very different from those of the 60's and 70's. We must hedge in casting judgment at Miller's decisions, at least some of them, which reflected the recommendations of professionals at the time. Yet as the article tells, Daniel's mother, was quoted as saying about her visits to Southbury Training School,

Inge said, "'You know, I go in there and it's like a Hieronymus Bosch painting.' That was the image she gave."

This is a good description of the institutions at the time.

God bless the older couple who took Daniel under their arms and loved and supported him. Apparently he now has a wing built onto their home where he lives.

The article ends with the following.

"Some wonder why Arthur Miller, with all his wealth, waited until death to share it with his son. Had he done so sooner, Daniel could have afforded private care and a good education. *But those who know Daniel say that this is not how he would feel. "He doesn't have a bitter bone in his body,"* says Bowen. *The important part of the story, she says, is that Danny transcended his father's failures: "He's made a life for himself; he is deeply valued and very, very loved. What a loss for Arthur Miller that he couldn't see how extraordinary his son is."* It was a loss that Arthur Miller may have understood better than he let on. "A character," he wrote in Timebends, "is defined by the kinds of challenges he cannot walk away from. And by those he has walked away from that cause him remorse." (emphasis added)

Daniel, who "suffers" from Down's syndrome as the story relates, "doesn't have a bitter bone in his body...he is deeply valued and very, very loved." How very sad for Arthur Miller. The lost relationship, the communication of no value to Daniel. God bless Daniel for his heart of forgiveness, and apparently irrepressible love for his father. As the article relates, who knows what plays were not written by a man the article states could be the greatest American playwright of the last 100 years. What great good he might have done in his own life, the life of his son and the life of his family. The article also gave me a new appreciation of Daniel Day-Lewis (I hated him in *Gangs of New York*, or I should say his excellent acting made me hate him!), who married into the Miller family and as the article relates is the "most compassionate about Daniel. He always visited him."

The Arthur Miller family is a famous family in America, but they are just another family in Daniel (their son's) mind. A family who he loves although he lives with a couple who loved him for who he was. A family like many families whose patriarch feared Down's syndrome, probably would have aborted the child had the option been provided to the father. A family probably coming to grips with their legacy, informed, yet misinformed.

Why is it that when we look back on situations such as the one with Daniel Miller, the son of Arthur Miller we look back with regret for what might have been. We judge Arthur Miller for not being a father to his son because his son had Down's syndrome. We praise the family who came alongside of Daniel and took him in. But I suspect the Vanity Fairs of the world will also support abortion of persons like Daniel. They will blindly talk about choice, or those who "suffer" with Down's syndrome, not

45

knowing about what they speak. People who know other people who have Down's syndrome tend to like them, tend to think they are nice people, tend to think they are loving people, tend to think they are friendly people. But in the future we may never know this because of our efforts to wipe out people with Down's syndrome.

The article ends once again with the statement, "A character," he (Arthur Miller) wrote in Timebends, "is defined by the kinds of challenges he cannot walk away from. And by those he has walked away from that cause him remorse." Will the Christian Church walk away from the challenge of Down's syndrome, the challenge of disability or with integrity will we say that we cannot walk away? If Arthur Miller committed a "crime" in his relationship with his son, it was a crime of reflecting society. Perhaps he went where the rest of society is going now. What is Vanity Fair's response for his taking this path? It is probably our response. It is lamentation, shaking our heads in sadness, and perhaps judgment. I doubt Mr. Miller had any notion that his relationship with his son would be the subject of a Vanity Fair article, or discussed by an obscure Christian blogger.

May Arthur Miller's name forever be linked with the term Down's syndrome and the name Daniel Miller.

It seems that Daniel Miller was born and Arthur Miller saw Down's syndrome not Daniel Miller. This should be a warning to me, a warning to all of us, lest we make the same error.

In our world today, Daniel Miller is anticipated. Daniel Miller is conceived, Eighty percent of Daniel Millers will be aborted. Down's syndrome was the challenge Arthur Miller walked away from, hopefully with remorse. Our society is running headlong toward the elimination of people with Down's syndrome.

Lamentation, sadness and judgment will be the response of those in the future to what we are doing to people with Down's syndrome now.

Monday, August 20, 2007

Wyatt, Doc and difficult friendships

I like to wake up on Saturday mornings and watch old cowboy movies. This past week Wyatt Earp was on. There are two scenes that struck me. One, is when Wyatt and Doc Holiday meet for the first time. Doc asks Wyatt, "Do you believe in friendship?" He responds, "Yes" and their friendship begins. The movie portrays scenes from that friendship over the years. At one point, Doc and his girlfriend Big Nose, get in one of their typical drunken fights where they try to kill each other. Wyatt breaks the fight up and attempts to sober Doc up. As he begins to regain his senses, Doc says, "Its not easy to be my friend, but I will be there for you when you need me" or something to that effect.

Do you have friends like that? Friends it is not easy to be friends with? Some of my intellectually disabled friends are like that (I have a greater tendency to not work on relationships with nondisabled people if they are hard to be friends with for some reason). Sometimes helping my friends with intellectual disabilities, being friends with them is "messy." They have problems that I can't solve, and they impolitely do not keep their problems to themselves. They tell me their problems, make demands on me, and expect me to help them or solve their problems. Even keeping in contact with them is difficult because they don't follow the social etiquette I am used to. They will call me at 11:30 at night or 6:30 in the morning. They will call me 7 times a day or everyday of the week. My response has been to tell them "Please don't call me after 10 or before 7 unless it is an emergency. I will also tell them, "Please just call me once a week just to talk." I have gotten to the point that I will tell them, "You have already called me once this week. Unless this is an emergency, I will talk to you later." I may even have to hang up after ensuring there isn't an emergency. It might seem unkind, and perhaps it is, but it is what I have come to. But I like the fact that others in my church are facing the same challenges in their friendships with the people with intellectual disabilities who attend our church. These individuals are now on their radar screen. They are also someone else who can be called once a week just to talk for a few minutes.

Some of the messiness of the friendship comes from the social skill differences of my friends with intellectual disabilities. Some of the messiness comes from differences in my friends' life experiences that I may not be not used to. My friends with disabilities have to deal with...

-Access (busses they reserve to take them places), and

-conservators (who may or may not be very interested in them, but nonetheless have control over their lives),

-unscrupulous people who sell them things (cell phones can be the biggest pain)

-being alone except for people who are paid to be with them

-dealing with human services and human service rules (in other words, the government)

-a lack of friends

-too much time and too few things to do

-and so on

In attempting to be a friend to some people, I find myself in the position of negotiating, or being in the middle, or whatever. They are not friends who I can call to come over, or meet for a ball game, who then go home and solve their own problems. They can be high maintenance.

The whole social skills thing is another aspect of the difficulty of some friendships. Some of my friends I am sure impact the potential of friendships with others. People I love have told me that friends of mine are "weird." Those who are not afraid to be politically incorrect and tell me what they really think will sometimes say that, which makes me think that others with whom I am not as close probably think that as well, but just don't say it to me.

So as Christians, what do we do about this? Are we called to befriend those who are more difficult to befriend than the average person? Are friendships about us only? Do we befriend others to benefit them? Is friendship something that is easy? I must admit that I have at times asked myself Doc Holiday's question. I have wondered if I believe in friendship, or just friendship that is easy for me.

Monday, August 13, 2007

Less honorable need abundant honor

"...And those members of the body which we think are less honorable, on those we bestow abundant honor." (1 Corinthians 12: 23)

So, a man with intellectual disability lives for 60 years. He gets up in the morning, goes to a job, comes home, and spends time with friends or family, and goes to bed. This scenario is somehow different from people without intellectual disability who get up, perhaps go to a better job by comparison (more responsibility, more money, etc.) come home to family or friends and go to bed. How is the life of the person who is a waitress or a mechanic or a teacher or a professor or a doctor different? Is the difference based upon how much money they make or their contribution to others? Distinctions are artificial.

So we react when "stay at home mothers" are regarded as less than working mothers. Then we decry the effect on children of poor parenting. If some salary figure is our criteria for life well lived, stay at home mothers are criticized. If well adjusted children are our criteria, then working mothers are criticized. The criteria we set will determine whether we are successful in the evaluation. But I must look critically at those inside and outside of the group I am evaluating if I am being honest. For example, the need to be served might be the criteria to elevate someone to inclusion (special honor) not only a reason to exclude.

Self-sufficiency, the Bible would imply, causes people to not trust in God, to think they don't need God. Yet how do we convince self-sufficient people that they need God? Perhaps we put them in situations where their presumed self-sufficiency is inadequate. Put them in

48

situations where they are once again forced to trust in God and not in their wealth (for example). People in need, people who need to be served have the potential on many levels to teach us about faith. Those *we think* are less honorable might actually be worthy of honor for a variety of reasons.

    1. Through their own faith

    2. Through the way they cause others to try to reconcile disability and faith theologically and philosophically

    3. Through the service they demand (causing one to decide whether or not he will serve God)

    4. What are the essential elements of being human or being made in the Image of God

    5. What is it that makes a life valuable or well lived

    6. Why should I or my life be considered more valuable than that of a person with a disability

    7. God's sovereignty

    8. Support within/among the Body of Christ

    9. The ability to teach lessons about faith might require special honor.

So the giving of honor might be less an artifact of our simply being obedient (although that is sufficient reason) but might actually be due to people, if we use the correct criteria to do the evaluation. In thinking about having honor or giving honor, we might define honor in the following ways (the first five definitions from Webster's Third New International Dictionary, 1966):

1. good name or public esteem
- so people may have no good name or receive no public esteem, but we would give it to them
- we give them a good name through our social capital
- we recognize their contributions such that they receive public esteem

2. a special prerogative
- so we give them special prerogatives in overlooking social skill differences in the same manner we would overlook the social errors of our loved ones
- we facilitate the opportunity to provide honor by giving the opportunities to make decisions about their own lives, rather than approaching with a we know best attitude

3. person of superior standing or importance
- we begin by recognizing them as people as having equal standing and

importance
- recognizing strengths we may begin to see superior standing
- through relationships we may begin to see importance

4. one that is of intrinsic value
-we honor by fighting for the disabled person's intrinsic value, that is, value that is not determined by ability levels, etc.
-we honor by having a realistic picture of our own value, intrinsic or otherwise

5. an evidence or symbol of distinction
-we honor by giving the same symbols of distinction to those who are disabled that we would give to anyone
-we honor when relationships with persons with disabilities are no longer a symbol of distinction

Our society decides about what it will choose to honor and then honors it. We honor physical appearance and athletic or other abilities. The Bible calls upon us to think differently about what honor means. One distinction of being a Christian is that within the Body of Christ, we reject the worlds criteria for honor, and honor whom we choose to honor. Paul chides us to give special honor to those whom we would typically think are less honorable.

Perhaps there are things worthy of honor if we would see people through God's eyes, using God's evaluative criteria. Perhaps we are to treat those we think are less honorable with abundant or special honor because in the deliverance of that honor we will begin to see the honor we should have been giving but missed in the first place.

Monday, August 06, 2007

Learned helplessness and learned unhelpfulness

Learned helplessness results from a period in which someone encounters failure and as a result just gives up. It is a motivational problem. People will say, "I'm tired of fighting" or something to that effect.

Learned unhelpfulness is the result of someone being taught that all they need to do to help their neighbor is to pay their taxes, or contribute some money to a group that is doing something. People will say, to use the words of Ebenezer Scrooge in Dickens's *A Christmas Carol*,

"Are there no prisons? . . .And the Union workhouses?" demanded Scrooge . . ."Are they still in operation? . . .The Treadmill and the Poor Law are in full vigor, then?" . . . "Oh! I was afraid, from what you said at

50

first, that something had occurred to stop them in their useful course," . . ."I wish to be left alone" . . . "since you asked me what I wish, gentlemen, that is my answer". . . "I help support the establishments I have mentioned – they cost enough: and those who are badly off must go there."

Those having the potential to help, instead look to the government because they pay taxes, or look to some organization because they give money. As a result then are unhelpful on a personal level.

In the end there is a confluence of learned helplessness and learned unhelpfulness. Those needing assistance may be totally frustrated with government and other bureaucratic structures from whom they have been endeavoring to receive help resulting in their feeling helpless and wanting to give up, while those who could help have learned to lean on bureaucratic structures to help those in need, thinking they need to do little or nothing other than that, resulting in their becoming unhelpful.

As Christians, we should know better than to rely on the government to help people in need. Sure we can support and/or advocate for government programs, however, we recognize that services are rendered when caring is needed. As Christians, we should also know better than to assume that all we need to do is to send a check to someone and we are then relieved of our responsibility towards others. Statistics indicate that the majority of Christians do not even tithe their financial resources, so that we are giving too little financially to charitable and church organizations, and expecting others to also do the grunt work of helping others, whether it is through governmental programs or relief organizations.

Its like the perfect storm of uncaring coupled with deep need. Perhaps the only way it could get worse would be for the government to cut programs as then the **learned unhelpful** would be relying on governmental programs that were not in existence, and the **learned helpless** would experience a further loss of motivation to attempt to fight for limited governmental resources.

To my mind, the answer is for me to get involved with my neighbor. I must tell you that that involvement is not often clean or easy. I have a friend I am trying to encourage and support who looks to me for solutions and I have none. I sit with him and talk through the issues, I am his friend, I try to encourage him in the midst of the frustrations with the system, but I don't have the answers. What I do have for him is encouragement and friendship. He knows that when we get together for coffee, that he will be meeting with someone who cares about him, who listens to him and will try to help him if we can arrive at a course of action. Will I be able to help him to move forward, I hope so, but I make no promises. However, I also do not wash my hands of him in the

51

assumption that the government or other agencies are taking care of him. I know better. I cannot do everything, but I can do something and what I can do I try to do and I think that is encouraging to him. It helps him to continue to battle the helplessness that the system is unconsciously trying to teach him. It also helps me through my friends encouragement to battle the unhelpfulness that the system is unconsciously trying to teach me.

Human service is always messy and not easy. The degree to which human service becomes regimented and easy is the degree to which it is excluding helpers, removing freedoms, and teaching helplessness. To paraphrase Dr. Julian Rappaport, when I use convergent thinking to solve human service problems I prove that I do not understand the problem.

So find those around you who are being devalued and encourage them. Then look in the mirror and ask yourself if you have bought the lie that helping is the government's or some agency's responsibility. Have you been programmed to be unhelpful?

Wednesday, July 18, 2007

Write love

My son, Josh, turned me on to an cool story of love, acceptance and forgiveness. Check it out TO WRITE LOVE ON HER ARMS by Jamie Tworkowski, available on the internet.

In the story it states,

"We often ask God to show up. We pray prayers of rescue. Perhaps God would ask us to be that rescue, to be His body, to move for things that matter. He is not invisible when we come alive. I might be simple but more and more, I believe God works in love, speaks in love, is revealed in our love. I have seen that this week and honestly, it has been simple: Take a broken girl, treat her like a famous princess, give her the best seats in the house. Buy her coffee and cigarettes for the coming down, books and bathroom things for the days ahead. Tell her something true when all she's known are lies. Tell her God loves her. Tell her about forgiveness, the possibility of freedom, tell her she was made to dance in white dresses. All these things are true. "

Why is this interaction with the girl in the story, the love showed, the kindnesses expressed, the forgiveness of God explained, all of these acts of love, why are they important?

Are they important because of who the girl is or who she might be? If she were to become a great poet, would those acts be now justified? If she was to be saved from her addictions would those acts be justified? If she were to become a loving mother, would the acts be justified? If she were to become a Christian, would the acts be justified?
OR

52

If she were to be unable to escape her addictions would those acts be unjustified?
If she remained an addict for the remainder of her life, would those acts be unjustified?
If she were never to become a Christian, would those acts be unjustified?

Can you see acts of love and kindness and forgiveness are of value within themselves? The recipient of those acts is largely irrelevant. Sure our heart goes out to a woman who condemns herself in profane terms, writing her indictments with a razor on her skin. But what of a woman who has been socialized to believe that she is worthless, or would be better off dead, or should have been the focus of an abortion to prevent her life? Does our compassion change if the woman has Down's syndrome, or a birth defect of some kind?

I believe the story shared at the website is a true story, and may God help that woman to escape her addiction and her self abusive behaviors and find forgiveness. But may God also help His church to escape her addiction to comfort that leads to exclusion, exclusion which is really a form of self abuse through the exclusion of people God loves and wants in his church, and may He through the church's repentance provide forgiveness leading to repentance.

In the story, the girl condemns herself by writing f*** off on her arm. What is the church writing on the arms of persons with Down's syndrome or intellectual disability or mental illness? I pray that as the website says, we are writing love on those people for the sake of writing love on those people. That is the end. For the benefit we receive when we show love to another without any expectations or for no other reason than the showing of love.

Saturday, July 14, 2007

How to ask questions?

Michael Oliver is an author in disability who I really enjoy reading. He makes me think. In his book with Bob Sapey, *Social Work with Disabled People* (2006, third edition) he relates two sets of questions asked of persons with disabilities. One set from a 1986 disability survey and the other a set of alternative questions he (Oliver) developed in 1990. He makes the point that respondents are influenced by the way surveys ask questions. In particular, he relates that the particular survey done in 1986 causes respondents to think of themselves as inadequate by the way questions were asked. I want to juxtapose the two sets of questions so that you can see the difference clearly. These questions and the discussion surrounding them can be found on pages 60-61 of the book.

1986-What complaint causes your difficulty in holding, gripping or turning things?
1990-What defects in the design of everyday equipment like jars, bottles or tins causes you difficulty in holding, gripping or turning them.

1986-Are your difficulties in understanding people mainly due to a hearing problem?
1990-Are your difficulties in understanding people mainly due to their inabilities to communicate with you?

1986-Do you have a scar, blemish or deformity which limits your daily activities?
1990-Do other people's reactions to any scar, blemish or deformity you may have, limit your daily activities?

1986-Have you attended a special school because of long-term health problem or disability?
1990-Have you attended a special school because of your education authority's policy of sending people with your health problem or disability to such places?

1986-Does your health problem/disability mean that you need to live with relatives or someone else who can look after you?
1990-Are community services so poor that you need to rely on relatives or someone else to provide you with the right level of personal assistance?

Oliver advocates for what he calls "the social model of disability". He states, "The argument for a social model of disability is that the causal relationship begins with the reactions of mainstream society to people with impairments that oppress and exclude them. Part of this oppression is the imposition of an understanding of disability that blames the individual" (p. 60).

I had the opportunity to address a small group of people this past week at a community college. During the question and answer time at the end, a gentleman asked an interesting question. "Why do you think people with disabilities don't go to church?" The question, although a good one, reminded me of some of the questions above.

What is it about people with disabilities that causes them to not be church goers?
What is it about being disabled that makes you not want to go to church?

The answers I provided seemed unsatisfactory to several in attendance. You see my answers related to church attitudes, or leadership attitudes, or changes which needed to occur within the church. Those unsatisfied wanted me to provide answers about the people with disabilities. The only answers I could provide were things like, people don't like to be around other people who are impatient with them, people don't like to be around other people who don't think they are important, people don't like to be around other people who wish they weren't there, people don't like to be around other people who don't want to have to change the things they do in order to make a more accepting environment. Or even something as simple as people will not go places where they are not invited to go. The answers had little to do with the people with disabilities and much more to do with the unaccepting environment. I could tell the questioners rejected my response saying they couldn't or wouldn't believe that churches were like that. Obviously churches are loving and caring and accepting places. Therefore if disabled people were not in churches in numbers reflecting the community, there was something wrong with the disabled people.

Thursday, June 28, 2007

"Don't hate the player, hate the game"

"Don't hate the player hate the game" is a saying that you will sometimes hear people say. The idea is, for example, good looking guys tend to date good looking girls. That is just the way it is. So I shouldn't hate a good looking guy (the player) because the good looking girls like him. I might hate the fact, however, that good looking girls and good looking guys like each other (the game).

So what could this possibly have to do with disability... bear with me.

It seems in society today people with disabilities are ostracized, and misunderstood, and just generally not treated very well. At least not as well as those without disabilities (the game). I hate the game. I hate the fact that that is the way of the world. But should I not also hate the player?

My faith is clear that I shouldn't hate anybody, so I do my best not to. But if the player says that I treat people the way I do without thinking, because that is the way I have been socialized he is worthy of disdain.

At the recent Social Role Valorization training I attended, Dr. Wolfensberger stated the following:

55

"Collective unconsciousness can be so vast that even the most global societal policies may be undeclared, unexplicated, unacknowledged, and even denied. Thus for many people to all work toward a bad thing requires no deliberate or conscious conspiracy. While this is well-known by social scientists, most citizens are not aware of how they themselves can be totally unconsciously acting out undeclared, large-scale, societal policies in their own daily lives" (from "A leadership-oriented introductory social role valorization (SRV) workshop, February 27, 2007)

It is one thing to recognize the game and just shrug your shoulders and say, don't hate the player, hate the game. It is quite another to be a player in the game and be so unaware that you are working toward a bad thing. To be unaware and yet working on the side of the bad thing. Churches need to wake up to their participation in the bad thing. Discrimination is the way things are, it is the game, but players have a choice to play or not in the discrimination game.

Changing the game begins when you wake up as a player.

Friday, May 11, 2007

...and to love mercy

In Micah 6:8, the famous passage talks about loving mercy. I have been thinking a lot about this passage lately. What might it mean to love mercy? I suppose I could love the concept of mercy, not giving someone something they might deserve, or forgiveness. But I am tempted to think about loving the acting out of mercy. I love that God is merciful, and I love that people are merciful to other people, sometimes.

Why would I love mercy?

If I have experienced mercy, I will love mercy.

If I want others to know about God and receive His mercy, I will love mercy.

If I want to be shown mercy, I will love mercy.

If I accept God's mercy and give myself to Him, I will love mercy.

If I understand mercy, I will love mercy.

If I understand worship, I will not only love mercy, I will do mercy.

Again

If I understand worship, I will do mercy.

Mercy implies an object, a person to whom mercy is shown. Jesus on several occasions, makes the statement "But go and learn what this means...I desire mercy not sacrifice" (Matthew 9:13). You might think that He had said just the opposite when you look at how churches do worship. We talk about the "sacrifice of praise." Oh, please. I think it may be more of a sacrifice on God's part to listen to it, than it is a sacrifice to give it. I suspect our singing voices will be much better in Heaven. We focus on sacrifice. God focuses on mercy. We raise our hands in praise (which is fine to do). He wants us to do that but to also look around for someone to whom we might show some mercy. You see, we show our love to God by what we do for other people. James 1:27 says that true worship is to look after widows and orphans. As I have been the recipient of mercy, I offer myself to God "as those who have been brought back from death to life" (Romans 6:13). God's greatest gift to me is mercy. Perhaps my greatest gift to God is mercy as well. Obviously, I cannot really show mercy to God, but I can show mercy to people, the ones to whom He gives mercy, his greatest gift. In the most positive of ways, I become like God, when I show mercy to other people.

When it comes to worship, what does God need from me? Sure in heaven, we will worship in various ways, but we will worship in a different form. You see there aren't any poor or disabled or disenfranchised people in heaven. There will be those who were poor or disabled or disenfranchised while they lived a human life on earth. Perhaps they will have a memory of their poverty or disability or disenfranchisement while they lived out their human life. But there will be no one who is poor or disabled or disenfranchised any more in heaven. Our worship there, will therefore no longer need to have the mercy component it must have here on earth. I can sing songs to God for eternity when I get to heaven. While on Earth, I need to take care of widows and orphans. I need to show mercy to people as an act of worship while I am here on Earth. My worship should be significantly different as an earthling.

This has been a revelation to me. I have commented elsewhere in this blog that I am confused by worship. I have been confused by church, music based, sermon based worship. But when my son goes out of his way to take a man with disabilities out to lunch, by making the man's day, by filling his stomach with great tasting good food that he would not otherwise be able to afford, I am not confused about the worshipful nature of that act. It is an act of worship, as God desires mercy.

I have shown you, O man, what is good and what the Lord requires of thee...to love mercy.

Sunday, February 18, 2007

57

Comments about the Ashleys of the world

Regarding the story of the little girl Ashley (who was subjected to surgery to remove her ovaries and breast buds so she would remain small and easier for her parents to care for), demeaned with the name, "pillow angel" a term which from a normalization perspective is sick in and of itself, I would like to make two points.

First, we cannot marginalize people and then criticize those who are left alone to care for marginalized people for their decisions. I wonder if the adults in Ashley's life felt supported in her care, anywhere. Sure the wrongness of the surgeries stands on its own merits. We can criticize them. However, if we hope to avert a rash of such medical treatments toward people who inconvenience their families by their very lives, the community, and I would say the faith community, the Christian Church needs to come along side of those families and individuals who face the challenge of severe disability in their lives and provide support. Why aren't the little Ashley's of the world in the Sunday School classes of most churches? Yet we will criticize those who perform abusive surgeries. Where is the church at the birth of such children? Yet we will criticize the decisions of those facing the birth of a child with a disability who choose abortion...at least as a church I hope we will be critical of such people (I'm not sure we actually are). Obviously, the laws are not going to prevent families from stopping tube feeding, or performing radical surgeries on family members. However, if we as the community provide support to people challenged by the unknown of disability in their lives, those faced with the kinds of decisions the medical profession increasingly offers, will be less likely to abort, or create people who are further disabled by surgery, because they do not see themselves as facing their challenges alone. They see the experience of others in their community whose child with disability may be a value added to their families, or their churches or their communities. But those children have to be present and they have to be supported to change the minds of people tempted to do the wrong thing.

Second, the decisions relative to performing the procedures on Ashely were condoned by a group of medical ethicists at the hospital where the surgery was performed. Well, **medical ethicists are lost**. I would love to know, for example, how many of those on the medical ethics committee who made the decision to go forward with the surgery, even know a person with a profound intellectual/physical disability. I wonder if any have friends with such disabilities. I wonder if any ever spent the day with a person with a severe disability. Decisions are made on the basis of ideas ethicists have about who those people are, and I would suspect they have largely never gotten past the notion of people with disabilities as "other." My goodness, the medical profession has

58

become rabid over Down's syndrome being prenatally diagnosed and those detected being aborted. These doctors are listening to medical ethicists when they say such abortions are humanitarian because they prevent a suffering, or poor quality life.

So let's point out the madness of the reasoning, and the surgery, and those who defend decisions by medical ethicists. But let's also take away the argument that the families faced with the challenges of raising children with severe disabilities are in it alone, by coming alongside of such families with acceptance and support.

Tuesday, January 30, 2007

Why I need my brother with intellectual disabilities

In a previous post I questioned the spiritual maturity of those who would not know why they would need their intellectually disabled brother in Christ. This question was raised in reference to the 1 Corinthians 12 passage where it is written that those parts of the body which we may think are unimportant are actually absolutely essential. Perhaps you might not know yourself why your intellectually disabled brother in Christ is absolutely essential. Perhaps you might want to call my bluff.

Well, let's think about this in reverse. That is, rather than starting with the disabled brother and thinking about what he might bring as a body member who is absolutely essential, let's first think about what are absolutely essential components of the Christian faith. Absolutely essential components might be servanthood, faith, or love. I think most would agree that love is an absolutely essential component of the Christian faith. After all, the Bible says, "God is love" (1 John 4: 8, 16). Now we wouldn't look at love as being not important, we would see it as being absolutely essential. However, we might look at those parts of the body of Christ who teach us about love, or demonstrate live as not being important, most likely because we don't know what love is.

People with intellectual disabilities, as a group I would say, love others pretty unconditionally. They as a group really do teach me about what it means to love others by the way that they love others. They are truly excellent examples to me of how I should love my neighbor.

So let's put this together. Persons with intellectual disabilities are thought by many as not important, not a priority for ministry. They are not considered a critical part of the body. However, they may be the best examples to others of what it means to truly love others, to love God. Therefore, as verse 22 states, "On the contrary, those parts of the body that seem to be weaker are indispensable..." Why might those parts be indispensable? Because they teach us about God. They teach us about God not because of what they cause us to do for them (although that may be a part of it). But more so, they demonstrate for us the most critical aspect of the Christian faith, and that is love. I need people with intellectual disabilities in my church so I can learn about love by watching them love others. I learn about acceptance by watching the way they accept others. I may reject them, but in a very Godlike manner, they will accept me. I may reject them but in a very Godlike manner, they will love me.

I think the Church has not learned a significant lesson about what love is partly because they haven't had the parts of the body of Christ which would demonstrate what love is for them.

Sunday, January 07, 2007

Doing God's work alone

This past Sunday, a group of us went to see a showing of "The Nativity Story." I was impressed by the movie, and really enjoyed it. One thing that hit me that I really hadn't thought about before, was how alone Mary and Joseph were in their knowledge about the Christ child that she was carrying. To the degree that others did know that she was pregnant, their responses would be largely negative. Ultimately when they left for Bethlehem, the were once again alone with the knowledge of what was happening to them, to the world. Obviously they had both been visited by an angel, but as far as human support, human encouragement, only Elizabeth was in any way encouraging to Mary, understanding to some degree what was happening to her. Nevertheless, on they went to Bethlehem, alone, responding in obedience to the direction of the Lord. Ultimately, they received affirmation in the form of the Wise Men's visit from the human world.

I was encouraged in regards to working with people with disabilities from that interpretation of what was shown in the movie. Often we work alone, with little encouragement or understanding. Yet we are responding to the call of God. In the same way that Mary and Joseph finally received affirmation from the Wise Men, from people, but they relied on the Lord for their affirmation their encouragement. We must learn to do the same. Ultimately we will receive affirmation for our work, often alone as we are being obedient to God. But we must learn that in spite of what people do or do not do to affirm or encourage us, we must continue our work knowing we are doing the will of God.

Tuesday, December 19, 2006

You decide who I am

A student of mine, stopped by tonight during office hours. We had an interesting discussion about issues related to the class, but in the midst of talking she made a very interesting point. Basically people are who they are perceived to be. So, you approach a young woman and just see her as an attractive woman. I approach the same woman and see her as my daughter. You project a person who is attractive, but strange to you. I project a person who is as important to me as just about anyone else in my life. She is an attractive stranger to you. She is my daughter to me.

A man approaches you who has Down's syndrome. Perhaps he is not even much of a person to you, or someone who has a poor quality of life, or someone even to be feared. To me he is Ryan, my friend. I am aware of his disability in the same manner he is aware of my height (I'm 6'7"). His Down's syndrome doesn't add or detract from our friendship and neither does my height.

People become what they are projected to be by their environment. My student told me of a group of students she knew who were put in a program basically for trouble makers. Those around them then perceived them as such, as did they of themselves. They now saw themselves as trouble makers and lived up to the part.

I am reminded of the story (might be apocryphal) about the teachers who were given their students locker numbers and told the numbers were the students IQ scores. Students then proceeded to achieve on the basis of their locker number.

If I invite people with disabilities into my church, their perception of themselves will change. They will see themselves as worthy of friendship, wanted, valued. As a church member I also will learn to see them as worthy of friendship, as wanted and as valued. Exclusion, or absence of those people projects the image of unimportance, irrelevance, other, among other things. No wonder parents of children attending Christian schools will fight children with disabilities being in their Christian school. What have they learned to project on people with disabilities? How has the Church taught them to perceive persons with disabilities?

It goes to comments I made in an earlier entry to this blog. Others can be a detriment or a value added. It has more to do with me, with my perceptions, with my projections than it has to do with another's characteristics. I know people who love particular people with specific characteristics and others who dislike those same people. What is different? The object of the perceptions is the same. What those making the perceptions of other bring to the interaction is what is different. That is why it is so important to change churches, to make them more open. As we do that, perceptions will change so that the same man who was once ostracized is now accepted because the environment changed.

Wednesday, November 29, 2006

Men and women

This past week I was speaking to one of the classes I teach about the way people with disabilities are perceived, often negatively, by those around them. This is in spite of the fact that they typically think they are doing fine. Their only experience is their life experience and as far as they are concerned they are ok. In thinking through that, I came up with a metaphor, which might be helpful to some people in terms of understanding the point I was trying to make.

Now, I am a man. I was born a boy, and have grown up male. All I know is what it is like to be a male. Of course I love people of the opposite gender. I first loved my mother, then loved my wife and for the last 19 years have loved my daughter. I love those women, but I have no idea of what it is like to be a woman. I have no idea of what it is like to be three of the closest people to me in my life. I have some ideas of what it might be like to have me as a son, or as a husband or as a father, but I really don't know. Women tell me what they are thinking sometimes, but I really don't know what it is like to be one. Obviously, they don't know what it is like to be a man either. My mother, wife and daughter only know my thoughts to the extent to which I share them with them, and I have been told by them at times that I don't understand (ostensibly their women's perspective). I am sure that that is the truth.

However, imagine that I decided that because women are not men, their lives are in some way diminished, disabled. They think they are just fine as women, however, I think I know better. I therefore impose my beliefs on them. I think I know what it would be like to be a woman, and if I were a woman, I would be upset that I am not a man. I convince them that they have a poor quality of life, or get them to believe that their physical womanness is an impairment of which they should be ashamed. Perhaps I conclude that their differentness from me is not a difference, it is an impairment to which discrimination is attached (some of you may argue that this actually occurs, and I would be hard pressed to disagree). But to continue to press this metaphor, instead of me as a man seeing women as part of the natural diversity of humanity, as my equal yet in some ways different from me, imagine that I see them as "other," as very different from me. Not only that, imagine that I think they are dissatisfied with their lives as females and that they would choose death over being a woman, so deep is their wish they could be a male like me.

Can you catch where I am going with this metaphor? I think there is a lot overlap with the way in which people with impairments are perceived, particularly those with disabilities that they are born with. I only know what it is like to have my level of intellectual ability. So I assume those with a lower intellectual ability level would wish to be me. I only know what it is like to have my other characteristics, good vision, healthy, etc. And because I am satisfied with my life having my characteristics, I assume that those who don't have my characteristics are dissatisfied with their lives. That because they are not me, that they are in some way suffering, or depressed, or something else negative in character.

You might say that this sounds foolish, however, this perception drives the movement to prenatally diagnose and abort babies with disabilities. Take Down's syndrome for instance. We are told by the medical profession that obviously, people with Down's syndrome suffer, are dissatisfied with their lives because they don't have normal intelligence, or other characteristics that we (people without Down's syndrome) have. At least that is what people think who are behind the prenatal diagnosis and abortion movement. They take the lives of infants with Down's syndrome out of "compassion" for what the persons with disabilities are not.

But just as certainly as I don't know what it is like to be a woman and a woman doesn't know what it is like to be a man, I don't know what it is like to be a person born with Down's syndrome. All I do know about that life experience is what they tell me about that experience. And what do they tell me? They tell me that they are happy with their lives. Many would say that they don't think they even have a disability (something they perceive negatively, probably through their socialization). Yet I believe my daughter when she says she is happy (even though I don't know what it is like to be a woman) but I don't believe the person with Down's syndrome when he or she tells me she is happy because I say that I would not want to live with that disability if I had it.

In the same way that I don't know what it is like to be a woman, I don't know what it is like to be a person with a disability. In the same way that a woman does not know what is like to be a man, a woman without a disability does not know what it is like to be a person with a disability.

May God forgive our society for projecting its negative perceptions on people with disabilities and then killing them on the basis of our negative perceptions through abortion, infanticide and other approaches. May God stop us as well.

Tuesday, September 26, 2006

The "embarrassment" of disability

In the book *Defiant birth: Women who resist medical eugenics* the author Melinda Tankard Reist takes on the notion of prenatal diagnosis leading to abortion through the stories of women who having received the diagnosis that the child they were carrying was determined to be disabled, but chose to have the child anyway. Of course she relates stories of those who were misdiagnosed, however, the thrust of the story is the experience of women who gave birth to children who were born with various disabilities. These disabilities include anencephaly (a disability which typically takes the life of the newborn within hours or days) and of course Down's syndrome. There are many amazing lessons to be gained. One, for instance relates to carrying a baby with anencephaly to term. Overwhelmingly, doctors would advocate for abortion of such children as they will die soon after birth anyway. Tankard Reist, however, says that if you knew your child would die in an hour or a day, would you choose to kill your child or would you enjoy the hour or day you had remaining with your child? Mothers spoke of their child living his entire life in their arms, of celebrating the 1 day birthday, or the trip home from the hospital. They also spoke of the impact for good the birth of the child had on their lives.

One story really touch me. Written by Elizabeth Schiltz about her experiences carrying, having prenatally diagnosed, giving birth and raising a child with Down's syndrome. She relates that when she took her baby out into the community there were actual comments made like "Why didn't you have prenatal diagnosis?" She said that many of the stares she received seemed to give the same message. There is a kind of embarrassment with goes with choosing to have a child with a disability, or simply having a child with a disability under any circumstances. Let's think this embarrassment through a bit.

Why would someone be embarrassed about anything in their lives? Perhaps I do something foolish and I don't want to be laughed at. Perhaps I do something wrong and I don't want to be found out. Other reasons could be thought of as well. The bottom line is that I am concerned about what those around me think about me, or my behavior, or my decisions. Teenagers in particular struggle with worries about the perceptions of their peers. As a parent I have often made a special effort with my kids to deliberately be goofy, or silly, or dress oddly in public so that when people look at me strange or if my children say, "People are looking at you" I can respond, "I could care less what people think of me. Am I doing anything wrong? (with my goofiness or whatever). If not I am not going to let them determine what I will do." They are on to me now, and know better, often saying themselves, "I don't care what people think about me." That is good, I think as it develops self confidence, but there is something even better that could happen. What if people would come up to me and say, "I like the way that you express your individuality." That would be an even more powerful witness to being a free spirit.

But that is what Christians, of all people, need to be doing. When we see a child with a disability, we should treat it like any other child we would meet. We should delight in her, play with him, tease with her. If I approach a family in my church or community who has just given birth to a child with Down's syndrome and say, "I am so sorry, I will pray for you." I don't bless that family, I embarrass them when there is nothing to be embarrassed about. They have received the gift of a child that God has given them, often in the face of incredible pressure from the medical profession to abort the child, and our response is to embarrass them for their heroic choice. Tankard Reist cites a statistic that 86% of babies prenatally diagnosed as having Down's syndrome are aborted by their parents. Do you, does the church add to the certainty that those children will be aborted by our embarrassment of parents, embarrassment of people with disability? As stated elsewhere in this blog, are we complicit in the abortion of babies with disabilities through our lack of caring or priority giving to the lives of persons with disabilities?

Those who would reject parents of persons with disabilities for choosing life or would reject people with disabilities themselves should be embarrassed, should be ashamed of themselves, not the other way around. We need to "not be conformed to the patterns of this world but be transformed by the renewing of our minds" ala Romans 12. What have you done in your life to contribute to 14% of families, moms and dads who chose to give life to a child with Down's syndrome?

Friday, August 18, 2006

The why of disability

In the last week, I have had 2 separate discussions with friends about the question of why people have disabilities (particularly congenital disabilities). The one setting was at an international conference in Montreal. There were professors from Belgium, Netherlands, and several important people from the disability world in the United States in that group. The second group was with some close friends of mine with whom I meet regularly, one a psychiatrist, the other a professor and philosopher.

In the first setting I asked whether they felt disability was the result of the Fall, or was just a part of the natural range of human diversity, or something other that hadn't occurred to me. I was chided for even asking the question in the first place. "Who are we to questions God" was the response from one member of the group. I feel like I can ask questions of God about anything. Particularly because my question is one of trying to find understanding, not trying to question God's wisdom (although I would ask those questions as well if I had them). God is big enough to take our questions and either answer them or guide us through the process of further trust in him without a specific response. I left that discussion thinking that surely these people had thought about this question even though the weren't very interested in discussing the possibilities.

In the second group, the answer given to me was more of a "what difference does it make" kind of response. Now as far as I am concerned, it makes no difference in my day to day interactions with people with disabilities. However, there are many spurious notions of the why of disability floating around out there and there are people who ask the question for a wide variety of reasons. If I say that disability is not the result of the parent's or the person with disabilities' sin (see John 9) to use a reason sometimes provided in Christian circles then I must look to other reasons. Is the reason the syrupy sentimentality about specialness? Are people with disabilities actually angels who are unaware? Are they there to teach us something, i.e. living object lessons? If I am going to refute these ideas, do I simply say "I don't know what the reason is but it not what you say it is?" I can test some ideas against the truth of scripture (e.g. the result of sin notion) which can support or refute an idea.

One of my friends in the second group said that it is not the event in itself that is important but the fact that God is with us through the event. He cited stories about the twin towers incident on 9-11 and how God's presence was made real to the fire fighters through prayer and encouragement when they took brief breaks from their heroic efforts. I heartily agree that God is with us through all the circumstances of our lives. That is not an issue for me.

I guess the reason why this question is important to me is that if I am to say that your reason for the why of disability is not biblically sound, I need to also say this is what the biblically sound reason is. I also do recognize that we are to trust in the Lord and not lean on our own understanding (Proverbs 3:5). If we do that, God will indeed be with us and as the verse says will make our paths straight.

So this is not a point of faith for me; my faith is not tied up in whether I get an answer to this question. But it is a point of understanding. An understanding largely of who God is through the work of his creation.

Sunday, May 21, 2006

Community Integration

This week I am headed up to Montreal for a conference on social inclusion of persons with disabilities, particularly those experiencing intellectual disability. As I plan to attend the conference I am increasingly more confident about the role the Church has to play in the community integration of persons with disabilities and their families. It is pretty easy to make the case for Christian churches as the place where disenfranchised, devalued individuals can find integration into the community.

If you think about the Church, it exists to worship and serve God, to do what is right as well as it can understand it, and to support its membership. We have also received a call to go out into the world and make disciples of all nations, so there is an outward focus as well. In each of these areas, the inclusion of persons with disabilities makes perfect sense. They worship God, they try to do what is right, and are quick to help others if given the opportunity. I have found that they also do what they can to speak to others about God, or at least have a positive witness. Through simple efforts on the part of the Church, community integration might also be facilitated.

The secular human service world is pretty much desperate to find ways in which persons with intellectual disability can be integrated into the community. All the while, there is the ubiquitous presence of churches. Those in human services, particularly those in academia who prepare human service workers are often unchurched or have a negative perspective towards all things religious. On the other side, the Church is blind to persons with disabilities, quite often, and is blind toward things related to disability. Over the years, I have been trying to help the secular see the potential of things religious and the church to see the potential in things "disabled." God willing, one day, the two will come together and the outcome will be beneficial for all three. The secular will see the benefit of integration through the church, the church will see the benefit of being obedient to God in including persons with disability in the church and the persons experiencing disability will have the benefit of knowing what it is to be integrated into the community rather than being ignored or discriminated against. As I have said elsewhere, one day the involvement of persons with intellectual disability in churches, their referral to a church by a secular agent of the state may become as obvious as taking an aspirin for a headache.

Saturday, April 29, 2006

Removing the feeding tube

I just heard that a lifetime friend of mine who had fallen into Alzheimer's disease has possibly had her feeding tube removed. Both she and her family are absolutely wonderful people. They have been a model for me of love and caring in an extremely difficult situation. But apparently the disease has progressed to the point that the decision to remove the feeding tube has been made.

I must admit that I am very conflicted on this whole issue. Knowing these friends the way I do, only adds to my conflicted feelings.

On the one hand this is the active taking of a life. There is no way to remove food from a person without having the effect of taking his life. So this is a conscious decision to take a life, to kill someone to put it bluntly. When I state it in this manner it seems obvious that to remove the feeding tube is wrong.

Yet, if a person is at the end of her life as my friend is, is it humane to deliberately take her life? The fact that I would even entertain such a question makes me wonder about the degree to which I have bought a secular, liberal society's understanding of the value of life in its various forms and its various stages. Clearly my friend is not suffering by any measure that can be made. So the suffering that is being alleviated is not hers. Who knows where her mind is at this point in time? Is she better off dead? The death process will be made "easier" through the delivery of pain medication. The apostle Paul when confronted with the choice between life and death says that he doesn't know what he should choose. He says to die is gain. Should I usher others into death because I believe to die is gain? I hardly think so.

For myself, I would of course hate to be a burden to my family. Particularly me as a large person would be difficult to care for, to move around. However, I also would not want the taking of my life to be at the hands of my family. Because society would allow my wife to remove the feeding tube from my body, does not mean that I would want my wife to have my death on her hands no matter how humanitarian she might think she was being. You see it is one thing to remove various life supports from me such as medicines or other dramatic measures to keep me alive. It is quite another thing to stop feeding me. If food is keeping me alive than I am no different than anyone else. I am no different from children with severe disabilities. Your decision to stop feeding me now becomes based upon your judgment of the value of my life.

What criteria might you use to make a determination of the value of my life? Perhaps you might use a return on investment criteria, or my potential contribution, or something of that sort. The question is why would you enter into this discussion in the first place? Why would you enter into a discussion of how to determine whether someone's life is worth living? Particularly when you cannot get the perception of the person themselves who are living under that set of conditions.

Additionally, as soon as we enter into the discussion, we affirm that there are some lives worth living and some which are not and those who would take life win the point. Perhaps a better position would be to simply say that I will not have this discussion because I know where it leads. Are we unwilling to say that all life is valuable and precious, or can we be brought to a point where we will say that a particular life no longer has value, based on a set of criteria which we would probably not be willing to see more broadly applied?

I have mentioned before that I am reading a book called "By trust betrayed" which is about the taking of the lives of persons with various disabilities during the time of the Nazis in Germany. Yes there was great evil involved in the practices which led to the deaths of hundreds of thousands of persons with disabilities. But there were also many who felt they were providing humanitarian aid to people they perceived as suffering. So there were those who honestly felt they were humanitarians of the highest order (the difficulty of their decisions only adding to there love for the people they chose to euthanize) when they sent people with epilepsy or schizophrenia or intellectual disability to their deaths. It seems that there was also the proverbial "slippery slope" where the killing of the most severely disabled led to the killing of less disabled and less disabled, etc.

Are people better off dead? Would we be willing to have the process we moved through to make decisions to stop feeding someone be broadly applied? Are we willing to have death on our hands, independent of absolute love and desire for the best for a person that went into such a decision? Is it really heroic on our part to make a decision for death for a loved one who we perceive is living a life not worth living? Should I put such a decision on a loved one?

These are the questions that swirl through my mind as I think about such situations.

Friday, April 14, 2006

Crash

I finally had the opportunity to view the movie *Crash*, recent winner of the Academy Award for best picture. I found the film very thought provoking on a variety of fronts, however, one scene in particular struck me.

Throughout the film, you get to know a character who is an reflective/thoughtful African-American man who is the brother of a city lawyer and a car thief. You also learn that he does 3 things which the film portrays as uncharacteristic of a black man 1) he loves hockey, 2) he has a developing interest in country music, and 3) either he is Catholic, or simply has an interest because he carries around a St. Christopher statue that he puts on the dashboard after he steals cars. Anyway, in the scene which interested me, an off duty white police officer, a young idealist who has recently raised complaints about racism on the LA police force, picks up the car thief who is hitch hiking. In the course of the conversation, the black guy mentions that he was in the area of the town ice skating because he had always wanted to be a goalie. The white idealist doesn't believe him. The black man says he is developing an interest in country music which once again the white guy doesn't believe. Then the black guy looks up at the dashboard, and there is the same statue that he always carries around. He just starts laughing. The white guy gets angry and tells him to get out of the car, he thinks he is being mocked as no black man, likes country music and wants to be a hockey goalie. The black guy says to hold on as he reaches into his pocket to get the statue that he always carries of St. Christopher. At that point, the white guy tells him to keep his hands where they can be seen, but he keeps digging in his pocket to get the statue. As he pulls it out of his pocket the white guy shoots and ultimately kills him. The statue falls out of the black guy's hand.

As an observer, you sit there stunned. How could this happen? The complete disconnection between two people is perfectly illustrated. It is as if each of them approached the other through the socially constructed stereotypes they had been socialized to believe and when the black man in particular, did not meet the stereotypes of the white man we end up on very uncomfortable ground, where we don't know how to act or relate. In spite of the evidence otherwise, we act on our stereotypes. In the off duty cop's mind, the black man was obviously in the area of town, not to ice skate, but to rob or be involved in some sort of criminal activity.

How do we see persons with disabilities? What stereotypes to we bring to our interactions with them? What do we do when they do not meet the stereotypes we have for them? For those of us who are working to change the Church, what negative stereotypes do churches and those in leadership bring which result in the demise of those they would claim to help. In reality, the white cop was appalled at racism when he saw it. In the same way, the Church speaks of all people being equal and loved by God. But ultimately, when confronted with a real person, the white cop's racism came through as well. He wasn't specifically harassing people, and was even trying to help people who had been victims of racism (another of the movie's powerful scenes). But inside, he was capable of killing another person largely on the basis of his racist stereotypes which were just below the surface. The church also has discriminatory stereotypes, particularly about people with disabilities, which are "killing" people through their exclusion.

In the same manner that Crash expertly puts the finger on racism and race relations, we must do the same with discrimination against persons with disability where ever it might appear, but particularly within the Church.

Monday, April 03, 2006

Crash again

In the previous post, I related the scene from the movie Crash about the white cop and the black hitchhiker. Please revisit that description.

Another aspect of that interaction intrigued me. I suspect that the hitchhiker thought he was connecting with the cop, or at least thought he was attempting to connect with the cop. He talked about how he liked hockey, which he was socialized to think was a characteristic of white people. He also gave the impression he was developing an interest in country music. Once again, a good old white boy, driving an old car, the hitch hiker thought he was connecting with the cop when in reality he was illustrating his misperceptions about who white people are (true the cop was listening to country music on the radio).

We do the same thing with people with disabilities. We assume we know something about them because of the things we have been told, the way we have been socialized.

My daughter Amy and I love the film *Good Will Hunting* ("How do you like them apples!?). One of the scenes which we love is when Robin Williams' character confronts Matt Damon's character who has intimated that he understands what it is like to have the life experience that Robin Williams has had. Williams' character asks whether Damon knows what the Sistine Chapel smells like because he has read about Michelangelo, or what it is like to hold a dying friend during a war because he has read *War and Peace*, or to go through the cancer of a loved one because he knows something about cancer. Williams also asks whether he (Williams) would know what it is like to grow up as an orphan (like Damon) because he has read Oliver Twist. The answer to all of these questions is obviously NO. Yet the Damon character acted as if he understood Williams without any life experience.

We do that. We do that all the time with people with disabilities. I must constantly remind myself that many of my friends experiencing intellectual disabilities see themselves as **totally normal**. My friends with Down's syndrome see themselves at **TOTALLY NORMAL**. They are living their lives and are pretty much happy with their lives. Others, however, think that they know what it is like to be disabled so they want

71

to "alleviate their suffering" through abortion. They think they must be upset with their lot in life. They think that their disability consumes them. I don't know how to say this any more clearly.

THEY SEE THEMSELVES AS NORMAL.

There is nothing immoral about their disability or their perception of themselves in that way. It does no harm to me or anyone for them to see themselves as normal. It doesn't cost any more money for them to see themselves as normal. Yet we project our ideas on them and attempt to interact with them on the basis of our stereotypes and constructions of who we think they are.

What has the Church intimated about how it feels about people with intellectual disabilities? Do our actions indicate that we think they are just people? Does the Church's interactions in any way indicate that it sees people with disability in the way people experiencing disability see themselves? Or is the Church like the Matt Damon character, who having no experience, thinks he knows something? Matt Damon had an excuse as he was an impoverished orphan living in slums. What is the Church's excuse for not knowing or understanding?

What will it take for the rest of us to see people experiencing disability through their own eyes?

Friday, April 07, 2006

"Don't be conformed to this world..."

Romans 12:2 says,

"Don't be conformed to this world, but be transformed by the renewing of your mind, so that you may prove what is the good, well-pleasing, and perfect will of God."

It takes courage for pastors to embrace a ministry to persons with disabilities. I mean to **REALLY** embrace such a ministry. It causes ministry structures to change in order to be inclusive of all who might want to participate in the programs of the church. It takes courage because there will be resistance to change generally, resistance to people who haven't yet and perhaps never will master social skills, and many congregational members may feel uncomfortable. At least they may at first. Some may complain and claim they are not "being fed" (meaning, I guess, that the bottle has fallen out of their mouths). The response is not to exclude, but to change the way that things are done such that more individuals can be involved. The fact that current ministry structures do not include persons with various disabilities implies that they were developed without the involvement of persons with disabilities in the first place.

For example, there is a church that I know of whose youth program is held on the second floor of a building with only stairs to the second floor. This is more than just an ADA issue. Clearly there are times when ministries will be designed for specific groups (recovering alcoholics, victims of various forms of abuse) but the more "generic" programs should be reflective of a perspective that errs on the side of being inclusive of all who would choose to attend.

People with disabilities, particularly those with physically obvious differences (like Down's syndrome) are an easy target. I can see the outward evidence of their disability in their facial appearance. I can link their intellectual disability quickly to a physical appearance and dismiss them. It is harder to design ministry that aims at and fosters a wider range of "normal."

I have heard pastors wonder aloud, "What do you expect me to do?" Well, I expect you to speak about persons with disability from the pulpit, to advocate for their inclusion in the programs of the church. To encourage the congregation to get out there and bring them in. I first expect pastors to use their pulpit to develop awareness. I would then expect them to be involved in the ministry, if only making an occasionally appearance, or taking the time to interact with class members. I remember a pastor of mine, Dr. Paul Cedar, once chose a man with developmental disabilities to be his weekly prayer partner for midweek Bible studies. This was a year long commitment. This spoke volumes to the congregation about who he felt persons with disabilities are. I expect pastors to **not** be conformed to the patterns of the world as they are reflected in the structures of the church, but to be transformed by the renewal of their minds. What would a church look like who truly included all individuals who would choose to participate? What demands would be placed on the congregation to ensure that persons who do not have a driver's license got to church? It is easy to say you will include me if I come when you know full well that I have no ability to get there other than perhaps hours on a bus.

Then an issue that I continue to struggle with is what would inclusive programs look like? I don't think that the whole church should revolve around any particular group of potential members, but what changes might be implemented that would both indicate to the congregation that these individuals are a priority, that they are worthy of our time, and also would not exclude them on the basis of contrived criteria for program involvement? To what degree is intelligence (for example) a criteria for involvement in the Christian church? If it is a criteria, what does that imply about our programs, who we want to be involved in our programs, who we think the church is for? Clearly intelligence (continuing to use this example) is important for attending college, or being able to perform in some jobs. But is intelligence critical for church involvement? Is intelligence critical to being a follower of Christ?

We need to step back and consider the way we do things in the Christian church. We need to reflect on the degree to which our programs, our structures are reflective of something other than a renewed mind, under the control of God's Holy Spirit. Are we doing things because they are the best way of doing things or are we doing things because we either cannot or will not be transformed by the renewing of our minds?

Friday, March 17, 2006

"They'll know we are Christians by our lack of experience"

It struck me this week how inexperienced the average person who attends a church is about persons with disabilities. I know a wide variety of Christians at various stages in their spiritual development who attend various denominations within the larger Christian church, but I always am somewhat surprised about how little they have been around persons with disabilities of various types. Now I wouldn't necessarily have the same expectation of those outside of church, however, it occurs to me that the lack of experience, knowledge, interactions of Christians with persons with disabilities, rank and file Christians, is further evidence of the Church's lack of inclusion of persons with disabilities in local churches. Can you imagine having a church in the Greater Los Angeles Basin, where I live, and having no experience with people of Hispanic descent, or people who are primarily Spanish language speakers? Wouldn't you think it strange for people to recoil at people with that background when the region enjoys such a significant Hispanic population?

The US census tells us that 20 percent of the population experiences a disability, but I can introduce a Christian person to someone with intellectual disability and it is an entirely new experience.

As I have said elsewhere, we should be leading the way in reaching out to devalued people with love, and inclusion and respect, and service, but we have missed it somehow, and do not even think it strange that our experience in this area is so limited. It is an indictment on us as a Christian church that we lack experience with such individuals who should be in our midst on a regular basis, at least once a week you would think.

Thursday, March 09, 2006

Listening to the spirit of the world

A frequent respondent to this blog who contributes under the name "impossibleape" wrote the following.

"Our church administrator told me today that if the Holy Spirit directs them to serve the disabled they will but apparently the Holy Spirit has no more interest in my children than the board members do."

You know, I am very skeptical or have become very skeptical of those who claim to have such a connection to the Holy Spirit that He frequently whispers in their ears, particularly when He whispers things which are contrary to the revealed Word of God in the form of the Bible. It appears to me that the spirit they are listening to is attempting to subvert the Word of God. It occurs to me that because the Holy Spirit inspired the word of God, maybe those who claim to be hearing his voice are rather reflecting the voice of someone else who is whispering in their ears. It could be the spirit of this world which is a scary thought. Actually I wonder if the spirit they are listening to is an even more debased spirit than others as the secular world has done much to include and integrate persons with disabilities, particularly in public schools.

In relation to the issues we discuss on this blog, there are too many churches, pastors, leaders, administrators of churches, etc. who are listening to a spirit of the world. How could one truly be seeking to hear the Spirit of God on this issue and express no interest, no priority? How evil to blame our lack of caring and love on a lack of prompting by God's Holy Spirit? In other words they are saying, "It is the fault of the Spirit of God that I am not caring for persons with disabilities. It is not the desire of God's Spirit that I do so."

Matthew 12:31-32

"Therefore I say to you, any sin and blasphemy shall be forgiven men, but blasphemy against the Spirit shall not be forgiven. And whoever shall speak a word against the Son of Man, it shall be forgiven him; but whoever shall speak against the Holy Spirit, it shall not be forgiven him, either in this age, or in the {age} to come.

Mark 3:28-30

"Truly I say to you, all sins shall be forgiven the sons of men, and whatever blasphemies they utter; but whoever blasphemes against the Holy Spirit never has forgiveness, but is guilty of an eternal sin."

Luke 12:10

"And everyone who will speak a word against the Son of Man, it shall be forgiven him; but he who blasphemes against the Holy Spirit, it shall not be forgiven him.

Sure each of us are prompted in various ways to minister and to use our gifts in different ways. However, we are talking about an agent of the Church. The church that is saying it has **not** been guided by the Holy Spirit to respond to a group of potentially hurting people who are in need. I don't know who these leaders think people experiencing disabilities are or where they came from. That perhaps they fall from the sky, or crawl from under a rock. NO, they are parts of families and as the church ministers to families it needs to minister to **all** the members of the family. The Bible says we are to minister to those who are poor. Do a need a sign from God, or the Holy Spirit to speak to me in an audible voice to minister to the poor when the Bible is replete with allusions to me helping the poor? If a church leader told you that he hadn't received the prompting of the Holy Spirit to minister to the poor, what could you think other than that he is out of touch with God's Word and God's Spirit? If he said God Spirit hadn't directed him to share salvation with all people, only some, what would you think?

No, let's call this what it is. It is disobedience.

Wednesday, March 01, 2006

"We'll take you and not you"

I was hit today with something quite obvious, but I hadn't thought about it in this way before. It struck me that churches/pastors will at times say that ministry to persons experiencing disabilities is not a particular priority. We have probably all heard that at one time or another in the past. But the obvious thing that hit me again today was that I (as a church, pastor, etc.) will look at your family, a family that includes a person experiencing disability and say, "Ministry to you, the person over there experiencing disability, is not a priority for our church." It is not like we are saying ministry to white or black or brown or other entire groups of people is not a priority. We are looking within families and saying that these individuals in your family are a priority for ministry and those others are not a priority for ministry. I first observed this with Christian schools who can be notorious for not serving students who would benefit from special education. But it is even broader than that, actually separating families by prioritizing some members of the family over others.

It also struck me that the ones we don't choose to serve are potentially the more difficult ones to serve because they don't fit the way in which we have designed services, designed ministry. The classic example for me which illustrates this point is the church who wouldn't allow a high school student who used a wheel chair to be a member of the youth group because the youth group met on the second floor of a building with no elevator. So rather than design services which meet on the first floor, or develop access to the second floor, we choose not to include those who do not fit our designed ministries.

It is interesting that the Department of Rehabilitation used to have a criteria, I guess still does, for receiving services. The criteria was that you had to be able to "benefit from services." So if you needed services for an extended period of time or forever for that matter, you were deemed ineligible because you couldn't benefit from services. You could potentially benefit from services, just not those provided. Ultimately through the novel thinking of Madeleine Will, the past Assistant Secretary of Special Education for the federal government, the definition of services to include ongoing services opened up the Department of Rehabilitation to those who could benefit from services over the long term. The people didn't change, the criteria for delivery of services and the types of services provided were changed.

This is a change that needs to find its way into the church. There are those who would argue that people experiencing disability cannot be integrated in to existing church programs. This excuse is used as a reason for exclusion. In my mind, the answer is not exclusion, it is the redesign of services such that those who might be able to benefit would indeed benefit. Don't tell me that you will not serve people because they don't fit your structures, change your freakin structures. A discriminatory church which has been in a discriminatory rut for perhaps over a century will not change easily, but it is not the people who have the problem, it is the discriminatory church that needs to change.

This is hard coming because it requires a great deal of courage on the part of the leadership, and that courage is not as prevalent as I wish it would be. Ministry is hard and it is about time that the rank and file church attendee learned that. Rather than dodging the difficult issues of ministry for fear of making attendees uncomfortable, we should be saying "We choose to include people experiencing disability, and it will make us change the comfortable ways we have been doing things to date." I wonder how many rank and file church members think ministry is easy, because they haven't been challenged to do it. I wonder how many would embrace the changes that would be required to truly include all of the people who would desire to attend church and participate in the programs of the church.

Wednesday, February 22, 2006

"decisions to continue or terminate are never medical decisions"

I recently reacquainted myself with an article by Roberts, Stough and Parish, written in 2002 entitled, *The Role of Genetic Counseling in the Elective Termination of Pregnancies Involving Fetuses with Disabilities* (published in the Journal of Special Education). I want to give you a few quotes from the article, interspersed with some of my comments. The authors state,

"...most prospective parents seem to consider Down's syndrome as involving severe intellectual disability. In actuality, 90% of all individuals with Down's syndrome fall within the mild to moderate range of functioning."

The perception of who persons with Down's syndrome are, has been one of the greatest misperceptions. It has taken on the status of "common sense" as social constructions often do. It has been reported that nearly 90% of babies with Down's syndrome, when diagnosed prenatally, are aborted.

"A woman's intention to terminate or continue a pregnancy did not appear related to her overall level of knowledge about disabilities...as the level of knowledge increased, the choice to continue the pregnancy was more likely...The women were asked if they had been encouraged to meet with the parent of a child with a disability during the prenatal screening process. The majority of women (91.3%) indicated that they had not been encouraged to meet with a parent by either the genetic counselor or any medical personnel."

Medical professionals and geneticists in particular I would bet have little knowledge about the day to day lives of persons with a variety of disabilities, including persons with Down's syndrome. Yet they are in the position of influencing vulnerable families about decisions relative to aborting children with Down's syndrome. I have mentioned elsewhere in this blog that the only suffering most people with Down's syndrome face is that of discrimination (beginning with the medical profession at the point of prenatal diagnosis). To address the societal discrimination persons with Down's syndrome face, with medical alternatives is entirely inappropriate. The group who is discriminated against avoids discrimination by having their lives taken, not by changing the society.

The article, also indicated that 72 % of participants had some Christian affiliation, yet 0%, NONE, NO ONE, reported the church as one of the "Sources of information women viewed as helpful during the genetic screening process." In 87% of cases, "doctor recommended" was most often the influence in seeking genetic counseling. Can you imagine if the church celebrated loved and accepted people with Down's syndrome? Prenatal diagnosis would signify not a terrible tragedy with

78

the only seeming alternative being abortion, but a new opportunity, a new adventure for the family. In particular, if the church were there being supportive, understanding, it would be a great blessing not only for the family but also for the church and the larger community.

Such suggestions to seek out knowledge are probably not going to come from institutions who support abortion of any child as an aspect of choice, particularly a child with Down's syndrome. But what if individuals with Down's syndrome and other disabilities were present in the church in numbers reflective of the community. What if parents and family members of persons with disabilities were known to people in the church. Would that have in any way stemmed the decision to abort because the "level of knowledge" had increased.

"Women who had knowledge of resources and programs that assist with the education, training, and care of a child with a disability were more likely to consider continuing the pregnancy. It may be that as women become more informed about the associations, agencies, and individuals available to assist people with disabilities, they start to view the task of raising a child with a disability as less overwhelming."

What programs is the local church providing generically, that are present in all churches, that would in any way cause prospective parents of a child with Down's syndrome to consider continuing the pregnancy? This article never mentions churches as any kind of attenuating agent in the decision making of prospective parents. Can you imagine if all of the Christian prospective parents in the study stated, "We are going to keep our baby with Down's syndrome because of the way the people with disabilities and their families are enfolded and celebrated within the Christian church."

"However, most women reported that they did not receive information about disability resources or quality-of-life issues from their genetic counselors. In addition, they did not believe that their counselor presented them with both the positive and the negative aspects of having a child with disabilities. This finding suggests that pregnant women make decisions based on limited information even after participating in genetic counseling."

Where would someone go to gain such information? What if the church became a clearinghouse for programs and services which would paint disability in a positive light? God asked Moses, "Who makes man's mouth" in response to his complaint about his inability to speak. It is arguable that God makes persons with Down's syndrome. We as a church, however, don't seem quite as happy about that fact as we might be. We have failed in celebrating the diversity of humanity to the point that prospective mothers would perhaps reconsider abortion of a child with Down's syndrome. What information, experience does the church provide about persons with disabilities and their place in the church and the larger society? People are dying because people think they will have a poor quality of life. How does the church contribute to the perception of someone having a good or poor quality of life?

The article cites Rothman (1993), as making the following statement:

"decisions to continue or terminate a pregnancy are never medical decision. They are always social decisions"(Rothman, 1993, p. 63)

Does the society of the Church contribute positively or negatively to the social decision making of people? Whether they are Christian or not, how does what we, the Church do, to influence decisions about whether to abort or not abort a child with a disability?

Thursday, January 19, 2006

The ultimate in discrimination

My friend and colleague, Rev. Bill Gaventa recently recommended a book to me and I am glad he did. It is, Hans S. Reinders' *The future of the disabled in a liberal society: An ethical analysis* (Notre Dame Press). I am only about half way through it, but I have thoroughly enjoyed what I have read thus far. For those of you who do not like to read philosophy, it is a bit thick, but it is definitely worth the effort. I want to provide an extended quote from page 46.

The context is the attempt to try to understand the reasons for abortion of children with disabilities in the context of "prevention" of genetic disorders.

"The aim of the proposed terminology is to suggest that, in principle, we can attack the consequences of a disease from two sides: not only by combating the disease with the diagnostic and therapeutic means that medicine provides but also by changing the social and cultural environment that makes for the cause of disability or handicap. The latter may be the objective of social and political reform rather than of medical intervention. The distinction between types of genetic disorders is important, then, because it generates different moral arguments. Preventing the birth of a disabled child because its life will be devalued as abnormal is surely morally different from preventing the birth of a disabled child that will suffer from serious illness. Even if in both cases their lives may be burdened by distress to similar degrees, their distress is very different in kind. Furthermore, being devalued as abnormal in our society may be seen as constituting a case of discrimination, which means that prevention in that case takes on a completely different meaning. *For it can be argued, given these different meanings, that in some cases prevention is a dubious response to a social evil.* At least that is what I think many people in our society will believe to be true. *Instead of confronting the agents of discrimination, one aims at preventing its victims from being born.* Consequently, people in our society may be worried about preventing disabled children for reasons of abnormality, even if at the same time they may accept that parents decide not to have a mentally disabled child in order to avoid serious suffering due to illness. *If the cause of the suffering is society rather than nature, the more appropriate response would be political rather than medical.* This indicates in which sense disabilities and handicaps caused by different kinds of genetic disorders may raise different sets of moral questions." (emphasis added)

Reading this, I can't help but come back to the notion of the church's protective function. We have the ability to provide succor with the potential effect of normalizing the lives and experience of persons with disability. Or by choosing to ignore or not prioritize ministry to persons with disability, we can be complicit in the discrimination which leads to practices such as abortion of such people. As Reinders states, the solution to alleviating the suffering of a significant group of persons with genetic disorders/disabilities is of a political or social nature. If the church would normalize persons with Down's syndrome, for example, the arguments for prevention of these lives through abortion would be harder to substantiate. We would also be all that we should be to the community, potentially having a dramatic effect on the understanding of who people with Down's syndrome are. People would have to say that persons with Down's syndrome suffer from discrimination, but only in environments outside of the Christian world. Within the Church and its agents, they are just people.

Tuesday, January 10, 2006

disabled Body of Christ
A student in one of my classes recently shared the passage from Corinthians about the Body of Christ. The passage states,
"The eye cannot say to the hand, "I don't need you!" And the head cannot say to the feet, "I don't need you!" On the contrary, those parts of the body that seem to be weaker are indispensable, and the parts that we think are less honorable we treat with special honor. And the parts that are unpresentable are treated with special modesty, while our presentable parts need no special treatment. But God has combined the members of the body and has given greater honor to the parts that lacked it, so that there should be no division in the body, but that its parts should have equal concern for each other. If one part suffers, every part suffers with it;

if one part is honored, every part rejoices with it. Now, you are the body of Christ and each one of you is a part of it" (1 Corinthians 12:21-27).

We touched on this passage back on March 30th. However, thinking through the notion of the body again, and even the title of this weblog, it occurred to me that we are a disabled body. The Body of Christ is a disabled body. Why is that? I would argue it is because we have selectively not included or even have cut off parts of the body, people with disabilities who would desire to be participants in the Body of Christ. It is as if we as the Church (using the Body of Christ metaphor) are limping around without a foot, or are seeing with only one eye or are missing the fingers of one hand. In the same manner that a person might become used to a missing aspect of their anatomy, the Church has become used to functioning without all of the members of it's body. It would be interesting to try to determine whether there was a point in the life of the Church when we actually 'cut off' that part of the body, or whether it was in some way 'born' without all their body parts. To push the metaphor further, the Church might not know what it is to walk with two feet or see with both eyes or have a hand with all of the fingers intact. That is what I have alluded to in the past in this weblog regarding that we really don't know what the Church could be if we included all of those who would choose to participate. We have grown used to being a disabled Body of Christ, grown used to being an incomplete body.

Can you imagine cutting off your foot because it wasn't a priority to have it as a part of your body? Can you imagine thinking, "I will get by with one eye because it will be too expensive to try to live with two eyes." To me, that is what we as the Church are doing. We are by choice deciding to be a disabled Body of Christ that does not include all of the parts.

Tuesday, December 13, 2005

Down's syndrome Genocide

In a fascinating article, the National Review discusses an article in the Washington Post entitled, "*Down's syndrome Now Detectable In 1st Trimester: Earlier Diagnosis Allows More Time for Decisions.*" Couching the issue of prenatal diagnosis and abortion as a **women's health issue**, the article states, "This is a big deal for women. It's going to have a big impact on care for women, not just in the United States but throughout the world." In a crazy example of doublespeak, the genocide of persons with Down's syndrome is a solution that is going to have "a big impact on care for women." This is not the genocide of an entire class of people, having a particular characteristic, which the Washington Post article didn't even attempt to overstate, "The syndrome results when a baby has three, rather than two, copies of the 21st chromosome, causing distinctive physical features, developmental problems and an increased risk of a variety of health problems that usually shorten the child's life span." The taking of Down's syndrome life is so prevalent, that euphemism (the substitution of an inoffensive term for one considered offensively explicit) in terms of describing who persons with Down's syndrome are is unnecessary. We are taking the life of a whole class of people because they have, "distinctive physical features," "developmental problems," and an "increased risk for a variety of health problems." Step back for a moment and think about this. If this doesn't cause you great concern, it should. People with Down's syndrome are some of the nicest people you will ever meet. But we choose to kill them, to wipe them out in the name of a "**big impact on care for women**." It is sick.

In response to this article, the National Review online posted its own editorial entitled, "*Defining Life Down: Are we okay with eliminating a class of humans?*" This article does a pretty good job in defining the issues and confronting us with the reality of the situation, we are "**eliminating a class of humans**."

Through training I have received from the Syracuse University Training Institute or Human Service Planning, Leadership and Change Agentry I have become sensitized to the issues. We are on a fast track to increased devaluation and termination of the lives of persons with disabilities. But my real question is, "What about the church?"

We, the Christian Church, are embracing the sins of the culture in direct opposition to the obvious and "most central themes of the Scriptures" (as Jim Wallis states in *God's Politics*, 2005). "Social location often determines biblical interpretation" (also Jim Wallis). Our social location is anywhere where people with disabilities aren't. No wonder we think we can exclude them with impunity in the face of God's commands.

Tuesday, December 06, 2005

Pride sucks or "I am better than you!"

I have been thinking a lot about pride as it relates to a variety of areas in my life, but particularly in relation to persons with disability.

If I were honest with myself, I think I would say that I believe I am better than my intellectually disabled friends. Its shameful to admit that, but I believe it is true. I am smarter than most, I am physically better off than most, I am wealthier than most, I have more opportunities (which of course I feel I deserve because of my efforts, my hard work), and on and on. The only thing which in any way reigns in my self-absorbing pride is the fact that God tells me that I am not better than anyone else. God tells me that we are all equal. In fact, the fact that I believe I am better, may make me worse than many others, particularly those I feel I am better than.

But I don't think that my problem is restricted to me (unfortunately). I honestly believe that in their heart of hearts, most of those who attend a church and call themselves Christians hold the same perspective as I do about how I/we, rank in relation to those among us who are disabled. I/we, like to say that we are all equal at the foot of the cross, but I (for example) have a Ph.D. and many of my friends are intellectually disabled, so obviously that can't be true. I/we say that we want to evangelize the world, however, I/we won't go out of our way to bring a disabled person to church so that can't be true. I mean, either I don't think the disabled person is worth my time, worth my effort to be picked up (because I am too busy to pick him up, or I have plans after church, or something else related to me and my importance) or I honestly do think they are my equal or perhaps even my better and do go out of my way to pick them up.

On several or more occasions the NT states that salvation is a gift, "so that no one can boast." So I/we don't boast about my having access to the most important thing, the point of life, because it is a gift, but I/we am quick to boast (although through socialization, not out loud) about all the other things I/we am able to do, which are of course, once again based upon my/our own efforts. I boast by my actions or by my inaction. I boast by my unwillingness which is only unwillingness because of the pride I have which makes me feel that I have more choices than I probably actually would have if I weren't so full of pride. One might think these other things that seem so important, are the most important thing the way I/we tend to rate these other things in importance by my/our behavior. The most important point in life is free, it is a gift so that no one can boast, but I/we exclude people on the basis of things which are not important. I/we don't brag about my/our salvation because it is a gift. But my intellect, my behavior, my physical stamina, my health, my good looks (if I had them) are of course not a gift, so those things can be the basis of differentiation amongst people.

I see myself through such a strange perspective. If I see God through a glass darkly, I see myself through a brick wall. We chuckle at the pride of others when we see it, because we see others the way they really are as compared to the way they think they are, we think. We also think we see ourselves clearly. I think that if it weren't for God in his mercy protecting me from seeing myself as I really am, I would be stymied to the point of being totally incapacitated by my pride, my sin, my self-centeredness my total disregard of God's purposes. But instead, he allows me to live on in some fairyland of totally unsupportable ideas of who I am.

Particularly who I am in comparison to others around me, and particularly in comparison to those who I see as below me, not worthy of my time or effort. Those who are "not a priority for ministry at this time," as I have heard too many times from Christian church leadership. What does it mean if a person or a group of persons is not a priority for ministry at this time? It seems to obviously imply that I, in my pride, can determine who is worth the effort (see Sept 28 entry), and unfortunately, for too long persons with intellectual disabilities have not been worth my/our effort.

Can you see how this is a problem of pride? Pride in individuals like me and pride in the church as a whole?

But there is something that I can boast about with total confidence. That is that God loves me, the way I am, full of myself and my importance. But God loves my friend with disabilities the way he is, full of himself and full of his importance. I wish I loved my friend like God loves me and my friend the same. I wish I believed in the importance of my friend with disabilities like God believes in the importance of me and my friend the same. I wish I could be willing to give my life for my friend with disabilities like God gave his life for me and my friend the same. I wish my behavior reflected the principles of equality that I say I believe in. I wish my behavior reflected the importance of all people before the cross the way that I say I believe in the importance of all people. I wish my thoughts about myself and my friends with disabilities reflected the thoughts of God about me and my friends with disabilities being both the same.

Tuesday, November 29, 2005

The Theological Voice of Wolf Wolfensberger 1

I have been reading The Theological Voice of Wolf Wolfensberger, which is a book of Dr. Wolfensberger's writings on disability from a theological perspective. Dr. Wolfensberger is renowned for his work in areas related to human rights, education and other issues impacting particularly persons with developmental disabilities. However, this book (edited by Bill Gaventa and David Coulter) is an absolute must read for persons interested in notions of intellectual disability and disability from a theological perspective. The next few entries will interact with some of the thoughtful discussion provided in this volume.

In "The Prophetic Voice and Presence of Intellectually disabled People in the World Today" (a presentation made by Dr. Wolfensberger in 1976) the following statements (they really should be read in context) are made.

"So I asked myself, what are the prophetic signs which appear to be unique or very special to our day, which are very different from what they have been at other times. . . Where and how is the Spirit active today in a way that is different from the way it may have been in other eras?

As I posed these questions to myself over the past few years, I began to read both the signs of dysfunctionality and of prophecy in a different and clearer fashion, and I read one very, very powerful prophetic message, coming from intellectually disabled people. For instance, I considered that it should not be unexpected if divine messages about the present patterning of offenses should come from people who, in their roles and identities, are exactly the opposite of what our era idolotrates. Who and what is the opposite? The opposite is a person who is not intellectual, not scientific, not technological, and not academic; who does simple instead of complex things; who cannot cope with complexity, and technology which passes him by; and who, possibly, is despised for lack of modernity and intellectuality. Is that not the retarded persons of our age?

But if it is, is there any evidence that God has thrust retarded people into a prophetic role? I submit to you that there is indeed . . ."

The article goes on to list 10 signs to substantiate the possibility that persons with intellectual disability are indeed carrying a prophetic message.

-Intellectually disabled Persons are Becoming Much More Public and Visible

-Retarded People are Becoming Internationally Known

-Non-Handicapped and Handicapped Persons are Sharing Their Lives, Often Living Together

-Retarded Persons are Gentling Others

-The Prophetic Manifestation of the Presence of God via Retarded People

-Retarded People Speaking in Tongues

-Retarded People may Withstand Their Culture

-Retarded People May Be Parodying Intellectualism

-The Dance of Spiritual Joy

-Retarded People Are Beginning to Be Persecuted and Martyred

No doubt Dr. Wolfensberger's writing on this topic will cause you to think through, to consider his position. For each of the signs he describes the sign and how he has seen it evidenced. His perspective is very interesting. Under the sign, "Retarded People are Beginning to be Persecuted and Martyred," he makes the statement,

"The logic is compelling: the world has always tried to put to death God's prophecy, and it is the nature of God's will that prophets must be prepared to be martyrs, and disproportionately they are. The **moment retarded people in significant numbers become bearers of the word of God, the principalities and powers will converge upon them to fight and stifle that form of prophecy that is so specially powerful all because of its much more miraculous nature, and because in some ways, it goes beyond what any other type of prophecy has said before** (my emphasis). . . we have never been told in systematic prophecy that human intellect is universally bankrupt, and that millennia of technological development is at an end."

There is a connection here, I believe, with our earlier discussions in this blog of Down's syndrome, prenatal diagnosis, etc. It is not unusual for persons with developmental disabilities, yes, intellectual disability, to change those around them. Personally, I recognize a kind of a prophetic voice about the importance of love and caring and genuine friendship. These kinds of principles fly in the face of the calculations which are driven by technology . . . "Will this person have a good quality of life?" . . . "Is it cheaper to test infants for PKU, or just to deal with the disabilities which will result if we don't?" . . . "What do the percentages tell us about whether or not parents carrying a particular gene will produce a child with a disability?" . . . "Is it more cost effective to spend millions of dollars on political campaigns, or to provide housing subsidies to persons on fixed incomes?" . . . and so on.

And where is the moral compass in this situation? Where is the salt that gives the world its flavor? Where is the light on the hill? Wolfensberger makes the claim that persons with intellectual disability are prophets to the culture, to the church. You may not agree but it makes you think.

I am confident that Jesus would be hanging out with the unwelcomed people with intellectual disability and other disabilities in the group homes and care facilities.

Tuesday, August 23, 2005

The Theological Voice of Wolf Wolfensberger 2

I have been reading The Theological Voice of Wolf Wolfensberger, which is a book of Dr. Wolfensberger's writings on disability from a theological perspective.

In "An Attempt Toward a Theology of Social Integration of Devalued/Handicapped People" (a paper presented in 1978) Dr. Wolfensberger takes on the notion of segregation by whomever of a group deemed as different in some way. This principle has particular relevance to the church to the degree that it acts to segregate persons with various disabilities from the general congregation. The following comments are made about how segregation begins.

"In truth the one single characteristic of a person, or of a group, that can override all other shared characteristics of people in being used as the justification of segregation can be utterly trivial. It is remarkable in itself that one single characteristic can be presumed to differentiate people so totally, i.e., in that this characteristic can override everything else, even thousands of other characteristics the segregators and the segregatees share. If we just contemplate this one little reality, we may be stunned by its magnitude, especially when we consider that this one overriding characteristic can be something as minor as skin color, the shape of one's ears, left-handedness in Japan, or something of this nature. Even when the characteristic is not trivial, it pales in comparison to the massiveness of the shared characteristics...segregatory congregation also signals back to society that the one characteristic that the congregated people supposedly share with each other is more important than all the thousands of characteristics they share with the segregators.

Now there are times when some forms of segregation make a degree of sense because the point of segregation is relevant. For example, we wouldn't expect to see persons with intellectual disability studying medicine in medical schools. Their difference would be a point of relevant segregation from the field of medicine."

What, however, are the relevant characteristics for segregation from a local church?

1 Corinthians 1: 27 and following states,

"But God chose the foolish things of the world to shame the wise; God chose the weak things of the world to shame the strong. He chose the lowly things of this world and the despised things - and the things that are not - to nullify the things that are, so that no one may boast before him. It is because of him that you are in Christ Jesus, who has become for us wisdom from God - that is our righteousness, holiness and redemption."

Who has the Church chosen? What are the relevant characteristics that are so different from the rest of us that we see fit to exclude them from out midst? God chooses "the things that are not." Who do we choose?

Monday, August 29, 2005

The Truman Show

I was watching the movie The Truman Show tonight. I have always found the movie very interesting. Anyway, one of the main characters in the movie, Kristoff, the guy who created the reality television program called "The Truman Show" makes the following statement.

"We accept the reality of the world with which we're presented."

An interesting statement. In terms of the real world, I agree and I disagree with the statement.

I agree in that I don't think that I have abilities and deficits other than the ones I have come to know after nearly 50 years of being me (although I do think higher and lower of myself then I should at times). I also recognize that the world I live in is a dangerous place, and there is such a thing as evil. For me to think otherwise is a fantasy.

I also cannot project my life experience on another, or compare my life experience with another's and have any notion that how I view his life is how he will view his life. My life experience is reality to me in the same way that another's life experience is reality to him. I will at times look at others and imagine how they might feel about a particular life experience, but I really don't know the process they have gone through to understand their life and am therefore very limited in my understanding.

I disagree in that I don't have to accept the reality of the world with which I am presented if I have the fortitude to change it. The "reality of the world" for persons with disability, for example, does not reflect the reality of who they are. They may finally give in and submit themselves to the reality thrust upon them. They can also fight them with the assistance of others who also reject the reality of the presented world because it needs to be changed.

Sunday, July 31, 2005

Mark 7/Isaiah 29

This people honors me only with lip-service
while their hearts are far from me.
The worship they offer me is worthless,
the doctrines they teach are only human regulations.

That is how Jesus' quoting of a passage from Isaiah 29 is reported in the Jerusalem Bible. Jesus goes on to say, "You put aside the commandment of God to cling to human traditions. How ingeniously you get around the commandment of God in order to preserve your own tradition."

I recently visited a church where they were celebrating work done with orphans in Africa. This church has been instrumental in building and supporting this orphanage. As the slides of beautiful African children were shown in the background, the comment was made, "We are all the same in God's sight. We need to care for these children because we are all the same in God's sight." I couldn't agree more. The work this church is doing is wonderful. They are making a great impact on the lives of children a half a world away.

But what about the people in need in their own back yard? As I looked around the congregation, I saw one man who appeared to have a form of cerebral palsy. But beyond that, he was the only person in the room that I could detect as having any form of disability.

It seems that we get around the commandment of God to preserve our own traditions. In this case, the tradition is to be involved in overseas ministry which is an outstanding tradition. But the commandment of God says we should also touch our neighbor. Our traditions of overseas ministry may have given us the perspective of less responsibility at home, particularly towards underserved people in our community.

The work I observed that the church was doing with the African orphans was beautiful! But I still wondered why that church could not see the people with disability in their own community.

The traditions of the church really do need to be shaken up because they are getting around the commandment of God. All people are created in God's image and are loved by God. But the "difficult" ones are not in churches. Why are the supposedly easier people to serve the ones who are in church if we really do believe that the commandment of God is to love everyone in the same manner that He loves us. Why are the supposedly easier people to serve the only ones that I could really prove are created in God's image by their presence in a church? I must argue too, that persons with intellectual disabilities are not really harder to serve. Someday the church will discover that.

I am reminded of the passage in Matthew 23, where Jesus is putting the hammer down on the scribes and Pharisees. In regards to tithing, he says in verse 23, "These you should have practiced without neglecting the others." I don't think it is too far out of context to say that without neglecting the important work with African orphans, we should also be working to include persons with disabilities in our communities in our own churches.

You want to buck tradition? Start bringing the people with intellectual disability to church.

Thursday, July 14, 2005

"A More Perfect Society"

In the July 2005 *Christianity Today*, there is an editorial piece by Angela Beise entitled, *"A More Perfect Society: Why I wouldn't want to live there."* In the article, Ms. Beise describes an interaction with an itinerant teacher she used for her son with disabilities while she was living in France. She begins the article by stating that in France, the "the society in general isn't friendly to the disabled. In our area of Paris alone, there are 300 special needs children on a waiting list for a place in a school." She then goes on to state the following.

"As she (the teacher) was leaving our house after a therapy session, she advised us to apply to a couple of schools that are specifically for children with Down's syndrome, even though Michael does not have Down. Then she made the shocking statement, "Schools for Down children are starting to take children with other syndromes since Down is becoming so rare," she said. "Now that tests can tell so early in pregnancy that a baby has Down, few people are choosing to have them."

Amazing when our choices come home to roost. A world without people with Down's syndrome. I know a lot of people with that particular syndrome, and I pray that people like them will always be in the world. They are some of the kindest, most friendly people you could ever want to meet. But our world misunderstands who they are and in the name of "quality of life" chooses abortion. They are comparatively easy to be rid of as well. Not to say that abortion is easy, but the diagnoses which have become routine make an unborn child with Down's syndrome easy to identify.

And doctors are telling us that they should just be aborted or at least offering tests for Down's syndrome should the conditions be right (they are required by law to do so!) and another pregnancy attempted. Other groups who I refuse to even mention in this blog talk about choice in pregnancy. **All I can say is this is evil.** Can I be more blunt than to label the complete obliteration of persons with Down's syndrome from the world as nothing less than evil? One need only read about the history of doctor recommendations in relation to institutions for persons with intellectual disability to recognize that they can be not only wrong, but contributors to outcomes which reflect the very worst that man is capable of.

As a medical student (I later flunked out of medical school) I took a class in genetics. The genetics professor was giving a lecture on Down's syndrome, as it is caused by having 3 copies of chromosome 21 instead of the typical 2 copies. In the discussion, he made the statement, "It is important to remember that people with Down's syndrome are people." For a moment I rejoiced at his statement. But then he followed it up with, "And some of them may actually develop a personality." One of the greatest things about persons with Down's syndrome is their wonderful personalities. I wondered how many people this guy actually knew with Down's syndrome to be able to make such a ridiculous statement. But these are the kinds of people who are making recommendations to families about Down's syndrome in terms of prevention and abortion.

These are the people who are delivering the diagnosis to parents and families with a total lack of understanding of who these individuals are.

I can criticize doctors and I can criticize the French (that actually seems to be in vogue now) but I wonder where the church is in all this. What is the church's position on Down's syndrome, for example? Would most pastors even know what it was, or the effects it has on individuals, or what to say to families who had a child with Down's syndrome born to them?

I wonder if the church in its attitudes towards persons with disability and its lack of knowledge about persons with disability may actually support a position of aborting children with Down's syndrome, or at least a position that the abortion of a disabled child is somewhat more understandable, or less worthy of condemnation than the abortion of any other child.

As sad as I was to see the piece in Christianity Today because of the story it told, I was also happy to think that maybe stories such as the one told by Ms. Beise would be another step in waking the church to its responsibility towards all of humanity.

The abortion of children with Down's syndrome is nothing more than a new form of eugenics. Perhaps we are not out to purify the human race, at least not overtly, but the systematic abortion of a particular group of people, people who are lovely people generally, because we don't understand them, or have no experience with them, or project some feelings we might have about what their lives might be like on them, all of which are misinformed is evil and wrong. It is time for the church to rise up in defense of these individuals. The church should be providing counseling about what Down's syndrome is, and include persons with Down's syndrome routinely in the congregation. Church people should be at the beside at the birth of a child with Down's syndrome and begin their interactions by saying, "Children with Down's syndrome are a gift from God! Bring them to us, we will love them and their families."

Thursday, July 07, 2005

"Bring them to me"

That is reported as Mother Theresa's response to those who would abort their babies. That is, have the baby and she would take the responsibility for caring for those children who escaped abortion.

Those should also be the words of the Christian church in response to a wide variety of disenfranchised people, but in particular, persons with disabilities. Bring them to us, bring them to church. You know, it is one thing to be against abortion, or mistreatment of people for whatever reason. It is quite another to want to offer solutions to problems, particularly when they involve a commitment of time on your behalf. A ministry to persons with intellectual disability provides "teeth" to arguments which would support the lives of persons with disabilities. One could never accuse Mother Theresa of just being against abortion. She was against abortion with a solution in hand.

As Christians, we need to do much better in supporting our rhetoric, or maybe I should say in supporting Jesus' rhetoric. As I related in the April 20, 2005 entry from Kierkegaard, "Yes, it is even dreadful to be alone with the New Testament." Particularly if you are endeavoring to follow it in what it teaches. Such an effort first requires that you take the time to find out what it says, and second that you do what it says. Neither of these are particularly easy.

But if we claim to be following Christ, there should at least be evidences that we are making the effort to understand what He said and making the effort to do what He has told us to do. What might those evidences look like?

It might begin with more clarity about what the scriptures say about disability. I am completing a survey of church members from a variety of denominations about disability, and if one thing comes through it is the confusion about who persons with disabilities are. To me this is a reflection of the confusion in the leadership about who persons with disabilities are. Christian leaders need to rise up and take on understanding disability and sharing that theological understanding with others in leadership and with their own congregations. In spite of the presence of persons with disabilities in the community, the presence of persons with disabilities in the scriptures, there is surprisingly little theological writing to guide an understanding of who these folks are from a theological perspective.

Then, because we don't know who they are, we don't know what to do to serve them. At least Mother Theresa had a notion of who a baby is and what her or his needs would be. We don't know who persons with disability are or what their needs are. Sometimes I hear young adults talk about babies as if they are from another planet or something. They speak as if they would be totally unprepared to deal with a baby should they have one. Their speech reminds me of those who are unprepared to deal with a person with a disability. In the same way that a baby being born into a family is totally natural, the enfolding of a person with disability into a church should be natural. Interestingly, you will find that those young adults generally do pretty well with their new baby when it comes. The church would do well to.

So I would say to parents of persons with disability, "Bring them to me (the church)" and let us prove our rhetoric with some action.

Tuesday, July 05, 2005

John 5

The pastor of my church gave the most interesting sermon this past Sunday. He preached from the book of John, chapter 5. He had many great insights which I am sure I will write about at other times in this blog, however, one insight he had was the setting for the miracle which is described in the beginning of the chapter. He talked about how the city of Jerusalem would be packed out because of the feast of the Jews, which meant that the area around the Bethesda pool would likely be more crowded than usual. He related that the physically disabled individuals in addition to perhaps not having the greatest hygiene in the first place, would more likely than not be surrounded by their own excrement and urine. No doubt a setting which would be a real affront to the senses. But the amazing thing was that Jesus was there, in the midst of the poor, the suffering and the filth which had to have been in the setting. The passage is not entirely clear why he was there, or whether he went to the pool directly as his destination. Jesus does notice the man whom he eventually heals, who for some reason caught his eye. He had been disabled for 38 years, the passage says. Jesus also approaches him with an interesting question, "Do you want to get better?" he basically asks, but that is for another blog entry.

Imagine, the Son of God, the Savior of us all, goes to a place of misery and filth and hopelessness and superstition, and heals an ungrateful man in the midst of it all.

Kind of reminds me of what he has done to me, although my misery and filth and hopelessness and superstition and ungratefulness is well hidden, at times even from me.

We serve an amazing God. Oh, that I could be more like him in ministering to those most forsaken and most helpless. Those whose last thread of hope is a superstition. Those who desperately need my help yet will be ungrateful and even try to cause me problems for my trouble in helping them (as the man does in reporting Jesus to the "Jews."

The standard set by our Lord for our service is exceedingly high (or low). We are to have his mind in us. He emptied himself and took the form of a servant. He was equal with God, but didn't consider his equality a thing to be "grasped." I sit and shake my head in amazement.

Monday, June 27, 2005

Beards and Pipes

I was provided with the opportunity to write an instructor's manual for perhaps the premier textbook in moderate to severe disabilities, Martha Snell and Fredda Brown's *Instruction of Students with Severe Disabilities*. In the edited text, there is a chapter on the "Promise of Adulthood" by Dianne and Philip Ferguson, well known experts in the field of special education who are not only professors of special ed, they are parents of an adult son with disabilities.

Anyway, in their chapter they tell the following story.

"We remember working in a large state institution for people with severe disabilities some 25 years ago. This institution closed in June 1998, but at the time, a number of people who worked there had apparently gotten only part of the message about treating people as adults. As a result, over a period of months, all the adult men on the ward grew beards and smoked pipes. Nothing else changed in their lives to encourage their personal autonomy, much less their membership in the community. The beards and pipes were simply empty symbols of adulthood that had no grounding in the daily lives of indignity and isolation that the men continued to lead."

This quote made me think of experiences I have had at church. I remember giving a talk about poverty to a group of adults with mental disabilities and a homeless man. I had an inkling of what it was like to be living in poverty from some of my life experiences, however, many of the members of my audience were living in poverty on a daily basis and had been for years.

I guess the point is, I can think that I am doing something which reflects a change in my perspective, a change in my understanding of something, but is what I am doing really reflect a growth of understanding or only that I have so much further to go. When I go to church I hear people talking about God's love, and caring for your neighbor, and the widow's mite, and love for the poor, but I don't see a lot of poor people, at least disabled poor people at church. And when they do show up, they are unexpected. It's as if the congregation is taken aback, "We didn't expect to see you here" or even "What are you doing here?"

The men in the institution had beards and pipes but no autonomy, and nothing had really changed. But the people allowing them to smoke and grow their beards probably thought they had reached a new stage of understanding. Our "beards and pipes" in churches are that we speak of care for the poor, or God's love, or that we are all equal in God's sight, yet there are a lot of people who might be equal to me in God's sight but are never in my line of sight.

Bob Bennett, one of my favorite singers has a song called "The doing of the thing." In talking about helping those in need, he describes how he could, "mistake the very song I sing for the doing of the thing." What do we in churches mistake for the "doing of the thing?"

Friday, June 24, 2005

Not really a *new* way to discriminate

Last night we had another meeting in Redlands Ca. relating to a group home for medically fragile, developmentally disabled adults. A group of neighbors to the future home were there and they claimed their major cause for concern was that the group home developer represented himself as adhering to the homeowners association agreement, and then changed the home by putting doors on the sides of the house so the wheelchair bound residents could exit the building in case of fire. They were appalled that he would be dishonest in this manner.

Now I agree that he may have done this, not be entirely honest. He may have signed the homeowners' agreement with the full knowledge that he was going to make alterations to the home, and that was not entirely truthful. But I also sat there amazed at the people who were using this argument to discriminate against persons with developmental disabilities. They spoke of property values going down, and how the neighborhood would be devalued, of how their children would be unsafe and how the house would be poorly kept all due to the placement of the home in the community. They even had the nerve to ask whether people would be "peeing in their bushes."

As a boy, I grew up in a predominantly white neighborhood of Southern New Jersey. There were very few African Americans or Hispanics, or other persons who weren't white who lived in my neighborhood. I can clearly recall hearing adults talk about how the property values would go down, how the homes would not be properly cared for, how they feared for their children should anyone other than a white person fill any vacant house in the neighborhood. I can even remember people speaking about an unwritten agreement that homes would not be sold to anyone other than a white person. This is correctly referred to as bigotry or racism.

Yet, although there were those in the meeting from groups who have experienced significant bigotry and racism, they didn't connect their behavior to that of others who experienced discrimination.

Now imagine I developed a homeowners' association, and somehow we were able to establish a rule about homes that would somehow prohibit persons of ethnicity X from living in the neighborhood. However, a person of ethnicity X wants to live in the neighborhood. In order to live in the neighborhood, the person of ethnicity X comes in and makes the change required for him to live in the neighborhood, and the homeowners' association comes down against him for breaking the homeowners' association's rules. Can you imagine the charges of racism or bigotry? Those charges would be justified, unless the homeowners' association reflected on their rules and said, "We have made a huge mistake. We didn't intend our rules to be discriminatory against group X." If, however, that same homeowners association said, "We don't care, we have a homeowners' association and those are the rules," we would begin to wonder about their motives.

Well, the homes in question do not allow for particular types of modifications. In this case, the doors which were added to the sides of the house, to allow for the exit of the wheelchair bound residents were against the homeowners' rules. So in effect, persons having the types of disabilities of those who will live in the group home are excluded from the neighborhood. It was countered that the backside of the house is wheelchair accessible. The association rules indicated, however, that no ramps were permitted to be added to the front of the house. As one person commented, "If I am going to spend 500K for a home, I'm going in the front door."

Can you see how this is a civil rights issue? I can write seemingly innocuous rules, which are largely to protect the aesthetics of the neighborhood, which in reality can be discriminatory against a particular group of people. Not people who want to paint their house purple, but people who want to go into the front door of their house, or be able to get out in case of a fire.

By the way, to my knowledge, there was only one pastor of a church who attended any of the meetings, and he is the parent of a son with a disability.

What ever happened to doing justice?

Tuesday, May 03, 2005

We must work the works: John 9:3-5

Nearly a year ago, I related the following in a blog entry:
John 9:3-5 says,
"Neither this man or his parents sinned" said Jesus, "but this happened so that the work of God might be displayed in his life. As long as it is day, we must do the work of him who sent me. Night is coming when no one can work" (NIV).

Jesus said this in response to his disciples asking about a blind man they encountered, "Who sinned, this man or his parents?" They were wondering who's sin caused the blindness.

Merril C. Tenney, the Bible scholar wrote that this passage might be translated in a different way. Here is Tenney's translation.

97

"Neither did this man sin, nor his parents" said Jesus. "But that the works of God should be made manifest in him, we must work the works of him that sent me, while it is still day; the night cometh when no man can work."

One of Tenney's points with his translation is that the works of God are made manifest in persons with disability by the things those around them do. The works of God were not made manifest solely through the healing of the man by Jesus. An interesting perspective to consider. An interesting plumb line for evaluating the response of the Church to persons with a variety of disabilities.

This morning, Kathi and I had the pleasure of having coffee with some friends who are parents of a daughter with Down's syndrome. They related the story of how their daughter will engage in a game of "keep away" with a couple of boys in the neighborhood. Invariably, the game becomes those two boys keeping the ball away from their daughter until the game finally ends. Independent of whether or not the gal with the disability recognizes that she is being taken advantage of in the game, it is obvious that those two boys are not working "the works of him that sent me while it is still day." Now its not that the boys are being particularly evil or something, but they certainly are not being kind to the girl. Working "the works of him that sent me" would probably look a lot less competitive in this case (I have nothing against competition), and reflect, I don't know, fairness, encouragement; evidences of works of God.

People with disability in our midst, provide us the opportunity to work the works of God. Don't hear me wrong. They are not in existence so that I might gain some brownie points with God. That would belittle the importance of their lives and accentuate the importance of my life. I see no evidence from scripture that I am to do either. However, as with the opportunity to help any person who needs it, the chance is provided to work the works of God. At times I will work the works and at other times I will receive the benefit of someone else working the works. The take home lesson, I believe, is that we are all surrounded by opportunities to serve others and we need to take advantage of those opportunities. We are all equal before God.

In response to a letter about his Lord of the Rings, J.R.R. Tolkien penned the following,

"Frodo indeed 'failed' as a hero, as conceived by simple minds: he did not endure to the end; he gave in, ratted. I do not say 'simple minds' with contempt: they often see with clarity the simple truth and the absolute ideal to which effort must be directed, even if it is unattainable. there weakness, however, is twofold. *They do not perceive the complexity of any given situation in Time, in which an absolute ideal is enmeshed. They tend to forget that strange element in the World that we call Pity or*

Mercy, which is also an absolute requirement in moral judgment (since it is present in the Divine nature). In its highest exercise it belongs to God" (emphasis added) (From Carpenter & Tolkien (1981), The Letters of J.R.R. Tolkien, #246, pp. 326)

There is a depth to the situations of my life. I may not be attending to the depth but it is there nonetheless.

Friday, April 01, 2005

I don't need you

Think about what has been happening in the Schaivo case as it relates to other persons with disability whose lives might be determined unworthy of continuance due to a quality of life determination. Paul wrote,

"The eye cannot say to the hand, 'I don't need you!' And the head cannot say to the feet, 'I don't need you!' On the contrary, those parts of the body that seem to be weaker are indispensable, and the parts that we think are less honorable we treat with special honor. And the parts that are unpresentable are treated with special modesty, while our presentable parts need no special treatment. But God has combined the members of the body and has given greater honor to the parts that lacked it, so that there should be no division in the body, but that its parts should have equal concern for each other. If one part suffers, every part suffers with it; if one part is honored, every part rejoices with it. Now, you are the body of Christ and each one of you is a part of it" (1 Corinthians 12:21-27).

How often in the church, the household of faith, the body of Christ, do we turn to our neighbor and say, "I don't need you!" Our neighbors are defined as people who "seem to be weaker." Interesting caveat. They *"seem"* to be weaker for whatever reason, however, the Bible indicates that somehow these persons are "indispensable." It would appear to me that they are weaker, justifying my statement, "I don't need you!" but in actuality, they are "indispensable." It also says that the parts that "we think" are "less honorable we treat with special honor." Another caveat in the statement "we think," the implication being that although we think them less honorable, they are to be treated with special honor. God has "given greater honor to the parts that lacked it so there can be" get this, "no division in the body, but that its parts should have equal concern for each other." No division, equal concern. Equal concern about or for what? It would seem equal concern at the most basic level for life.

In the Schaivo case, they have music playing, flowers around her and a stuffed animal in her arm, but they are starving and dehydrating her to death. Is this having "equal concern for each other?" Who are we comforting with these amenities? Supposedly the woman's life is being taken because she is in a persistent vegetative state and would not appreciate such things. Please, if there is any notion that these things are comforting to her, reinsert the tube as she has the ability to appreciate music and beauty!

It occurs to me, that the church has for so long excluded people with disabilities that it has less problem than it perhaps should when a disabled person is starved to death. Or even if it has concern, it seems hollow in light of its lack of effort to include persons with disability prior to the point of life sustaining measures for a brain damaged person. If the church truly has concern for such individuals, why aren't there more brain damaged persons going to church? A pastor friend of mine has said that for a church to have a ministry that includes persons with Down's syndrome for example (as that is the form of disability most often tested for via amniocentesis in efforts at "prevention" of intellectual disability leading to abortion), we give teeth to our arguments against abortion. We say, "Don't abort those children and bring them here, to our church to become a part of our church family, after they are born."

But I don't see as many persons with Down's syndrome attending church as are represented in the community. Instead, I hear horror stories of churches discriminating against persons with Down's syndrome and other disabilities and their families.

The church is a part of the problem in this whole issue. Disability has been constructed *by the church* in such a way that we feel comfortable saying to a disabled person "we don't need you." I look at this incident and am concerned, but I look at what might be the result of years of the church's lack of concern and am really concerned for what the future may hold.

Would we as Christians even miss, would we even know they were gone, if persons with intellectual disability, for example, were systematically starved to death? We see Ms. Schiavo being starved to death and we become greatly concerned about the life of a person with a severe disability. But our track record says that really, as a whole Christian church, we don't seem to give a damn about persons with disability.

Like participants in a liturgy, we stand before the Lord, and tell those with severe disabilities who are **not** in our midst, "WE DON'T NEED YOU!" That is, until we are confronted with the natural results of our indifference.

Wednesday, March 30, 2005

What to make of current events

I must admit that the recent events regarding taking the life of a severely disabled person concern me. However, it isn't just the events regarding the woman in Florida, it is also the discussion which surrounds her life and the battles of those around her. For example, this morning a bioethicist spoke of how the practice of removing a feeding tube occurred commonly across the country. He specifically referenced it happening to aborted infants who were born alive and children born with Down's syndrome. If you recall, the starving of children with Down's syndrome was an issue during the Reagan administration with the whole baby doe affair. I am aghast to think that our medical profession does such things.

Now I recognize that people should have a right to determine whether or not extensive efforts should be made to keep someone alive, particularly someone who has specifically requested that such efforts should not be used. However, feeding someone has now become included in extensive efforts. People are also permitted to make decision about others by caveat, without any documented permission given.

When people have lived life without the experience of the differences referred to as disability, they think they know how they would respond should they at some point experience disability. However, that is like trying to think about what it would be like to be a cat when you have been a dog all of your life. You think you know what you would do as a cat, but you really don't know, and you may find that your will to live as a cat is much more than you ever expected when you were still a dog.

Another concern to me is where these decisions about the life of another will go. If I have a severe disability, do I have a poor quality of life when the quality of life I have is the only one I have ever known? Can I look at a person in desperate poverty and say that they have a poor quality of life? Can I look at a person with Down's syndrome and say they have a poor quality of life? I have gone out of my way to ask quality of life questions to persons with disability, and almost without fail the response is that they feel they have a good quality of life. I have also at other times in this blog referred to the interview Christopher Nance did with Ray Charles. Nance asked, "What is it like to be blind?" Charles' wise response was, "What is it like to not be blind?" Quality of life is in the eye of the person having the life experience. . .not those observing the person.

We must be very careful about projecting our perspectives of poor life quality on others who may not agree with our point of view, or may agree at one point and not at another. Joni Eareckson relates the story of how she would have said that she wouldn't have wanted to live with the differences she now faces prior to the accident that changed her.

However, now having become accustomed to her life, she feels she has a good quality of life.

So, although I don't want to get into people's business when such decisions are on the line, I am very worried that our laws allow for starving another to death on the basis of subjective notions of disability and quality of life. Persons with severe disability are easy targets.

Thursday, March 24, 2005

Christian social constructions

Are we a reflection of what social constructions say we are? At times we may desire to be a reflection of social constructions, at other times, not. For the Christian, we have been given this archetype construction of who a person should be in the form of Jesus. Any Christian worth his salt will say that his greatest aspiration is to be like Jesus. The social construction of a "follower of Jesus" is something that was new at the time of Jesus, but has developed over time as Christians continue to grow in their understanding of who Jesus was and is. Douglas (1970) states that social construction theory explains a process whereby a reality is developed through the creation of knowledge. To the Christian, the reality is being a "Christ follower" which is built upon the knowledge which comes from revelation, wisdom and faith. If we truly understand this knowledge, we are able to look upon an individual and have some notion of how that individual lines up with the plumb line of "Christ follower."

There are those who would say that people are much more than a reflection of social constructions, whatever they may be, but for the Christian, the desire is to reflect the social construction in significant ways. For example, Jesus modeled ways in which a person would love his neighbor, love his enemy, and love and worship God. Christians themselves might mimic the ways in which Jesus prayed, by repeating the Lord's Prayer, making it their own. Christians might mimic Jesus' dedication by devoting daily time for prayer, Bible reading and reflection. Christians might also look at specific behaviors and language that Jesus used in reference to a particular life issue he confronted. For example, one might study Jesus' interactions with persons with disability in order to reflect the language and behaviors Jesus used in reference to persons with disability. The example of this interaction provides a knowledge set basic to a social construction of who persons with disability are, what disability is, and the responsibilities of persons in the world toward both disability and those who have "disabilities." Jesus' life and teachings might be said to be the basis for a Christian social construction of disability.

For Christians, the degree to which they represent this social construction of disability, reflects the degree to which they emulate Jesus in this particular area of life. If they do not represent this social construction in this particular area, they do not represent Jesus. The Christian social construction is prescriptive in a slightly different way than typical social constructions.

As we are socialized as people, we come to believe particular things about how the world works. Some notions are ingrained in our psyche. Every American child knows to "look both ways before crossing the street" or "don't pet a strange dog." But also built into that psyche deliberately or otherwise are "there but for the grace of God go I" or "don't stare" or "they can't help the way they are" or "they are God's special angels" or "they have a poor quality of life." These perceptions are communicated just as clearly as others although not perhaps as consciously.

For Christians, a whole series of behavioral social constructions are built into members of succeeding generations biologically and spiritually. Much of this "knowledge based reality" is indeed knowledge based. However, much of it is not and when examined shocks the person who had carried such a misperception all of his life.

I once went backpacking with some so-called friends. One of the group put a large rock in my backpack just before our decent down the mountain. Imagine my surprise to find that I had been carrying that rock for 8 miles. Upon recognizing that I had the rock in my pack, I promptly removed it and tossed it aside. We shouldn't press this metaphor too far, however, I was surprised because I had examined the things which found their way into the pack. I was surprised because something had gotten by my observation. In a life immersed in culture, we should not be surprised what notions, what ideas about reality, what social constructions fill our minds. It is only when we sit down and open our packs, when we engage in reflection in the light of what we know about our faith, that we see the incongruity of the rock in the backpack. But to recognize that a rock doesn't belong in a backpack, I need to know what does belong in a backpack. I don't throw out my dry socks, or my matches, but I definitely throw out the rock.

Christians haven't been examining the contents of their backpacks, at least as they relate to persons with disability. If they had, they would have found that not only were they carrying rocks, they had neglected to pack dry socks and matches. How do we know this? It is because of the prescriptive nature of the Christian social construction of disability which points us to the knowledge which can be gained from studying the revelation of the life of Jesus, the wisdom which can be gained from life among people with "disability" and the understanding of one's own faith, who is invited to faith, and what the requirements of faith are.

Douglas, J.D. (1970). Understanding everyday life. In J.D. Douglas (Ed.), *Understanding everyday life: Toward the reconstruction of sociological knowledge* (pp. 3-43). Chicago: Aldine.

Tuesday, February 22, 2005

Metaphor as metaphor vs. metaphor as reality

The Bible is filled with various metaphors useful in illustrating a point for Christians. Everything from the notion of God as our Father, to us as sheep, are actually metaphor for the purposes of instruction or the assistance with understanding. God is our Father as most of us have had fathers, most of them have been loving, and we can relate to the notion of Father. Apparently God wants to relate to us as a father to his children as well, or he would have chosen some other metaphor to teach us about who he is and how he wants us to relate to him.

There are other metaphors in the Bible, which when taken out of context can result in people being misunderstood and potentially ostracized. For example, the Bible will at times talk about people as being spiritually blind. It is a great metaphor as all one who is sighted needs to do is close her eyes to recognize that she would feel at a great disadvantage. The idea is, that spiritual blindness is similar to physical blindness in its effect on being able to find one's way. However, physical blindness is not spiritual blindness. A person who is physically blind is not necessarily spiritually blind. To equate the two would be a great disservice to the person who is a physically blind Christian.

At other points, people are given a disability by God for greater or lesser periods of time. Paul is blinded on the road to Damascus. Zechariah is unable to speak because of a lack of faith, Nebuchanezzar loses his mind because of his pride and vanity. However, not all who are blind are blind to catch their attention because they are persecuting the church. Not all who cannot speak are that way because of a lack of faith. Not all who deal with various forms of mental illness are that way because they were full of themselves. In fact in the overwhelming number of cases, blindness, speech or mental illness have nothing to do with an individuals behavior at all.

Unfortunately, the exceptions have resulted in Christian social constructions which make them more of the rule. As with the disciples we asked "who sinned?" when we see a person with disability. We ask, "What is God trying to teach you?" when we see a blind person, or think of the destructive lifestyle one must have lived to experience mental illness. We over generalize the experiences of a few people in history.

Whether it be the misapplication of a metaphor or the overgeneralization of experiences of people shared in the Bible, we must

104

be careful in our application to people with disability. Metaphor is useful when it is taken as metaphor. The life experience of another is useful when taken within the full picture of the other person's life.

Friday, October 22, 2004

Attitude development

In the classic book on curriculum theory, *Basic Principles of Curriculum and Instruction* (1949) Tyler discusses four chief means by which attitudes "commonly develop." He states the following.

"The most frequent method is through assimilation from the environment. The things that are taken for granted by the people round about us, the points of view that are commonly held by our friends and acquaintances are illustrations of environmental attitudes which are frequently assimilated without our having been conscious of them.

A second and perhaps the next most common method of acquiring attitudes arises from emotional effects of certain kinds of experiences. In general if one has had satisfying experiences in a particular connection, he develops an attitude favorable to some content or aspect of that experience while if he has had an unsatisfying effect from the experience, his attitude may become antagonistic.

The third most frequent method of developing attitudes is through traumatic experiences, that is, experiences which have had a deep emotional effect. Thus, a youngster may develop overnight a great fear of dogs from one experience in having been bitten by a dog.

Finally, a fourth method of developing attitudes is through direct intellectual processes. In some cases when we see the implication of a particular object or process, we are led to develop an attitude favorable or unfavorable to it from the knowledge which we gain from this intellectual analysis". . . Unfortunately, attitudes formed through definite intellectual processes are not so frequent as those obtained in other ways. Of these four methods of developing attitudes, the third is not likely to be useful to the school. Traumatic experiences involving the intense emotional reactions are too hard to control to be used systematically in an educational program. Hence, schools will have to lean heavily upon the use of a process of assimilation from the environment, of developing attitudes through emotional effects of particular experiences, and through direct intellectual processes" (p. 76).

Once again, attitudes develop through
a process of assimilation from the environment
emotional effects of particular experiences
direct intellectual processes

In thinking about societal attitudes toward persons with disability as reflected in social constructions, the attitudes developed in different people in different ways. Traumatic experiences must also be factored into the mix, although we cannot use them necessarily to develop attitudes. I would suspect that by and large, most attitudes are developed through assimilation from the environment. Among some informed groups, direct intellectual process has probably had some impact. Some people might have had emotional effects from experiences, but using myself as an example, experiences might cause negative effects, or might cause one to devote his life to these persons with disability (in their inclusion, education, etc.).

"Several generalizations may be suggested regarding learning experiences for developing attitudes. In the first place, the school and community environment should, so far as possible, be modified and controlled so as to promote desirable attitudes. In many modern communities there is disjunction between the school and the home, the school and the church, the school and the rest of the community with regard to the attitudes that are developed. The environments are inconsistent; values, points of view are taken for granted in the press that are denounced in the pulpit, the values emphasized in the motion pictures are in conflict with those which the school seeks to develop. There is a great need for seeking to modify the environment of the youngster throughout his experience in order to help him develop desirable social attitudes. This means increasing the degree of consistency of the environment and helping to reinforce the emphasis upon social rather than selfish attitudes" (p. 76-77).

As I think through the various environments from which attitudes might be generated, I am not sure which one I would choose as the model I would want to proliferate. School, community, home, church, press, pulpit, to some degree each of these attitudinal repositories beg for the modification and control Tyler alludes to. The church distrusts the public school which distrusts the community and so on. Teacher training becomes more rigorous because the community distrusts the school as it is the teachers' fault children aren't performing as they should. Schools point to homes. Once the appropriate attitude is found, the job is to try to align everyone to that attitude.

Sometimes that alignment can be orchestrated through law, at least aspects can. I can force integration with the hopes that when people are together, attitudes will change to reflect what they learn through the integration experience. Forced integration might be thought about in a variety of ways, but I am thinking about integrating persons with and without disability. As far as the church is concerned, I must rely on the good will of the people. If my church has too much of something different, I will simply go to another church which has more of the same that I am used to. People who are willing to take the risk of having their attitudes changed can often be the ones to lead the way in altering social constructions, however, that doesn't always work as they are typically marked as being different (meaning open minded) and not all open mindedness is good.

Even within families, the experiences you might think would soften attitudes toward or at least cause dissonance with the social construction isn't always perceived that way. Rather than seeing the construction as unreflective of reality, they define the situation with the construction until they are beaten into submission by the dissonance between the construction and reality. A price was paid for the information gained from that experience. As long as the experience of disability is deselected or remote, the social construction is employed unchallenged. The saddest thing, however, is when the construction is embraced by parents and significant others and fed to the person with disability. The negative self-perception the person with disability gains becomes the filter through which they define themselves, their social interactions, their ambitions, and the world.

Friday, October 01, 2004

Deconstructing intellectual disability: an intro

In a recent issue of World magazine, Andree Seu has an editorial entitled, "House of mourning: Funerals are opportunities to hear the best, and worst, of theology." He states, "A collective spiritual insight almost breaks through, then is submerged again . . .But I am not here to deconstruct funerals." Probably all of us have had this same experience. If you haven't, you probably need to study up on your theology a bit. But people's ideas of death are not unlike their ideas about disability. It's like, they heard something somewhere before, can't really recall when, but they are sure it is in the Bible or something, and whatever the sentiment, it kinda makes them feel better about the situation. So we have people looking down on us from heaven, we have spirits still with us, we have people who haven't really died, we have people being reincarnated, and so it goes on.

But the same kind of ridiculous ideas pervade in spiritual discussions of disability. Children with disability are special children from God. Funny how nobody wants them if they have the choice and often will choose to abort special children from God. If they were actually special children from God, perhaps the church would be more interested in serving them.

107

Or parents are told that they are special in that they were "chosen" to have a child with a disability. It would seem that chosen parents would be valued more than they are. It seems too often that "chosen" in reference to parents means "You are on your own, baby." That is, you were chosen, I wasn't so it is up to you to figure out how to help, integrate, educate, etc. you child.

Let's work through some of these misguided issues from a theological perspective. We will attempt to take on each one (that I can find) and address them. Let's see where we end up?

Tuesday, August 24, 2004

Deconstructing disability: role perceptions/subhuman animal

More from Dr. Wolf Wolfensberger(1972), wrote about what he called deviant role perceptions. These were ways in which persons with disability were sometimes perceived. The word "deviant" should be thought of in terms of differing from the norm (American Heritage dictionary). The word deviant itself can be very charged in its connotations. I thought it might be interesting to examine each of these role perceptions briefly and think about the applications for today. The following are from Wolfensberger.

1. The deviant as sub-human animal

Considering the perceptions of persons with disability in the past, particularly during the time when institutionalization was prevalent, persons with severe disability appeared to be being perceived as animals. Some of the evidence included abuse resistant environments, easily cleaned environments (even to the point of being hosed down), extensive soundproofing, objects placed out of reach, and many locked areas. The types of foods served seemed to imply a lack of discrimination in those who were eating them. Similarly, rooms were without windows or windows were highly placed and those living in the institutions would be unable to see out of them.

People spoke of keeping clients, rather than interacting with people. We see protected nurses' stations reminiscent of a scene out of "One Flew Over the Cuckoo's Nest." Residents are not expected to learn or develop appreciably. People also spoke of "garden variety intellectual disability" or even referred to a person who was profoundly disabled as a "vegetable."

There was the abrogation of human emotions or sensibilities such as shame, or modesty. Even as late as the 1970's severe aversive stimulation was used as a "training" technique, in particular with people with autism.

The implication was that such severe aversives were necessary as the trainees had no feeling of pain or sensations were diminished in comparison with non disabled persons.

How do these perceptions persist today? I honestly think that the situation has improved for persons with more mild disability. However, this perception lingers in the perceptions of persons with more severe types of disability. I have been in situations where a young woman with profound retardation had her diaper changed by an open door during the passing period at a junior high school (that is, until I shouted at the teacher to "Shut the door!"). I have been in other situations were private student information was posted on the wall of the classroom, or the students' privacy was not protected in other ways. I have heard teachers speak about students in negative ways in front of the students because "he can't understand what I am saying anyway."

One of the first things one should do in visiting an environment populated with persons with disability is to look carefully at that environment. The appearance of the environment will provide an indication of what those who are managing the environment think of those who populate it. You will learn whether those in charge think those in the environment are safe or dangerous, are in control or out of control, should be treated according to their age, are learning or are being maintained, are sick or healthy, are people or otherwise.

Wednesday, September 08, 2004

Deconstructing disability: role perceptions/menace
More from Dr. Wolf Wolfensberger (1972).

2. The deviant as a menace
At the turn of the 18th to 19th century, a variety of things happened relative to persons with disability. The birth of institutions 50 years prior (a very positive thing at that time) caused parents to come forward with their children with disability so they might be served by these, "palaces . . . for the indigent and infirm, the chosen friends of our Lord Jesus Christ" (Edouard Seguin, 1854). People at the time began to wonder at all those who came forward. Then there was the urbanization of America where persons who were successful in an agrarian society were not in the cities. The IQ test identified even more with low IQ's. Although these people had always been in the community, they were somewhat hidden. However, this growth in the numbers of persons with disability appeared to be a real growth, an epidemic. At that time, the public was aroused to fear.

Persons with disability became associated with the social problems of the day (crime, degeneracy, poverty, etc.), and were vilified. The institutions changed becoming places of segregation from the community, for protection of the community, and segregation of the sexes of those with disability, to stop their out of control reproduction.

It is important to note that there is often evil perceived in what is not understood. Evil has been perceived in persons with disability through the centuries. Earlier in this blog, we noted how the disciples of Christ asked who sinned that a particular child was born with disability. Jesus refutes this notion, however, sins of parents or of the disabled individuals themselves as the cause of disability is a wrong notion which lingers in the church today. If I feel that a person who is dysmorphic in appearance is that way as a result of sin/evil, to some degree I will treat that person as a menace.

The proof that these attitudes pervade can be seen when someone attempts to place a group home for adults with intellectual disability in the community. Although these homes tend to be better maintained than the community average, fears of violence or sexual perversion on the part of the persons with intellectual disability enrage the community and people attempt to keep the homes out. The thing that always amazes me, is how these perceptions of persons with disability as menace, are so close to the surface in society's thinking, and how quickly they are verbalized with little evidence to support them. People suspect that this is the way these different looking people are, and when someone mentions their irrational fear, they just pile on.

People truly do see evil in what they do not understand.

Monday, September 13, 2004

Deconstructing disability: Role perceptions/object of pity

More from Dr. Wolf Wolfensberger (1972).

3. The deviant as an object of pity

Once it was understood that persons with intellectual disability were not actually a menace, their perception largely changed from a menace to an object of pity. They needed to be placed in environments where they might be protected. A medical model replaced the educational model. So health became the primary concern, not education.

I can remember working at an intermediate care facility for kids with severe to profound intellectual disability, where one of the children was given a new pair of tennis shoes. As with anyone, after a few hours, the student developed a blister on his heal, which then began to bleed a bit.

Once this came to the attention of the nursing staff, all educational programming was canceled for that student indefinitely into the future till the blister healed. After all, you couldn't expect the poor child who has already experienced so much to have to endure going to school.

This experience illustrates this perception. There are few demands for growth, no "risks" are taken, and the person is infantilized. This is a demeaning position for one to be in. Later in the development of the disability movement, one of the rallying cries was that people need to be afforded the "dignity of risk." That is, that if someone is constantly protected, he will never grow. Risk is not embraced in a cavalier fashion, like life is some extreme sport, however, dignity does come with risk. It's like the first time your parents gave you the car keys. Risk was involved but it was a calculated risk, an informed risk which moved you to a new level of responsibility. Imagine if you were 25 and were still waiting for your parents to trust you with the car keys. You would feel angry and humiliated at the paternalistic protective environment you would have to endure.

Christians often will, with the best intentions, make comments which illustrate this perspective. We see a person with disability acting in an inappropriate fashion, and someone says, "He can't help the way he is." Well, nine times out of ten he probably can help the way he is, and needs to be told to "cut it the heck out!" I remember a great scene in the movie "Almost an Angel" where a guy in a wheel chair, upset about the fact that he is disabled, acts obnoxiously in a bar. A character played by Paul Hogan (Crocodile Dundee) tells him to quit acting like a jerk. The guy doesn't act right, so Paul Hogan sits in a chair, so he is at the guy's level, and punches him in the nose. That is so refreshing in that Hogan sees the man in the chair as a man, not as a disabled man, and treats him like a man.

Another comment sometimes made is that the person with disability is "suffering from his condition." Now there are people who actually suffer from disabling conditions, and I would in no way belittle that. However, to many persons with disability, their condition is the only experience they have in life, so they don't suffer from the loss of some capacity as a person who might have acquired a disability later in life would. If I project suffering on another person, I will either inappropriately see him as some sort of hero, or an object of pity. Neither of these characterizations apply to the average person born with a disability and do little to normalize them to the general society.

And then my personal unfavorite, "There but for the grace of God go I." So, the obvious conclusion is that you have experienced the grace of God, she didn't. The sentiment I understand. Yes, perhaps I should be grateful that my life experience is what it is. But I do little for the person

111

with disability or myself for that matter in just celebrating that I am not disabled. A better reaction would be to celebrate the grace of God to you by doing something to help, befriend, support, or do something positive with the life you have received.

It is also interesting to contrast this statement, however, with the response which Paul relates when he asks God to take away his "thorn." Paul says that God relates to him that, "My grace is sufficient for you." If that is indeed the case, Paul might be able to say, "Here by the grace of God go I" as he carries his disability.

Somehow there is something which is not entirely negative about disability that we as people just don't appear to get.

Tuesday, September 14, 2004

Deconstructing disability: Role perceptions/sick
More from Dr. Wolf Wolfensberger (1972).

4. The deviant as sick
Another role perception described by Wolfensberger, is the disabled person as "sick." They are a diseased organism. As stated previously, that is why a medical model was adopted to treat them. People with disability are patients, not students or residents. Decisions are often made by medical personnel. It is true that there are many areas in which medical personnel are the best to make a particular decision, however, often they are not.

I once had the opportunity to work with Dr. Richard Koch. Dr. Koch at that time, was the director of the national collaborative PKU study (phenylketonuria, an inborn error of metabolism which without treatment can result in severe intellectual disability). Even in the midst of the powerful research he was doing which ultimately affected the lives of thousands of persons experiencing this genetic disorder, his perspective was that the medical profession had very little to offer most people with disability. They could provide a diagnosis most of the time, but beyond that, it was the job of educators to improve the lives of the persons with disability.

Educators have at times adopted this same perspective, referring to their services not as education, but as "educational therapy."

The take home lesson of this particular role perception is that people with cerebral palsy are not contagious and neither are persons with Down's syndrome. The appearance of having a cold has to do with aspects of their disabilities (although I guess they could at times also have a cold). People do not "suffer" from Down's syndrome in the same way that someone suffers from the flu.

Additionally, there isn't a medication, for persons with Down's syndrome or cerebral palsy or most other forms of disability that makes it go away.

The life experience as persons with Down's syndrome is their life experience. How could a person with Down's syndrome, a congenital genetic syndrome, know an existence other than that which they were born with? Those who are less disabled intellectually, might realize they are different, but I suspect such thoughts are atypical.

Personally, I can imagine what it might be like to be blind or regularly use a wheel chair, but I really don't know. I do have some experience of feeling different because of a lack of math ability. Such a problem is hardly comparable to blindness or other disabilities, however, it can be used for a point of discussion. I am amazed at people around who understand things which I don't, but I really don't know what it is like to understand those things. My son, for example, was doing advanced calculus as a high school senior. I don't know what it is like to have that level of math ability. I guess I can imagine being able to understand something that I don't understand, but that is about the limit for me. As a medical student, I could imagine being able to take in all of the information provided, commit it to memory, and then retrieve it as necessary to answer questions on a test or from an instructor. However, the fact that I flunked out of medical school indicates that I was in a place that was beyond my ability to do those things. I know that I largely only think of myself as different when the environment that I am in makes me feel that way (e.g. medical school). In other environments, I appear to have a level of understanding beyond many of those who are in the environment with me. In those environments, I have the ability to either accentuate my strengths in comparison to another's weaknesses, or attempt to integrate them with myself and myself with them. I have a notion of what it is like to be them and they have a notion of what it is like to be me, but we really don't know.

I can remember my father used to talk with frustration about a comment my grandmother would make when she was feeling depressed. She would say, "Nobody knows how I feel." My father, a person with severe diabetes, chafed at that statement, saying, "Well, nobody knows how I feel." Which really didn't help my grandmother.

I believe this is the same for most persons with intellectual disability. They don't know how I feel and I don't know how they feel.

One thing I have to get through my head, however, is that their disability is their life experience. They are not sick, they have a different life experience. If I treat them as if they are sick, I project on them something which they are not feeling and I illustrate my own ignorance about what their life experience actually is.

Wednesday, September 15, 2004

Deconstructing disability: Role perceptions/object of ridicule

More from Dr. Wolf Wolfensberger (1972).

5. The deviant as an object of ridicule

Elsewhere in this blog, we have discussed the film **Freaks.** This film used sideshow performers as the actors. It was taking these individuals who for whatever reason chose this means of livelihood and put them on the big screen. The reaction of the "normal" people attending the side show in the film provide the true indication of how these persons were portrayed. One woman screams and faints. Hardly the response one would have when visiting other parts of the circus.

The "freak show," however, was not something new even in the 1930's. Wolfensberger speaks of medieval society, or the court of Montezuma as being populated with persons with characteristics different from the norm, with these same individuals "housed after the manner of a modern park z00" (p 23).

I can remember when imbecile, moron and idiot, terms I had come to laugh at when uttered by Moe, Larry or Curly, took on a different meaning. They were actually the labels for persons with intellectual disability at the time the Three Stooges films were made. Now I still love the Three Stooges, but I tend to cringe when one calls another an imbecile as I consider the use of the term in the time that those films were made. It would be like me saying, "You profoundly intellectually disabled person" to someone I was upset with. Wolfensberger speaks of the "moron" jokes that were prevalent around the time of the writing of Normalization. Take your most offensive racial slur and come up with a series of jokes using that term, and you get a feel for the inappropriateness of that term to those experiencing intellectual disability.

I can remember a time when I read a newspaper article to the group of intellectually disabled friends I meet with each Sunday. We call our group the "Light and Power Company." Anyway, the article spoke of how someone referred to a member of our group (that was why I was reading the article, to help them through the offensive nature of the article) as a "retard." I was struck by how the person to whom the label was referring, said, "They shouldn't use that kind of language in the newspaper."

So chide someone if they say someone else is retarded, or is a retard. That word takes a group of wonderful people and stigmatizes them indirectly. It supports negative aspects of the social construction of who

114

persons with disability are.

Tuesday, September 28, 2004

Deconstructing disability: Role perceptions/eternal child

More from Dr. Wolf Wolfensberger (1972).

6. The deviant as an eternal child

Unfortunately, much work in psychology has led to the perpetuation of this role perception. We have measures of intelligence translated into "mental age" apparently because such a measure will help professionals in programming. So we hear people say that Johnny has a mental age of 12 or the mental age of 11 months. Even people who are not professionals talk about a person as having the mind of a 6 year old.

We see people as never growing up. Therefore, we place them in childish environments with decorations unfitting for their age. At times we even see adults with disability housed with children, the obvious thinking being that they are functioning at the same age level.

As a reaction to this, beginning around the 1970's, professionals have developed the term "chronologically age appropriate" as a description of programs, interactions, environments, etc. for persons with disability. We want these aspects of their lives to reflect their chronological age, not their supposed mental age. There are a variety of reasons why we would want to do this.

Persons with disability simply by virtue of the fact that they have a disability are often stigmatized. Disability is not seen simply as a characteristic of these individuals, it is a negative characteristic which limits typical positive interactions which might be enjoyed between people. This of course depends upon the mindset of the person without disability, however, at the very least, stigmatizing factors may cause one to pause. They cause one to wonder, thinking that something is not quite right. These stigmatizing factors may be overt, or discovered through further interaction. In order to facilitate normalization in interactions, we do well to not add stigmatizing factors to people who may already be devalued by social constructions.

Back in the early 80's (before I knew better) I once worked at a camp for adults with intellectual disabilities. The theme of the camp was "cowboys and Indians." We rode horses, shot guns, made bows with arrows, Indian jewelry and headdresses, and barbecued. The problem with this was that the persons with disability who attended the camp were adults, some in their 50's with intellectual disability. They had a great time at the camp, but the following week, some were walking around

Pasadena California with headdresses on carrying a bow and arrow. Now they wouldn't be a danger to anyone (as hard as we tried, we weren't very good bow makers), however, what we did in holding a camp that was not age appropriate was to send them into the community with artifacts that they carried around which did little more than stigmatize them. Can you imagine walking down the street and seeing a fifty year old guy with a bow and arrow and a headdress (made out of construction paper no less) walking toward you on the street in Pasadena? I suspect your response wouldn't be to think, "I gotta get me one of those head dresses" but rather "What is wrong with that person?" By engaging in activities which were not age appropriate, particularly those which produced artifacts that the people carried around for the next 3 weeks, we hurt their potential for positive interactions with the general public by stigmatizing them.

By contrast, there is a fellow who attends my church. Let's call him Chuck (not his real name). Now I have know Chuck for probably 10 years now. He is a good looking young man who dresses well. He regularly attends church with his mother, and I believe he works in some sort of sheltered setting. The point is, you would never pick this guy out of a crowd as being someone with a intellectual disability. So in every first interaction, he has the opportunity to sell himself to you (if he cares to) as the great person that he is. In discussion you would quickly learn that he has a disability, however, you would also learn that he is a great guy. Contrast that with the people I helped to stigmatize with the construction paper head dresses. Certainly your approach to them would be different. You would approach thinking these persons have intellectual disabilities.

But the typically reply is, "But they enjoy the juvenile activities." Well, there may be juvenile activities that I enjoy as well, but I am careful to whom I share that interest of mine, or at the least, I have competence in other areas to overcome the deviance of my preoccupation with some juvenile activity.

The poster child for the competency/deviancy hypothesis (I first heard described by Dr. Marc Gold) was Dennis Rodman, the outstanding NBA player. As long as Rodman got 17 rebounds a game, he could behave poorly and act crazy. He really was an outstanding rebounder and defender. But as he aged, his competence (rebounding) began to wane, while his "deviance" (acting crazy) remained the same. Ultimately, he was unable to play any more in the NBA. It is arguable, however, if he had been a better "citizen" he might have lasted longer as there would have been less deviance to be overcome by competence.

Persons with disability, at times due to their disability and at times due to the social construction of their disability, carry around "deviance" which must be compensated for with competence. Age inappropriateness on the part of the person with disability only adds to their perceived deviance, requiring more competence of some type to overcome it. If the captain of the football team starts carrying a Spongebob Squarepants back pack, it will be cool. However, if the person with intellectual disability who attends the same school tries to initiate the style, he will be devalued because of the lack of competence he has to counterbalance the deviance.

So by way of instruction, when you interact with a person with intellectual disability, independent of the severity of their condition, the way you interact, as much as possible the content of your interactions, the environment for your interactions, etc. should be as age appropriate as is possible. Your language might be simple in style and content, however, it is not age inappropriate or demeaning, and reflects a respect for the person's age.

Monday, October 04, 2004

Deconstructing disability: Role perceptions/holy innocent

More from Dr. Wolf Wolfensberger (1972).

7. The deviant as a holy innocent

The notion of persons with intellectual disability as being holy innocents is a perception which permeates Christianity. We hear of people being "God's special children" or "Angels unaware." No doubt those who use such characterizations are in some way trying to elevate the perspective of persons with disability, or encourage the parents or families of these persons, however, if they are God's special children. . .

Why do we fear them?

Why don't we want them in our own family?

Why aren't Christian churches working feverishly to bring them into the fellowship?

Why aren't Christian schools looking for every possible way to serve them?

You see, those who say they are God's special children, really don't believe they are. If they actually did, their behavior would change toward them. I don't agree that they are God's special children, but if I did actually think that I would base my perspective on scripture, and it would hopefully impact the way I live. It's like saying "We are all the same in the eyes of God." Well, if you believed that, you would be as interested in bringing persons with intellectual disabilities into your church as you would business professionals.

But there are other issues with the holy innocent perspective. The holy innocent is incapable of voluntarily committing evil or doing wrong.

117

They are simply misunderstood. By saying such things, you remove their humanity in that the Bible is crystal clear that we have all sinned and have hearts that are "desperately evil." I do no favors when I act in a paternalistic manner when I see a child doing something wrong by saying that he can't help himself.

When a friend of my son's was young, he had an anger problem. When I confronted his parents about the problem, they replied that people just get angry in their family and that he can't help himself. My response was that he will help himself when he is at my house or he won't be welcome there anymore. Can you imagine an employer of a person with a disability who does something inappropriate in the work environment gathering customers together and saying, don't mind him, he is a holy innocent and really either can't help himself, or is basically unable to do something wrong. They would indicate their position on his perspective by no longer frequenting the store. By holding persons with disability to the same high standard for behavior as others, we challenge them to grow and our high expectations will spur them on to do better.

A friend of mine with intellectual disability called my home once when my son was younger. He had been trying to reach me, and as we all face at times trying to reach someone, was having trouble. He became frustrated and started swearing at my son over the phone. My son was old enough to take it in stride, and told me of the interaction. My response was to contact my friend and tell him that if he ever swore at my son again he would no longer be my friend. My friend was just a man, a man who had lost his temper and needed to be called on it. Since that time, he will still get frustrated with me at times, but he won't swear at anyone in my family because I applied the same standard to interactions with him that I would with anyone.

The holy innocent also has about it an infantilizing aspect. When preschool children do something wrong, although we correct them, we tend to smile inwardly. At times their misbehavior is almost cute. That same perspective is often applied to adults with developmental disabilities. But we do them no favors if we treat such behavior as cute. A general public which has little tolerance will not look on the behaviors as cute. In fact the behaviors might actually support the social construction they have assimilated from the environment.

Last evening in a class I am teaching, a student commented to me that persons with disability, specifically intellectual disability have a "special relationship with the Lord." My first response was to tell her that so did she and so did I, however, I then went on to ask where in the Bible does it indicate that persons with disability have a special relationship with God? She mentioned several verses which have been cited in this blog which indicate that God is particularly interested in the "things that are not." But once again, when it was all boiled down, we ended with the position that somehow simply because a person has a disability, they become a holy innocent, a special child of God.

Even though those who use this phrase mean well, we have to get them to either, 1) stop using it, 2) justify it from scripture, or at the very least 3) get them to act as if they really believe it is true.

Thursday, October 07, 2004

Deconstructing disability: the tragedy of disability

In the following passage, Jesus seems to worry less about the tragedy which befalls the victims, and more about repentance.

Luke 13:1-5 "And some were present at the same time reporting to Him about the Galileans, whose blood Pilate mixed with their sacrifices. And answering, Jesus said to them, "Do you think that these Galileans were sinners beyond all the Galileans because they suffered such things? No I say to you, But if you do not repent you will all perish likewise. Or those eighteen on whom the tower in Siloam fell, and killed them, do you think that these were sinners beyond all men who lived in Jerusalem? No, I say to you, But if you do not repent, you will all perish likewise."

This passage has always impressed me as it gives an insight into Jesus' thinking about people suffering "things." In this case, death, but arguably the principles evidenced here might be applied to other areas of suffering. The principle seems to be that bad things happen to people independent of whether or not they have committed particular sins in a particular area. Bad things happen to good people. The Gallileans were murdered, it appears, and the 18 happened to be in the wrong place at the wrong time and died as a result of the tower falling. Jesus' response is that these things happen, but the question is repentance. If you don't repent, you will experience a similar result. It appears that the similar result is that you will come into God's presence via death in an unprepared manner: you haven't repented.

So it appears that the response to tragedy is preparation before it occurs and some level of acceptance when it does occur.

What about the "tragedy" of disability? Earlier in this blog, we discussed the difference between congenital and adventitious disability. In some ways, it is the adventitious disability which is the most tragic. If I have been able to see and now cannot, I mourn the loss of my vision. However, if I have never had vision, I really don't know what I am missing. If I develop Alzheimer's disease, I lament the loss of my faculties. However, if I have never had the faculties in the first place, I once again, don't know what I am missing.

119

The congenital disability might be tragic to family members, but in many ways they are reflecting their impression of the unknown, the "death" of the normal child who was not born or the mistreatment the individual might expect from society, not the perceptions of the actual child born. He will never be a doctor (assuming he would have wanted to be one anyhow), or he will never be a football player (assuming he wouldn't have rather have been a musician). The fear of the future born out of ignorance (in a positive sense) cause the suffering. There is the 'chronic sorrow" described in the literature when persons with some forms of disability do not progress through the normal life changes that people typically move through (graduation, marriage, child bearing, etc.), and these notions might also impact the suffering of family members. But the picture isn't typically a bleak as anticipated. People with intellectual disability do live on their own, or with supervision or in group homes. They do have jobs which they are proud of, and they do make contributions to the community through their work and tax paying. So knowledge about the future life of persons with disability does provide positive expectations to counteract the negative.

The impressions of the child born about himself, his world, are that he is who he is. I personally dream about what it would be like to be a great musician. I see pianists and hear guitarists and think it would be fun to be that good. But I don't lament not being able to play the guitar or piano. I don't know what it is like to be a musician, let alone a great one. The child born with disability has nothing with which to compare his experience. It will take many years before he understands that he is "different" if he ever does. Typically these understandings of differentness come from the manner in which he is treated, they are social constructions reflected in behavior, they are not necessarily due to anything specifically about him. They are caused only indirectly by his disability, and need not be the result of disability at all.

Friends of mine who are intellectually disabled, I would suspect, do not feel intellectually disabled when they are with me, because we just have the same kinds of interactions I would have with anyone else. We talk about their work, their joys or frustrations with life, we joke and are serious. It really isn't any different than conversations generally that I would have with any other person. However, they relate that there are people who interact with them differently because of their disability. Those people talk down to them, or treat them like they are stupid. But that is more of a reflection of those people than it is a reflection of the person with intellectual disability.

Most forms of disability should be treated as irrelevant characteristics of the individual in most social situations. Do I act differently with people on the basis of their skin color? I shouldn't. Of course I am careful in taking them into situations where people will act with hostility toward them on the basis of prejudice based on skin color. But that has no impact on my interactions 99% of the time. The same is true of persons with intellectual disability.

As I look at any person, I see them as a collection of strengths and weaknesses. I support them in areas of weakness (assuming I have the ability myself to do so) and leave them alone in areas of strength. I don't look at a person and on the basis of something I see with my eyes, assume that they are disqualified in a particular area of life. This perception influences the manner in which I characterize disability. That is, do I see it as a tragedy or as an aspect of human diversity which like any other human difference has positive and negative aspects associated with it?

If I see persons with disability as evidences of diversity, I become more focused on their repentance than I am on their tragedy. As a result, I see them as more like me than different from me.

Monday, August 30, 2004

Deconstructing disability: the tragedy of disability (continued)

If you have been reading this blog, you might think that I live in some kind of a dream world in relation to understanding many of the hardships involved in having a family member, particularly a child with disability. I have spoken of the social construction of disability and have tried to break that down. It is true that many of the problems which people face relative to disability are related to the perceptions of those individuals and their families by the community. The community has a misinformed notion of what disability is, what it means, etc. However, many of the difficulties which accompany disability are hard reality, they are not constructions of society.

The research literature indicates that a child with a disability is a significant stressor on a marriage. Siblings are changed as a result of growing up with a disabled brother or sister. Some forms of disability are accompanied with severe, bizarre behavior problems difficult to understand let alone manage. The difficulty of finding and managing psychotropic drug regimens, which can create another whole range of behavioral and other issues, is a significant problem. So there are many realities associated with being a person with a disability or parenting a person with a disability which can be quite difficult.

What does the Bible say about these difficulties?

Paul describes how a "thorn in the flesh was given to me" (2 Corinthians12:7-9). Some speculate that he might have had epilepsy or more likely a visual problem. So, Paul himself actually had the thorn, not

121

a son or daughter. Paul says, "I entreated the Lord three times that it depart from me." This would be the typical reaction of anyone with a "thorn in the flesh" but God didn't remove the thorn/provide healing. Rather, he says that "He said to me, My grace is sufficient for you, for My power is perfected in weakness." He goes on to say, "Because of this, I am pleased in weaknesses, in insults, in dire needs, in persecutions, in distresses, for the sake of Christ. For when I am weak, then I am powerful."

The research literature describes one of the most common questions of parents at the birth of a disabled child is "Why God?" But verses like Proverbs 3:5 remind us to "trust in the Lord with all our hearts and not lean on our own understanding." This was further illustrated in the book of Job. Job is beset with terrible catastrophes which have taken his family from him, taken his livelihood from him, and left him covered with boils and a nagging wife. After much questioning and accusations on Job's part, he finally meets the Lord. After some tough questions from God, Job responds (Job 42: 1 and following) "I know that you can do all and no purpose is withheld from you. Who is hiding counsel without knowledge? So I declared, but did not understand things too wonderful for me; yea I did not know. . .I have heard of You by hearing of the ear, but now my eye has seen You; Therefore I despise myself, and I have repented in dust and ashes." It is interesting that although the story relates the difficult questions Job asks of God, he doesn't ultimately condemn him for asking questions. In fact, he condemns his friends for condemning him. But the point here is that the Bible speaks of how God is in control. Our key response might be to repent as described in yesterday's blog, but the take home lesson is that God is in control.

Paul also says in Romans 8:18, "For I calculate that the sufferings of the present time are not worthy to compare to the coming glory to be revealed in us." That is hopeful, but it doesn't help a lot when I wake up to my son having smeared his feces on the wall. It excites me to think the future will be better beyond my comprehension, but the present may still suck. I need God's presence to get me through the present as I in faith look toward the future.

The fact that God's grace is sufficient and that He is in control are a great comfort to Christians with disabilities or Christian families with a disabled family member.

Tuesday, August 31, 2004

Deconstructing disability: aging

A colleague of mine, Dr. Nancy Contrucci and I met briefly today to discuss common research interests. In the midst of that discussion, we began talking about prefall/postfall notions of disability. She brought up the issue of aging.

In the post fall condition, aging carries with it the idea of diminishing faculties (trust me, I know) be they physical or mental. The question is what were the prefall conditions associated with aging? One must assume that many of the reasons which can result in diminishing faculties were present pre fall. I can still fall and hurt my knee, or bang my head and hurt my head. Obviously there was the possibility that I could make decisions which could be detrimental to me even though they might not have caused death as did the decision toward disobedience. Pain receptors were pre fall, I would assume, in order to teach us safety. Bleeding and clotting I would assume, were pre fall to heal injuries the body received in life. Redundant bodily systems were present to compensate for loss. New fingernails could be grown should one be injured and fall off, and baby teeth were shed when adult teeth came in.

Yet, I would assume only one set of adult teeth came with any adult, and nerve damage was irreparable. You probably couldn't inadvertently get a stick in your eye and hope to grow another.

Obviously there was a dramatic difference before and after the fall in innumerable ways. However, did the immune systems which are built into people to fight disease only arise after the fall when disease could kill? Was blood clotting only necessary after the fall as no one was ever injured before? Did no one ever stub their toe and loose a toenail before the fall?

These are important questions because they speak to the role that human differences, expressed by social construction as "disabilities" may have in God's design of human beings.

We must always keep in mind that an omnipotent God is not surprised by anything in his creation, so the notion of disability, whether congenital or adventitious (the result of aging or disease, injury, etc.), is not something that took him by surprise, and bodily correction of injury appears to be planned for to a significant degree as evidenced by the systems for repair observable in our bodies. We experience repair when our systems return us to a place of normalcy as compared with the rest of people. If our systems cannot bring repair, we might be characterized as experiencing disability or in more severe cases death. This disability might be short term, like a broken arm, or last indefinitely as in intellectual disability. We know for sure that death came as a result of the fall, so someone severely injured prior to the fall must have either experienced healing, or was maintained in a living state while continuing to experience the injury, which hardly sounds like paradise.

Friday, August 27, 2004

Deconstructing intellectual disability: etiology and social constructions

The etiology of disability can basically be categorized in three different general areas. There are disabilities caused by genetics, disabilities caused by trauma and disabilities caused by the environment. Questions related to the cause of disability can dovetail with the understanding of the why of disability.

The notion of disability caused by genetics may seem to be the most "God caused" notion as the cause of the disability is built into the makeup of the parents of the child who has the disability. Often, these disabilities seem to arise "out of the blue." Although the biological basis of such disability is as predictable any other cause effect sequence, they don't seem to be so, particularly if the disability is the first appearance within a family.

A geneticist/professor of mine used to state that each of us carry about 11% of out genetic make-up which if paired with a spouse who also has that same 11% genetic component will result in disability or death in the offspring. I suspect this percentage was an estimate on the basis if his experience, however, it causes one to pause in thinking about the various factors which would result in the pairing with another person (how a couple met, etc.) and the coming together to have a child with that other person. The take home lesson, is that each of us carry the potential to produce offspring with disability, genetically, if the conditions are "right." The reason why this potential is carried around in our genetic complement is a question for theologians. We will be discussing this question, however, let's be clear on who we are talking about when we speak of persons experiencing disability.

Elsewhere in this blog, we have discussed the notion of the range of variability within the population. That is, the "normal" variation within the population. We note that Jesus, for example, was intelligent and physically strong, however, we also note that he was not necessarily remarkable in his physical appearance. Jesus himself reflected the range of normal. The question remains, however, what is the normal range? That is a difficult notion to nail down as normal, above normal or below normal is often environment specific.

I remember as a high school student, I was able to make the high school basketball team. That to some degree indicated that I was in the upper echelon of boys playing basketball at that particular school. When I went on to college, I found that the players on the basketball team were better than those at my high school. My skill level was suddenly much more average (and that was at a division 3 school). Should I attempt to play at a division 1 school, or for the sake of discussion at the professional level, I would not only be unable to compete, I would probably appear "disabled" by comparison with the athletes at those levels. So depending upon what particular portion of the population, within which particular environment, I can appear disabled, average or even above average.

Within our society we do a variety of assessments to attempt to determine what is the average for persons having particular characteristics (age, ethnicity, even urban or rural life experience among others). Depending upon what the characteristic is that we are assessing, we then develop interventions to take those who are below a particular level up to or above that desired level in order to facilitate life success. Now in our society we do not do basketball assessments, however, if we did, such assessments would identify those who are in the gifted range, those in the above average range, those in the average range, those in the below average range and those in the "disabled" range in their basketball ability. The fact that people are not being labeled as having a "basketball disability" is a reflection of what our society values in terms of assessing in all individuals. It's nice if you are good in basketball, however, it is in no way required. When we meet someone who is good at basketball we celebrate that in the same manner that we would celebrate any strength in an individual. However, we don't commiserate with families who find that their child does not have basketball ability as such ability is not valued by all people in society.

For people with disability, particularly intellectual disability, one of the issues where they often evidence of weakness is social skill. Obviously social skill is something which is wildly divergent across groups and cultures. Social skill is perhaps the most difficult of skills to master particularly as a person's range of accessed environments increases. Using the same range of ability level that we used with basketball, we will find that there are those who are gifted in the area of social skills, there are those above average and so on. However, in contrast to basketball ability, social skills are valued by society and one is personally included or excluded on the basis of their social skills. Society is very unforgiving in the social skill arena.

One way to increase the range of normal is to change the environment. In some ways the notion of disability changes as the environment changes. I suspect there are actually families for whom basketball is life to whom a family member who lacks basketball skill would be considered tantamount to having a disability. Unfortunately, individual Christians and churches often reflect society in a negative way.

At times, churches can be more disability regarding than the secular world. This should never be the case. If disability can largely be a social construct, then the environment reflecting the social construct can change.

We have seen this occur for a segment of American society. In my lifetime, homosexuality has gone from psychological disorder to mainstream. It has been changed as a social construct among some groups of people.

But what of areas of disability which are not socially constructed? The question is whether disability is part of the design of humanity or an aspect of the fall into sin. For a moment let's move away from the "gray" areas of disability which may be the result of a social construction. So we are talking about perhaps the most severe of disabilities, including more severe areas of intellectual disability, or severe physical or sensory related disability. However, even these forms of disability must be segregated. The social construction of deafness has developed to the point of becoming tantamount to a cultural difference rather than a disability. Blindness has not developed in this manner, however, people who are blind are finding their way into the mainstream on the basis of their own significant efforts, those who have advocated on their behalf, and technological advances. Even those with severe physical disability are making significant progress in deconstructing severe physical disability as a social construction. Yet you only need to go to IHOP with your friend with severe physical disabilities to find out that if physical disability is a social construction, it is still firmly entrenched. However, if the example of blindness is any indication, there is the potential for greater inclusion and acceptance in the future. The Americans with Disabilities Act has helped in the deconstruction of physical disability, however, there is still a long way to go.

So the remaining area of disability to be considered is severe intellectual disability which once again is caused by genetics, trauma and the environment and is the focus of this blog.

Wednesday, August 25, 2004

Love and trustworthiness

I remember as a 19 year old, some of my earliest interactions with persons with disabilities. As a student at Wheaton College, I became friends with a woman in a Friday evening social group we ran for adults with disabilities named Paula. Paula had Down's syndrome with the accompanying intellectual disability and sweet disposition. She liked to draw pictures with markers.

126

One day I heard that Paula was in the hospital for headaches. I remember going to the hospital and walking into her room. She gave a friendly greeting and we began a conversation (I don't remember what it was about). I was having a nice visit, when suddenly she began wildly flopping around on the bed. I had seen people have seizures before but this was something different. She was aware and crying as she would flail which isn't something you typically see with a seizure. I got the nurse, and after a minute or so she stopped and lay still again. I stayed and was able to continue the semblance of a largely one sided conversation.

When I left the hospital room I as very angry with God. It wasn't enough that he made this young woman intellectually disabled, he also had to give here severe headaches on top of it all? It didn't make any sense.

To those who have faith the resolution I came to will make sense while to those who don't it may seem a cop out. But as I worked through this experience I came away with two characteristics of God that the Bible was crystal clear on and even to this day, I cling to these when I don't understand what I see around me. Those two principles are that God is love and that God is trustworthy. He loves me and he loved Paula and both of us can trust him, even though neither of us was quite sure about it at the time.

In the last few years of my life I have found that Proverbs 3:5 is the piece of wisdom which most encourages me, and gets me through situations when I am struggling. It says, "Trust in the Lord with all your heart, don't lean on your own understanding. In all your ways acknowledge him and he'll make your paths straight."

The growth in my trust in God took a major hit and then made a significant jump in 1975, and has continued to grow to where it is now. In the same way that I was somehow a part of Paula's spiritual journey (through interactions, Bible study, etc.) she through her disability became an important part of mine.

Thursday, June 24, 2004

Disability as a social construction

I have been working on a video series about the lives of adults with disabilities. We are in the early stages, but you can get an idea of what it is about by visiting "dislife videos" at my web page, jeffmcnair.com

Anyway in the process of interviewing "Mark" one of the subjects of the movies, I asked the question, "Do you have a disability?" To me the answer is obviously "Yes" as it would most probably be for you as well. However, Mark responded, "I don't know. I try to work hard and I am not as bad as some people and I have friends. I don't know."

127

So there I was, Mr. Loves the Disabled People, shot down by a guy who felt he wasn't sure he had a disability. I saw him as disabled.

What was my evidence he had a disability?

Well, he had been in special education classes all his life.

His IQ was lower than the average, probably a full standard deviation lower because of the services he was receiving.

He had an assistant who came in to help him with budgeting and shopping.

He had a job coach who made an occasional appearance at his job.

He can't read very well if at all.

His social skills are good, but not perfect.

He received social security income.

What was his confounding evidence which might cause him to wonder whether or not he had a disability?

He tries to work hard.

He has friends.

He isn't as bad as some people (the example he gave was that he didn't use bad language or start fights).

I also observe that he lives pretty much on his own.

He is able to get around the community on his own.

People care about him.

He is quick to help someone out as long as it doesn't interfere with his work hours.

He is interested in his own spiritual growth ("Jeff, do you think I am doing better than I used to be?").

It sounds trite, but I am not so sure he has a disability either.

You might reply, "Well obviously he can't do a lot of the things people without disabilities can do!" (Thanks for helping out with that comment). But I would reply that there are many things I can't do that he can do. He can bench press about 200. I can't. He can work for 11 years collecting carts at a Sam's club store, and go to work with joy, and come home fulfilled. As a university professor, I don't always feel that way. He can trust others in a way I can't. He can live without things I think I can't live without . . . and so on.

Its interesting that at the Department of Rehabilitation (a state agency which assists with jobs and job training) if you no longer need their services, you are said to have "medically recovered from your disability." I like that. So if you are a person with cerebral palsy who goes to Rehab, and they help you get a job, in their mind you no longer have a disability. You have medically recovered.

What would it take for a church to not see a person with a disability as a person with a disability? Is there the possibility that such a person

128

could "recover" from their disability in a Christian church setting? Many of the criteria which cause a person to be labeled as disabled are irrelevant in a church setting. Must a person be able to read to be a Christ follower? What are the entry level social skills required to be a Christian? If there is a difference between the criteria for being a Christian and being a member of a church, should the criteria for being a Christian change or should the criteria for being a member of a church change?

I was once involved with a church where a 60 year old adult with intellectual disability was member. He had worked at the local university for 40 years as a pot scrubber. At the church, he was "permitted" to serve communion. He was a real asset as the aluminum communion plates they used sometimes got stuck together, even during the actual communion service. He could pop them apart quickly without spilling a drop or a crumb. One day the leadership of the elder board was changed, and my friend was no longer permitted to serve communion. The reason given to me? "He has the mind of a 6 year old." All those years of competence did not dispel the social construction that he was a disabled person, not a person.

He was seen as a retarded man, not a man.

Tuesday, May 18, 2004

Divergent thinking part 1

"There is more than one way to skin a cat." Actually I will have nothing to do with a cat or his skin, whether or not he is wearing it. But to put it another way, we need to think divergently, rather than convergently. "In praise of paradox" (1981) is an article by Dr. Julian Rappaport which makes this point. He states that social problems, social issues are different from hard science issues. I can calculate the answer to a Physics problem (well, I cant, but at least I know there are people who can do those kinds of calculations). There will be a single correct and a multitude of incorrect answers. Social issues are not like that. As Rappaport implies, we may come to two conflicting solutions to the same problem. For some people one will work, for others another and for others, neither will work. I think divergent thinking is sometimes difficult for Christians. We will at times carry over our morality orientation towards the black and white to other areas of life. We take differing positions, at times positions based upon interpretation, experience, understanding or knowledge, and assume that is the only correct position.

I recall the pastor of a church I attended for five years when I lived in Illinois stating that if someone really got into the Bible, she would see that the perspective of this particular church was the right one and they would come to believe what he believed. He related how people had come to this church and stayed because they realized that the perspective taught there was the truth! I asked whether anyone had ever left that church for another church. Or what of all the other Christian churches in that community. Were all those people disillusioned? The implication of his perspective was that they had all fallen away. Of course I am not saying that anything goes, however, I have come to believe that people can have a different perspective from me on a world of issues and still be Christian.

This same point is true of ministry to people with various disabilities. The church can fall into the same problem that the state has fallen into in that it offers a limited menu of services. You can use those services or you can go home. It's like going to McDonalds and trying to buy a hot dog. You aren't going to get a hot dog at McDonalds, so if that is the outcome you desire, you will not be able to reach it.

I have taught a class at the university on the portrayal of individuals with disability in film. Just like in all the Disney cartoons the mother dies, in most disability movies, the professionals look foolish because they offer services which don't meet the need. Some examples:

In Benny and Joon, the psychiatrist wants to put Joon in a home, instead she lives on her own.

In Cuckoo's Nest, Nurse Ratched wants McMurphy to be the model patient, when through his antics he frees the other patients, particularly the Chief.

In My Left Foot, mom keeps the gifted Christy Brown, a person with cerebral palsy at home and educates him against recommendations.

Similar themes arise in Lost in Yonkers, or Slingblade, or Dominick and Eugene or The Other Sister, or Rainman.

The messiness of human service makes us uncomfortable. You can't send the autistic boy to the Sunday school class like you would the cute little nondisabled youngster. The adult with intellectual disability cannot always be expected to sit quietly in the church setting. The other day at our church, a developmentally disabled adult happened to stand up (he was sitting in the front row) at just the moment the pastor began to preach. He stood there for about 5 minutes looking up at the pastor as he spoke, and I am sure that he thought the pastor was talking directly to him. Finally the light came on and he sat down.

That is the problem, but that is also the excitement. Work with persons with disabilities is filled with challenges and the unexpected. Social skills are up for grabs, and the traditional menus which churches have used for ministry can be tossed out the window because many disabled persons are living under a different set of rules, rules that they don't even understand.

So, creativity is the mark of the special educator, or the person in ministry to persons with disability. Convergent thinkers need not apply.

Saturday, May 15, 2004

Divergent thinking part 2

Continuing with the ideas of Dr. Julian Rappaport from the previous post, another problem with convergent thinking in human service is that single solutions create another whole set of problems. The menu driven limitations of human service agencies will solve some problems, however, such limited options provided to problems to which they don't apply, exacerbate some problems and create others. How about some examples.

If the only option for Sunday school is to have children sit in large groups on the floor of a room, then there will be many children who will never benefit from Sunday school.

If the only option for ministry to adults with intellectual disability is fully including them in the regular adult classes at the church, then some of these adults will never learn about their faith.

If the only option for persons with disability is to go to another church, then there will be many people with disabilities who along with their families will be unchurched.

If the only option for service in the church is something that requires a physically intact body, then those with out such bodies will not be able to serve.

If the only singing, dancing, reading, speaking that is permitted from the stage of the church is perfection, a total emphasis on excellence, then there will be few who can participate.

If the standard for social skill for the congregation is too high, many will be excluded.

In each of the above areas, escaping from the convergent requires creativity. What if there were actually options for children in Sunday school? Options for adult ministry including reverse integration where adults without disability attend the class geared to the level of understanding of those with intellectual disability. I have taught such classes for a long time and I always learn something.

We have to find ways to open up our churches to persons with disability. We need to look for options for service for all members, while at the same time reserving particular opportunities for service, for persons with disability who are perhaps limited in the ways they can serve.

131

Recognizing that persons like my friend Gavin, an adult with severe cerebral palsy who uses a wheelchair and is blind is a powerful witness when he sings before the congregation. It doesn't matter that he won't be releasing an album any time soon.

Also, expanding the range of normal to include a variety of not entirely appropriate social skills which are tolerated (not without efforts to improve them) because it is more important to have the individual at church than it is to have his social skills be perfect before he is admitted. I have had disabled friends with their hands touching or scratching every imaginable part of their body, but I welcome them because after shaking theirs, I can always wash mine.

Be divergent, be creative.

Sunday, May 16, 2004

Reject the lies and work the works

Susan Dolan-Henderson in her article "Mainstreaming Justice" (Sojourners, 2000) makes the following comments.

"Need and dependency are so hated by our society that euthanasia and assisted suicide have been put forth as better alternatives than interdependence. We need health care, pain control, and support for families to empty euthanasia and assisted suicide of their terrible attraction." How evil that people will come to us, to our American society and say they are in pain or depressed to the point of wanting to take their own life, and we reply, "I'll help you take your life." In effect we say, "You are right. You are not worth any effort from me or others." Not all of these people are on their death bed. As a respected friend of mine, Dr. Rick Langer once said to me, "These are not people who are sustained on life supports, they are those who if they are not killed today, might go to McDonalds."

Then later in the same article she writes,

"We are all only temporarily-abled. Illness and disability can strike at any time. The disabled and chronically ill remind us of how much in life is beyond our control. It is theologically and ethically appropriate to see God as having a preferential option for the disabled and ill, and thus for the church integrally to mirror this preference and work for justice concerning their well being. Throughout the New Testament, the church is called to be a community of interdependence. Care of the chronically ill and disabled is not a one-way street."

Perhaps as an American, or perhaps just as a person, I resist the above statements more than I care to admit. I think I would do just about anything to be able to die quickly. Not because I necessarily fear death, but because I don't want to be a burden to my family. I don't want to be dependent on others in any way because dependency is weakness, and as a MAN I don't want to be weak. I am happy to help others who are disabled or weak, but I don't want to be in need of their help because I am disabled or weak. The Bible tells me God's strength is shown in my weakness, but I think that deep down I think God's strength is shown in my strength. I think I might actually hate some forms of weakness. God tells me that the first will be last, but I think that the first will be first. I see the way Jesus responded to his critics while I in my bravado study to devastate my detractors with a witty counter attack.

"For what I do is not the good I want to do; no, the evil I do not want to do - this I keep on doing" (Romans 7:19).

I have bought the lies. . .

My wife's grandmother, a woman who is a true servant of God, raising Godly boys, and impacting our family for what I suspect will be many generations (the Lord willing) is dying as I write this. Her malady has been progressive in nature. Family members have used this opportunity to visit with her, help her, love her. I don't know how aware she is, but I hope she has awareness of these people who love her as they gather around. In better days, she was a person who always did for others. Her sugar cream pie was the stuff of legend. Through her life ending disability, God has provided the opportunity for her loved ones to gather around her and support her, the opportunity to manifest the works of God in her (see April 26 entry). We have the opportunity to work "the works of him that sent me, while it is still day."

While it is still day.

This part of the verse hit me. I have the opportunity to work the works while it is still day for me, and I have the opportunity to work the works for disabled individuals like my wife's grandmother while it is still day for her, and I have the opportunity to work the works while it is still day for the world.

So reject the lies and work the works while it is still day.

Friday, May 14, 2004

The "bleedin' obvious"
In the British sitcom, "Fawlty Towers" Basil Fawlty (John Cleese)makes the comment ostensibly to his wife (but actually under his breath)about an observation she has made. He states, "Contestant, Sybil Fawlty, category, the bleedin' obvious."

Sometimes, people's questions of how to act toward individuals with disability although seemingly unknown to them, to me is the "bleedin' obvious." Recently my wife, Kathi, made a presentation to a group of women at a Christian women's retreat. When she concluded, a participant raised her hand with a question. She asked, "A disabled woman attended our church, and even became a member, but we haven't heard from her lately. What should we do?" For a moment Kathi was taken aback. "Well, do you have her phone number?" "Yes" the woman replied. "Well, why don't you call her?" At that the woman took out a pen and paper and wrote the suggestion down. "Maybe you could take her out to lunch." "Wonderful" the woman replied excitedly.

For some reason, common sense goes out the window when people with disabilities are involved. Should a friend of ours need a job, we respond that we will do what we can to help. However, should that person use a wheelchair, we ask if he has contacted the state agency that assists with job identification. I even knew of a situation where a young woman with intellectual disability was sexually abused and raped. The people at her employing agency just sent her home that Friday because the state agency who works with disabled people wasn't open till the following Monday.

A friend of mine, an intelligent doctor once said to me that he would love to help out adults with disability, but he didn't have any training. He honestly felt he didn't know what to do.

However, I have seen glimpses of the same helplessness in myself. When I was a church leader, a family in our church was rocked by the husband being arrested and sent to jail. When asked what I might do to help this family, the words came out of my mouth, "I don't know how to work with the family of someone who is in jail." Almost as soon as those words escaped my lips, I recanted saying, "Well, I guess they will need help with child care, and with basic home repairs, and maybe money will be a bit short." Even with the most rudimentary thought one quickly comes to solutions.

Yet at times I think Christians don't even give interactions with persons with disabilities the most rudimentary thought.

"What do disabled people need?" they might say. Well, probably somebody to give them a call now and then, or take them out to lunch, or give them a ride to the mall, or include them in a holiday celebration.

"But what would I say?" they might say. How about, how are you doing, or did you see the Lakers game, or nice weather we are having, or tell me about your family.

"Should I help a person who is blind with their lunch, or a person who uses a wheelchair with the door?" they might say. How about asking, do you need some help with your lunch or with the door?

Innumerable other situations might be imagined with equally difficult answers. "What if they spill their food?" Maybe clean it up. "What if they fall down?" Maybe help them get up again. "What if they use bad language? (those with emotional problems)." Maybe tell them, please don't use bad language. "What if they need something?" Maybe ask them what they need.

Sometimes I feel like Basil Fawlty.

Monday, May 10, 2004

Changing perceptions to reality

Seymour Sarason the 'father of community psychology' along with John Doris wrote in *Educational handicap, public policy and social history* (1979), the following:

"Behind all the ways physicians view the retarded infant is the assumption that it creates a social-interpersonal disaster. This 'diagnosis' says far more about the value systems of our society than it does about the retarded infant."

In 'Disability, cultural representation and language,' Barnes (1995) writes,

"In most developed societies it is now widely recognized that the severe economic and social deprivations encountered by disabled people cannot be explained simply with reference to individually based functional limitations."

These two quotes, separated by 15 years indicate how the perception of an individual influences the life experience of that same individual.

In the first quote, we see the notion of a family member with disability as a disaster. It will take a wise family, who, at the birth of an infant with retardation are treated with pity, comments about how the family will be prayed for, that the parents or child are somehow special, specially selected (or some other inanity), are able to see past all the furor to a reasoned understanding of their disabled child.

Unfortunately no preparation comes with a disabled child's birth. Parents and families are forced to rely on the limited experience they have gleaned from life up to that point. Sometimes there is real life experience with a friend, or family member with disability. More often, perhaps, honest parents of children with disabilities will relate that they gave little or no thought to children with autism or intellectual disability in their community until their child was diagnosed with such a condition. That this would be the experience of unchurched community members, from a Christian perspective, might not be surprising. However, for Christians to share that same lack of experience or concern should cause Christians to pause.

A lack of knowledge or experience would imply that persons with disabilities and their families have not been in the "congregational midst" in the local church. Should a child's only knowledge of people with intellectual disability or other disabilities be what she learns in the public school setting? Interesting how this important aspect of moral understanding hardly appears on the radar screen of Christians.

In the second quote, we see that the experience of persons with disability cannot be explained solely on the basis of their functional limitations. That is, it might be concluded that their experience has been imposed upon them by society. I am reminded of the days when it was thought that persons with Down's syndrome were unable to learn. You might reply, "I don't believe it. When did that happen?" Well as recently as 1972 there was a court case in which the State of Pennsylvania took the position that a child with Down's syndrome could not benefit from a public school education. Ultimately the court decided that it was easier to attempt to educate such children than it was to prove they could not be educated, and special education as a right was born (public school education became a right in 1979).

The individuals who were ultimately educated, who learned to read, and develop skills sufficient to be employed and live on their own were the same before and after the court case. What changed were the opportunities provided and the perceptions of the people around them.

In each of the quotes provided, the authors are advocating change in the environment in which persons with disabilities find themselves. To what extent is the local church a positive or negative reflection of prevailing cultural values about disability? How might a Christian community be different such that the life of an individual with disability is not a family disaster, or limited by anything other than the person with disability's own functional limitations?

Friday, May 07, 2004

The little children metaphor

There are several places in biblical gospels where Jesus tells his followers to somehow resemble little children. In Luke 18:16 he says to let the little children come to him because the kingdom belongs to such as these. He also says we must receive the kingdom like a little child. In Matthew 11:25, he praises God because he has hidden things from the wise and revealed them to little children. In Matthew 18:3, he says if you humble yourself like a child you will be the greatest in the kingdom.

So. . .

we should receive the kingdom like little children
hidden things are revealed to little children
we should humble ourselves like little children
the kingdom belongs to little children

In considering Jesus' audience, poor, malnutritioned, largely uneducated, third worlders, the level of their children would be arguably even lower than the adults. This audience strikes me as not being that far a field from intellectually disabled adults of today. Jesus was no doubt speaking figuratively when telling his followers to be like little children.

Yet in my interactions with intellectually disabled adults, little children, in many ways, intellectually, it gives me pause. I consider the joyful manner in which they receive gifts. I ponder the things which they understand about the Lord and about their faith and wonder about the things which might be clear to them yet confuse me (ostensibly an educated person with wisdom of the world). I reflect on the humility they must consistently engender to receive the kinds of services and supports they receive. I disagree with the following statement, however it makes a point, in that few people would really say they "need" their disabled friend. If I need you, then you can make demands on me and I must capitulate to you in order to gain what I need you to provide, or I need to receive from you. In over 25 years, I can't remember a time when a intellectually disabled person refused to help me when I asked for assistance. But to be in constant need from others forces humility on you, and in some ways causes you to be humble like little children. Ultimately the kingdom of God belongs to such as these. Belongs to those who receive it like a little child, are humble like a little child, and receive the revelations that confound the wise, like a little child.

There might be a principle here, that persons with average to above average intellectual abilities can be deluded into thinking that they are self sufficient. This level of conceited arrogance which we all have to some extent, interferes with many aspects of our spiritual growth. That is, I won't believe unless I understand something, I don't want to humble myself and serve others, I really desire that they serve me, I must receive my faith along with other gifts from God with humility. I struggle in all these areas, particularly in receiving my faith as a gift. As Watchman Nee says, I look in the wrong direction, looking at myself as the source of my knowledge, my success, my faith, my acceptability and reason for belonging.

I find people with intellectual disabilities don't face that same problem as much. For example, they are used to not understanding things, to having to be humble to receive help. If you tell them that God has given you a gift, they will respond in humility, not second guessing what He wants in return or if he even is. They set an example for me.

To my thinking they often respond as a little child would.

Tuesday, April 27, 2004

The
Church

From "Surprised by Hope" by N.T. Wright

I have been reading *Surprised by Hope* (2008) by N.T. Wright with some friends. I have found it a fascinating book. As the subtitle states, it deals with "Rethinking Heaven, the Resurrection, and the Mission of the Church." Here is a quote that grabbed me.

..."To hope for a better future in this world - for the poor, the sick, the lonely and depressed, for the slaves, the refugees, the hungry and homeless, for the abused, the paranoid, the downtrodden and despairing, and in fact for the whole wide, wonderful, and wounded world - is not something *else*, something extra, something tacked on to the gospel as an afterthought. And to work for that intermediate hope, the surprising hope that comes forward from God's ultimate future into God's urgent present, is not *distraction from* the task of mission and evangelism in the present. It is central, essential, vital, and life-giving part of it. Mostly, Jesus himself got a hearing from his contemporaries because of what he was doing. They saw him saving people from sickness and death, and they heard him talking about a salvation, the message for which they had longed, that would go beyond the immediate into the ultimate future. But the two were not unrelated, the present one a mere visual aid of the future one or a trick to gain people's attention. The whole point of what Jesus was up to was that he was doing, close up, in the present, what he was promising long-term, in the future...

The point of the resurrection, as Paul has been arguing through the letter (1 Corinthians), is that *the present bodily life is not valueless just because it will die*. God will raise it to new life. What you do with your body in the present matters because God has a great future in store for it. And if this applies to ethics, as in 1 Corinthians 6, it certainly also applies to the various vocations to which God's people are called. What you *do* in the present - by painting, preaching, singing, sewing, praying, teaching, building hospitals, digging wells, campaigning for justice, writing poems, caring for the needy, loving your neighbor as yourself - *will last into God's future*. These activities are not simply ways of making the present life a little less beastly, a little more bearable, until the day when we leave it behind altogether...They are part of what we may call *building for God's kingdom"* (pp. 192-193).

I want to pull a few sections out of this passage and touch on them a bit. Wright says, "Jesus himself got a hearing from his contemporaries because of what he was doing." This is so important in the life of a church in relation to disability issues. You can criticize me all day long about being closed minded or intolerant, however, if I am working to love, encourage and befriend people with various disabilities, well, it might just cause you to be silent. Unless completely foolish, people are still impressed by what others do over what they say they will do. Wright says that a significant reason that Jesus himself got a hearing was because of what he was doing. Why should people listen to you or your church? Is there any reason that a family member or friend of a person with a disability or a person with a disability herself should listen to you on the basis of what you are doing?

"The whole point of what Jesus was up to was that he was doing, close up, in the present, what he was promising long-term, in the future." How does what you or your church doing point to what you are promising long-term in the future for persons with disabilities both on Earth and in Heaven? Are you promising them a future where they will be a full member of the Body of Christ or are you promising that there is no place for them in the Body of Christ, in the Kingdom of God? We have the ability to provide a glimpse of the future even if we are not seeing a person physically healed. We bring glory to God by providing a glimpse of a future where disability is largely irrelevant. I say largely irrelevant because it appears that there will be vestiges of our Earthly life in Heaven (e.g. Jesus' stigmata). My love, my acceptance, my caring, independent of your personal characteristics are a glimpse of the future. It is no wonder if people with various disabilities are not drawn to church. We give them a picture of a future without them through their experience of a present without them.

Wright also states that, "These activities are not simply ways of making the present life a little less beastly, a little more bearable, until the day when we leave it behind altogether...They are part of what we may call building for God's kingdom." He makes the point that our physical bodies are redeemed. Our existence is not merely a spiritual existence because this cannot be supported by scripture. So he claims there is some kind of a link between our physical bodies now, and the new bodies we will receive in the New Heaven and New Earth. I am confident that I don't understand what this means. However, there is a long term aspect of the things we do as people if we will only be aware of it. I think the effects are multifaceted for our own lives and the lives of others. They build God's kingdom in myriad ways.

Tuesday, December 02, 2008

The moral "where with all"

While in Cape Town at the IASSID conference, I attended two presentations relative to personhood of people with disabilities, in particular intellectual disabilities. One presenter quoted Dr. Hans Reinders using the phrase "precarious personhood." It is a good phrase, pointing to the tenuous nature of the lives of many people around the world.

A second presenter used the phrase "traditional moral philosophy" as kind of the point of appeal for personhood, implying that traditional moral philosophy will bring us to the awakening we need to love our brothers and sisters in spite of their perceived, negative, personal characteristics. I felt like she was Peter Pan asking me to throw myself out the window because she says I can fly. I raised the question, "If just about everywhere in the world, pretty much forever, people have been excluded on the basis of their disability, to what traditional moral philosophy are you appealing? Our traditions have failed us at every turn. Our secular and at times religiously informed moral values have been traditionally unhelpful and problematic. To imply otherwise is to evidence an intellectual disability. You are therefore appealing to a morality that is basically not present." Strangely, she agreed.

Such morality is not present in the majority of parents until a child with a disability is born to them and even then not always so. It is not present in schools where special education teachers force inclusion on children but do not live lives inclusive of their own peers with intellectual disabilities. Our only hope is to appeal to settings where the morality we desire is present although perhaps dormant in many situations like the Christian church. We have the opportunity to lead the way in the development of values that will value people with disabilities. In many ways it is not natural for societies to have such values...they must be taught. Or better yet, they must be modeled by us for society because we as Christians can at times talk a good game, but can't back it up. At least not yet, and for sure not universally. Pockets of brilliance do not an argument make, however, but as the pockets grow, more will want to reflect what they see.

Wednesday, September 10, 2008

Universal design and the Christian church

Universal design is a recently developed principle. It is defined by The Center for Universal Design website as, "The design of products and environments to be usable by all people, to the greatest extent possible, without the need for adaptation or specialized design." If you visit their web pages they provide the definition as well as 7 principles with explanations.

One of the lessons of universal design, is that changes that are made, say for example in an environment, for the expressed purpose of making things easier for a disabled person, end up often benefiting everyone in that environment. This is illustrated in the webpage provided above.

I was thinking through the universal design principle the other day, and it occurred to me that universal design should be a basic

145

characteristic of the Church. I suspect in its purest form, if the church were all it should be, it would be a perfect example of universal design. That is the case because the Body of Christ is comprised of people with varying abilities. The church was envisioned for humanity, so it must be designed, be comprised of structures, evidence practices, develop programs, that reflect the variety of humanity. The degree to which we do not see universal design principles within the church, in many ways is evidence that it is not all that it should be. Let's consider the principles of universal design briefly in reference to the church.

1. "Principle one: Equitable use
Provide the same means of use for all users: identical whenever possible; equivalent when not. Avoid segregating or stigmatizing any users."

The church should facilitate equitable use. That means access to the programs of the church, all the benefits of church participation. The implication therefore is that programs and benefits might have to be altered such that all people can have access to them. If there is not access, the person is not wrong, the program is wrong or needs to be altered in some way. Wheelchair use should not mean that I cannot be a youth leader.

Programs and practices of the church should also not segregate and stigmatize people, particularly on the basis of perceived negative characteristics. Down's syndrome does not mean that I cannot be in the Sunday school class.

2. "Principle two: Flexibility in use
Provide choice in methods of use. Facilitate the user's accuracy and precision. Provide adaptability to the user's pace."

Flexibility implies flexibility in the delivery of information, in the social standards (no I am not talking about sin, I am talking about social skills). By understanding "users" we understand that responses can be very different. We understand, for example, that faith development is a process that is not exclusively knowledge based, so that programs that facilitate faith development are sensitive to where people are in their faith, and the contribution of knowledge to faith development. We also do not offer "once size fits all" worship, or Sunday school, or music. We may find that people will prefer the faith development activities designed for persons with intellectual disabilities, for example, because they are connected with real life and are less potentially esoteric. Worship alongside of a person who is atypical changes the nature of worship from quiet listening to a sermon, to service, or patient love, or a variety of

146

other goods. Do we ever assess user's pace in sermon delivery? Do we ever assess faith development in individuals who have listened to sermons for 20 years as a means to evaluate our programs? Sometimes I feel like if I am not understanding something that has become programmatically entrenched in the way the church has always done things, that I am at fault. But it may not be so. Universal design would say that there are others who have the same questions as I, but the programmatic "heavy hand" squelches questions of why.

3. "Principle three: Simple and intuitive
Eliminate unnecessary complexity. Be consistent with user expectations and intuition. Accommodate a wide range of literacy and language skills. Arrange information consistent with its importance. Provide effective prompting and feedback during and after task completion."

Are programs of the church simple and intuitive? I know that often in programs for persons with intellectual disabilities, the knowledge based orientation of the programs makes them unnecessarily complex. Somehow complexity is a high value in knowledge based approaches. But what are the user expectations of the typical church member? Are they being addressed and do we even know whether or not they are?

I have often wondered about the way church programs accommodate literacy skills (let alone language skills). How do we make material accessible in a manner that is not demeaning for those for whom literacy is an issue? I have also wondered about the notion of arranging information consistent with its importance. In training persons with severe disabilities, there is the concept of functional curriculum. That is, teachers ask themselves whether it will make any difference in the person's life if they learn a particular thing. This notion is something that churches should consider in program development. Do we ever evaluate the comparative importance of the information we are sharing or do we just blindly teach our 3rd grade Sunday school class? I remember looking through a children's picture Bible, where there was a picture of Absalom hanging by his hair from a tree! What is the point of this in terms of importance of relevance of the story to children? Once something is learned, how to we ensure learning is maintained, or do we simply move onto the next thing?

4. "Principle four: Perceptible information
Use different modes (pictorial, verbal, tactile) for redundant presentation of essential information. Provide adequate contrast between essential information and its surroundings."

How do we make relevant information perceivable, and how do we help people to understand what is relevant? Do we highlight or point out for people that this is the focus, this is the lesson, and how do we facilitate understanding?

In our current churches, we have lots of video and lots of music, etc. Is that the way to make specific content relevant because there is a difference between being culturally relevant (via technology for example) and personally relevant in terms of helping people understand what is essential. The video screens are not essential, although they may assist in bringing what is essential to the notice of those viewing. I am confident, however, that there is confusion about whether the information or the video screens are what is essential to many people.

5. "Principle five: Tolerance for error
Arrange elements to minimize hazards and errors: most used elements, most accessible; hazardous elements eliminated, isolated, or shielded. Provide warnings of hazards and errors. Provide fail safe features. Discourage unconscious action in tasks that require vigilance."

What hazards or errors might characterize a church that is trying to include people with disabilities? In the past hazards and errors have been the focus on social skills of attendees, on the potential perceived contribution of attendees, on the demands people by virtue of their disabilities may make on attendees, the failure of leadership in recognizing the priority that should be placed on ministry that involves service. Past errors have also been related to resistance to change.

People might also need to be prepared to see errors within themselves so that they can be aware of them. "We are going to have people start coming here who are autistic. Autistic people sometimes make strange noises that largely will make us feel uncomfortable, because we have not been around them enough to have their noises no longer bother us. But we will get better over time as we become acclimated to them and them to us. What we cannot do is reject them, because that is sin and we don't want to sin."

6. "Principle six: Low physical effort
Allow user to maintain a neutral body position. Use reasonable operating forces. Minimize repetitive actions. Minimize sustained physical effort."

How can the effort to do church attendance be minimized for persons with disabilities? Whether it be not having to ride the bus to church, or just getting around? We also need to teach average church members the truth, biblically and theologically about what disability is so that they do not cause the goofy ideas that have grown out of ignorance to persist. I know of people with disabilities who will not go back to church because of the things said to them there. Things about sin and disability or sufficient faith and disability, or just a blatant lack of understanding of what life is like for a person with a disability. I will also say that many people, church people, Christian people who use the handicapped parking spots should be ashamed. I literally know of people who have come to a church, but did not stay because all of the handicapped parking spots were used. You might say, "You should be celebrating that! All the spots are filled." Yeah, but I see the mirror hangers that someone holds onto from the broken leg they had a year ago and that isn't right.

7. "Principle seven: Size and space for approach and use
Provide a clear line of sight to important elements for any seated or standing user. Make reach to all components comfortable for any seated or standing user. Accommodate variations in hand and grip size. Provide adequate space for the use of assistive devices or personal assistance."

People should have access to what they need at a church, whether it be physical, intellectual, or emotional. I was speaking to a friend the other day with a hearing impairment. He asked the church whether they could provide an interpreter so he could attend Bible study, and they said they couldn't. But then he asked whether there was someone who could disciple him, teach him the Bible one on one, because he can understand one person at a time in a one on one conversation and they once again said no. That is just stupid. One on one is called discipleship and churches do that all around the world. His church was blocking his access to God's word because they would not facilitate approach.

So much more could be said on these points, however, I think the take home lesson, is that the Christian church should strive to be the model of universal design. It should be the example that people use whenever they discuss such principles. I believe that it is God's intention that the church be a place of openness and acceptance. A supple place where the environment is much softer than the community. Where people come and can cease their fighting and relax in love acceptance and accommodations as appropriate. A place that does not nullify the word of God by its traditions (Mark 7:13).

Saturday, July 19, 2008

The ultimate in legal rejection
Sometimes I post things on this blog and people don't believe me. "It can't be as bad as you suggest" they sometimes say. It is always my

prayer that I am wrong, that there is much more going on than meets the eye. But, for example, if there are 100 churches in the area of the country where I live (the Inland Empire of Southern California) who are working to reach out and include people with disabilities, then that means that only 10-12% of churches in my region of the country are reaching out to people with disabilities.

At times, we are also doing just the opposite, and at times the ridiculous nature of what we are doing is hit by the light of day. Why would the story about a child with autism's relationship with a local church be noteworthy? Was it because the church had dramatically changed the way they do things such that these individuals could be involved? Could it be that special programs were developed so that children with autism could be involved at the church? Those stories could be written, but all it takes is one of the following stories to short circuit the wonderful work of other churches.

The following is in reference to an article is by Terry Gruca, a reporter at wcco.com. In it she describes how a church took out a restraining order to prevent a 13 year old boy, who is a big guy from the description given, from attending the church because he becomes violent or has loud outbursts. If such a child attends church, at least the church in the article, he is to be arrested.

As comedians sometimes say, "I couldn't make this stuff up." But this is not funny. This is tragic. It says that for some people there is NO place within the Body of Jesus Christ. If fact if you attempt to be a part of the Body of Christ, we will arrest you.

Talk about resistance to change.

This church is representing to the community that my Lord and Savior, Jesus Christ, would arrest disabled people for attempting to go to church. I wonder about the violence and loud outbursts. I mean loud outbursts are 50% of the reason why this young man would be arrested for attending church.

All I can say is God bless and God protect the mother of this man for her desire to take him to church, and her faith in God, in being unwilling to reject God in the way that would be self-describing followers of God have rejected her.

"Sure you are critical of this situation, but what would you do, Jeff?"

Let's assume for a moment that the young man is violent and it remains to be seen what violence means in reference to a person with autism. But even so, does violence justify a person being excluded from the Body of Christ? My answer is NO. Don't expect me to have the young man working with the babies or children, however, I will create a place for potentially violent people so that they can be a part of the Body of Christ. I will not file restraining orders against them.

This is so very sad. May God forgive his church for such acts.

Monday, May 19, 2008

Missing love

I just completed *Resurrecting the person* (2000) by John Swinton which I would highly recommend, particularly if you are interested in ministry to persons with mental illness. Many of the issues apply to ministry to anyone, whether or not they experience disability.

In the final chapter of the book, Swinton says, "Perhaps the strangest thing about this process of liberation is its ordinariness" (p. 207). The process of liberation is the change that needs to come over the church such that it will embrace persons with mental illness (in this case) but also persons with various differences in general. The ordinariness is in no way ordinary largely because it is not typically present. However, when you come to understand what the basic changes need to be, you find that they are quite ordinary.

When distilled down, the change that needs to occur is that we need to love our neighbor. It occurred to me that when we have "difficult" people in our midst, like those with severe mental illness, our lack of love is highlighted, it is felt like putting your finger in a wound. However, I wonder if the fact that we are missing love for the difficult group is evidence only that we lack love for those people, or is it an indication of a greater lack of love for all people, unless they are easy. Easy to love people are those who cross my path, tell me everything is fine, make no demands on me, ask me how I am doing, shake my hand or pat me on the back and then leave me alone. Those are the kinds of people I like to populate my world with. They are the easy to love. The other end of the spectrum are those who have poor social skills, or want my money, or want my time, or cause me to have to do things like help them in the bathroom, or wipe their snotty nose, or call me all the time, or disrupt my meetings and so on and so on. They are hard to love. I don't like to populate my life with those kinds of people because they don't leave me alone. Too often, I think, the church is populated with the former and not the latter.

But it is pretty obvious who of the two above will grow me as a person, will grow me as a Christian. I am not called as a Christian to social niceties, independence and being left alone. I am called to messy relationships with difficult people who are unsatisfied with my helping, no matter what I do. I do not learn love through unfettered

151

independence. I learn love through messy relationships, and difficult people, and those who do not praise me for my minimalist love efforts.

However, as I look at the church, it appears to be designed around and largely populated by people who want to be independent, and grow in their independence. I don't want to be a part of the vine, in a relying on others sense, I want to be a branch alone. I don't want to be a part of the body, in a dependency sense, I want to be a foot alone. As I am successful in my independence, I will move further and further away from love. The ideal of love is replaced by the ideal of independence. Those who **are** dependent are also disdained because of the demands they make.

However, what might 1 Corinthians 12:9 mean? Paul asks God to remove his thorn, his disability.

"And He has said to me, "My grace is sufficient for you, for power is perfected in weakness." Most gladly, therefore, I will rather boast about my weaknesses, so that the power of Christ may dwell in me."

How is this premise acted out in churches? The power of Christ dwells in Paul through his weakness. This is something to try to flesh out in another blog entry, however, could the reverse be true? If I boast about my strength, could it be that the power of Christ does not dwell in me? If I am independent, if I am unconnected with others through my own and their need, does the power of Christ not dwell in me? Our independence, our disconnectedness from those who would potentially sap our strength for love and service is a symptom of a disease that has permeated the church. "But now faith, hope, love, abide these three; but the greatest of these is love" (1 Corinthians 13:13). Are we missing the greatest thing? Are we missing love?

Monday, March 10, 2008

Curse the deaf stumble the blind

Leviticus 19:14 states, 'You shall not curse a deaf man, nor place a stumbling block before the blind, but you shall revere your God; I am the LORD" (NASV). It is striking that we are warned to **not** do something to someone who would not be able to detect us as having done that thing to him. A deaf person cannot hear me cursing him. The blind person cannot detect me putting a stumbling block in her path. In the case of the deaf person, he would not know that anything had happened to him although those around him would realize that someone has cursed him. In the case of the blind person, she would recognize that she tripped over something and fell down, but she would not necessarily attribute her own misfortune to the actions of another person. However, in each of these cases, we know what we should do towards these individuals. If we are unsure for some reason, the passage tells us what to do. Typically, if someone makes rules such as these, it is because people have cursed the deaf person or put the stumbling block in front of the blind person. It is not hard to imagine people thinking this is great sport, great fun.

I would extrapolate this message to others to whom we might do something who wouldn't realize that we were doing a bad thing to them.

I think there are many things like this that we as Christians, that we as the church do to people with intellectual disabilities. Like the deaf, we curse those with intellectual disabilities in ways that they don't realize we are cursing them. We exclude them, and then speak among ourselves about how their presence would be disruptive, or wouldn't allow us to do programmatic things the way we would choose to do them should they be present. We curse them in a way by treating them as children, or in not treating them as peers. Like the blind, we may put barriers in their way that they do not see or are unable to overcome. Barriers such as social skill expectations or relational expectations or knowledge based performance expectations. When they trip over these they fall down, when they need not have fallen if we had just changed our expectations.

Thursday, February 21, 2008

Normality

Here is another great quote from John Swinton's book, *Resurrecting the Person*. He writes,

"The task of a liberating church is to reveal signs and pointers to remind the world that the way it *is*, is not the way it *should be*, and that loving "the outsider" is not an act of charity, or a function of "specialist ministries," but is, in fact, a "new" way of being human. In remembering God's actions in history and in the life, death, and resurrection of Christ, the Christian community is drawn into a new way of living and seeing the world. This way refuses to forget the pain of the oppressed, or the degradation of those who are excluded and fragmented by the types of social forces that seek to provide a picture of "normality" that bears little resemblance to the coming kingdom. Such a community embodies the fact that God has not forgotten the world" (pp 125-126).

Normality bears little resemblance to the coming kingdom. Whatever that definition of normality might be. Whether it be...

normality in terms of race
(is your church all one color of people) or
normality of socio-economic status
(is your church largely upper middle class people) or
normality of intelligence

(is your church all educated people), or
normality of social skills
(is your church all people with good social skills), or
normality of reality
(is your church devoid of people with mental illness), or
normality of ability
(is your church lacking people with various disabilities).

The only normality that should be present within the church is a normality of desiring to follow Jesus Christ to the degree you are able to understand it. If that were truly our bottom line, then Christian churches might look a whole lot different then they currently do.

Normality is also reflected in our church structures. How else could you have the major weekly meeting of the church be something that is so social skill intensive. Our structures not only reflect normality they then enforce normality, in a relatively constrained way. That is, it doesn't take much in terms of difference for you to stand out in a church, it seems. And we should **not** embrace that, we should reject that. Openness to differences in people should be a characteristic of the Christian church. If we were what we should be, we would be so counter culture that we might risk persecution and death on a cross.

When it comes to people with various differences, various disabilities, to what degree does the church show the world how it "should be" not just reflect the way it is. It is sad that even our attempts at being what we perhaps should be, are attempts to copy the secular world (inclusion for example). We could be so much more creative, so much more giving, so much more inclusive, so much more radical in our loving approach. In reality, however, in many ways we lag behind the programs (like inclusion) that the world offers.

A bit more from Swinton, "The church is a community of friends that is charged with the task of reminding people with mental health problems that God has not forgotten them, and reminding those who would oppress them, wittingly or unwittingly, that God is with and for those whom they reject and marginalize" (p. 126).

Monday, February 11, 2008

An alternative structure

I have been doing some thinking about the two reasons for most churches weekly coming together for a worship service. One main reason is the preaching from the Bible. A second main reason is the coming together as the "Body of Christ" a time when we are all together. At the moment, the typical church's focus is the former, preaching from the

Bible. Therefore those who would in any way interfere with that reason would be excluded. The second reason should cause us to change our programs in such a way that all people could be included. The coming together is the priority. It seems on some levels that these two reasons can be mutually exclusive. It is difficult to do traditional worship and preaching if people are present who are noisy or disruptive, and how can we be the body if not all members of the body are permitted to be present.

It seems, therefore, that there needs to be some new structure, or variation on existing structures that needs to be created. Because the time of preaching will typically hit the majority of the church population it needn't be changed as a way of sharing the Bible. In even the most inclusive settings, not every class that includes the teaching of the Bible would be relevant to every church member. There would no doubt be differentiations among classes such that knowledge is accessible for all the membership. It is important to recognize that a structure like the typical preaching part of the typical worship service will remain a significant means of facilitating growth in knowledge about the Bible.

The change that needs to occur, therefore is that there needs to be a structure in which all people could be included, and this could be called the meeting of the body, or corporate worship, or whatever would be the most meaningful. It might precede the typical preaching, but be separated by a time during which those who do not necessarily benefit from the preaching can attend programs where they will be fed. **There is a stigmatization associated with groups of disabled adults exiting the traditional service prior to the sermon.** Perhaps the worship service could be divided into at least two parts: one is meeting as a group for the purpose of the body being together, and the other being a time of sharing from the Bible that hits most of the people in the congregation, with simultaneous other opportunities for Bible study that are designed to facilitate understanding for specific groups.

Wednesday, February 06, 2008

"Don't taze me bro!"

This past weekend I was up in Seattle, and while I was there, I visited a very large and growing church. The music was great and the preaching was as well. But there was something very different from any other church I had ever attended before, and that was the presence of security. Everything from young men with shirts that said "Security" on them to a armed police officer who sat just to the right of me. As the preacher spoke, there were even two security guards who sat in the front on either side of the stage watching the audience the whole service. Afterwards, I approached a group of them and asked, "I am from

Southern Cal, and couldn't help but notice the presence of security here at this church. What specifically are you looking for?" The kind response was that there are often protesters outside of the church, at times there are people who are drunk, or on drugs who would come into the church, and the security guards are there to watch for that. In speaking to my daughter, she indicated that the pastor is very controversial, i.e. a conservative Christian (that is controversial I guess, for a city like Seattle, which apparently has the country's largest statue of Lenin in it which gives you an indication of some of the thinking there).

But it struck me again, What could call the security guards into action within a church service?

Could screaming or loud noise? How about behavior typical of someone with intellectual disabilities milling around and refusing to take his seat? Could we hear, "Don't taze me bro!" coming from a disabled person at a church with such a security presence? If they were not compliant, would they be dragged from the room? What does that tell the community about who we are? As Christians do we want to have the face to the community that we are tough on those who would disrupt our meetings? Of course we are permitted to have security guards at church, as well as uniformed off duty policemen. I just wonder what this communicates. A part of it strikes me as legalism on steroids, or the preservation of tradition (quiet worship services) on steroids. You see my question is, if there are drunk people around the church, does that change the way we do church or do we just beef up security so we can continue doing church in the same manner? I wonder the same thing about people with say, mental illness. **If there are people with aberrant behaviors around the church, do we beef up security or change the way we do church?** The increased presence of security in that church is one way of changing the way to do church. But is that the direction in which we want to change if we are indeed going to change? People with various disabilities could no doubt be the focus of the security guard's attention at a worship service, in particular if they were unknown to them. What would be role of security in such a setting?

Monday, January 28, 2008

The disability corrective

As I commented on my last entry, I was visiting a church in Seattle. As I was waiting for the gals in our group to use the ladies room I approached the information desk of the church. "Do you have any programs or make any efforts to include people with disabilities here?" I asked the man behind the counter. "Not really" he replied. "If you call us a week ahead of time, we will have an interpreter for you." That seemed reasonable to me, at least the interpreter part although I was once again struck by the ignorance about disability in such a growing church, that that could even be the case in such a church.

I then went into the actual service, which was great. It struck me though that as the pastor was parsing out the 14 different kinds of grace, that there was a disconnect between what he was saying and what the church was practicing. We can talk about God's grace all day long, and the multitudinous ways in which we are shown grace by God, but at some point wouldn't you think that we should show grace to other people? It struck me that if you don't do what you say you **should** be doing, or imply you **are** doing, from your pulpit, in your church's documents, and in the scriptures you claim are the guiding principle of your very life, then why should I trust you? You have indicated to me that you are two faced at worst and blind to the ramifications of what you are saying at best. You are saying one thing and doing another.

I recognize that I as an individual am a sinner so you can count on me to be a liar, inconsistent in doing what I believe and so forth. When people notice those things in my life they will comment to me as a way of helping me. You know, I do the things I don't want to do... (see Romans 7). I suppose the church is the same way because it is made up of a bunch of sinners. But it just strikes me that we have not yet gotten fed up with our own (as the church) duplicity in saying one thing and doing another. Where are the exhorters?

It occurs to me that the presence of persons with disabilities (once again my experience is with persons with intellectual disabilities) would be a **corrective** to a whole variety of inconsistencies and double speak that goes on in the church. The pastor could say "God loves us all the same," and then we could see our neighbor with severe intellectual disability, or mental illness sitting next to us at church and conclude "I guess He does and this church does too." We don't see them because these people are nowhere in our lives. Even as Christians they tend to be nowhere in our lives unless they are members of our families. People become advocates when someone with a disability is born to them. Where was their advocacy prior to that person entering their family? We tolerate the pabulum that comes from the pulpit about love thinking it is enlightened. However, we learn love when our actions as individuals and as church are consistent with the words that come from the pulpit.

How exactly would that look? I'm not sure. I know the principles I would like to see inform what that would look like. I do have ideas of how that would look, and have attempted to facilitate how that would look in settings in which I am in charge. It is my hope, however, that those trained in pastoral ministry would grapple with this and develop programs and structures for the church that could be employed. I am happy to be a part of that discussion, and I will offer my ideas to any church leader who wants to grapple with me on those issues. I have received a few calls over the years. The bottom line, however, is that it demands programmatic change. It will take courage on the part of leadership to do things that are truly different. But then, our rhetoric, our claims about God and grace, our speech about love and acceptance will not be in disagreement with our actions as it currently is in our churches.

May God lead us to a place where our words and actions are consistent.

Tuesday, January 29, 2008

Walk by faith not by sight

In 2 Corinthians 5:7 we read the phrase that we "walk by faith not by sight." Lately I have been thinking about how knowledge focused the Christian church is. Just think about the way we do everything from the worship service to Sunday School, to Bible study and it is all about knowledge. You might respond, "Duh...it is called Sunday SCHOOL and Bible STUDY." But I would respond that perhaps we have the focus of Sunday school and Bible study, and even the Sunday morning worship service wrong. You see, like you I have heard "walk by faith not by sight" probably a thousand times to the point that it just rolls off my tongue. I get it that I am supposed to have faith. But it struck me that I wonder whether I really do get it. "Walk by faith not by sight." What does that really mean? Is my church teaching me to walk by faith?

Well, we are to live by faith not by sight. But everything the Church seems to do from an educational perspective is all about walking by sight. We have an emphasis on knowledge which is simply a form of sight. We have an emphasis on knowledge development/sight development over faith development. We act as if sight and faith were the same thing. But Paul clearly distinguishes the two. How does one develop one's faith over just developing one's sight? Well I develop sight by increasing the ability to see things. I can help people to understand things by for example parsing out or unpacking scripture. But I wonder about the degree to which this unpacking leads to faith development. The assumption is that it does. We look for pastors who can explain the scriptures to us clearly. People with advanced degrees in theology.

The verse, however, seems to say that we don't live on just what we see, we don't live on just what we understand, we don't live on just what we can explain to others. As someone who is 52 years old and who has been in church and a Christian all my life, there are few things I can hear in a sermon that are really brand new. I delight when I learn something

158

new, but new knowledge doesn't mean a sudden boost in my faith. I just think, "Oh, I hadn't thought about that before."

Faith development is harder it seems. It challenges me to do things that I perhaps would not choose to do, or to be consistent in doing things that I would rather not be consistent about. I do those things because I know they will develop my faith. They will take me to a place in my walk with God that I haven't been to before. Attending church can be one of those places of consistency, however, I think the church has missed all it could be in taking that consistency in attendance and truly making it into faith development in the lives of the attendees. It is almost like we treat people like they are going to school rather than attending church. Additionally our measures of faith seem misguided by notions of knowledge, of living by sight.

People speak of blind faith as kind of the ultimate put down of those who are religious. Clearly we are to have the knowledge to explain the "hope that is within us" but there is an aspect of faith that is experiential. If my experience with faith is like school, then I should expect that I am developing as a person who is living by sight. If my experience with faith is faith challenging or faith facilitating, or causes me to step out "blindly" I will develop as a person living by faith. When was the last time that your church challenged you to really step out in faith in anything other than your giving money to that church? Is that all faith relates to? Why am I not challenged to step out in other areas related to faith development, like loving people who are really hard to love, like bring people to church who will make others uncomfortable, or people who will make demands on me? Why are churches always begging for Sunday school teachers? These experiences at least in part point to the same thing. We are too often developing people who live by sight and not by faith. What is in it for me (sight)? How will this cause me to grow (faith)? The questions that people learn to ask are very different if they are living by faith.

Monday, December 31, 2007

Exercising your love muscle

I haven't worked out in probably 3 months. I am not looking forward to starting up again, but Monday is the day. Anyway, it is tough getting into shape. You recognize how you have been a slug, and your body rebels. It hurts for a while, but ultimately once you get into shape it is great. You look forward to your workout each day. But until you decide to do it and then stick to it, your muscles will always hurt because you are always starting over again. Once it becomes a pattern in your life, it is easy.

Love is like that. If you always love people who are easy to love, it is like sitting on the couch all day. You never push yourself, and anytime you are confronted by someone who is in any way difficult to be with or to love, it "hurts" and it is hard. Perhaps people have poor social skills, or are unkind or make demands on you because of some need they have.

Your choice is to say, "This is too hard, I quit" or to stick with it and like exercising a muscle, it begins to get easier.

I can tell you that after 30 years of befriending persons with intellectual disabilities, loving them is much easier for me than it would be if I had never had any interactions with people with such differences.

The answer is to be with people with differences as you will be stretched. You will learn to love people who may be different than the typical. You will grow and develop and over time it will get easier.

But for love to happen, the decision has to be made that I am going to love other people even if it is difficult for me. If I am committed, over time it will get easier...it is a principle that can be counted on.

Thursday, November 22, 2007

Child find

Perhaps the most pivotal law in special education in the United States, is PL 94-142, the Education for All Handicapped Children Act. There are several important precedents that were set by the legislation, however, in order to serve the children with disabilities, they first needed to be found. One critical component of the law, therefore, was called "child find." I can remember posters that were placed around the community that said something to the effect, "Do you know a child with a disability who would benefit from a public school education. Please refer them to ..." and so on. So as the government got into the business of providing special education services it had to first find the children to be served.

Fast forward 30+ years. The church should be in the "child find" business when it comes to children with disabilities. There should be signs around our communities saying something to the effect, "Do you know of a child with a disability, or of a family with a child with a disability would enjoy worshipping at a Christian church? Come to --- church where you will be welcomed and embraced. We want you and your family member with a disability to feel welcomed, and loved. You have a church home!" How about that for child find? Better yet, let's just call it person find... "Do you know a person with a disability looking for a church home?" I plan to approach people at my church for permission to put such signs in my community.

You see, there are churches with disabled members. Some have become disabled during their tenure attending a particular church. Some people with disabilities will arrive at a church, and the church hopefully tries to figure out how to include those people.

I want my church to be one that recruits people that other churches do not want to recruit.

I want my church to be the "child find" or "adult find" or just simply "person find" church. **Let people start with us.** We can then not only serve them at our church, should that be their desire, but we can also talk to other churches to get the other churches to serve those individuals as well. So if a person from the Catholic, or Baptist or whatever faith comes to my church, I can say, "You are welcome here!" If they respond, "I wish there were a Baptist church locally that would serve us" we can respond, "Let us help you to become involved in that church." We could then contact that church. If they are open, great. If not, the people are welcome to stay at our church until the Baptist church in the community is more open.

Why did the state have to find children under PL 94-142?
Because the state had not been serving the disabled population in the public schools.

Why does the church need to find children, adults, people with disabilities now?
Because the church has not been serving people with disabilities.

People with disabilities and their families probably as a group think that they are not welcome in churches. For us to sit back and say that we would accept them if they came is insufficient. We need to demonstrate to them our change of heart through our efforts to ask them to come. We have to go to them. We have to ask them to come.

Monday, September 10, 2007

Forms of faith expression

I have been thinking about the ways in which faith can be expressed by an individual. I was once an elder in a church, and when we would interview potential members, we would look for key phrases both positively and negatively. For example, if we asked the question, "If you arrived in heaven, why should you be let in?" we would look for responses like, "I believe that Jesus saved me from my sins" or "Only because of faith in Christ would I be allowed in" things of that sort from the positive side. Negatively, if someone said, "I have tried real hard" or "I have been a good person" these would indicate that the person didn't really understand the work of Christ, and at the very least needed some instruction on those aspects of the faith.

But what of the person who cannot communicate via words, spoken or written. What if they lack the intellectual ability to understand the work of Christ even to the point of saying that "I have done bad things and Jesus has forgiven me." How does one with that level of disability express faith?

Well, we don't allow anything to count as faith, but I think we should look for indications of faith amongst those people. First of all, God can be trusted in this whole discussion. He will love the people I am trying to love more than I can even imagine, so he is out for their best. I think I am wanting to affirm people at their level that they are expressing faith when they are expressing faith. This can get a bit weird where we are projecting things on people. Where, for example, people make random statements, or speak incoherently, or other random behaviors which those of us without disabilities take for expressions of something totally apart from what they might actually be doing. But there is a level of awareness that might be achieved by those who are helping people with disabilities in their faith, which can encourage and guide them.

I remember for example trying to teach a man with intellectual disabilities the Lord's prayer. In the beginning I would have him repeat the phrases after me. Each time the things that he said were unrecognizable to me as the statement I had just made. But then I began to realize that each of the statements was consistent and unique. So if I said, "Our Father" he would respond with an unintelligible, yet unique phrase which he would always repeat when that was the phrase he was to produce. "Who lives in heaven" same thing, unique and consistent phrase. I came to the conclusion that he was repeating the Lord's prayer, however, he was repeating it in a way that I could not understand due to his speech impediment, but I am sure was understandable to God. I have known others, however, who produced random statements in response to learning a Bible verse who I am sure had no idea about what they were saying.

Another aspect of this is the ability to respond to the degree you are able, or to the degree you have been given the opportunity to respond. So I know people who have grown to love coming to church. Sure there are social components to church attendance (which is obviously NOT the reason for many attending church who are not disabled), however, the desire to come to church, to be with other Christians, even to be in "God's house" are all evidences on some level of a faith commitment. I have

162

mentioned at other times in this blog Fowler's book on the Stages of
Faith. There are stages I will probably never attain myself, however, there
is a stage at which I am currently functioning, and hopefully I will grow
in my faith. That is the same for persons with intellectual disabilities. We
help them at the stage where they currently function and attempt to assist
them to grow in faith. A critical aspect of this is I need to look for
expressions of faith, not so I can judge, but so that I can reinforce and
facilitate the spiritual development of those with disabilities.

Friday, September 07, 2007

Kindly platitudes versus the truth

I read a story the other day sent out by a person in the disability
community whom I respect. I won't share the story here, but the jist of it
was that a religious leader said something that was encouraging when
others were being discouraging about this leader's child with a intellectual
disability's presence in the worship service. Obviously the words that
were shared made the parent feel good, good enough to share the story
with others. Some of the reaction from others, also leaders in the
disability community was also positive. I just kept silent.

You see, it doesn't help if we share platitudes, no matter how kindly
they sound or how kind our intentions are if they aren't the truth. I have
been in settings were a severely disabled person was screaming or
making very loud noises while someone was trying to teach a class. Kind
people around will say, "He's praying" or something to that effect. Well I
have been around a lot of people with severe to profound disabilities, and
I will tell you that many do not have the intellectual ability to pray, or to
talk or to understand a great deal of what is going on around them. Some
scream for a particular reason and some just scream. For me to even say
they are praying when they are screaming is really to demean them, to
treat them like some kind of a child or something because if I was
screaming you wouldn't think I was praying. The point is, if someone is
screaming, they are screaming they are not praying. If someone is
swearing, they are swearing they are not praying or something else. The
question is, how do we make places for people who because of the
severity of their disability will scream or swear or do whatever it is that
they do?

Could I be in a worship service where someone in the audience was
screaming? Not if I am supposed to sit quietly and listen to someone
teaching me. Worship would have to change, or the teaching would have
to change, or the person would have to get quieter or be removed. As a
church, our response has been that the person has to be removed or get
quiet. My response is not to say they are praying and should stay when

163

they are screaming. My response is that the way we do worship needs to change, or if it is a teaching situation, the teaching situation would need to change such that a person who is screaming would be able to be a part of the teaching situation. Now not everyone should be a part of every teaching situation. I have trouble enough with teaching or taking college classes when the students are quiet. There are settings where screaming people are not welcome because of the situation. Unfortunately, church worship services as designed, are such places. There is a problem with that. The one time during the week when we gather as Christians, the church service, is the most socially restricted of any of the times we gather as Christians. Worship has largely become a time where I sing, or sit or stand, but otherwise I am to be absolutely silent (I recognize that is not the case for all Christian worship gatherings, however, largely it is).

It would seem that the largest gathering would be the time when there would be the MOST latitude in behavior, or openness in what is accepted socially. So if I attempt to be a part of the larger gathering but can't because of my disability, I would have to argue that it is the Church's fault. Particularly when as a person with a intellectual disability, there is literally no other place for me to go, no place for me if I am a screamer, or whatever my social difference is. My best hope is to be where the most people are, and unfortunately that is where the most restrictions on behavior are present.

We have got it entirely backward. Sunday morning worship should be the most wide open time. It should be noisy and joyful. Maybe there is some instruction, but it is understood that there is going to be a lot of activity in the midst of the instruction. People might be walking around, or talking to each other, or even interrupting the speaker with questions. But it is a jubilant time where we celebrate our gathering together as all Gods children with our slight or significant differences. Then if you want to parse out the scriptures in a quiet place, we go to a classroom, and that is were particular behaviors are required. You might have to know Greek for a class or you might have to be a parent or have some other characteristic. That is the place for discrimination, not the greater group gathering of the church. And there should be a place for everyone in one of those smaller classes or groups. Literally, anyone who would come to church should have a place where he can be himself (in terms of differences of disability) and be accepted. That is were we need to go in terms of changed structures.

It does no good and it is untrue to say people with intellectual disability who are screaming are praying. Don't offer platitudes no matter how kind, about who they are. Rather, make a place for them and open things up a bit. Worship settings should not be the most brittle, the most socially restrictive of all church settings.

164

Thursday, June 28, 2007

God's works and God's grace

In the past I have commented on the John 9 passage about working the works of God. The implication is that we have the opportunity to "work the works of God" we have the opportunity to be his hands to people here on Earth. Recently I was thinking about that verse in combination with the 2 Corinthians 12:9 passage were Paul is told by God, "My grace is sufficient for you" when he asked to have the thorn in his flesh (some form of a disability) removed. If you put these two verses together, you come up with an interesting lesson.

One of the greatest works of God is the provision of His grace in a multitude of ways to people. It occurred to me that one of the implications of God's statement, "my grace is sufficient for you" could be that one of the ways in which God makes his grace sufficient is through the works of Christians, through the work of His people. God's grace goes way beyond those things that people do, and is not dependent only upon what people do. Yet there might be an aspect of this connection that people are or are not recipients of an aspect of God's grace because of what the Church does or does not do.

The Joni and Friends organization has reported the statistic that 95% of people with disabilities are unchurched. That implies that in as much as 95% of the disabled population, the Church is not taking advantage of the opportunity to work the works of God, to be agents of His grace, to be sufficient to people with disabilities. It is a very sad statement. We have the potential to be agents of God's grace and we choose not to be. We have the potential to have the "works of God" manifested through us and we say, "Never mind."

Friday, May 25, 2007

The servant and devaluing roles

I was thinking again about the training I received in social role valorization. As Christians we are called to be the servant of all. The servant role is, in our society, a devalued role. There is value in being served, not in serving. Serving implies that someone else is "better than me" where being served implies that I am "better than someone else." At least that is what I think our society might say. Politicians like to refer to themselves as public servants, but I think most would agree that is more rhetoric than truth.

Jesus, however, saw things differently. In John 13, he was interested in teaching a lesson to his followers when he washed their feet. "You do

165

not realize now what I am doing, but later you will understand." Peter understood the ramification of Jesus taking on a devalued role (at least he thought he did) and would have no part of it. Jesus responded, "Unless I wash you, you have not part with me."

It is amazing, but Jesus forever changed the meaning of washing someone's feet (no doubt, a common although devalued role in his time, as once again evidenced by Peter's statement). I suppose in non-Christian societies, it would still be considered demeaning. In Christian societies, it has ever since been associated with servant hood and being like Jesus. The devalued role has now become associated with something beautiful, and it is an example. Jesus even labels is as such "Now that I, your Lord and Teacher, have washed your feet, you also should wash one another's feet. I have set you an example that you should do as I have done for you...Now that you know these things, you will be blessed if you do them."

In our society, serving persons with severe disabilities might be considered a devalued role. Teachers of students with severe disabilities will have the experience of being told by their own families, "Why would you waste your time with those kids?" For that matter why would anyone "waste their time with such people?" If the church would embrace persons with severe disabilities (I mean SEVERE disabilities) we would change the meaning of such service. We would bring it honor in the same way that Jesus did via his example of service. We would be in the honorable position of setting an example such that others should do as we have done for others. So we would make the role valued by our desire to do it.

Jesus' washing of the disciples' feet also brought honor to them. Peter recognized that Jesus should not be washing his feet. However, by Jesus washing their feet, he not only taught a lesson to them about servant hood, he brought honor to them. Imagine being one of the 12 people who ever lived who had the Lord of the universe humble himself to wash your feet. Pretty elite group. The point, however, is that I bring honor to people when I serve them. Those I serve may be just as lacking in understanding as Peter was, but I understand what I am doing.

I understand that I am setting an example.

I understand that I am elevating that form of service.

I understand that I am demonstrating the worth of those I serve via my service.

I understand who I am in relation to the person whom I am serving. They are not above or below me, they are my equal.

If I allow myself to be inconvenienced, or better yet, choose to inconvenience myself in the name of service to another who society has devalued, I contribute to the valuing of that person. Particularly if I am a person of stature in the community.

It is amazing to think about the depth of meaning than can come from a valued person washing the feet of others. It is amazing to think of the depth of meaning I have the potential to bring to a situation when I as a person who has value in society's eyes, serve those who society has devalued. Perhaps I will bring value to them. Cool.

Tuesday, April 10, 2007

Helping those who can't repay you

Luke 14:14 "Although they cannot repay you, you will be repaid at the resurrection of the righteous."

When I am speaking to groups, I often ask the question, "When was the last time you did something for someone who was unable to pay you back?" I also always give the caveat that I am not talking about your elderly parents (whom you are paying back) or your infant children (who will hopefully pay you back). I am talking about strangers or strangers who have become friends over time. People with whom you would typically think you have no particular reason to develop a relationship...no reason other than Jesus' words in Luke 14 and elsewhere that your life as a person will be evaluated at least partially on what you did for those people. Well I guess I do have a reason if I am going to be evaluated on that basis. In fact that is probably the major basis for the evaluation of my deeds in life. In Matthew 24 the difference between people will be as obvious as the difference between sheep and goats, at least obvious to the Lord. If you look at the response of the sheep (the good guys, although I personally do have an affection for real goats, not the scriptural illustrative type) they appear to be somewhat oblivious to the fact that the people to whom they were showing kindness, ostensibly without repayment, were in fact Jesus in many different forms.

It is interesting that earlier in the Luke 14 passage, it even cautions you that the people you help might repay you or may be able to repay you and so you will be repaid. It is almost as if you should avoid helping those who can repay you (not really, but there is a priority on the non-repayers). Wow, so we as Christians should be seeking those people out. I should be thinking, "Sweet! I got to help someone who has little ability to help me back!" It sure gives you a different perspective on helping.

I was talking to one of the pastors at my church the other day, a really great guy. I think in the course of our discussion we both concluded that within the group of people with whom he works, it is not necessarily the superstars that he has helped who are the "jewels in his crown" so to speak. They were probably in pretty good shape anyway, on the fast track to successful lives. But rather it is the autistic man or the intellectually disabled woman that he has helped who are his glory, his claim to fame. He can proudly state, "I helped a man with intellectual disability be a loved and respected member of a group of Christian peers. I helped an autistic woman feel like she had a place where people wanted to be with her, where she was accepted."

But I guess in the cosmic, kinda spiritual world of things, those people give us the greatest of all gifts. They allow us to please our Lord through our actions. But hear me clearly. The opportunity for service to another human being is what I am talking about. The Christian life is not about earning credits toward my salvation (which I already have through faith in Christ). It is not about pity or charity or whatever. It is about being like God in showing mercy and facilitating justice in the lives of the powerless. The ultimate result of being with devalued people is that I see myself for who I am. In a Micah 6:8 way, I learn to walk humbly with God and with my fellow human beings.

Monday, April 09, 2007

Traditions of the church

Mark 7 is the passage where the famous verse in Isaiah is quoted by Jesus. He says,

"These people honor me with their lips but their hearts are far from me. They worship me in vain; their teachings are but rules taught by men."

That section has always grabbed me as I wondered how I am guilty of that indictment, and also about how the church is guilty of that indictment. However, as I read on in the passage, there are several other comments by Jesus that really grabbed me. He is talking about the practice of "corban" but I think the passages still apply. Think about these sections as they may relate to the church's ignoring of persons with disabilities, the exclusion of people with disabilities, the traditionally often heard perspective that people with disabilities are not a priority for ministry. In verse 8

"You have let go of the commands of God and are holding on to the traditions of men."

And then in verse 13

"Thus you nullify the word of God by your tradition, that you have handed down. And you do many things like that."

Jesus confronted the theological experts over their tradition of corban. He says "you have left the commands of God and are holding

168

onto the traditions of men." The Jews had fallen into generations of missing the point and doing the wrong thing. Sound familiar? What is the result? "...you nullify the word of God by your tradition that you have handed down."

The church has left the commands of God and are holding on to the traditions of men in regards to people with disabilities. In fact in some ways, the traditions of men have changed and the church remains entrenched in a past form of the traditions of men. And what is the result? We are nullifying the word of God. No wonder that when a friend from the East coast was asked to receive counseling from pastors at a particular church, he responded "They do nothing for people with disabilities. Why should I receive counseling from them?" It would be as if someone had recommended in Jesus' time that someone go to the Pharisees to receive counseling in the practice of corban. The leaders presented themselves as representing God, however, as Jesus says, "you have let go of the commands of God...you nullify the word of God by your tradition." We as the church, nullify the word of God through our discriminatory traditions. We nullify the word of God through our prioritizing traditions. We nullify the word of God by our distancing of persons with disabilities in our traditions. We nullify the word of God by making church membership only accessible to those who can meet criteria based upon intellect. I wonder how people ever evidenced a faith in Christ prior to our times of saying the right phrases. All people had to say to Jesus was I believe and he accepted them. Today you have to behave a certain way, have certain social skills, memorize certain statements, assent to certain theological positions, and so on and so on. Now understand, I am not saying we just become a place where people believe in anything. At the same time, however, if our traditions are contrary to the word of God, and are actually nullifying the word of God, we have got to scrap our traditions.

Our traditions are exclusionary, and discriminatory, and intolerant of people with individual differences. It makes for an interesting Bible lesson when you are teaching people who don't have the greatest of social skills or don't quite understand how the traditional dynamics of a class should be acted out. But it also is very refreshing to be in a place where you comments are valued, whether they be about the impact of the Bible verse you are teaching, or to ask you for a dollar, or to discuss hot dogs and pizza.

It is time, in my humble opinion, that we step back and examine our traditions within the church. Tradition is not always the best reason for doing something. Tradition may be the absolute wrong reason for doing something, particularly if it nullifies the word of God.

Monday, March 12, 2007

40 years but no membership

I was having a conversation with a friend the other day who related an interesting yet sad story. Apparently, she had an uncle who was a pastor, who had a son with Down's syndrome. Anyway, the man with Down's syndrome was a regular attendee of his father's church for nearly 40 years. My friend related how he loved the church and loved God. The man literally would sleep on his hymn book every night. The sad part of the story was that the man was never offered membership in the church. My friend's assumption was that he wasn't offered membership because he was unable to memorize the church's creed, or relate particular faith statements in a manner sufficient to justify his actual membership.

What does a person need to do to express faith in a way that will lead to acceptance in the Christian church? Is faith only expressed through achieving some level of intellectual knowledge? Or can I love God and love my church so much that I literally sleep on my hymnal, possibly as an act of worship?

Obviously we don't give away the farm to anyone who believes anything, but we can also be exclusive in the most negative of ways. I suspect that the man, now a resident of heaven, didn't have the same criteria applied to him there. So he could be a member of God's family in heaven, but not a member of his local church.

Thursday, March 08, 2007

"Does the church let you to do that?"

Because we facilitate a class for persons with disabilities at our church, Kathi and I often receive phone calls from people interested in our church because we attempt to include people with disabilities.

Yesterday, Kathi got a phone call from a woman wondering about the ministries at our church. Our group called "Light and Power" which is specifically focused on adults, was the point of her question. She described her son's disabilities, and then asked whether he would be welcomed in the class. Kathi replied that the class includes both people with and without disabilities.

"Really?" she replied. "Does the church let you do that?" (That is, mixing people with and without disabilities).

Kathi replied, "Sure!"

She then asked, "What time does the Light and Power group meet?"

"We go to the regular church service at 9:30, and then..." Kathi replied.

"Does the church let you to do that?" she interrupted. (That is let the people with disabilities go to the regular church service).

"Yes" Kathi replied.

Obviously, this woman's response is a bit funny, but it must also be informed by something. Something that has grown out of her personal experience. Perhaps she and her adult son have been told "You aren't allowed to do that at this church" when she wanted to have her son in a regular church class, or attend the regular worship service. The confused responses of this mother of an adult son is an indictment. Imagine someone honestly wondering whether an organization (the church) which claims to represent Jesus would allow people with disabilities to attend the regular church service, or even house an integrated (people with and without disabilities) class on the campus.

Its a little funny but its a lot sad. It is particularly sad in that this mother herself may be a person who experiences a disability. Her questions and responses kind of make me think that is the case. Also I find that those with mild disabilities often will be turned away with excuses like that. Those without intellectual challenges would typically speak up. Others without the ability to argue their point are more easily turned away. Which is another insidious aspect of her responses.

Hopefully she and her son will soon be attending our church.

Friday, February 23, 2007

Walking on water

In the book, *The road to Daybreak* (1990) Henri Nouwen relates the following story, attributed to Tolstoy.

"Three Russian monks lived on a faraway island. Nobody ever went there, but one day their bishop decided to make a pastoral visit. When he arrived he discovered that the monks didn't even know the Lord's Prayer. So he spent all of his time and energy teaching them the "Our Father" and then left, satisfied with his pastoral work. But when the ship had left the island and was back in the open sea, he suddenly noticed the three hermits walking on the water - in fact they were running after the ship! When they reached it they cried, "Dear Father, we have forgotten the prayer you taught us." The bishop, overwhelmed by what he was seeing and hearing, said, "But, dear brothers, how then do you pray?" They answered, "Well, we just say, 'Dear God, there are three of us and there are three of you, have mercy on us!'" The bishop awestruck by their sanctity and simplicity, said, "Go back to your island and be at peace."

Nouwen then comments in regard to three handicapped alter servants at the L'Arche community where he was staying,

"When Louis saw the three handicapped altar servers, this story came immediately to his mind. Like the three monks of Tolstoy, these men may not be able to remember much, but they can be holy enough to walk on water. And that says much about L'Arche."

You see, we are confused by this. Faith is so linked with knowledge and intellect by Christian society, that we cannot imagine a person of great faith not knowing the Lord's prayer by heart. How can someone be a growing, believing, faith filled Christian if they lack basic intellect? But that is the lesson of the story, isn't it? Nouwen saw the connection. We don't. The men in the story were in a place where nobody ever went. When the bishop finally did go there, he saw their limitations in regards to how he understood church should be. With his limited yet prideful understanding of "church" he attempted to change the three monks. They, in their humility took what he had to offer hoping it would help them to grow toward their Lord. But in reality, it was they who should have been the teachers. When they ran to the ship, it was to regain the knowledge they had never quite gotten, not to teach the bishop how to walk on water.

I am beginning to understand the truth of this story. The simple faith of my intellectually disabled friends outpaces my own faith in so many ways. Rather than putting them into the prideful straight jacket I call Christian faith, a straight jacket they will never be able to wear due their limitations, I should learn from them, remove my straight jacket and allow them to soften me.

He has shown thee, O man
What is good and what the Lord requires of thee
But to do justly
And to love mercy
And to **walk humbly with your God.**
Micah 6:8

Sunday, February 04, 2007

Come as you are... if you are the way I want you to be

It is sometimes hard to believe what people will do within the Christian church regarding people with disabilities. If you follow what I write here, you might think that I overstate the changes that need to occur within the church. Just by way of example, here is an email I received this morning, and my response. I suspect it relates to a student who has some form of learning disability...a mild disability. It is sad but it continues to be the reality.

172

First the email...

"Can someone please provide feedback on the following issue: Student attends a private religious high school. Even though she has a documented disability, the school will not provide her accommodations in theology classes based on the fact that "Jesus said "come as you are." Question is asked Are theology classes exempt from ADA? And what other Bible references may be used as counter point."

My response...

Hello all-

No accommodations for the theology class because Jesus said, "come as you are." I think my first question would be is this person actually serious. Is this some example of a bad joke. Unfortunately I have had sufficient experience with people with disabilities and the Church to know this probably is real. It is particularly troubling that the person teaching this class is teaching theology, not mathematics or reading or something.

Obvious responses come to mind. What if the door was not disabled accessible, or there were steps up to the classroom because the school did not comply with ADA. Would there be a requirement to make the door larger or build a ramp, or is that another example of "come as you are." What if the lights need to be brighter because of a visual impairment, or some sort of audio was needed for the class. Is the answer "come as you are?" Other types of disabilities, such as learning disabilities are not different. But I suppose, the Bible is clear that those with disabilities in the scriptures all always brought themselves to Jesus. No one lowered them through the roof, assisted them to come as they are, or Jesus never went to places where people with disability (like a disgusting, bubbling pool) were to help them. Does Jesus ever come as he is to them? Might that example of Jesus be employed as well.

What is so sad about the "come as you are" comment is that it is meant to include every one. Everyone as they are is to be accepted. It is clearly NOT meant to be a command for exclusion.

I have come to the point that I am intolerant (yes, I am admitting I am intolerant) of responses such as the one given. Let's just be honest and say that the teacher doesn't want to be bothered with people with disabilities, doesn't want to do the work (much or little) to accommodate a person who wants to study theology, and that all this other excuse is just a smokescreen for discrimination.

The sad part of this story, however, is that 1) the teacher of Christian theology thinks she/he can make the statement she/he does, 2) such people are teaching our children Christian theology, and 3) this is not

173

totally uncommon within the Church. I hear of such stories and recognize how far we still have to go.

I would refer the teacher to the John 9 passage where Jesus heals the blind man, which states that we must work the works of God, so that God's glory might be seen. What about 1 Corinthians 12? Apparently this teacher doesn't think all members of the body are important, even though Paul says they could be absolutely essential. I am also reminded of Ezekiel 34 where the teacher is like a sheep who bumps out the other sheep. I could go on and on.

Perhaps the best solution would be to introduce that Christian theology teacher to her/his Bible.

Just some quick responses.
McNair

This is a perfect example of how we as Christians separate the teaching of theology from theology, or the teaching about love from love, or the teaching about the example of Christ from living the example of Christ. I mean this student is probably a person with a learning disability. That is, she/he had the potential to understand the content of the class, but just needs some accommodations (things like assistance in taking notes, or alternative assignments, or the like). I also think this is a perfect example of why we desperately need people with disabilities within the church. They make us live what we say. I remember talking about poverty when I had a homeless man in the group. It challenged me to really examine what poverty is and who poor people are.

I am only pretending to teach about who God is (theology) when my starting point is diametrically opposed to one of the most basic characteristics of who God is (love and acceptance of people)? It is a malaise of the Church.

Monday, January 15, 2007

Church of the merry-go-round

Impossibleape, a frequent contributor to this weblog made an interesting comment to the December 12 posting. He writes,

"there comes a day when we shouldn't have to be spoon-fed another bible lesson, comfortably entertained and made to feel that our hearing the word (again and again and again) is enough."

He is so right. You see, church is understood as going to a church service and hearing the pastor preach a sermon, singing some songs in worship and then praying. Perhaps we then go to a Sunday school class where we study the Bible some more. We end up like experts on the study of baseball who play very little baseball. I sometimes even wonder at the regular "altar calls" which happen many weeks at church. I would bet that 90% of those in the congregation are already saved.

Is that what church is? Is that what the church is about? Hearing many sermons, as good as they may be, singing many worship songs, and prayer? Obviously that is a *part* of what church is, but it definitely is not exclusively what it should be. But that is what church has become for too many people. Then someone with a disability comes and the attendees get confused about how they are supposed to do church when a noisy person with a intellectual disability is in the audience. They see the mentally ill person in their midst as someone who needs to be excluded. "How can we get through the lesson on love if that person is so distracting?" "If that person is involved, we can't do church in the way we have always done it?"

I don't think that is what church is supposed to be. Perhaps a small portion, but not the majority. And when we do get people saved, we ruin them by letting them think that that is what church is supposed to be.

Why are churches constantly begging for people to work in the children's Sunday school classes? Why are people with disabilities not a priority for ministry in ALL churches? The problems are related. It has to do with the structures of the church and how they demand something which is not what the church should be.

I personally do not now nor have I really ever understood what worship is. Is worship little more than me becoming emotional at a particular song whose lyrics or music connect with me? Is that what worship is? Should I disconnect my intellect from the lyrics of the music or disconnect my aesthetic appreciation from music and lyrics and try to be swept away by what I am experiencing? Should I actually choose my church on the basis of the style of music presented? Is that what church is? Is that what worship is? Such an approach to church, to worship, is debilitating in that it provides a substitution for a more demanding way of doing the harder worship like taking care of widows and orphans (see James). Don't get me wrong (if you are even still reading), I am absolutely not saying we should not sing songs of worship to God.

But please do not confuse songs of worship with other acts of worship. Singing songs are the easy way to worship. Your singing will be made a more beautiful act of worship if you have worshipped in other ways as well, ministering to those who are disenfranchised, working with children, loving your neighbor. Clapping to the music is more enjoyable if a severely disabled adult is clapping along, off time, with a huge smile on his face.

Sermons and Bible studies are of value in themselves. However, teaching on 1 Corinthians 13 without anyone in the room who is particularly difficult to love, is easy. Is love easy? You might think so.

175

I don't need another sermon on 1 Corinthians 13. I need people who challenge me to live and love in the manner described in 1 Corinthians 13. By that I am not claiming that I entirely understand the passage. I am saying that I need to put what I do understand about the passage into practice. Challenge me to love a mentally ill woman. Have her in the church in my midst. Have the leadership clamor to understand what to do with her. Then we will all really learn about love, and the extent to which we are willing to love others who are difficult to love. When am I really going to be playing baseball rather than just talking about baseball. What do I do with church structures if I know that there are difficult to love people who are not entirely welcome because we don't know what to do with them under our current structures? Our response is the status quo.

I sometimes feel like I am on a horse tied to a merry-go-round. The horse was desperate to run, but it just kept going around and around, covering the same ground, doing the same thing. Eventually the horse turned to wood and now just mindlessly keeps going around and around and around. It used to be a horse, was originally a horse. But now it is an inanimate object just going around and around and around. It still looks like a horse (it's doctrine is correct) but is it inanimate (it's love is not correct). Maybe life can still be breathed into the wooden horse and it can run once again instead of being bound to the merry-go-round.

The church needs new structures needs new love and inclusion, like the horse needs to get off of the merry-go-round.

Monday, January 08, 2007

Interdependence

My daughter Amy just returned from the 2006 Urbana missions conference in St. Louis. She showed us a video of clips of the speakers, one of whom intrigued me with his comments. His name is Oscar Muriu and he spoke on the topic of "The Global Church." It is well worth listening to.

Several of the points he made about the global church touched me in reference to persons with disabilities in the church. He said, the purpose of maturity as a Christian is not independence but interdependence as we are a body. He gave the example of the liver saying "Now that I am all grown up, I don't need the lungs or the body anymore." His point being that as we grow we recognize our need for the rest of the parts of the body. A lack of need for all parts of the body is a sign of immaturity. Should the liver say it didn't need the lungs, we would correct it saying, "No, you just don't understand how things work in a healthy body." Our interaction would be like that with a child who will understand as he grows. Thinking one is independent and doesn't need the rest of the body

176

is a clear indication of immaturity. With maturity comes the understanding of the need for interdependence.

Muriu spoke of his interaction with Western pastors. He would question them asking, "Why do you need the African church?" (he is an African pastor). Their response was that they didn't know why they needed the African church. This once again shows a lack of maturity, a lack of understanding of how the body works. Why does the liver need the lungs? To exchange gasses. Why does he liver need the kidneys? To clean the blood. There are reasons for why parts of the body need each other. The fact that I as the liver don't know why I need the lungs or the kidneys only points to my ignorance and my need for maturity.

Why do I need my intellectually disabled brother in Christ? Why do I need my mentally ill sister? Why do I need my paraplegic brother? If I don't know, as a point of maturity I should strive to find out. Perhaps the best way to get at the answers is to have that person in my midst, to work to include that person.

Oscar Muriu spoke of how the Western church appears to be in decline. I wonder, could it be in decline because it is not healthy because it has never included the parts of its body which would keep it alive? Muriu asked why the African church, for example, would want to drink from the poisoned chalice of Western theology if the result is a declining Western church? Great question. Could a part of the slow poison which is causing the decline of the Western church the lack of involvement of persons with disabilities? I am foolish enough to think it might be, because the body has been attempting to live without all of its parts. Parts that 1 Corinthians 12 states are absolutely essential. How can a body live for long without absolutely essential parts? Perhaps it would gain life if the absolutely essential parts were reattached. Could the church potentially even recover if the parts were remade body members?

Society is gradually on a path to destroy all the parts the church has rejected in the past. The world is killing persons with disabilities through abortion, infanticide and euthanasia. What type of church will survive if there are no people with Down's syndrome in the world? What type of church will survive if all quadriplegics are assisted with suicide? The world is removing the possibility of being the whole Body of Christ for us and we are complicit in a sort of slow, self-inflicted, church suicide. We are the liver who thinks it doesn't need the lungs.

And the world is willing to take our lungs away from us.

We lose people with disabilities in the world at great peril to the church.

Wednesday, January 03, 2007

Lesson from Wilberforce

I have been reading some brief booklets on famous people. These are put out by The Trinity Forum. The first one I read was entitled, *William Wilberforce: A man who changed his times* by John Pollock. In the Foreword, J. Douglas Holladay reflects on Wilberforce's life, and develops a summary of the "seven principles that illuminate what it means to live a life of significance today." He states,

"Wilberforce's whole life was animated by a deeply held, personal faith in Jesus Christ...

Wilberforce had a deep sense of calling that grew into the conviction that he was to exercise his spiritual purpose in the realm of his secular responsibilities...

Wilberforce was committed to the strategic importance of a band of like-minded friends devoted to working together in chosen ventures...

Wilberforce believed deeply in the power of ideas and moral beliefs to change culture through a campaign of sustained public persuasion...

Wilberforce was willing to pay a steep cost for his courageous public stands and was remarkably persistent in pursuing his life task...

Wilberforce's labors and faith were grounded in a genuine humanity rather than a blind fanaticism...

Wilberforce forged strategic partnerships for the common good irrespective of differences over methods, ideology or religious beliefs..."

Wow, if we could only live a life as significant as Wilberforce. His issue was largely stopping the slave trade. Our issue disability and the church.

The one principle that really jumped out at me, however, was the one which states, "Wilberforce had a deep sense of calling that grew into the conviction that he was to exercise his spiritual purpose in the realm of his secular responsibilities." How does one exercise spiritual purpose in the realm of secular responsibilities? Wilberforce was a politician so he used his political platform to unabashedly champion against the slave trade, informed by his Christian principles. I am a special education teacher, or a rehabilitation counselor, or a parent who works in the business world, or a pastor or Sunday school teacher. Do I see my secular calling as an opportunity to exercise a spiritual purpose? Note, I am not necessarily talking about sharing the "four spiritual laws" every day during lunch. Rather I am talking about expressing the need for people religious or not to care about their brothers and sisters who experience a disability. I am particularly calling on those who have a secular responsibility based upon their training, or experience, or knowledge to express that secular responsibility in the climate of a spiritual purpose.

I have often spoken to secular groups of special education teachers, or caseworkers, and asked, "When was the last time you did something for someone who couldn't do something back for you?" Something, that is, for which you weren't paid to do. You see, I think that like pastors, we confuse the things we are paid to do with the things we are not paid to do. Yes as the Wilberforce statement makes clear we are to work toward a spiritual purpose through our vocation, however, we should not allow our vocation to be the only place where we use the training we express in secular responsibilities to be evidenced. The world is desperate, I believe, for people who care for their neighbor, just because they care for their neighbor. They don't care because they are paid to care.

Churches are desperate for Christian professionals to express their secular responsibilities in both the secular world and the religious world, the public square and the church. In both places, spiritual purposes need to be achieved.

What if we could soften the church and soften the secular world toward individuals experiencing disability?

Friday, December 29, 2006

Social looseness

Have you ever been to a dinner with a person to whom table etiquette is extremely important? Now I am not talking about wiping your mouth on the table cloth, or grabbing food off of your neighbor's plate, or spitting or swearing. I am talking about the fine points of where the fork needs to lie, or how to hold your glass while you are drinking, or how you cut your piece of meat. I get really impatient with people in such situations. I think they are focusing on things which comparatively aren't really important, particularly when the points of etiquette are used to judge. I find I would rather not eat than have to eat with people who are constantly judging me on my table manners (which aren't that bad, I don't think).

I think some people with intellectual disabilities must feel that way about their church or other community group experiences for that matter. They are constantly being judged on their social skills (which are often not quite there because they do not understand the subtleties of many social interactions). I must say that the more I am with such people with intellectual disabilities, the less their lack of understanding of social structures bothers me. Now I am not talking about moral rigor. We should as a church and as individuals hold the line on issues of morality because that is a point of obedience to God. However, the social creations to which we have been socialized need more looseness. Particularly in the church, our social structures should be loosened in the name of

179

acceptance. The environment needs to be softened because out of love and acceptance, your presence is more important to us than a particular socially derived pattern of social behavior.

Why do I say this? Solely because such social structures are used as a point of exclusion.

A person talks out in a group too much so he can't be a part of the group (obviously we should be quiet when in groups)

Someone misunderstands the level of familiarity he should display, so he is excluded (obviously I should not stand too close to people)

I am more open/less guarded with my verbal expressions so I should be excluded (I shouldn't express that I love you or that I am angry with you because we just don't do that sort of thing)

I cannot understand your subtle expressions of rejection so I should be excluded (you try to avoid me, and I just don't get it)

I talk to you about my work and you just aren't interested so I should be excluded (you try to move away and I follow you)

I repeat my comments about things which are really interesting to me and you get tired of them so I should be excluded (you tell me I have already talked about those things)

My nose runs and I don't wipe it so I should be excluded (you are tired of handing me tissues)

I need assistance with many of the things which are a part of being in a group so I should be excluded (I just take up too much of your time when you want to also be with others)

All of these are like the person at the dinner table judging my eating while I am doing my best, just trying to be a member of the group eating at the table. I want to be there because I want to be a part of a group, I want to be loved, I want to love you. You turn me away because I don't hold my fork right, or lay my knife on my plate in the right way.

I am reminded again of the verse in Romans 12:2 which says, "Do not be conformed any longer to the pattern of this world but be transformed by the renewing of your mind. Then you will be able to test and approve what God's will is - his good, pleasing and perfect will" (NIV). We should not reject needy people, particularly on the basis of what is tantamount to table manners. Could it possibly be God's good, pleasing and perfect will to reject people on the basis of their social skills, their table manners? NO. Could it possibly be God's good, pleasing and perfect will to become a bit more socially loose, and overlook the social skills of others in the name of love and acceptance of those who truly need love and acceptance? ABSOLUTELY. I need to once again reject the patterns of this world and once again be transformed by the renewing of my mind.

Monday, December 11, 2006

Church of England supports killing the innocent as long as it is "with manifest reluctance"

The headline states,

Outrage as Church backs calls for severely disabled babies to be killed at birth

The article begins...

"The Church of England has broken with tradition dogma by calling for doctors to be allowed to let sick newborn babies die."

Some other quotes from the article...

And the Bishop of Southwark, Tom Butler, who is the vice chair of the Church of England's Mission and Public Affairs Council, has also argued that the high financial cost of keeping desperately ill babies alive should be a factor in life or death decisions.

Morality is a financial decision.

In the Church of England's contribution to the inquiry, Bishop Butler wrote: "It may in some circumstances be right to choose to withhold or withdraw treatment, knowing it will possibly, probably, or even certainly result in death."

The church stressed that it was not saying some lives were not worth living, but said there were "strong proportionate reasons" for "overriding the presupposition that life should be maintained".

The bishop's submission continued: "There may be occasions where, for a Christian, compassion will override the 'rule' that life should inevitably be preserved.

So now we are advocating taking the lives of babies who were able to survive prenatal diagnosis and abortion out of Christian compassion. But we are not saying that their lives are not worth living. This only condemns us further as we are taking lives that are worth living. Why would we as Christians even want to enter into an argument as to whether or not lives are worth protecting, are worth living? We are not going to convince the detractors, and entering into the argument only justifies the argument on some level.

The church said it would support the potentially fatal withdrawal of treatment only if all alternatives had been considered, "so that the possibly lethal act would only be performed with manifest reluctance."

So as my life is being taken, I can smile knowing that those who are killing me are doing so with "manifest reluctance." You see they really don't want to kill me, but their Christian compassion informs them that they are forced to do so, ostensibly because the Spirit of the Lord is whispering in their ear, ***"Kill the baby. Kill the baby.***"

The submission says: "The principle of humility asks that members of the medical profession restrain themselves from claiming greater powers to heal than they can deliver.

So saving lives or attempting to do so shows a lack of humility. Using their argument, it is prideful, therefore it is sin to attempt to save the life of a disabled newborn.

There are those in the United States who aspire to be Europe in so many ways, not the least of which is the post-Christian culture there. Now the remnants of the Church are making determinations on the quality of life of disabled newborns. To whom do they think they are appealing with such pronouncements? Will people now begin coming back to the Church of England because of its stand on euthanasia? "I go to that Christian church because they kill the disabled babies!" "That's the kind of Lord that I want to serve!"

We have a choice to make as Christians about people who are experiencing disabilities. To date, we haven't been the greatest advocates for them, for their lives, for their inclusion in fellowship with us. Will we follow the Church of England and take the final step of preventing their lives? Killing disabled newborns is only the tip of the iceberg, and would most definitely place us on the proverbial slippery slope. Will the church now come out in favor of physician assisted suicide? After all, it is expensive to support people who experience depression, and wouldn't Christian compassion call for the taking of the lives of the depressed as long as we evidence manifest reluctance. "Manifest reluctance." What a morally sinister phrase that is.

Who will be left to protect the fragile, the devalued, the vulnerable if not the Church of Jesus Christ? Once the Church of Jesus Christ goes over to the side of death, death will come unrestrained to any and all. It will justifiably come to us. Christians themselves will be the target of death. It is not like Christians have not been the target of death in the past. We play into the hands of our adversary, the evil one, when we become what Dr. Wolf Wolfensberger refers to as "deathmakers." Particularly when we kill the innocent, and claim we are killing reluctantly out of Christian compassion.

This is desperately evil and a horrible disgrace.

Tuesday, November 14, 2006

New wineskins/church structures

I was thinking about the whole new structures for the church in terms of a verse out of the book of Mark. Specifically Mark 2: 21-22 which says,

No one sews a patch of unshrunk cloth on an old garment. If he does, the new piece will pull away from the old, making the tear worse. and no one pours new wine into old wineskins. If he does, the wine will burst the skins, and both the wine and the wineskins will be ruined. No, he pours new wine into new wineskins (NIV).

As I thought about this, I wondered about new wineskins/old wineskins and new structures/old structures. At times it seems to me that the inclusion of persons with disabilities into traditional church structures is tearing the old structures. The old structures are being torn:

-through frustration of leaders, persons with disabilities, and their families

-because of advocacy of people who "get it" for persons with disabilities

-from people being uncomfortable

-because of need for providing "extra" support to persons with disabilities

-over challenges to the traditional excuses for doing nothing

-through tolerance for a very limited set of social behaviors

-by confusion over theological "curriculum" versus theological "practice"

-by groups breaking up over membership of persons with disabilities

-because of the desire to maintain the status quo

-and so on and so on

I think the old structures are being challenged by the Spirit of the Lord who has finally gotten the attention of dense people like me.

I guess you might develop new structures through the changes that the presence of excluded people bring. I mean, the reason that we know old wineskins don't work, is because people tried to put new wine into them and the old ones burst. We know that we shouldn't use unshrunk cloth for repairs, because people have ruined old garments by sewing unshrunk cloth into them. But perhaps there needs to be a time when structures get torn and burst for a while. In that way, we will then see that we need new wineskins, new structures to house the new inclusiveness we are evidencing for all people. We are in the sewing new cloth patches on old garments and putting new wine into the old wineskins phase. Hopefully, this will not lead to our rejecting the new wine, but rather to us making new wineskins to house the new wine.

The Way online, makes the following statement.

The parable of the wine and the wineskins is about putting new wine into a suitable vessel or container, and there are two vessels or containers that the Holy Spirit dwells in today:

The Church.

The believer.

So to use their example, we need new wineskins within the church and we also need new wineskins within each believer. I think they are mutually effective on each other. Believers will effect the church and the church can effect believers.

Monday, November 06, 2006

Church structures

The Oct. 31, 2006 posting entitled "Value Added" touches on the notion of church structure. This is something I have dealt with a bit in other entries in this blog. But I have been thinking a lot more about it lately. Where do new structures come from? Where will new structures come from?

Although I speak of the structures of the church not necessarily being helpful to inclusive ministry for persons with disabilities, I must admit that I am not entirely sure of what kinds of structures I would advocate for. For example, if you look at the "Value Added" entry, I describe a woman with mental illness attending a local church. It is clear that the existing structures are not working. I think that our typical response would be to exclude her from many of the activities of the group. That is what we have typically done. I know that because I don't see a lot of people with mental illness attending church. If they were in our midst, that would imply that the structures have changed in some way.

Changing structures begin with the decision,

"I want people with mental illness to be able to attend church."

"I want people with disabilities to be able to attend church."

Once that decision has been made, the rest becomes just logistics. How will I be able to include people with mental illness? How will I remove the exclusion (as Arthur Seale says) that keeps people with disabilities from being enfolded? Once again, the fact that the people with mental illness or other disabilities are not in our midst implies that we have not made the basic decision that all such people should be able to attend church.

Now there may be people out there who are clever enough to plan changed structures ahead of time. I don't claim to be clever, but I have a few ideas. But largely, the structures will develop as we work to bring people into church, as we work to make our programs no longer exclusive. Even as we strive to understand what ministry is.

In the Sept. 18, 2006 entry, I quoted Vanier's statement about the rectitude of doctrine vs. the rectitude of love. Instead of studying love, how to love, the different types of love, how much better to attempt to get love right relative to a person who is mentally ill, who wants to be in our midst.

"No, you can't be in our group because we are studying about love. We will not be able to cover all the material, or you might distract us too much should you attend. We want to be able to complete the love passages by the end of the month, so I am sorry but you can't participate."

But by having a person with mental illness in our midst and making the decision to keep her there, we will develop structures that will work. **I repeat that the structures haven't developed in the past because we haven't made the decision to include in the past.** I am also sure there is not a single answer; there are many ways in which inclusive ministry might be done.

New structures will develop when the existing ones are no longer working. I would argue that **if people with disabilities cannot be in the typical Bible study group, then the typical Bible study group is all wrong**. The person with the disability is not wrong, the structure, the "way we have always done things" is all wrong.

Please, for Christ's sake, invite the person with the disability into your group, remove the exclusion, and work to see what structures He will develop in your group that serve all. If God truly believes what Paul wrote...

On the contrary, those parts of the body that seem to be weaker are indispensable, and the parts that we think are less honorable we treat with special honor (1 Corinthians 12:22-23)

...maybe we should believe it as well.

Thursday, November 02, 2006

Deja Vu all over again

Well it happened again. I was visiting a dear friend of mine, Ed, and went with he and his great family to his church. The worship service was amazing and I was touched by the pastor's revealing sermon on forgiveness, healing and moving forward with God. She was so insightful, so right on, and it caused me to really reflect on who I am. I will be chewing on her message fro some time to come.

Anyway, afterwards we went to the welcome area where I met several others in leadership. At one point, I related to another gal in

185

leadership about my interest, my passion for people with disabilities to be embraced by the church. Earlier, in a Sunday school session, her husband, another pastor, spoke of how ministry shouldn't be like a buffet where we pick and choose what we will and won't do, or who we will or won't serve. Which of God's requirements we will or won't respond to. I related that I would be quoting him (but based upon his response, I won't). I told him about the church and people with disability relative to his statement about the buffet. He appeared to become very uncomfortable when I said THE church, not necessarily HIS church, was disobedient in regards to those with disabilities. After sitting through a training earlier where he spoke of first impressions at church and putting on the positive face to the public even if you don't feel like it, he suddenly expressed a great interest in getting out of the conversation. He was particularly interested in getting home so he could watch football on TV. So in other words, "Don't bother me with the needs of desperate ignored people in my community, I have a football game to watch." Deja vu. So the ignorance perpetuates.

Prior to him joining the conversation, his wife had been literally pummeling me with questions. It was like when I mentioned disability I turned a switch on for her...

Who are these people?

Where are these people?

How did you find these people?

How can we find these people?

What does your church do to help them?

What kind of programs do you have?

I could barely get a response out before she was asking another question. Her interest was so exciting and so encouraging. But in a moment, we moved from her sincere interest in disability to his, the pastor's, trumping and surpassing interest in football.

I think it was an old Phil Keaggy song that said,

Seems as if we've lost the nerves for feeling
and no one's in the mood to want to know
I've got news for you this is not a game
I've got news for you are you listening?
I've got news for you we are all the same
and when that is understood we can start to live again

Will this particular church ever get it, relative to persons with disability? I sure hope so. It is a fantastic church with its finger on the pulse of culture, it seems. The messages I heard from the leadership both touched me and moved me. My deepest prayers are with it for its success and growth. I would definitely be going there myself if I lived in the area. No doubt!

But it will **NEVER** achieve all that God intends for it if it is more interested in football, or music or presentation or whatever else than it is in seeing ALL Gods people. ALL.

I truly do love what God is doing among young people in churches through the use of music and technology which are so much a part of what those in their teens through 30's are about. But without a deeper change, they are making the exact same mistakes that the churches they are replacing made. It is generational ignorance. They see themselves as hip. They think they are novel and up to date. They are not.

They are the exact same thing all over again.

But how about something **truly different**. How about including **all of God's people**. It seems we and particularly many in church leadership are oblivious to and don't want to know about disability. Especially if the Eagles are playing on TV.

Thursday, November 02, 2006

The rectitude of doctrine vs. the rectitude of love

I had the pleasure of attending a conference last week at the University of Aberdeen in Scotland. The conference was hosted by Dr. John Swinton, and featured Dr. Stanley Hauerwas, a theologian/philosopher and Dr. Jean Vanier, writer and founder of the L'Arche communities.

I asked Dr. Vanier why he thought it was that the church has not been as responsive to persons with disabilities as L'Arche as endeavored to model. His response was that we as a church are focused on "the rectitude of doctrine" when we should be focused on "the rectitude of love." The rectitude of doctrine vs. the rectitude of love is something worth thinking about. No one is implying that doctrine is unimportant. Rather, doctrine can be dry and harsh. Love by comparison can be soft and accepting. In the case of persons with disabilities, we need love and doctrine to be as correct as possible.

May God open our eyes to the rectitude of love.

Monday, September 18, 2006

More from the Aberdeen conference

As I related, I recently attended a conference at the University of Aberdeen. There were two featured presenters, Dr. Jean Vanier and Dr.

187

Stanley Hauerwas. Both of these men are professional heroes of mine. I could not believe that I would have the opportunity to meet them both at the same conference, particularly as the second day of the conference was with an intimate group of about 30 people with Vanier and Hauerwas.

Much of the focus of the conference was on the work of Vanier, particularly through the L'Arche communities. The second day of the conference was specifically dedicated to what the L'Arche communities have to say to the church. Dr. Hauerwas gave a presentation that day, in which he lauded Vanier's work, and the example of L'Arche as in many ways prophetic, as prophesy to the church. Allusions were made to L'Arche as in some ways being similar to a kind of monastic community. A question from the group of 30 particularly made that connection, which Dr. Hauerwas affirmed had occurred to him.

I then asked a question which I will have difficulty repeating here exactly, although Dr. Hauerwas' response will be much easier to reproduce. I asked something to the effect, "Although I have tremendous respect for Dr. Vanier and the work of the L'Arche communities around the world, don't you think the manner in which people in these communities interact with persons with disabilities should be like the "normal Christian life", the way in which we all should interact with such people? I mean, to set this community up as approximating a monastic model, only implies that it is not for everyone, as I for one will not be joining a monastery. Most people will not. Shouldn't this be the way we all should be interacting with persons with disabilities, within the church?" I actually thought I was asking a kind of a "soft ball" question, but his response shocked me. He said something to the effect, "I don't know, you have to ask Dr. Vanier." I can only assume I was misunderstood. I hope I was misunderstood. Otherwise, the love and compassion evidenced by people at L'Arche towards persons with disabilities, causes a world renown theologian and philosopher to reply basically that he doesn't know if that is the way Christians, or the church are to act towards people with disabilities.

A light came on for me.

This was a perfect example of what is wrong with the Church today. A brilliant man, one of the few theologians who has taken on disability and has written pretty powerfully about it, didn't know whether we as Christians, within the church, should be showing the love and caring demonstrated in L'Arche communities towards persons with disabilities. Maybe he was thinking of people living together in the manner of L'Arche, I don't know. But his answer was almost breath taking for me in illustrating how disconnected the church is about people with disability and who they are. Perhaps he needs to know more people with disabilities, perhaps he is afraid of people with disabilities. Clearly he holds those like Dr. Vanier who have done incredible work in this area in high esteem, but that can be a big part of the problem.

I have shared with the classes I teach that I have been told many times by a variety of people how wonderful I am because I work with persons with severe disabilities. I am a bit sick of that praise, however. I am at the point where I respond, "If it is so wonderful, why don't you do it too!" Don't praise me and dismiss yourself. I wish you wouldn't praise me at all. Just you do what you can, so that all of us loving and supporting people with disabilities will become the normal Christian life.

And theologians will not be stymied by the question of whether I should love my disabled neighbor.

Saturday, October 07, 2006

Biblical language

Dr. Stanley Hauerwas writes of how groups define themselves by their narrative. The Bible is obviously the narrative for Christians and in the Bible, one can hardly read the Gospels in particular without bumping into people with disabilities. In many occasions, Jesus heals them. Dr. Bob Pietsch has written how the Jewish leaders needed only have a man with a "withered hand" in a room of people to "trip up" Jesus. That is, they knew He would see the man and then that He would heal him. Jesus on another occasion sends out his disciples, and later the 70, with the power to heal people with all types of infirmities (Luke 9). When in prison, John is told that the proof that Jesus is the Messiah is that the sick and disabled are healed (Luke 7:23).

Jesus and other biblical writers change how we think about things. They redefine words as illustrated by the following.

Foolish – one who hears words but doesn't put them into practice (Matthew 7:26)

Good – one who bears fruit (Matthew 7:17)

Servant – we are all to be servants of all (Mark 9:35)

Wisdom – the fear of the Lord (Psalm 111:10)

Strength – is Christ (1 Corinthians 1:30)

Poor – poor in the eyes of the world but rich in faith (James 5)

Humble – those who are lifted up (Luke 1:52)

We are also instructed to, give to the needy (Matthew 6:1-4), not worry about our lives (Matthew 6:25), and seek first the kingdom and righteousness (Matthew 6:33).

Each of the above establish criteria for followers that nearly all may participate in. These radical definitions provide access for the inclusion of nearly all people. In an effort to include all, Paul goes through a list of persons who would typically be excluded, ultimately going so far as to state that God chooses, "the things that are not" (1 Corinthians 1:26-31). Interestingly, this perspective and the above definitions benefit persons with disabilities.

In spite of this language, this narrative, such perspective changes are not reflected in many churches. These environments can have an effect positively or negatively on God's ability to minister within their midst. For example, in Matthew 13:58, it states that Jesus was unable to do miracles among them due to their lack of faith. While on the contrary, when the paralytic is lowered through the roof for Jesus to heal in Luke 5:17, the Bible says that when Jesus saw "their" faith, including the faith of those who lowered the man, he replied "Friend, your sins are forgiven."

Thursday, July 06, 2006

"The ministry is already full"

I heard an interesting, true story the other day. A person was being interviewed for a position as an assistant to a ministry to persons with disabilities at a local church. In the midst of the interview, the person from the church doing the interview asked something to the effect,

"Why does that ministry need to grow. The ministry is already full."

Now this comment is interesting and appalling from a variety of perspectives. How does one know when one's ministry is full? A room might be full or a theatre might be full, but what constitutes a full ministry? Are all the people who might be served already being served? That would be great if it were true. What if we were talking about children. "Don't bring your children to church, our ministry is full." Or High School students..."We will no longer be allowing you to bring visitors to the High School program because that ministry is full." Can you imagine, if the church was doing a ministry to a particular ethnic group, and the comment was made, "That ministry is full." In other words, we have enough of those people down here. "Our ministry to white Irish people is full (I'm Irish)." "We don't need anymore Irish people down here." I would never be allowed to get away with such a statement. However, because we are talking about people with disabilities, I as a person of authority in a church can say with confidence, "We have enough disabled people here. No need to bring in any more. The ministry is already full."

This is the discrimination which periodically rears its ugly head in the church and could easily be passed over if someone wasn't sensitive to the issue. The fact that someone could say such a thing is amazing.

Tuesday, April 25, 2006

Complicity: the state of being an accomplice, as in a wrongdoing

That is the way The American Heritage Dictionary of the English Language defines the word complicity. In atrocities, in discriminations, in poor treatment of the past the word might be used to describe the church. We look back on those times of complicity in the past and wonder how the church could have been so blind as to have missed the great evil, the significant injustice it was participating in at the time.

We congratulate ourselves at the fact that "we would not have let that evil happen!" I have often wondered what the blind spot of the church is today. What is the evil we are overlooking which we might stand up against? I think I might have one answer.

As I described in the last blog entry, there is great excitement that doctors may now be able to identify up to 90% of persons with Down's syndrome prenatally, and do it earlier. They claim this will save mothers the embarrassment of being detected as pregnant or the psychological dissonance of having felt the first kicks of the baby before killing it. Church people, leaders included, are often so oblivious about who persons with Down's syndrome are that they cannot even engage in a discussion. As a result, they mourn the birth of a child with Down's syndrome in the same manner as someone without knowledge. Down's syndrome is an unknown to them, though it needn't be, so they fear it, perhaps even fear those with the disability. But if those people were in churches, we might not only loose our fear, we might learn to see them as a blessing. **I can tell you that I do!**

I am not the parent of such a person although I would not fear being such a parent. I don't know how many people with Down's syndrome I have known, maybe 50, not a lot of people but I certainly don't fear them or their differences. I have actually come to love them and am drawn to them. They are sweet, decent people who enjoy life. They will rejoice or mourn with you with heartfelt empathy. They will go to school, maybe get a job, and live on their own or with limited support. You wouldn't have to try very hard to convince me that a great sense of humor is a characteristic of the syndrome. However, we, the church, fear what we don't understand, and are too damned lazy to find out what it is that we fear. If we did take the time, our perspectives would change.

The degree to which the church has not participated in dispelling falsehoods and telling the truth,

The degree to which the church stigmatizes and excludes people from the typical programs of the church,

The degree to which the church says that such people are not a priority for ministry to the point of putting it into their budgets,

The degree to which the church doesn't go out of its way to bring people with Down's syndrome into its fellowship,

The degree to which national church leaders are not speaking out against the evil of prenatal diagnosis and abortion of children with Down's syndrome,

Is the degree to which we are complicit in this evil.

We are complicit in this evil.

The good news is that God is a forgiving God. He is forgiving if we denounce our complicity and repent. It starts with you (as trite as it sounds).

Wednesday, December 07, 2005

Rob Bell's *Velvet Elvis*

Independent of what you might think of the "emerging church" movement, there are some interesting comments being made by those in one way or another who are involved in that movement. For example, Rob Bell (pastor of Mars Hill Church in Grand Rapids Michigan, an amazing church which I had the opportunity to visit a week ago with a dear friend, Dan Morton) in his book *Velvet Elvis*, wrote the following:

If the gospel isn't good news for everybody, then it isn't good news for anybody.

And this is because the most powerful things happen when the church surrenders its desire to convert people and convince them to join. It is when the church gives itself away in radical acts of service and compassion, expecting nothing in return, that the way of Jesus is most vividly put on display. To do this, the church must stop thinking about everybody primarily in categories of in or out, saved or not, believer or nonbeliever. Besides the fact that these terms are offensive to those who are the 'un' and 'non', they work against Jesus' teachings about how we are to treat each other. Jesus commanded us to love our neighbor, and our neighbor can be anybody. We are all created in the image of God, and we are all sacred, valuable creations of God. Everybody matters. To treat people differently based on who believes is to fail to respect the image of God in everyone. As the book of James says, 'God shows no favoritism.' So we don't either.

This is a controversial statement no doubt, but the point of the church surrendering itself to radical acts of service and compassion, expecting nothing in return is something we have lost to a significant degree. Yes there are pockets of radical service, however, we as an entire church body could hardly be characterized as being involved in radical acts of service, nor could we as individual members of churches be characterized as involved in radical acts of service (I count myself among these individuals).

But what is the example of our Lord? Somehow, I need to make the radical acts of service more important than the probably thousands of hours I spend with my children or on my own in sports activities, for example. If we are doing anything radically, we are missing the example of Christ in a radical manner.

Monday, November 07, 2005

Ezekiel 34 Part 1

Let's dance with a few sections of this passage, Ezekiel 34, thinking about the church as the shepherds and persons with disability as the flock. I have pulled a few of the sections of Ezekiel 34 out because of their particular applicability.

"Woe to the shepherds of Israel who only take care of themselves! Should not shepherds take care of the flock?"

I think the implication is that some sheep were taken care of and some were not. Apparently the shepherds took care of themselves and their families, however, there was a group of people who were ignored. Who were they specifically?

"You have not strengthened the weak or healed the sick or bound up the injured. You have not brought back the strays or searched for the lost. You have ruled them harshly and brutally. "

The weak, sick and injured were not strengthened, or healed or bound up. Additionally, they didn't bring back the strays (it seems the assumption is that they knew where the strays were) or search for the lost. Once again, it seems the assumption is that they knew they were lost. Instead, what did they do? They ruled them harshly and brutally. Now I don't know about brutality of the church towards persons with disability, but I have experienced and read about some harsh treatment on the part of the church towards persons with disability. Examples of that treatment are provided elsewhere in this blog.

So they were scattered because there was no shepherd, and when they were scattered they became food for all the wild animals.

Persons with disability often live at or below the poverty line. When you are poor, you live where other poor people live. There are many nere do well people who live among the poor and like wild animals they take advantage of the poor, particularly the mentally disabled poor. But why were they scattered? Because there was no shepherd. You don't know how often I hear church leaders excuse themselves from responsibility for persons with disability because of the their lack of funds. There are funds for other programs, oftentimes for programs for people who are not scattered or weak or sick or injured.

My sheep wandered over the mountains and on every high hill. They were scattered over the whole earth, and no one searched or looked for them.

I was floored to find out that 20% of the population of the United States are disabled. Not all are intellectually disabled, but disabled nonetheless. Why isn't the church looking for these people to bring them in. One could take the idea of being scattered as being lost, but one could also take it as that they are everywhere. They are on every high hill. But no one is looking for them.

Wednesday, May 18, 2005

Ezekiel 34 Part 2

Let's continue to consider Ezekiel 34 for a moment. It continues on, saying,

Therefore this is what the Sovereign Lord says to them: "See, I myself will judge between the fat sheep and the lean sheep."

You know, a significant number of persons with intellectual disability are "lean sheep" in that they live in poverty, often on fixed incomes. They are poor.

"Because you shove with flank and shoulder, butting all the weak sheep with your horns until you have driven them away."

I think there have been times when the fat sheep have shoved the lean ones away. Maybe not with shoulder and flank, but with words and attitudes for sure. With the power they exercise over all the sheep. They shove out by saying that such ministry is not a priority, or that they haven't the money to do such ministry or bring them in. In these ways they give a more holy face to their actions which shove out.

"I will save my flock and they will no longer be plundered. I will judge between one sheep and another."

194

Should God judge between the poor with limited resources and the rich with great resources, how do you think the rich will fare? Will God say that the poor and disabled were not a priority for Him either?

If the church was doing what it should, then

"They will live in safety, and no one will make them afraid. I will provide for them a land renowned for its crops, and they will no longer be victims of famine in the land or bear the scorn of the nations. Then they will know that I, the Lord their God am with them and that they, the house of Israel are my people, declares the Sovereign Lord."

I think it poignant the way this passage ends. I am not sure what the actual meaning of the last line is, but as stated it is a simple yet jarring statement. The implication is that you might not have recognized the obvious fact of the statement.

You my sheep, the sheep of my pasture, are people and I am your God, declares the Sovereign Lord.

The group we are talking about, are not sheep or something other than people. They are people, the Sovereign Lord declares. People are always a priority, or at least should be. In the Christian faith, if they are not, then what is being evidenced is not the Christian faith.

Monday, May 23, 2005

An Epiphany?

Epiphany: A spiritual event in which the essence of a given object of manifestation appears to be the subject, as in **a sudden flash of recognition** (1976, The American Heritage Dictionary).

Epiphany? Maybe not. However, I did come to realize something the other day. One would think that the church would represent the community in which it finds itself. the church taken as a whole, say all the churches in the City of Redlands, California where I live, should reflect the entire community, but individual churches may not represent the community at all. That is, sadly we have churches which are overwhelmingly white, black, Hispanic or Asian in the ethnicity of the members. We even have churches which separate themselves within the groups. So if I go to a church that is predominantly black, I assume that white people worship somewhere else. If I go to a church that is predominantly Asian, I assume that the Hispanic people worship someplace else. I am used to attending churches which do not represent the community in and of themselves. Why would Christians choose or even want such an option? To me it is disturbing that we as Christians cannot even worship with people of a different ethnicity than ourselves. There is truth to the axiom, that Sunday morning at 11:00 is the most segregated hour of the week. The church will have some explaining to do when it meets its Husband.

However, I guess I assume that there are not very many African American people who attend my church because they go to a different church comprised of mostly African American people. In the same way, the Hispanics attend the Hispanic church, and I guess, the disabled people attend the disabled people church. Perhaps I have the same lack of concern in that I don't worry (or care) about those of a different ethnicity who don't attend my church, as I don't worry about the disabled people.

There are two problems with this assumption. One is that most people with disability do not represent a different culture. They are the same as the rest of us. The other is that there is not a separate church for persons with disability (nor should there be, I believe), so the only option is to include them in the existing churches. I would argue that you should assume that if persons with disability are not in your church, chances are that they aren't anywhere, aren't in any church.

Why would your church be any different than any other in this regard?

So all you white, black, Hispanic and Asian churches, if their aren't white, black, Hispanic or Asian persons with disability attending your church, where do you think they are? Chances are they aren't attending any church. Do you care? Even if you do have some persons with disability at your church, do they represent the numbers you might expect in the community? Do you know?

"I tell you the truly, whatever you did not do for one of the least of these, you did not do for me" (Matthew 25:45)

If you are not doing anything, why would you assume that someone else is?

Friday, February 11, 2005

Understanding Social Support

Social support has been defined by Cobb (1976) in the following manner.

Social Support is "information" leading someone to believe
He/she is cared for
He/she is loved
He/she is valued
He/she is esteemed
He/she belongs to a network of communication and mutual
obligation

Cobb states that, this information fulfills social needs and protects from adverse consequences.

Robertson et al. (2004) observed that among persons with intellectual disability (in particular) living in community group homes, 3-4% had a **"neighbor"** with out intellectual disability. Overall, they had 3 or fewer persons in their social network (most often staff or family) and 10% had nobody.

I know I too can do much better in this area, but I provide an exhortation nonetheless.

If you were to ask me what a neighbor is (I hope you are not trying to justify yourself) I would refer you to Luke 10:29 and following where Jesus provides a good definition in the form of a parable. In case you are unfamiliar with the Bible, it is the story of the "Good Samaritan" which has become a part of culture, at least in America.

If you were to see someone lying along side of the road beat up and hurt, would you say, "I don't know what to do because I don't have any training" and then walk on? Of course not, you would do what you could do. Unfortunately, the most common excuse I have heard from Christian churches or Christian individuals as to why they aren't reaching out to persons with disability is "I don't have any training." Perhaps Jesus should have added that excuse in the story of the Good Samaritan. He might have said,

"But by coincidence, a certain priest was going on that road; and seeing him, he passed on the opposite side. A 20th century church member came upon the man and said to himself, 'I don't have any training, so it is not my responsibility to help this man' and continued on so he wouldn't miss The Simpsons. And in the same way, a Levite also being at the place, coming and seeing him, he passed on the opposite side."

At the NACSW conference, Jim Wallis (Call to renewal) spoke of an inner city worker who made the comment, "We are the people we have been waiting for" and spent herself working with persons in inner city Washington D.C.

Perhaps my altered version of the story of the Good Samaritan might be further changed in the following manner.

"But a certain traveling Samaritan came upon him, and seeing him, he was filled with pity, and said to himself, 'We are the people we have been waiting for. I am the person I have been waiting for.' And coming near, he bound up his wounds, pouring on oil and wine . . ."

If not you, who. If not now, when.

Friday, November 05, 2004

"Make the little children suffer," I mean, "Suffer the little children"

I was talking to a Catholic friend today. She told me how her priest didn't want kids with disability to come to catechism because they were too noisy.

"The little children were brought to Jesus for him to place his hands on them and pray for them. But the disciples rebuked those who brought them. Jesus said, "Let the little children *who are quiet* come to me and do not hinder them" (sorry, strike that) "Let the little children come to me and do not hinder them *unless they are disabled"* (sorry, my bad again) "'Let the little children come to me and do not hinder them, for the kingdom of heaven belongs to such as these.' When he had placed his hands on them, he went on from there." (some old texts say, "Suffer the little children to come to me")(Matthew 19:13-15)

I suspect the children in this case were perfect little angels, bright eyed and intelligent, without a blemish of any kind, and quiet, wonderfully quiet. They were also probably clean and dressed well, oh yeah, and with good social skills. You see a lot of children like that running around in third world countries, particularly 2000 years ago.

If it weren't for how wrong it is it could be laughable. "The kids are too noisy." I would love to go toe to toe with such a person and have him name 15 children with disability that he knows, and how much time he has spent with them which gives him the experience to make such claims to those under him. Have Christian leaders never heard the story of the little children and Jesus? And what was the point of them coming to him? So that he could place his hands on them, one would assume to give them a blessing.

Our response today is not only do we **not** want to bless them, we may actually want to curse them. "They are too noisy" or "They have bad social skills" or "They are a black hole for service" or "They will disrupt the other children." In contrast, imagine a catechism class where the teacher says, "Jesus allowed all children to come to him, and so will we. We all need to learn to accept and love all children, so as long as I am the Catechist, these children will be given access."

An accepting situation such as this truly will reflect that "the kingdom of heaven belongs to such as these."

No retreat.

Saturday, October 23, 2004

Broaden your mind, Malcolm, broaden your mind!

I was reading C.S. Lewis', *Letters to Malcolm, chiefly on prayer* and was struck with something Lewis wrote. Although the comment was

198

made in reference to liturgy/worship, I thought about it in terms of disability. Lewis says,

"Broaden your mind, Malcolm, broaden your mind! It takes all sorts to make a world; or a church. This may be even truer of a church. If grace perfects nature it must expand all our natures into the full richness of the diversity which God intended when He made them, and heaven will display far more variety than hell."

Grace perfects nature. That is an interesting concept. More perfection needed, more grace dispensed. God shows grace to all people, sometimes I think me above all. God shows grace to perfect our nature. The church is God's agent on Earth. How does the church fare in dispensing grace for the perfection of nature? In order to include me, God needs to dispense grace. I accept His grace but he gives it.

There are those who need grace from the church. It is their role to receive it, however, it is the church's, our role, to dispense it such that we can perfect their nature insofar as we connect them with God, with the Body of Christ.

Later in the same letter, he writes,

"My grandfather, I'm told, used to say that he 'looked forward to having some very interesting conversations with St. Paul when he got to heaven.' Two clerical gentlemen talking at ease in a club! It never seemed to cross his mind that an encounter with St. Paul might be rather an overwhelming experience even for an Evangelical clergyman of good family. But when Dante saw the great apostles in heaven they affected him like mountains. There's lots to be said against devotions to saints; but at least they keep on reminding us that we are very small people compared with them. How much smaller before their Master."

I, like C.S. Lewis' grandfather, in my pride and vanity tend to have an inflated view of who I am, and therefore of my arrival in heaven. Do I actually think everything will stop and St. Paul will be looking for me to have a cup of coffee and discuss some fine point that I think I have a handle on. This is the same Saul who met Jesus and became Paul who has been with the Lord for a couple thousand years. I agree with Lewis in agreeing with Dante, that encountering the greats of the faith will be like encountering mountains, and how does one interact with a mountain.

Actually I think I might have more of a chance of coffee with my mentally handicapped friends, assuming the elect do such things like coffee in heaven. If God allows us to keep memories of life in heaven (some He couldn't I would suspect in order to make heaven truly blissful), but if He does, I would love to have a conversation reminiscent of what one finds in Keyes' *Flowers for Algernon*.

Sunday, September 19, 2004

199

Church caused suffering

I have recently taken a position as professor of special education. In the midst of meeting other "new" faculty, we had a discussion about the suffering church. That is, those who as a result of their Christian faith are experiencing persecution around the world.

I mean in no way to minimize the suffering of any Christian, however, the church is causing some "suffering" itself. At those same new faculty meetings, we were each asked to share our interests. I shared my interest in opening up the church to persons with disability. As often occurs when I share my passion in a public forum, another faculty member, also the parent of a child with disability told me of how his heart was moved to hear of my passion. He was another of the many parents who cannot bring his child to church as they are not welcome. They are sometimes not welcome overtly, in that the church will tell parents their child is not welcome. They are also sometimes not welcome by default, in that the child is exclusively the parents' responsibility when on church property. The Sunday school will accept the child only if the parent accompanies him (not just for a short time, but forever), but otherwise, there is no place for the child.

Because of the stories I have heard and the things I have read, I can't help but believe that there are many churches where overt exclusion is occurring, and exponentially more where the exclusion by default is happening, even though those in leadership in the church must know that there are families with a child with disability who would chose to attend the church if some form of program were available.

However, the exclusion of persons with disabilities is so pervasive that it is common practice, and it really takes someone up in the face of the church, to rattle their cage to get something going. As I write this, I sit here shaking my head at the implication such exclusion gives to any who observe it about who the church is and worse yet, who their god is.

If it is too much trouble to include persons with severe disability in our churches, what does that shout out to those around us about the God we serve?

Friday, August 20, 2004

Ruminations on a model for churches

For years, I have wondered about the kind of model I would propose for supporting persons with intellectual disabilities in a local church. On the one hand, such a model needs to be natural; it needs to be something which is a natural growth out of the life of the church. Good people have proposed a variety of models which borrow from those developed by the state, state agencies, secular groups. This is not to say that these groups have nothing for the church, however, it seems the church, a church which really believes in helping other members and fellow men in general could come up with something more.

Recently, I have been ruminating over an idea which I think has some merit. It has partially grown out of interactions I have had with a homeless man I know. I can't say he would consider me his friend, although I have provided assistance to him on occasion, have gotten into shouting matches with him on the phone, and have discussed the relevance of the church to the problem of homelessness in general. Anyway, in spite of problems he faces with mental illness, his feeling is that if some family would take him in, that would be the start of a successful program that would put him on the path of recovery. The notion of average families helping disenfranchised people is what has struck a nerve with me.

I want people, regular people and their families to know persons with intellectual disability for the same reason others want white people to know black people and black people to know yellow people. That reason is that when such people get to know each other, stereotypes, fear, distancing, negative attitudes, fall away and are replaced by understanding, acceptance, empathy and caring. I want every family in my church to know a person with intellectual disability by name. I want the children of every family in my church to have had lunch with a person with intellectual disability and to know that person by name. I want every person with intellectual disability to know the phone number of a family in my church whom they can call when they have a problem, who will be there for them, who will care about their problems, who will help them out on occasion. I want that because that will change the person without disability, will change the person with disability, will change the church, will change the community and perhaps most of all, would be an evidence that we as a church are finally being obedient to the example of Christ provided for us.

DC Talk, the musical group, has stated, "a physical world creates a spiritual haze." That is so true. I never cease to wonder at the indignation of families of persons with disabilities, or persons with disabilities themselves at the treatment they receive from those around them. These same people were oblivious to the experience of disability till they experienced it themselves. But people without disabilities are only that way for a while, they will eventually have a disability of some sort either themselves or within their family. For example, I see a further degrading of my already poor eyesight, and if the Lord gives me 20 more years, I can't imagine what my knees will be like by then. The certainty of disability is right up there with death and taxes. Yet a physical world creates a spiritual haze. How might we cut through that spiritual haze?

Perhaps some sort of a program which links families with disenfranchised persons of various types might be the answer. Not everyone can make the commitment required to be a member of a L'Arche community, however, everyone can make some sort of commitment to a neighbor. People will be able to deal with more or less severe disabilities according to who they are. I for one can work with a mentally ill, homeless man, or another emotionally disturbed man whom I used to know because of who I am, my personality, etc. Others would be scared or threatened. But there are plenty of sweet adults with Down's syndrome, for example, who could use a friend, a family to fill their lives. The interaction would not be one sided either. Both would gain. There are children/adults with autism and their families who would gain from interactions with other families. Families who would take the time to learn how to baby sit for the autistic child sometimes. There are group homes in the community where sweet adults with severe developmental disabilities live, where a visit a couple times a month would make a huge difference. Yes there are staff at these facilities, but anyone who has ever been in a hospital knows the difference between being visited by the nurse and by a family member or friend.

So what am I proposing? As the title states, this is just ruminating, but some kind of linkage between persons with and without disabilities, particularly interactions in which regular families get to know persons with disabilities and their families. I would love to pull any 5 year old child at my church aside and ask, do you know someone with intellectual disability, someone with a disability? I would literally cry if I could consistently hear, "Yea, Rosa is coming to our house for a barbeque today!"

We can get there.

Monday, July 19, 2004

What would a church that always includes all types of disenfranchised people look like?

What would it look like organizationally?

There would have to be many channels of communication set up and open to deal with the many issues people would have both as persons with problems and with persons with problems. Because some of those who are disenfranchised are used to "working the system" there would have to be ways of checking their stories to both have some level of stewardship over the resources of the church, for reasons of safety for the members (children and adults).

Communication would be imperative in supporting such people with their various emergencies.

Communication would also help the church leadership to keep on top of the needs of all members of the church, particularly those who are disenfranchised. Perhaps particular pastors, leaders or lay people would be the first points of contact through whom someone might become enfolded.

What would be characteristics of the people there.

Church members would need to come to church prepared for the unexpected. Church services might become a bit more unpredictable due to the social skills (or lack thereof) in the membership. But the people in attendance would be just as genuine as those already in attendance in regards to their desire to worship, to grow, to change. Their backgrounds, disabilities, etc., might cause them to come out of a different background, however.

Other potential characteristics might include,

fresh - a certain unpredictability might also bring freshness to the situation

unpredictable - when things are unpredictable, they require another whole set of skills. You become less brittle in the way you do things. You have a plan and a program, but it adapts with the situation. The flexibility which results is a good thing.

accepting - because you are committed to enfolding all types of people, particularly those whom society has often rejected, your level of acceptance expands. You begin to worry less about how someone dresses or looks or smells. The range of "normal" expands as you meet more people who are outside of what is typically considered to be normal. For example, a friend of mine with intellectual disabilities talks a little too loud during the church service (a service for largely white people in an affluent suburb). I visit other churches in other settings and I find that behavioral standards for churches are different. An African-American pastor once spoke at my church and wondered out loud whether the people were paying attention because they were so quiet.

full - the church would be full of both people who are disenfranchised and those who desire to serve those people.

ministering - to others would be the rule of the day. I remember Lake St. Church in Chicago which did include many disenfranchised persons who required a high level of service to be eligible for initial or ongoing church membership (I believe). Not an entirely bad idea.

needs met without programs - sure there would be many programs within the church, however, much of the work of the church which should be encouraged on a one to one basis would happen naturally. Programs are not to be disdained, however, individuals or families helping others independent of programs should be encouraged.

prepared for this role - obviously people would need to be prepared for this role. There would have to be discussions about what is appropriate or inappropriate within a Christian church setting. As and undergrad, I took a course in "contextual theology" the jist of which should be a must for all churches. Can you have communion without bread, or grape juice? I sometimes wonder whether churches believe you could. Could you have a worship service without a sermon? Could you have singing without people with microphones up front? Preferences which seem almost wrong, are often far more the result of cultural differences, or even what people have become used to more than something ordained by scripture.

character of worship would change - at times in church I try to imagine what the persons with intellectual disability who sit next to me are thinking about what they are hearing. I listen to them sing the worship songs with the words projected on the screen and imagine how I would do singing those songs. If I look away from the words, I find I sound a lot like they do, remembering a few words when I sing. Obviously the entire character of the worship can't change to better include a few with disabilities, for example, however, I wonder what thought is put into planning for persons who are dyslexic or mentally handicapped, etc.

many would leave - finally, in such a church many would leave. They want their God to be predictable, and they want him to be worshipped in a predictable manner. Don't change the order of the worship, the songs sung, the version of the Bible, the social skills required, the way the offering is taken, or to some extent who they have to sit next to. If the church really started bringing in everyone, many would leave because I honestly believe that there are those who don't want everyone there. In fact they would rather have particular persons not there, then have their familiar worship experience disrupted.

More on this later.

Monday, July 05, 2004

A glimpse of a future

In my professional writing I have spoken of the potential the church holds as a place of support for adults with developmental disabilities. Here are a few of the things I have observed.

-Over 50% of developmentally disabled adults surveyed reported

attending church in the last seven days.
-Over 80% of churches surveyed reported having individuals with
developmental disabilities in their congregations.
-Churches provide a wide range of supports (money, food, clothing,
opportunities for recreation, education, social and emotional supports and
opportunities for service).
-As a rule, churches provide these services because a disabled person
happened to show up on their doorstep.

These observations reflect some of what is happening now. But what
of the future, where are we headed?

I think we are honestly on the crest of a wave that will lead us to a
different future for persons with disabilities in local churches.

I can remember as a boy growing up in the 60's, the world was a
different place in terms of racial integration. Over the last 40 years
though, things have gotten better. The church has become more accepting
as evidenced by people within churches becoming more accepting. (I
would say, however, that independent of the ethnic make up of churches,
the absence of persons with disabilities is pervasive). Maybe it is because
I attend a church in Southern California, a place which is truly diverse,
but I see more acceptance, more mixing in a variety of ways among
ethnic groups. This gives me hope for the future.

I hope for a similar future for persons with disabilities. I observe
churches being more open to these people. I know of a churches which
have full time pastors to address the needs of people with disabilities. I
observe a willingness on the part of my own church to make ministry
work. To do the extra which is required to include persons, children with
disabilities and their families. But we are not there yet.

At my church, we have had a ministry to adults with developmental
disabilities for about 13 years. Recently, however, as an outcome of a
National Organization on Disability conference we held at our church we
have been working to reach out to children. Although I knew there were
many who were unable to attend a local church because of the church's
unpreparedness and lack of focus, I have been surprised at how quickly
these families are coming forward. Our children's pastor reports getting at
least 2 calls a week from families asking whether it is true that our church
is a place where children with autism (for example) are welcomed. That
these families want a church home and are unwelcome because of their
child with disability is in my mind flat out disobedience to what the Bible
demands of us.

But I can foresee a future where churches will get past their lack of
interest, disobedience and perhaps even discrimination and include all
people. That they will see people. In the same way that you would visit a

205

church and wonder why there weren't any people from (fill in the blank) ethnic group, you would look around and wonder where the disabled people are in this church. That you would go to a church and notice, "Hey this church isn't accessible to people who use wheelchairs." Your child will come out of Sunday school and wonder where the children with autism or Down's syndrome were. Can you imagine your child saying, "They don't have any special kids at all in that Sunday school?"

We would be in a place where parents no longer had to rely on the state to facilitate integration for their child through laws (like the Americans with Disabilities act) or through Special Education teachers trying to cajole those around them to accept students with disabilities. No, the church would be leading the way in integration because the kids were growing up together in natural social settings, local churches, where accepting people naturally congregated together. The point of integration would not be the school curriculum where the child with disability may be at a great disadvantage, but growth and development as a Christian, as a "little child." In this area, the person with disability might excel above those without disability. They would then be integrated at a point of their strength.

I hope I live long enough to see that which I feel is just beginning.

Thursday, May 20, 2004

Church or state leadership

I have been thinking a lot lately about the differences between the way the "secular world" interacts, works with, supports persons with disabilities, and the way the "Christian world" does the same. Clearly, the secular is filled with Christians in various positions. I, for example, am a professor at a secular state university. Therefore, arguably the face of that university towards the public, in particular as it relates to the little department of which I am a part, may be impacted positively or negatively by what I do, what I fight for or advocate for. Hopefully we Christians are being "salt." So to separate the two worlds may be somewhat artificial.

I think, however, that it is still useful to look for distinctions between what the state is doing and what the church is doing. Historically, it is important to understand the impact, the effect the church has had on the state. Arguably the church was pivotal in the development of social services both in Europe and in America. Early human service programs of the 1800's were largely facilitated by religious groups. Particularly with the turn of the century and the increased urbanization, churches were being overwhelmed with the problem, and sought help from the state. Social work and human services can trace their roots to church advocacy.

206

Churches were also instrumental in ending sterilization practices in the United States. These groups were very vocal in calling for an end to these abusive and actually futile practices; people with intellectual disability in particular were not reproducing.

Obviously other groups and individuals have worked for societal change in recent years, but it seems to this observer that the secular world is currently leading the way. A couple of examples might suffice.

The Americans with Disabilities act focused the nation's attention on architectural barriers to persons with disabilities. I can remember as a young man attending a Baptist church in New Jersey, where the entrance to the church had beautiful granite steps which rose up perhaps 12 feet to the entrance. A wonderful Christian saint and gifted science teacher at our church, who had used a wheelchair most of her life had to be lifted by four men every week up those stairs and into the church. I'm sure Ms. Barto enjoyed getting to know the young men of the church as they did her (she used to wonder why our national anthem ended with a question). But in all the years I went to that church, it never occurred to anyone that some means of allowing Ms. Barto to enter the church independently might be constructed. I still don't know whether the church is accessible today. National leaders, however, recognized that lack of access is a form of discrimination. Public buildings must be accessible to persons who use a wheelchair. Even the curbs of our cities must allow for easy access.

I was excited recently to see a church in my town installing a elevator. I was excited because I met with them a few years back to assist in thinking through the development of ministries which would include persons with disabilities. They indicated that there was at least one boy who wasn't able to attend the junior high group, which met on the second floor, because he used a wheelchair and there was no elevator. They recognized that something had to be done to either move the junior highers to the first floor, or provide access to the second floor. I haven't been involved with them for several years, but apparently they arrived at a solution.

But I come back to my question of who is leading the way? Who is the example to the other? At the moment I would have to say the state is the leader.

For the past ten years I have traveled around the country doing presentations, mostly to secular professionals about the potential of the church as an agent of supports for adults with disabilities (my focus). You see, the state is constantly on the look out for ways in which adults with disabilities can be supported naturally in the community (I will give you more information about this in the future). I tell them about churches and the potential they hold. Often they are surprised and amazed. I wish I had a dollar for every time someone has said to me, "How come I have never heard about this before?" Well the reason they have never heard about it is that the secular trainers, universities, agencies, etc. don't talk about it (church/state separation, you know) and partially because there wasn't enough to talk about. Notice I keep using the word "potential." But my thought was that if I talked to enough secular professionals who really do want what is best for their clients, perhaps they will encourage churches to do what they should have been doing all along. Ironic isn't it? State agents contacting churches to, in Dolan-Henderson's words "see God as having a preferential option for the disabled and ill, and thus for the church integrally to mirror this preference and work for justice concerning their well being."

I don't know if I have had my desired impact on state agents or churches. I do think that the church as "salt" in this area, is somewhere between a flavorful spice and tossed on the ground to be trodden under foot.

Wednesday, May 19, 2004

The Christian imagination

Dr. Stanley Hauerwas has written, "The Christian imagination is constituted by practices such as . . . learning to be present to - as well as with - the mentally handicapped - who we hopefully know not as mentally handicapped, but as Anna and Boyce, our sister and brother in Christ" (The church and the mentally handicapped: A continuing challenge to the imagination, in *Dispatches From the Front: Theological Engagement with the Secular*, 1994).

He probably should have said that the Christian imagination "might be constituted," or "could" or "should be constituted." Because actually it is not constituted by the high ideals he mentions.

In reality the Christian imagination could be a significant part of the problem. Maybe not the imagination of "the church" as a whole, but the imaginations of individuals who comprise the church. Individuals who make up the church, well...

They imagine persons with intellectual disabilities as significantly different from themselves.

They imagine persons with intellectual disabilities as having a poor quality of life.

They imagine persons with intellectual disabilities as "black holes for service" as a pastor commented to me one time.

They imagine persons with intellectual disabilities as a threat to their regular Sunday school program, in that they will require super human efforts.

208

They imagine persons with intellectual disabilities as a threat to the development of their larger congregation in that their "notorious social behaviors" might scare off those who would choose to attend that church.

They imagine persons with intellectual disabilities as lacking faith, or experiencing disability as a result of some sin committed by their parents.

They imagine persons with intellectual disabilities as unable to contribute anything to the church, only being a drain on the church's resources.

They imagine persons with intellectual disabilities as being unable to grow spiritually.

They imagine persons with intellectual disabilities as being dirty or diseased.

They imagine persons with intellectual disabilities as being unapproachable by traditional social means like conversation, or phone calls, or lunch.

They imagine persons with intellectual disabilities as living in families who rue their existence, wishing they either had not been born, or were in some way different then they are.

They imagine persons with intellectual disabilities as being the offspring of parents who in some way were selected by God by some syrupy cosmic process to be the parents of the individual.

They imagine persons with intellectual disabilities as being "angels unaware" or "God's special children" or incapable of sin rather than being simply an example of the range of humanity.

They imagine persons with intellectual disabilities as suffering from intellectual disability.

They imagine persons with intellectual disabilities as dissatisfied with their lives.

After nearly 30 years of interactions with individuals with intellectual disability and a variety of other forms of disability I have come to the conclusion that people with disabilities are just people.

Friday, April 30, 2004

The Church and Disability

Ministry

Social healing

The gospels have many accounts of people with various infirmities or disabilities coming to Jesus and receiving healing. This is actually an evidence of him being who he claimed to be. Does this type of healing continue to occur today? I am sure it does, and I am not talking about the high profile evangelists making a lot of money from supposedly healing people. To its detriment, the church has at times approached people with various disabilities with only a "ministry" of healing. I have also known people who will never go to a church again because of the church's overemphasis on their need for healing, and the church's linking healing with the disabled person's faith or lack thereof. I have discussed this elsewhere in this blog, but I will only say that if your perspective on disability is that the only answer, the only truly Christian response to disability is healing, then you need to meet a man named Paul who wrote a lot of the Bible, who apparently had a disability and although he asked God for healing was definitely not healed.

But I think there is a great ministry of "healing" that the church can play in the lives of every person who experiences a disability and also a healing in the lives of families of persons with disabilities.

Dr. Hans Reinders in his excellent book, *The Future of the Disabled in Liberal Society* (2000), talks about the manner in which society addresses Down's syndrome. Basically he discusses the fact that typically, the suffering experienced by a person with Down's syndrome is not the result of the syndrome, it is the result of society's treatment of the person who has the syndrome. He goes on to indicate that we address a sociological issue with a medical procedure. That is, I experience discrimination because of my disability, so society's solution is to kill me (through abortion) not to address society's wrong attitudes about me or my disability. This, however, is the place where the church can have a particular impactful healing ministry.

If I am experiencing suffering because of the social consequences of my disability, then the church through its efforts can "cure" me of that suffering through what they do. I will still have my disability, however, there is the potential that I will feel much less of the social sting of my disability should the church step up and be what the church was intended to be to me.

So the church first of all comes to me and invites me in.

The church then welcomes me and is glad that I am there.

The church gives me opportunities to have responsibilities as that empowers me as a member of the church.

The church talks about people like me, people who face the issues I face, from the pulpit, particularly issues related to my disability in order to help me and those around me.

The church embraces me as a regular member, including me in all the social activities of the church.

The church socially softens to overlook many of the socially impacting aspects of my disability such as social skills, other behaviors over which I may not have control.

This overlooking is not an uncomfortable, don't know what to do kind of overlooking. This reminds me of times where I have seen people with severe intellectual disabilities doing ridiculous things in church like literally pouring the entire sugar bowl into their coffee cup. As they did so, those in the environment looked on helplessly. Whereas if someone they knew, or one of their children for that matter did such a thing they would correct them. Correct them, not reject them. I have a friend who due to a hearing impairment, speaks in a very loud voice during the sermon at church. If the person wants to say something to me, like "Can you help me get to the bathroom?" it is going to be said in a loud voice. I could try as hard as I wanted to get the person to not speak in a loud voice but it will never happen. So I as part of the environment, soften, the person doesn't feel condemned, and social healing occurs. In every way possible, I as a disabled person, am a regular member of the church, the social network of the church, the religious training of the church. The church interacts with me in a manner that understands that my disability will impact my life, but they first see me for me. Together we work through the challenges and inconveniences that my disability presents.

I believe the end result of such a relationship with a church is healing. It is the healing of the social issues which are typically many of the biggest issues I may face as a result of having a disability. I may or may not be healed physically, however, many of my social interactions are in fact healed.

Wednesday, October 29, 2008

Broadening the notion of "ministry"

I had the privilege of speaking in a class on suffering and disability at a local University this past Monday. The class went fine. Afterwards, one bright student approached me with her story. The child of deaf parents, she wondered about church ministry to persons who are deaf. Should interpretation of sermons into sign language be the extent of ministry with persons who are deaf? What a great question! So the only relevant aspect of being deaf is to be able to understand what is being said to you by someone translating. I am sure there are those who believe that, but I am not sure that I do. I suspect there are many other things that go along with being deaf that I have no understanding of and that if I treat deaf people as if the only important thing about their deafness is that they need to understand what I, or my pastor says, I am being very naive. Other similar questions flooded my mind like, "Are accessible restrooms the entire range of ministry to persons who use wheelchairs?"

The way the church typically responds, you might think so. I have several friends who have progressive MS. Is the extent of ministry to these people accessible restrooms, or a spot for their wheelchair in the church service? You might think so. When will the church, when will leaders in the church take on these issues such that those who experience the disabilities, and the rest of the congregation for that matter, become informed about what disability tells us about who God is, what the role of the church is, as well as thinking through the "whys" of disability. We may never know why, but we can sure explore the whys. Not knowing something has never kept Church leaders from speaking about it in the past. A rational exploration of the whys might be very helpful for all concerned and as with many things in life, the journey may be just as valuable as the answer. What does it imply to you as a disabled person, if I am struggling to understand the issues you face in your life from a Christian perspective? I think it implies at the very least that your issues are important and worthy of my consideration, my professional or pastoral efforts to understand, and at best that perhaps there are answers that might be found should I devote some or all of my energies to the issues.

Exodus 4:11 states,
The LORD said to him, "Who has made man's mouth? Or who makes him mute or deaf, or seeing or blind? Is it not I, the LORD?

Why would God do such a thing to a person? Because I know that God is love and God is just, there is something for me to learn if I will pay attention. God apparently deliberately makes some people mute or deaf or seeing or blind. I may never fully understand why, however, by devoting my energies to understanding perhaps God will reveal new lessons about himself that the Church has never learned but that God has for us to learn if we will only look.

Thursday, November 13, 2008

A new member of our group

This week at The Light and Power Company (our group that includes adults with various disabilities) we had a new attendee. He is a man, let's call him John, with profound intellectual and physical disabilities. John is largely non verbal, and doesn't move very much. I must tell you that I am delighted that through his father, John has decided to be a part of our group (I may be jumping the gun a bit as last week was his first week with us)! I introduced him to everyone as I typically do for anyone visiting, and asked him the question I typically ask visitors, "What do you like to do for fun?" I asked him and he didn't answer, however, his father told me that he enjoys music, so I was ready with a response for him. After introducing him, I instructed everyone to go over and introduce themselves to him and they did. John had his hand shook by perhaps 45 different people. I hope it wasn't too traumatic for him!

Over the past few days in thinking through John's presence in class, I am reminded about the story in Mark 2: 2-12 about the man lowered through the roof by his friends in order to meet Jesus, and I suppose to be healed. At least that is what I would think his friend's motivation was. Little did they know what the result of their assistance would be. "When Jesus saw their faith, he said to the paralyzed man, 'Son, your sins are forgiven.'" So they were going for healing and what they got through THEIR faith was much better...forgiveness.

This passage puts a whole new light on the presence of my new friend with profound disabilities. What will God do in his life if I and those around him are faithful? Like the friends in the story, his father had the faith to bring him to church, and ultimately to bring him to our group. In many ways, we now have the responsibility to bring him to God through our love and acceptance of him. I am also reminded of the verse in John 9:3-5, "Neither this man nor his parents sinned. But that the Glory of God might be seen in his life, we must work the works of him who sent me." So his presence provides the opportunity within our group and wherever we are with him to have the Glory of God seen in his life. What an amazing opportunity.

I will be honest in telling you that I don't know quite how the principles described in the two stories will be fleshed out in our interactions with John, however, you can believe me that I will be watching to see how they will be worked out. I anticipate seeing him each week, and in between should the opportunity arise, and look forward to seeing how God will act in his life and ours.

One final note. A member of our group and a longtime friend, Arthur Seale, grabbed John's father as he was pushing him out in his wheelchair. Arthur said something to the effect, "Your son is welcome and wanted here. He will never be too noisy, he will never do anything that would cause him to no longer be a part of this group." I didn't say anything, but inwardly (and probably outwardly) I was beaming. Arthur nailed it. This is the message we desperately want the church to give to parents and persons with disabilities.

Thursday, October 16, 2008

Great Expectations

I am often in situations where people with intellectual disabilities and those without who are their teachers, their care providers, their family members are together. Sometimes it is a therapeutic or educational situation and other times just typical life situations. It also seems, that those with the disability perform, to a certain extent, in accordance with the expectations of those they are with. So...

If they are treated as a child, they act as a child.

If they are treated as an adult, they act like an adult.

If they are treated as if they can't learn anything, they don't learn anything.

If they are treated with the expectation that they will learn, they do learn.

If they are treated as people who are just intellectually disabled, they act as such.

If they are treated as people who think, have opinions and are capable of thinking deeply they do.

I make concerted efforts, when I am instructing people who have intellectual disabilities, to try to stretch them, particularly if I am talking about spiritual things. I am always impressed how they will raise to the level of the discussion. They will often try to take what I am saying and translate it into a direct application to their lives. "So you are saying that I shouldn't listen when somebody tells me to ..." they will say. One gal I know who has Down's syndrome, will pause after you ask her a question, and often give profound insights. Too often, however, she is not given the opportunity to do so because the people around her think her pause a lack of understanding, and their limited expectations cause them to be impatient.

I believe I have shared this here before, but I have a friend who has severe intellectual disabilities, let's call him Fred. Fred would try to get my attention by nagging me with a question, the same question over and over again. Finally, one day, he asked me for a dollar. That got me to stop and pay attention to him for a minute. He learned that he could get me to stop by asking me for a dollar. Well many dollars have changed hands over the years, but at some point I stopped and began to have a conversation with him. I expected him to be able to converse with me on a variety of topics. At first our discussions revolved around his original repetitive question and asking for a dollar, but grew to discussion of his desire to marry his teacher, and his brother who lives in Hawaii, and his interest in baseball, and his favorite foods and so forth. When I treated

217

him as a real human being who would communicate with me on a variety of topics, he rose to the occasion. Had I continued in my interactions with him where I basically ignored him, he would have remained something quite less than what he was capable of.

So I have learned to try hard to raise my expectations of people, independent of their level of disability. Too often their low performance is due to what I do as the person who is in control of the social situation. It is the result of mistaken notions of the limitation of the person with disabilities.

Tuesday, September 30, 2008

What to do? How to begin?

I recently had the opportunity to teach a portion of the second Joni and Friends certificate program to be offered by them at the Christian Institute on Disability at Agoura Hills, Ca. What a great group of folks participated in the training. There was one person, however, who felt very put off by the things I was saying. The feeling was that I was just attacking the church. We talked and I think the person came to understand my perspective, that I was trying to improve the church's outreach to persons with disabilities by challenging those in attendance who in many ways self-selected to be taught important principles about developing ministries. As I shared with the one person who was having difficulty, "If you are in your church, I will praise your efforts. However, as soon as you enter the training, it is my job to help you to mold your ministry into the best it can be, using what are (in my opinion) best practices. I will therefore be critical." There are things we can do which do represent best practices, and there are things we can do that are not best practices.

For example, if we develop curriculum that implies that adults with disabilities are children, we are wrong because they are not children, and we demean them by communicating to them that they are children. I have been teaching adults with intellectual disabilities in ministry settings for 30 years, and I have yet to find the need to develop cutesy stories that I would never use for adults who are not disabled in order to educate those who have intellectual disabilities. We teach from the same Bible that the nondisabled adults use, studying the same passages, generally, that they study.

Now I am circumspect in the things that I teach because I know of the intellectual capacity of my audience. So for example, I don't see the need to teach the story about how David had the opportunity to kill Saul but didn't (1 Samuel 24:4) because that is irrelevant to their lives. I can teach about doing unto others (Matthew 7:12) and therefore make the same point in a relevant way. The Psalms, for example, provide a wealth of information that is entirely relevant to anyone, including adults with intellectual disabilities. For example, this past week, I taught on Psalm 116, asking the group whether God had ever saved any of them from death (v3)? There were those in auto accidents, those in hospital for surgeries and so on and they easily made the connection that God had saved them. Or had any of them been delivered from tears, or God kept them from stumbling into sin (v8). We then moved to verse 13 that asks "How can I repay the Lord for his goodness to me?" The answer is in verse 14, "I will fulfill my vows to the Lord." We talked about the fact that we have given our lives to Jesus. So that means we will try to do what is right, to do what Jesus would want us to do.

I don't need stories that are juvenile in nature to convey these truths to my audience. I talk to them as adults and they respond to me to the degree they are able as adults. And people will rise to the occasion. This past Sunday, for example, we were having a time of prayer for people in our group. One of our members is a 4th year medical student at Loma Linda university. He mentioned how he had important upcoming exams and wanted someone to pray for him. One of our men, a regular attendee, who I will tell you just to give you an idea of the level of his disability, spends his days in adult day care, immediately stood up and moved to the side of the medical student. He prayed, "God take care of him" ending with a loud "AMEN." He has learned how to pray for others who he is able to perceive are in need. He has been treated as an adult and has now developed the ability to treat others as adults.

But getting back to the initial point, we need to celebrate what we are already doing, but also improve what we are already doing. There are people out there who have thought deeply, have researched, have years of experience that we can benefit from. Yes there are those with years of doing something which may not be the best of practices. Hopefully God will provide the opportunity for assistance to those programs as the Christian church grows and develops in areas related to disability ministry. There is so much room for thought in this area.

But as stated above, the point is to begin and to even do things wrongly. Even if we are not doing things according to the "state of the art" we are moving in a direction and we can be directed. We will also see the logic of the correctives which might be suggested as well if we are "in the trenches" trying to figure things out.

There is really no excuse for inactivity in this area. Trust in the Lord and look to Him to direct you. Also recognize that as in any area of human endeavor, there are people who have gone before. Look to see what they have done. Evaluate what they have done to see that it treats people with disabilities with respect, does not demean them, and then emulate what you see as appropriate.

Saturday, August 09, 2008

Go and make vs. build and they will come

I teach a class that is called "The Exceptional Child." It is basically a class that is an introduction to disability. One of my assignments in the class is for students to contact their local church and interview their pastor about the priority the church places on recruiting and ministering to persons with various disabilities. All too often, students report that the pastor says that they have handicapped parking spaces and accessible restrooms, and that they also have areas for people who use wheelchairs. The typical comment is that "They are welcome and we would serve them if they came." In a kind of Field of Dreams model for ministry, you simply meet the basic requirements of the law in the United States (handicapped parking places and accessible restrooms) and people with disabilities will be so impressed that they will come to your church! Build the large bathroom stall and they will come!

I remember that was actually a principle I was taught as an undergrad in Christian Education (my major). "If you want to minister to widows, start talking to them from the pulpit and they will come." I guess that it makes a little sense.

As I sat in church this morning, however, my pastor was teaching on Matthew 28:16-20. The passage states, "Go therefore and make disciples of all the nations, baptizing them in the name of the Father and the Son and the Holy Spirit..." As he stated, it doesn't say, "Sit here and wait in Galilee and people will come." It says go to the nations. I am confident that relates to persons with disabilities as they are just members of the nations. We should go to them as we would go to any other member of the nations and invite them in. Jesus' command is "Go" not "Build it and they will come" or "We will serve them if they come to us." There is a big difference between going and sitting and waiting.

One other note, Titus 2:10 also states "Make the teaching about God our savior attractive in every way." I suspect this is not just a verse about knowledge, about the content of instructional lessons in the church. I don't think it just means that we should use lots of video screens and the latest technology, although I am not opposed to that. It is something different.

How would I make the teaching about God our savior attractive to persons with disabilities and their families? I could begin by accepting them, both the families and the people with disabilities. I might even talk about the life experience of people with disabilities from the pulpit because it gives the impression that those in leadership have thought

220

about both disability and theology as it relates to disability. It makes a difference. Human experience around disability and how an understanding of God relates to it is nuanced. There is a difference between being born with a disability or having some traumatic event in your life that causes a disability, or just kind of "rusting" (as I feel is happening to me) such that disabilities of vision or physical or memory just begin to happen as a result of age. Does God, does the Bible, does theology have nothing to say to these aspects of human experience? You might think it doesn't based on the amount of time that pastors dedicate to the subject. I could begin also by going out and trying to find persons with disabilities and their families and telling them about the priority that God seems to place on them and the importance of their participation within the church. The church desperately needs to discover that importance and reflect it in its practices.

Then, the teaching about our God and savior would be SO attractive, it would be hard to stay away. The church would be REALLY accepting people, really loving people as it was meant to. The church would be seeking out people who are "difficult to love" because of social skills, and that would be attractive to the community. The church would really be about acceptance and loving others as a reflection of its God and Savior and it would be hard to stay away.

Sunday, June 15, 2008

The 99 and the 1

I now have posted two blog entries where a person with disability and his/her parent were asked to leave a church service (and in the one case be arrested if they came back).

 I was sharing the story of the young man with autism and the restraining order with a colleague and friend, Dr. Danny Blair, and he responded that it is the 99 and 1 story. You remember it, from Matthew 18:12-14. In case you don't it says...

"See that you do not look down on one of these little ones. For I tell you that their angels in heaven always see the face of my Father in heaven. What do you think? If a man owns a hundred sheep, and one of them wanders away, will he not leave the ninety-nine on the hills and go to look for the one that wandered off? And if he finds it, I tell you the truth, he is happier about that one sheep than about the ninety-nine that did not wander off. In the same way your Father in heaven is not willing that any of these little ones should be lost."

So the example is to leave the "ninety and nine" to go after the one. Well what if the lost one, is really lost, like lost in autism, a disability that largely is a language disability (have you ever been in a setting where you can't speak a language that everyone else is speaking and even have difficulty communicating because you don't understand even the gestures people are using around you...if you have, you will know what it is to feel lost), lost in exclusion and lost in social isolation and perhaps lost spiritually as well. So you come to a church whose God has given the example of leaving the 99 for the lost one, and if you are able to understand the meaning of Matthew 18, you might expect that you would be welcomed.

But instead, perhaps you are asked to leave, or even arrested "for God's sake" (I choose my words carefully) if you attempt to not be lost. You have to wonder if that group has ever read the Bible they claim to represent.

As I have said elsewhere in this blog, I would love to have a person with disabilities evidencing some form of inappropriate social skill, like talking out, or standing up and sitting down, or making a noise, and hearing the pastor to say, "In the spirit of Matthew 18, let's see if we can tolerate, can live with this distraction and in a spirit of love continue on with our service."

As a person who played a lot of basketball, I have always been surprised at people who golf. When I was at the free throw line, I heard every comment possible screamed at me and people deliberately trying to distract me so I would make a mistake and miss the shot. But then there is golf where if you make a sound, even the people around you will shush you. Imagine people deliberately trying to distract a golfer? Both athletes are doing something that requires concentration, however, one has to do it with the roar of a hostile crowd. My point is not that we should heckle our pastor or any other teacher as she/he teaches. My point is that we have the ability to perform under a variety of conditions, and absolute silence is simply a preference it is not a necessity as a condition. I mean for goodness sake, visit an African-American church. We once had a black pastor speak at our church, and he made the comment something to the effect, "Speak up every so often so I know that you are listening" because everyone sat in silence like you are supposed to in most predominantly white churches. Great comment!

The presence of noise at a church service is a cultural thing, and cultural things can be changed, and at times should be changed in particular if they result in people being excluded. I can change the culture of my church, it is not a God ordained program for people to sit in silence, largely motionless for 40 minutes. We can change if we want to. So if people with autism or any other disability cannot fit our structures, our structures can change. And in a Matthew 18 kind of way, we can leave the ninety and nine behind and go for the one who is "lost," however he may be lost, be it socially, communicatively or spiritually.

What could possibly have been the point of Jesus telling the story of the ninety and nine and the one, if not to impress upon us the importance of the lost one? "...your Father in heaven is not willing that any of these little ones should be lost."

Are you? And if you are, what are you willing to do to see they, and their families will not be lost?

Friday, May 23, 2008

Stigma

When a person with a disability enters a room, people will tend to notice the differences about that person. Perhaps it is his facial characteristics as with people with Down's syndrome. Perhaps it is the fact that she uses a wheelchair for mobility. Perhaps it is some scar from an operation. Perhaps it is some other type of equipment that the individual uses to communicate or move safely, or breathe. These things stigmatize a person. That is, they cause those in the environment to think in a particular manner about the person who has the characteristic. If I show up in a wheelchair, people in the environment have their minds flooded with every idea, every notion they may have about who a person is who uses a wheel chair, be those notions correct or not. If a person uses a wheelchair, I cannot entirely help the fact that the environment will stigmatize them in particular ways. But I can do things that will help to remove the stigma or I can do things that will perhaps exacerbate the stigma. Let me give you some examples.

People with intellectual disabilities enjoy life as it is presented to them. Now I can present things to them via my disability ministry at church which gives the impression that disabled adults are really children. I can have them coloring pictures even though they are 50 years old. I can have them singing "Jesus loves the little children" even though they are in their 20's and 30's. I can communicate to those around the person with the disability that I believe that that person is not really an adult, she is really a child and because I am the expert in my church as the disability ministry guy, people will believe me and treat adults as children. Will the persons with disabilities enjoy coloring pictures and singing children's songs? Many will. However, I do not have them coloring pictures at church or singing children's songs because I know how this will stigmatize them towards others in the environment resulting in them being treated as children when they are not children. Instead, we will sit around tables like any other adult class at the church, sing choruses although they may be simple, which are typically sung in the church. If you walk into our class you feel like you are in a class for adults, not in a children's Sunday school class.

I think too many ministries for adults with intellectual disabilities convey the message through the activities that they do with those they are attempting to serve that these adults are children which is a great disservice to those to whom we claim to be ministering. Part of this problem is our knowledge focus in the Christian church. Sunday school is too often all about imparting knowledge, so if a person is intellectually disabled, then (it is thought) they need children's knowledge, delivered in a manner children would accept or be comfortable with. I would argue that knowledge should not be the primary focus of the Sunday school (even though it is called school) but it should rather be faith development. Faith development and knowledge development are two very different things. Is there knowledge associated with faith development? Of course there is. But I can become confused and end up just providing knowledge without worrying about faith development. Programs stigmatize adults with intellectual disabilities when they are exclusively knowledge based, partly because the accumulation or understanding of knowledge may be the weakest point for the person with intellectual disabilities.

However, faith development implies some knowledge, but also a lot of behavior. I can teach behaviors to persons with intellectual disabilities and it will likely result in faith development. For example, I can teach these people how to pray and then encourage them to pray daily, pray without ceasing, pray in faith. Will conversation with God via prayer increase their faith. I believe it will. I can teach them to fill their lives with uplifting media like Christian music or Christian video. Will that help them to grow in faith? I believe it will. I can also teach service and caring as a way of being like Jesus. In using these approaches, I am using the same approaches that those without disabilities should arguably use to grow their faith as well: doing something rather than just passively listening to something. As a result I am growing their faith in a manner that is not stigmatizing them by treating them as if they were children. I am also recognizing the fallacy of a overly intellectualized presentation of the faith that is too knowledge based for everyone in church, not just those with intellectual disabilities.

Friday, March 28, 2008

A lesson from *Pagan Christianity*

I've just finished reading a book that was recommended to me by a friend called *Pagan Christianity* (2008) by Viola and Barna. I have no doubt that it is considered a very controversial book, in fact it begins with the publishing company's statement that it doesn't necessarily represent their position on the issues it discusses. But in a nutshell, it takes many of the most foundational practices of the Christian church and traces their roots. Where did the practices come from and are they based on the Bible or were those practices adopted from the world.

I was intrigued by the book because I have long felt that there are many church practices, church structures which are an impediment to the full participation of persons with various disabilities. I personally cannot believe that a church based exclusively on Christian principles would be an exclusionary church, so I have wondered where many of our exclusionary practices have come from.

But after reading *Pagan Christianity,* it struck me that in disability ministry, we may be beginning to do or are actually doing exactly what Viola and Barna claim the church has done in the past. That is, build church structures (meaning church practices) that are based upon or mimic secular practices. For example, Sunday school looks surprisingly like regular school with just a different topic of study. The focus is just as knowledge based as the public schools are. You could further look at supposedly, "Christian schools" where people with disabilities are excluded and recognize that they may be Christian in some ways, but are also very far from Christian in other ways. In each of these examples, the Christian church has copied the way the world does things in both cases to our detriment.

But back to disability ministry. One of the first steps, it seems in disability ministry, is to do inclusion programs. Well, where did the idea of inclusive programs in schools come from? Clearly not from the Christian church. It was a development of the secular world as a way to integrate children with disabilities into the regular classroom. The secular world has found this has not entirely worked as a strategy because public school curriculum is so knowledge based. However, we in the Christian world, copy the knowledge focus of schools, then try to integrate children with disabilities into our knowledge based Sunday schools, and find we have difficulty in the process. The end result is that the children with disabilities are excluded, or at best just tolerated and treated as if we are doing them a favor by allowing them to participate.

But I would argue that the focus of Sunday school borrowed from the public schools is probably pretty much wrong, so the starting point takes us in the wrong direction. I have visited many classrooms where adults with severe intellectual disabilities sit while they are read a lesson from a teacher. Why do we do that? What do we think we are doing when we do that? If we want to engage people with intellectual disabilities, then let's think about how people with intellectual disabilities are engaged.

They have intellectual disabilities. They are not going to be engaged by sitting in a classroom and having dry knowledge dropped on them. They have intellectual disabilities. They are not going to make applications to their lives from content about Noah's ark or the 6 day creation of the

Earth. They have intellectual disabilities. If we were to copy the practices of the world, do you know what the most important skills are to be taught to adults with intellectual disabilities? They are social skills. NCLB has gotten us back into teaching content in the public schools to persons with intellectual disabilities, but by and large even the public schools have moved away from a knowledge based, content oriented approach to education for persons with intellectual disabilities. But we in the Christian church continue to copy programs that are basically irrelevant in their knowledge focus. Must I repeat again that the folks have intellectual disabilities. They are not going to get it. Then we borrow the inclusion practices of the public schools which again are probably not the best way to integrate someone (take for example people with intellectual disabilities...sure, let's integrate them at their point of greatest weakness) and we wonder at the problems we face.

As the Christian church, we can pretty much do **anything** in terms of faith development for our children. We can also pretty much also do **anything** in terms of working to include persons with disabilities in the structures of the church. So what do we do? We mimic the public schools. And as I have argued elsewhere in this blog, if our practices are exclusionary of persons with disabilities, then most likely our practices are wrong, perhaps not even Biblical in their roots.

So as we look to do faith development in children and in adults, we might consider developing models that go beyond the lazy copying of secular practices. Is the only difference between Sunday school and public school that I can pray in Sunday school? Are the goals just the same with only the content being different? Or could there be alternative methods leading to a qualitatively different outcome called faith development in our students, because we are working to develop something far different than just knowledge.

Is our goal for ministry to persons with disabilities no different than the goals of the public schools? Much of the data on the outcomes of inclusion in the public schools are not that great. People know each other's names and not too much past that. Is the goal for our teachers to be like the teachers in the public schools? Or would we prefer to see involvement in the lives of persons with disabilities as not just a job, but more of a lifestyle? Do not blindly look at the secular world, Christian, and just do what they are doing. Think Biblically. The secular world is doing some good things. But we have the potential to do greater, powerful, world changing, Spirit inspired things if we will seek God's guidance to do them.

Wednesday, March 19, 2008

Ministry to people with severe intellectual disabilities
What is the goal of a ministry to adults with severe intellectual disabilities?

I was having a discussion with someone the other day, and was talking about some of the pointless things that I have seen people do in the name of religious education of persons with severe disabilities. The person said to me, "Well those with severe disabilities in your class don't understand what you are talking about either." I was taken aback for a moment, because of course that was a true statement. I freely admit that persons with severe intellectual disabilities are not the primary target of any "lesson" I would teach, but that is also by my design. I am teaching lessons currently from the book of Psalms, and I freely admit that the severely intellectually disabled in our group probably don't understand 95% of what I am talking about. But their knowledge development, their understanding of a lesson is not something I am particularly worried about.

My primary focus for that group of people is that they can come to a place where they feel like they are a part, are a member of something. That they come to a place they call church where they are loved. A place where people are happy to see them. A place where they are given good food to eat, are largely served, and can go back for seconds. A place where they are listened to. A place where they don't need to sit quietly and just listen. A place where they can sing. A place where they can see friends. A place where they can make comments, whether or not they are relevant, and be congratulated for participation. A place where they are respected. A place where they are treated as peers rather than the object of ministry. A place where they are treated as adults. A place where they are valued.

That doesn't mean that we never work toward understanding of spiritual things with that group. But the gaining of knowledge is not much of a priority. We do work on teaching people how to pray through modeling, and some guided practice, but even then I am not sure they have any concept of what they are doing. They bring prayer requests and their requests are treated in the same manner as any person's requests, however, I am unsure of what they understand about prayer, for example.

So I guess I have come to understand ministry for this group of people quite differently. I think about the stage of faith they are evidencing. I think about how they enjoy being shown love, and how they demonstrate love for others and try to facilitate both. The focus of the ministry is not knowledge, or the understanding of principles in the same manner that it is for the typical Sunday school class or Bible study. A focus, by the way, that I perceive as being wrong as the predominant focus. We, however, in our knowledge fixation at church feel that that knowledge based religious education must find its way into the severely intellectually disabled Sunday school class. And I guess I simply do not agree.

With a mixed group like ours, we have highly educated individuals who attend (we literally have a brain surgeon) and people who are largely nonverbal and intellectually disabled. In other words, to some extent the full Body of Christ is represented. So we do do a lesson that will hopefully engage those who are able to understand it (which is the majority) while at the same time accepting those who may not understand the lesson as full members and full partners. Those individuals know, for example, that they can interrupt the lesson at any time and often do. In the same way that the lesson ministers to those who understand it as that is their intellectual level, the unconditional acceptance and ability to interrupt and receive interaction from the teacher at any time ministers to those with severe intellectual disabilities.

Tuesday, February 19, 2008

The reasons for ministry

I have been thinking lately about the reason for ministry to people, be they disabled or not, having any set of particular characteristics or not. Is the only goal of ministry only to tell people about Jesus in hopes that they will accept Him as savior? If so, then I feed people not because I would like to see starving people fed, I do it so they will become a Christian. I encourage people who are discouraged, not because I would like to see people not living in depression, I do it so they will become a Christian. I am loving to people not because I should be loving to people as a general rule, but because if I love them they will become a Christian. In other words, love and service and encouragement are not goods in themselves for me as a Christian, they are only good if they are linked to the "other shoe dropping" that is their becoming a Christian. That way of thinking about people bugs me. I think it probably also really bugs those who are not Christian working to love and help people who are in the world as well.

I just cannot agree with this perspective. If my kindness to another human being causes them to be open to my words about Jesus, that is great! However, I will show kindness nonetheless, and I will not remove my kindness if a person spends a lifetime of rejecting Jesus. So if I were to spend my life in a manner like Mother Theresa did, where I am working with the poorest of the poor, and perhaps saw only a handful of converts or perhaps none at all, was my life wasted? I would argue it wasn't because of the good I did in simply alleviating human suffering.

I am always responsible for what I do in any situation. I am hardly ever responsible for what someone else does. If, for example, you need medication for a terrible disease and I have it and I give it to you, that was a good in and of itself. I think in a Matthew 25 kind of way, God would celebrate that action I did. Should you also be open to Jesus through that action on my part, even better. I may use your willingness to listen to me as a result of giving you something that assists you in your life to share the truth with you. However, if you say that you don't believe in Jesus, I won't stop the medication as they are both goods (giving medication, accepting Jesus). They are not necessarily equally good goods, particularly for you (salvation is more important than healing) but they are both good. I think the problem comes when we don't see both as "good goods" and see the one, the helping as only a reason for the other. If that is the case, we become disingenuous in some ways. We are obviously interested in telling people about Jesus because we want the absolute best that life has to offer for them. But it can also make our helping appear encumbered to those who have not as yet accepted Jesus as savior. We can appear to have a hidden motive other than just wanting to see people's lives be bettered.

At the same time, I am clear as to why I love others. I will be quick to tell them that I love others because I want to be to them the way Jesus was and is to me. I love them not necessarily for what it does for them, I love them because of what it does for me. I want to love and care for other people because it helps me to grow as a loving person. It helps me as I am trying to model my life after Jesus' example. That is why I love. Should my life example be endearing to them, perhaps that example will cause them to want to know who this Jesus is so that they may follow my example to the degree that it reflects Jesus. But they will understand that I love them because I love them, just as Jesus loves me because he loves me. I will love them whether or not they reject Jesus. Jesus' love for me is not linked to anything endearing about me, anything special about me that people would point to saying, "You love him because he is ___."

The Bible is clear that Jesus died for us while we were still sinners. His example is to love us, in the hopes that we will want him. But while we are alive he will still love us independent of whether we love him.

Wednesday, February 20, 2008

Ministry to peers

Yesterday, I had the privilege of having a small cadre of people with expertise in disability and disability ministry in particular visit our Light and Power group at my church. They spoke with various people at the church who work with children, and then spent an hour and a half with our adult group. Afterwards we went to lunch and had a great discussion about many issues related to disability ministry for another 2 hours!

While we were at lunch, the leader of the visiting group made the comment, "Your ministry is different. You treat the people (disabled adults) as peers." The person could have hardly made a more positive comment about what we are doing, because that is one of the major goals of our adult ministry. We want to be the same as the women's ministry, the men's ministry or any other ministry in that we are in the ministry together and are all the same.

As I have said elsewhere in this blog, I may be the teacher of the group, and one of the more educated people in the group, but I am **definitely not**

the most loving person in our group,
the person with the greatest faith in the group,
the person with the most patience in the group,
the person who is most interested in spiritual growth in the group,
the person who is the most free in worship in the group, and so on
and so on.

And who are the people in my group? They are people with intellectual disabilities, persons with Down's syndrome, persons with intellectual disability.

I am confident that persons with intellectual disability are the most loving members of our group.

I am confident that persons with intellectual disability are those with the greatest faith in our group.

I am confident that persons with intellectual disability are the most patient in the group.

I am confident that persons with intellectual disability are the most free in worship in our group.

But because I am a person who is not experiencing an intellectual or other disability I and others like me might treat those who are experiencing disability as if they are not quite as good as me, not quite the same as me, not quite our peers. When we do that in the midst of ministry, it is particularly problematic. How would you, how do you feel about people in leadership over you who think that they are better than you? I don't find that a very endearing quality in people in any setting, let alone a ministry setting.

So to hear that comment from the person visiting our group was so encouraging to me. Thank God that that could be a characteristic that people would notice about our ministry.

Monday, February 18, 2008

Conversation with a man with glasses

"Hello"

"Hello"

"Can you see me alright?"

"Yes"

"You know I wasn't sure because you are wearing glasses."

"I know I wear glasses."

"Well because you wear glasses, I wasn't sure that you could see me but if you say you can, I guess you would know."

No comment

"You know it must be tough being a man who wears glasses, not being able to see and all if you don't have them. I don't know what I would do if I had to wear glasses."

"You would be fine."

"Well, I would hope so. But what happens if you don't wear your glasses, you probably can't see very well. That must be terrible. I am not sure I would want to live if I had to wear glasses."

"No, actually it's not that bad. You get used to it. Actually, I have spent most of my life wearing glasses so I don't really know what it would be like to see clearly without them."

"Well, God bless you for your courage. You are an example to me of succeeding in the face of terrible challenges."

"Sure there are some challenges, but you just live your life."

"Well there but for the grace of God go I, is what I always say.." hesitates, "Oh I didn't mean anything by that."

"No problem."

"I just never know what to say when I am around people who, you know, people who wear glasses."

"We are just people."

"Well, yeah, I guess so, but I just get uncomfortable. You know I have never had any training in how to work with people who wear glasses."

"Work with people who wear glasses?"

"Yeah, you know. Like glasses people education and all. But at my church we have a class for people who wear glasses!"

"That's great" disgustedly.

"Oh, I know! I understand that it is pretty innovative. But our church wants to make a place for everybody, even if they do wear glasses."

"Great."

"We feel like people with glasses should be treated like a regular member!"

"Like a regular member? You mean they aren't regular members, just like regular members?" (thx mh)

"Yeah, we believe God created all people to be loved and treated the same. That's why we have our special class for people who wear glasses."

"Why can't the people who wear glasses be in with everyone else? You are all pretty much working on the same kinds of things, believe in the same kinds of things, don't you?"

"Huh? What an interesting idea." Pauses. "Yeah, but if we did that, then we would have to make the text on the PowerPoint bigger, and would probably have to improve the lighting in the classroom, and what if a glasses person forgot his glasses? Then what do you do?"

"You could help him, support him."

"Yeah, but then the person helping him would not be able to pay attention to the lesson and would miss out on the teaching and all. It would also be distracting for the teacher. I think it is just too much to ask of a church group to sacrifice the teaching so that some glasses guy can be a part of the lesson if he is too irresponsible to remember to bring his glasses. No insult intended."

"But maybe if you made the type bigger, and the lights better, and people needed to help one another it would be better for everyone?"

Hesitates, then laughs. "You're kidding, right?"

Thursday, January 24, 2008

Leading worship for adults with intellectual disabilities

Eric Boyles is a friend of mine who helped me to see worship with adults with intellectual disabilities in a very different light. He is able to elicit participation in worship (or at least showed me that such participation is just below the surface with adults with intellectual disabilities). Eric would come to our Light and Power company group, and lead music/worship once per month. I remember one week, as he was beginning, just playing some chords and plucking strings on his guitar, he said something to the effect, "I feel like there are people who would like to give praise to God. If you would like to give praise to God, please do so." Very spontaneously, people across the group, representing all ability levels, would chime out. "I praise God for my family" "Thank you God for my job" "I praise God for Light and Power class" this went on for perhaps 10 minutes with Eric doing little more than asking the question, setting the occasion for the release of praise. I will admit that I had underestimated the folks in thinking that they would or perhaps could do such a thing.

At other times, Eric would elicit other forms of expression from the group, be it singing or suggesting a song, or prayer, or praise, or just being silent as he would lead. I learned a great deal about the level of participation one might facilitate with little more than praying and then setting the opportunity. Eric's appearance seemed to set the occasion for a deeper level of worship among those with disabilities. As he would express, he just tries to get out of the way and let God's spirit work.

He and I have also had interesting discussions about how persons with intellectual disabilities can set the example of freedom in worship. People with "social skill deficits" by definition, are largely unaware or unconcerned about how they appear to others. This is a real benefit when it comes to worship. If they want to raise their hands, or clap, or dance, or whatever, they feel the freedom to do so. Their presence opens things up a bit in terms of stretching the envelope. They are an example to the congregation.

Eric has also described to me how they are unimpressed with him as a worship leader. Perhaps a better way of stating that is that they are equally impressed with whoever is the leader. I am reminded of my grandmother, who when I told her that I received my Ph.D. said, "That's nice. I hope that makes you happy." She didn't demean me but she wasn't overly impressed. If people are not overly impressed with me as a leader, they once again facilitate my being able to get out of the way and allow God's spirit to shine through.

I asked Eric to write a song to go along with our current series of lessons on the book of Psalms, based upon the sit, stand, walk statement of Psalms 1.
See http://jeffmcnair.com/Biblelessons/Psalmslessons.htm

He wrote the wonderful song, "Sit, stand, walk." It is once again a perfect example of treating adults in a manner that is not juvenile. The song is simple, but at the same time profound. It is also a prayer which people can pray by learning to sing the words.

Monday, November 12, 2007

Leadership in ministry to people with intellectual disabilities

Who should be in leadership of Sunday School classes or groups for individuals with developmental disabilities? Typically it is people without disabilities although there may be a few leaders among those with disabilities in the group. Perhaps someone in your group with a intellectual disability immediately comes to mind. Perhaps we have people on the leadership team, some with specific roles. Others participate in leadership meetings because their input is valued, but one could ask why they are participants any more than anyone else. I think we need to be sure that leaders are in leadership positions. I am also confident that we could hurt feelings if someone was not invited to be involved in leadership because we felt they were not leaders. For example, there are those who would feel that they should be at any and every meeting and that their comments are essential to the functioning of the group. Others, might feel they are just missing out on a good time. But if the meetings are for purposes of discussing the future of the group, truly leadership meetings and not just social outings, there will be exclusion.

Because some of our group at my church have intellectual disabilities, and I am in a position of leadership in that group, I do not have a problem excluding them from the leadership meetings, as their disability on some level limits their contribution there. That is a judgment on their leadership skills, and their intellectual abilities which would imply that they are not gifted for participation in leadership, or teaching, for example (Ephesians 4:11). Obviously, I do not say there was no place for those people, only that their options could be limited by their disabilities and that would be a determination made by people with and without disabilities. I for one, have never been asked to sing before the church, or to have involvement in financial matters of the church. I have no problem with someone telling me that I am not gifted for those activities of the church because it is true, I am not. I also do not feel the need to have people with intellectual disabilities present in leadership meetings simply for reasons of political correctness. There are those with intellectual disabilities that I love dearly, and that I enjoy long conversations with, however, they will not be holding a position of leadership in our group. People with intellectual disabilities have very much to offer the church, but because of their intellectual or other disabilities, aspects of their service may be limited.

Another basic aspect of the disabled/nondisabled dynamic is that people with intellectual disabilities cannot help but look to people without intellectual disabilities for leadership. Every intellectually disabled member of the group at my church looks to a non-intellectually disabled person for leadership in areas such as finances, travel, work, relationships, spiritual issues, etc. I have no problem with that as well. That is our responsibility as those without intellectual disabilities toward our brothers and sisters in Christ who experience intellectual disabilities. It is, however, a fine line to try to walk.

In our group, we have in the past and will do a better job in the future, communicated that all of those without intellectual disabilities are in leadership, if only informally. We need to note that, support that and praise that. That aspect has been one of the greatest points of growth in

234

our group, for example, over the past year. I want people to be considered leaders in the class because of the positive impact their informal leadership has on members of the group. Others have a very quiet role in the group, but are leaders nonetheless through the way they come alongside of many people to talk and encourage them, love and support them. Those without disabilities are often totally invested in the group, and I think would do just about anything we could ask for the group. In that way they are an important part of the leadership. We, as those without intellectual disabilities, are responsible to help those who are intellectually disabled. Those without, or with less severe disabilities enjoy the group for themselves, but they also see it as a ministry role in a much different way than those with more severe disabilities typically see their involvement. I want to encourage the ministry view without disparaging the attendance view. I mean, I participate in groups where I am largely the recipient of ministry and that is fine. The key is that all should have the opportunity to be on both sides of the ministry equation (givers and recipients) although leadership in ministry might not be available to all.

Thursday, August 23, 2007

Social Role valorization and wounding

At the end of February, I had the opportunity to attend a training in social role valorization offered by Training Institute for Human Serve Planning, Leadership & Change Agentry in Syracuse NY. For those of you familiar with the work of Dr. Wolf Wolfensberger, his thinking was first published in *Normalization* in the early 1970's. The book was foundational to much of what has happened in changing the manner in which persons with disabilities are treated. In the early 1980's, Dr. Wolfensberger built on his normalization ideas and developed what he calls social role valorization. As a result of his work, there are many articles and books which have been written as well as an International conference held every four years. I would highly recommend the training.

Social role valorization begins by recognizing that people are devalued and wounded. In fact, the SRV training lists 18 wounds.

Wound 1: Bodily impairment
Wound 2: Functional impairment
Wound 3: Relegation to low social status/deviancy
Wound 4: Attitude of rejection-disproportionately/relentlessly the more rejecting party has higher values and is more likely to...
    1. Repress awareness out of consciousness "their faith tells them they shouldn't do it"

2. Harm is inflicted on the rejected party in unconscious, indirect and subtle forms

3. Negative behaviors are explained as having positive motives.

Wound 5: Cast into one or more historic deviancy roles...social status causes devalued roles or vice versa (we have touched on these roles in this weblog in the past)

So people can be considered...

1. Non human
    a. pre human
    b. no longer human
    c. sub human (animal, vegetative/vegetable, insensate object
    d. other "alien" non human but not sub human
2. A menace/object of dread
3. Waste material, garbage, discard, offal, excrement
4. Trivium
    a. not to be taken seriously
    b. object of ridicule
    c. jocular, jester, clown, etc.
5. An object of pity - accompanied by desire to bestow happiness on people and associated with the victim role. Person is "suffering"
6. A charity recipient
    a. ambiguous/borderline role of object of charity "nobility" in helping
    b. burden of dutiful caring "cold charity" entitled to only the minimum/should be grateful takers-not givers
7. A child
    a. eternally
    b. once again
8. As a sick/diseased organism (leads to handicap) "medicalization of everyday life", "psychiatrization of deviance"
9. In death-related roles: dying, already dead, as good as dead, should be dead, should never have lived

Wound 6: Symbolic stigmatizing, "marking", "deviancy imaging", "branding"

Wound 7: Being multiply jeopardized/scapegoated

Wound 8: Distanciation: usually via segregation and also congregation...major forms

Wound 9: Absence or loss of natural, freely given relationships & substitution with artificial/boughten ones

Wound 10: Loss of control, perhaps even autonomy & freedom

Wound 11: Discontinuity with the physical environment and objects "physical discontinuation"

Wound 12: social and relationship discontinuity & even abandonment
Reasons for relationship discontinuity
Wound 13: Deindividualization, "mortification" reducing humanness
Wound 14: Involuntary material poverty, material/financial exploitation
    1. stripping what you have
    2. preventing people from acquiring things
Wound 15: Impoverishment of experience especially that of the typical valued world
Wound 16: Exclusion from knowledge and participation in higher-order value systems (e.g. religion) that give meaning and direction to life and provide community
    1. lack moral guidance
    2. solace and comfort
    3. participation in community therefore reduced participation in society
Wound 17: Having one's life "wasted"...mindsets contributing to life wasting
Wound 18: Being the object of brutalization, killing thoughts & deathmaking

It was particularly interesting to see how these wounds tend to accumulate in the life of a person who simply has a bodily or functional impairment of some type. But the SRV folks would say that anyone who is devalued will experience these wounds to a greater or lesser degree whether your devaluing is due to impairment, or race or ethnicity, or religion or whatever.

The church needs to take the role of first of all recognizing the wounds of devalued people and then doing what it can to address the wounds in some way. I found it interesting that wound 16 is "Exclusion from knowledge and participation in higher-order value systems (e.g. religion) that give meaning and direction to life and provide community." That is, Wolfensberger has identified the exclusion from religion or religious groups as a wound that is inflicted on persons who are devalued. The training is very careful to present the material in a very empirical fashion. That is, they do their best to just present the facts. They simply say, "If you do this, this will be the result." So if you exclude people with disabilities from participation in religious activities, in the church, you wound them.

It was also noted in the training that people who are already wounded will often feel wounds, be they slight, more than those of us who are not devalued. I have noticed this fact with friends of mine whom I just suspected were very sensitive people. Yes they were sensitive, but I am coming to believe their sensitivity is due to their pain from being the brunt of so many of the wounds described above.

The church can do much to attenuate the wounding of persons who are devalued, particularly persons with disabilities, particularly by just preventing wound #16. Just as there is a kind of a cascade effect with many of the wounds, there might be a positive cascade effect as we attempt to alleviate the wounds. Facilitating church participation might be a significant start in healing persons with impairments, and lead to a diminishing or removal of the many wounds.

Wednesday, March 21, 2007

Spiritual Development

Picking up on the Nouwen related story of the 3 Russian monks, I was thinking about what "spiritual development" might mean and how it is achieved. I have known people with graduate degrees in divinity, who were spiritually lost. Their lifestyles were devoid of anything that would represent a Christian faith, or even a Christian world view. People who could quote passage and verse, or could share the thinking of Bonhoeffer, or explain Niebuhr's *Christ and Culture*, but lacked a basic faith.

I have also known people who could barely write their own names, perhaps have memorized a couple of Bible passages, but were an example of a profound faith in God that impacted every area of their lives. Their conversation revolved around God and church and faith. Their questions were largely about how they could grow in faith, or as one friend often asks, "Do you think I am doing better than I used to do?"

As I think about the kind of Christians I want to help develop, I would have to choose the latter. But I wonder sometimes about the kind of Christians our church structures are currently developing. I have said this before, but I am even more convinced that if we want to learn about love, we should learn by doing more than talking about love, or memorizing passages about love. We will produce a certain type of Christian when our knowledge is not developed in a more hands on type of a situation. Everything is one step removed from reality with the assumption being that if I read 1 Corinthians 13, I will be able to make the connection on my own. That I will generalize my learning, to use a special education term. But we have learned in special education that in order for some learning to take place, it must occur in the actual situation. That is, if you want to teach me to exchange money in a store, you need to take me to the store, or I won't learn. I cannot learn some things under simulated conditions...I need to be in the actual situation.

So I guess what I am advocating is a kind of a spiritual curriculum. A curriculum that is not knowledge based as in a public school classroom (what much of religious education looks like) but a different kind of approach. One that is more practical, more applied that teaches me in the actual situation so I don't need to generalize my learning. I am learning directly and will therefore be able to make the direct application.

Take love for example. What does a situation look like where people have to really make an effort to love others? What occurs in such a situation that changes people? What if I was taught about how to love people with challenging people in the room, in my midst? I will then either learn to love those people, or I will exit the difficult to love person or exit myself. Largely, in the past it has been the difficult to love person who has been asked to leave, and I have not learned the lesson about love. It is also useful to consider situations where we are not confronted with people who have been characterized as "difficult to love" and think about what people are learning in situations where "difficult to love" people are excluded from places where people are being taught about love?

People who act atypically, for whatever the reason (disability, sin, whatever) teach me about love. I think about the students I taught who were emotionally disturbed. In their ranting and swearing at me, I came to understand that their ranting and swearing were their disability talking. I wasn't always perfect, but I was softened by them, and learned to love them. Their ranting and swearing were less threatening to me because I came to understand them and love them in spite of their emotional disturbance. I was changed, I learned to love. I am now drawn to such people. I am still rejected at times, and I still am impatient, but I was forced to learn to love them, and I was the beneficiary of the lesson (I hope they were to some extent as well). The end result is that I was softened. I learned another aspect of the love of Christ. I could have studied love all day long, but the real learning came to me when I was confronted with people who caused me to put my head knowledge, and the faith I claimed to have into practice.

People with various disabilities will do that. I don't say that because I find them particularly difficult to love, but they will act atypically, they will take me out of my comfort zone, and as a result, I will grow. I want that growth for everyone in the church. For such growth to occur, there needs to be a change in the way that we do church, the way that we do Sunday School, the way that we do Bible study, the way that we do missions, the way that we do most things in the church. Instead of learning about how to love people, love people who others have not loved. In order to help the poor, don't have speakers come to tell you about the poor, have poor people come to your church and be in your Bible study. They may know a great deal more about faith and how it is acted out in daily life than you do with your 60K per year income. We may know the head knowledge, but they just might know the faith knowledge.

Tuesday, February 06, 2007

"Why should ministry to people with disabilities be a priority?"

I was very discouraged this past week. I had the opportunity to meet with a local Christian leader in the church about issues related to the church and disability. I wasn't talking about just one local church, we were talking larger. The leader made the comment in all seriousness, "Why should ministry to people with disabilities be a priority?" It wasn't a question asking for an answer, it was more a statement of this church leader's position on disability itself. People with disability were not a priority to this person, and her/his question basically was why should it be a priority for anybody? I would have answered, but the situation was such that any response I might have made would only have caused a digging in of the heals. Maybe that is partly why I felt depressed. The unrepresentativeness of my Lord and her/his Lord, Jesus Christ, and my remaining silent in the face of the comment.

I can tell you, that for me to remain silent in such situations is very unlike me, but for some reason I felt I should. I will probably have the opportunity to meet with this leader in the future, and perhaps I will have the opportunity to "bring her/him around" but it was almost breathtaking the ability of this person to simply dismiss people with just a statement. I could have countered by talking about the millions of people just in the United States, let alone the perhaps hundreds of millions in the world.

But that is where we are in the church right now. On a positive note, I think we are on the crest of a wave that is about to break over the church, and Lord willing through the Church, over the world as well.

But when people who are Christians make statements such as that,

I wonder about their faith,
I wonder about their compassion,
I wonder about their love,
I wonder about their trustworthiness,
I wonder about their knowledge of their Lord.

I am tempted to condemn them, but I just wonder. It's like they have given me a glimpse into their sin life, like I was a priest receiving confession, only they don't see their confession as sin. They see their statement like that of a racist sharing a racist joke with another racist. But there is such an assumption that I would obviously agree with their statement. "Of course, all Christians don't see people with disabilities as a priority for ministry." It's like that statement is irrefutable.

Well although I couldn't speak up in that situation (trust me it was very complicated), I will try to do better in the future. I am on a personal mission to refute the statements which have been used in the past, and apparently continue to be used to excuse church leaders from having a heart for people with disabilities.

So if someone says,

"Ministry to people with disabilities costs too much" I respond boldly, "How much does it cost? Do you even know or are you just making excuses?"

"Ministry to people requires a lot of training" I respond boldly, "What training is required to take a person with a disability out for coffee? Do you know anyone with a disability?"

"Ministry to people with disabilities is not a priority?" I respond (or will do better in responding in the future) "Maybe it's not to you, but it is to the person you call your Lord...Perhaps you should get to know your Lord a bit better before you make statements that reflect on how he prioritizes people."

Making priorities on some level shows weakness, as I cannot do all things at once. If God does prioritize people, He is a weak God who cannot do for us all, love us all, minister to us all all at once. We need to wait our turn. The God I serve is not a God of priorities. He is all powerful, all knowing all everything. I don't need to wait in line for him to discover me and then make me a priority. He created me the way I am. I wish those in leadership of Christian churches would get a better handle on that. Get a better handle on who the God they claim to serve is.

Tuesday, January 30, 2007

Second class ministers

Those of you who read this blog, know that I have at times spoken of the need for a movement of lay professionals to change the church. That is, professionals in special education, rehabilitation, social workers and others to step up and call for the development of disability ministry in their own local church.

Recently Kathi and I were doing an in-service for a local Christian school about why Christian schools should want special education generally and specifically how to do curricular modifications at the Christian school to allow students with various needs to be successful in the general education program. In the process of delivering the in-service, I got talking about the priorities that churches place, that pastors and leaders place on ministry to persons with disabilities.

It occurred to me that one of the reasons that professionals in areas of disability have not stepped up is that over the years is they have been made to feel that their work, particularly as it relates to the church is not very important. People will often say how wonderful it is to work with persons with disabilities, talking about how much patience it takes, however, they don't make the connection to applying those skills to the Christian church. I think that because there is little mention and little priority on ministry in the church, professionals may feel like second class ministers if they are involved in such ministries.

Churches see ministry to children or high schoolers or developing small groups for adults as very important. Disability ministry is less important in their eyes. So my desire to do such ministry is less important. I would be willing to bet money that at least one professional in disability attends every church in the United States. However, there is not at least one disability ministry in every church in the United States. Why might that be?

It could be that there is a disconnect in the minds of disability professionals between their work and potential ministry. I am sure that is often the case. However, I am equally as sure that pastors are not calling those professionals to use their gifts and their training in such ministry. There are people out there like me who arriving at a church with a Ph.D. and years of experience in disability ministry were told, "Its not a priority at this time." That is one way of telling someone that your ministry desires are second class. Another way is to have a highly trained person in your midst and see her expertise as irrelevant to the work of the church. it's like, "Its nice that you paint pictures" or "Its nice that you play basketball" or "Its nice that you have a BA, MA, PhD, or whatever in working with people who have been ignored by the church for hundreds of years." it's nice but it is irrelevant, in their minds.

That is why when Kathi and I were told that disability ministry was not a priority, I turned to her as we left the pastor's office and said, "It soon will be." We began to bring people with disabilities to church, sought them out in the community, and the ministry has become more of a priority. I think people think it is nice, but often don't know what to do with us. I wonder what would happen to the ministry at our church if we suddenly disappeared from the scene. It is getting better as regular members begin to open themselves to those with disabilities and begin to like the changes those people make in them. They find out the big secret that we in disability ministry already know...**Its fun** and people with intellectual disabilities (our particular focus) are really great people.

So you lay professionals out there, don't allow your church or its leadership to make you think that disability ministry and disability ministers (potentially you!) are second class ministries or second class

242

ministers. If we believe that all people are of equal value in the sight of God, our churches should reflect that fact. Our ministry priorities should reflect that fact.

And to you pastors who might be reading this, you need to confront disability professionals with their responsibilities in the church. You need to bring people with disability into the Church and support the efforts of those who do the same. Did Christ see people with disability? Very often these people are also poor. Did Christ have any interest in the poor? We read the stories of the extent to which Jesus went to minister without considering the context or the effort on his part to get with these people. Jesus' interactions with persons with disabilities are breath-taking, and they were intentional on his part. We trivialize these interactions when we use them simply as illustrations of spiritual principles. These were real people confronted by a real God, and these confrontations with real people by a real God are ubiquitous in the New Testament. So don't miss the priority Christ gives to these people as an example for you as a church leader in terms of the priority you should give to these same individuals who are living in your midst today.

If you say that people with disabilities are not a priority, you devalue people, you indict yourself and you diminish the service of those who do work with the disenfranchised and people experiencing disability.

Friday, December 15, 2006

Mental Illness in the Church

Here is the slightly edited text of an email I sent to some folks who are attempting to integrate a person with mental illness into their church group. I provide it as several of the ideas might be worth chewing on.

You guys have sure been giving your best in trying to integrate --- into the group activities. I really appreciate your efforts on her behalf.

In the midst of the difficulties, I hope you are debriefing with the rest of the group so that they can understand your heart in this matter and why you and the others have gone to the extent you have to try to make integration work. Perhaps the group may themselves come up with something that would work to include her to some degree. Ultimately, I think we must have a place for people like --- in the *church*. As people evidence more disturbed behavior, however, those places will become more circumscribed.

Should you decide to offer her a more circumscribed place, please try to come up with a place where she can regularly be with her age peers.

243

Perhaps she will not participate in all activities, however, I would recommend that there should be some place where she might be able to participate. Communicate to the group that a major part of the goal of that group might then be to act kindly toward her and people like her, attempt to overlook her negative or disturbed behavior and love her. It will not be easy, but it would be a stretching activity for those who would attend that particular meeting. I suspect the leadership themselves might feel less stressed about the situation as they are not attempting to offer the typical meeting or Bible study. They are offering a setting where Christian people are trying to reach out to a person who atypical, difficult to be with and possibly mentally ill. Because the rules for that sort of a meeting change, those involved in the meeting will also change their expectations. We will gauge our successes or failures differently. We will be looking at how a particular group member grows in her ability to interact or accept a person who is difficult. We will look at how people are becoming tougher in their ability to show love to difficult people. It would be understood that we are here in large part, to include a person who is difficult to be with and who will evidence difficult behaviors. It is a ministry. I taught kids with serious emotional disturbance for a while, and I know myself that if I am prepared to go into a situation with a person with emotional disturbance, for example, I am much more able tolerate various behaviors as I recognize that it is the disability that is being evidenced. I recognize that in this situation, I am doing my best to love this person in spite of his difficulties. Obviously not everyone would choose to participate in this particular activity/class/or whatever. However, you might find many who would be willing to step up.

I recognize your significant efforts to integrate --- and truly do appreciate them.

I honestly do believe there is a place in the church, or at least should be, for everyone who would want to attend, even if they are mentally or emotionally disturbed. To create those places, however, causes me to see my involvement in the church differently. So I don't always go to a Bible study group just to study the Bible myself, I sometimes go to be a part of a place where people with mental illness can go. I help to create a space where a person evidencing difficult behaviors can come and study the Bible. I recognize that I am in ministry by creating that space. I may not be leading the study, or even participating to a great degree, however, my being present, being accepting, not being so fragile or brittle, I am in ministry because I have created a place of acceptance for people who are largely deemed unacceptable. I fight the urge to just kick the difficult person out, out of obedience to God. God wants to love the difficult

244

person WHETHER OR NOT THEY GET BETTER and he wants to do it through his church, through me. It causes me to see my involvement in church differently. As Rick Warren says, "Its not about you." It truly is not about me as the focus. It is about me as the servant.

Tuesday, December 12, 2006

Value added

I had a discussion this morning with several friends who also are persons in leadership within a local church. They described difficulties they were having regarding their efforts at integration of a person who is mentally ill into the youth group. In the course of the discussion, they related how the person monopolized the discussion, implying I guess that content wasn't able to be covered and that others did not have the opportunity to participate as well. There were other issues relating to the hostility of the person when offered help and the frustration among other members of the group my friends were trying to serve. Their concerns were all legitimate concerns.

However, when I had the opportunity to chime in, I spoke of how in my experience, persons with disabilities change those around them, and changes them often for the better. In Jean Vanier's *Becoming Human* (2008) he states,

"That is why it is dangerous to enter into a relationship with the Lazeruses of our world. If we do, we risk our lives being changed" (p. 71).

Persons with challenging disabilities surely do change those who aren't currently experiencing disability. Take this youth group for example. At the moment the person has changed the group by causing much concern on the part of the leadership. The person has caused the leadership to look at the person and make the determination of whether the person is worth their efforts or not. It has caused the members of the group to wonder whether they want to continue to be a part of the group. The person has caused the leadership to make a judgment of whether the content or the person is more important. The person has caused the leadership to wonder how far they are willing to go. All this just because of the person's presence there.

But I think a significant part of the problem that people have in these types of situations is that they see the person who doesn't fit in easily as a detriment rather than as a potential value added. As a man of 50, I can tell you that I remember very little of the content of the Bible studies I have participated in (even those I've led!) but I remember a few of the people in the groups. The leadership is very hung up on the content of the Bible study/youth group, but I will guarantee you that what the members of that

245

group will remember for the rest of their lives is the person with mental illness in their group. Potentially they will also remember how a group of people in leadership treated that person, made that person feel like a part of the group rather than as a crazy person who needed to be tolerated. Perhaps they will learn how to interact with such people in the future because of the experiences they gained while in the youth group.

Perhaps the leadership might see the presence of this person as an opportunity to grow themselves and change the group members. **You see, this perspective sees people who present challenges to the status quo as a value added rather than a detriment.** I have the opportunity through the enfolding of an atypical person to promote real changes in the lives of those who want youth group to be only what they want it to be. I have the opportunity to challenge others with the trials and blessings of ministry. I have the opportunity to help others to understand service. These are the value added in addition to the obvious benefit of loving and supporting a person who is disenfranchised from all of the culture including the Christian subculture.

As is typical, however, rather than taking the opportunity to really change lives for a lifetime in a way that people will remember for a life time, I choose to lead a Bible study or youth group in the manner in which it has always been led. Oh we will have video games and lights and great music and great teaching. But instead of really demonstrating and thereby teaching others the benefits of truly loving others, those who are difficult to love, who won't get better and who will always be social skill deficient, who will always be mentally ill, I choose to make sure I get through Biblical passages about love and caring and acceptance.

One of my friends said that whenever someone tries to help the person with mental illness in the group, the person grabs a hold of him or her like a "freaking vise" (my translation). Well, duh? If I have been rejected because I am difficult to understand and someone finally shows me a little compassion, how would you think I would respond?

Please don't get me wrong. I am NOT saying that ministry to people with mental illness is in any way easy, because probably most often it is not. What I am saying is that the church must not reject those people, particularly when their behaviors are not dangerous, just annoying. I, we must model acceptance and see people who challenge us as those who most likely have been rejected by everyone (including us), those who need to be loved, and those who have much to offer to us, if only opportunities for growth.

Tuesday, October 31, 2006

The ALL principle

It is funny how our human vanity impacts our theology. I look in the mirror and have little difficulty understanding that I (in my vanity) am "fearfully and wonderfully made" (Psalm 139:14). Or I look in the same mirror and with little difficulty affirm that I (in my vanity) am created in the "image of God" (Genesis 1:27). Or I look in the mirror, and think about the delight that God must have experienced when he, "knit me together in my mother's womb" (Psalm 139:13). I mean, c'mon, look at me, isn't it obvious?

But then I look at someone born with a severe physical or intellectual disability and all of a sudden I am unsure about the whole fearfully and wonderfully made stuff, which never occurred to me when I was looking at myself. I wonder about the knitting together as clearly God would not knit like that (thinking about people born with disabilities). I may think like that, but God has something to say to me as well. "Don't think more highly of yourself than you ought to think" (Rom. 12:3).

I wonder about the impact of vanity on theology, in terms of 1)thinking I am a day at the beach and 2)in thinking that people with disabilities are a NOT a day at the beach. There are so many scriptural principles which include the word "all" but I have missed what I call the "ALL PRINCIPLE" as I am typically focused on persons without disabilities, people like me.

> Scripture doesn't say, using the examples above,
> "some of us are fearfully and wonderfully made"
> "some of us are created in the image of God"
> "some of us God knit together in our mother's womb"
>
> Scripture also doesn't say,
> "some of us have sinned and fallen short of the Glory of God"
> "some of us are loved by God"
> "we are to love some of the people around us"

All the teachings, all the promises, all of the scriptures, the reasons for Jesus' sacrifice, the whole thing is for all of us. Actually, it is for all of us or it is for none of us.

I honestly think that the church does not believe in the ALL PRINCIPLE. It takes most of what is in me to believe in the ALL PRINCIPLE. I have been socialized by society and by the Christian church to believe otherwise. It takes courage, because disability has been constructed by society and the Church to be something other than it is. I recognize that I am stepping out in faith when I believe in the ALL

PRINCIPLE. I will meet with opposition whenever and wherever I stand up for the ALL PRINCIPLE.

It is crazy but it is true.

Saturday, October 07, 2006

The gift of time

As I mentioned, I just got back from a wonderful conference at the University of Aberdeen in Scotland, hosted by Dr. John Swinton, which featured Dr. Jean Vanier and Dr. Stanley Hauerwas.

One of the ideas which came through at the conference was the notion of being a "friend of time" or giving "the gift of time" to persons with intellectual disabilities in particular, but to persons with disabilities in general. I believe it was Vanier who spoke about how those who are well connected in society have little time while those who are not well connected have a great deal of time available to them. The question is how to bring these two groups together. One way is for the well connected to slow down. To become a friend of time rather than a slave to time. It requires serious life changes on their part to make this happen.

Coincidentally, as Kathi and I were hurrying from flight to flight on the way home, at one point I exited the plane behind a man who appeared to either have hemiplegia or who had had a stroke. His slow movement caused the line to slow down quite a bit. It struck me even in that situation, that I needed only to slow down a bit to his walking pace to still get where I wanted to go. I was literally physically slowed down, and for a moment experienced "exiting from an airplane" from his perspective in terms of the time it took.

The conference conversation also talked about taking the time to just have fun together with others. Vanier spoke of how most of the time he spends with his friends with intellectual disabilities is spent "fooling around" with them. I was encouraged by this from such a respected man as that is how I spend much of the time when I am with my friends with intellectual disabilities. He said there is also lots of celebrating of little things in life, taking time to celebrate those things.

For about 5 months of this year, I was spending one evening a week (for about an hour or so) at a group home on my way home from work. We would talk, eat some ice cream, have a catch with a baseball, or they would encourage me as I try to learn to play the guitar. They are always there, ostensibly waiting for me as I hurry from place to place. Being with them was a chance for me to slow down and try to be a friend of time with them. I the connected one, being with those who are less or not connected.

Luke 12:48 says, "every one to whom much is given, of him much will be required..." Much will be required of the well placed in society, not the least of which is their time. I am well placed, but even the well placed know that they have time if they make it. Please don't tell me you are too busy, because I am too busy too. But I have the ability, partly because I am well placed, to become a friend of time, and give of my time to those who would enjoy my company. It is a choice I have to make. It begins with me being realistic with myself, and calling myself into account for the choices I make.

Wednesday, September 20, 2006

Its about relationships

Kathi and I had a great time yesterday. We had lunch with one of the pastors and his wife from our church, and our PAID ministry support person and her husband. It was great time. The pastor, Kurt, asked me where I would like to see our church in 15 years. As I thought through that question, and listened to the discussion that ensued, I was once again impressed with the fact that what are needed are not programs but relationships. It is not about building programs that include people, it is breaking down the barriers that exclude people from existing programs. Ben (the husband of our ministry support person, Rachel) talked about how he wished that people with disabilities were just known by others in the church, to the point that needs would be met on a simple interpersonal level.

We all talked about the distancing that can come from programmatic approaches to helping persons with disabilities. That whole question is something that I have thought about a great deal and I have come to the conclusion that we need both. We need to be people who introduce those with disabilities to those who haven't experienced them yet in order to break down the "otherness" feeling that many nondisabled persons have about those who are experiencing disability. That is all about relationships and experience and personal interactions. Those types of engagement will lead to experiential knowledge which will break down many of the barriers which have been constructed. Why do I not feel uncomfortable with people who act atypically? Probably more than any other reason is because I have been around many people over my lifetime who have been atypical actors. I have know people whose behaviors range from those with very minor social skill deficits where you just notice a very subtle difference, to those who smear feces or publicly masturbate, or violently punch themselves in the face. Through experience, I have learned to redirect them, or try to give them alternatives to their current behavior when asked to do so. But largely, I have learned to accept them. Sure, I get mad at people and enjoy the company of some over others. But the opportunities I have been provided through my experience have allowed me to see the person behind the atypical behaviors. By seeing the person, the otherness starts to fade. But these changes that have been wrought in my perspective came over time through personal interactions.

There is still a place for programs that focus on inclusiveness of persons with say, intellectual disabilities. Places where they can have the scriptures explained to them in a clear but not demeaning manner. Where they are treated as adults, but given information at a slower pace. But I think I would even sacrifice those types of settings (as useful as they are in building spiritual knowledge and understanding in persons with intellectual challenges) for simple ongoing interactions with other people. Many of the lessons we teach in our Light and Power class, for example, could be facilitated by friends explaining the sermon to friends. Additionally, as people experience more severe forms of intellectual disability, their church involvement does not revolve around some sort of spiritual formation. It relates to them coming to a place where they are loved and accepted. Where they feel a part of something while they have a donut and coffee.

So I think where I would like to see my church in say 15 years, is a place where there are many relationships between people independent of their differences. Where differences perhaps cause you to do a little planning (assisting a person who uses a wheelchair, for example) but doesn't in any way stifle relationships. Yes, there are structural changes which need to occur in the church, but rather than just prescribe structural changes from the outside, people will desire to see changes when they see their friend Sally excluded from opportunities for service or whatever within the church. Their righteous indignation would fuel the desire open things up. But as Kurt (the pastor at our lunch) said, it has to get into the DNA of the church. DNA is very difficult to change.

Monday, July 24, 2006

Inclusion vs. nonexclusion

I had the pleasure of having lunch with a friend of mine, Arthur Seale. In the midst of our discussion, Arthur made the comment something to the effect that rather than working on inclusion, we should be working on preventing exclusion. He and I then went off on a variety of ideas about how in a variety of places (the church in particular in our discussion) develops places of inclusion instead of preventing exclusion. So for example, we say, "Disabled person, you can participate by being involved in this program created for you, or you can participate in this

250

program where the people will not exclude you." Such statements are a far cry from inviting someone to full participation in the church. Imagine if you were joining a church and the places in which you might participate were described in such a circumscribed manner.

"You can be a member of this group because it was designed for people with your personal characteristics. This is the place for disabled people. However, you cannot be involved in this other group because the people either
1) will not accept you because of their prejudiced notion of who you are,
2) are not willing to alter the way they do things, their structures, in order to accept you,
3) are not willing to do anything extra to facilitate your participation,
4) are uncomfortable with your personal hygiene, your appearance, your manner of dress, etc."

Now obviously we wouldn't expect men to be members of the women's group or vice versa. Nor would we expect children to attend the high school group.

Our efforts should be at carefully looking at the structures of our church and removing those things which would exclude people who should be a part of whatever group they would typically be a part of. So I would expect all of the men with intellectual disabilities to be a part of the church's men's group. There is no reason for them not to be involved. And if we truly do believe that we are all equal in God's sight, we should be making the same efforts to involve them that we would for men who are not experiencing disability. It is not like they are damaged goods or something, so we should not treat them as if they are...and we do treat them like they are.

I was reading the John account of the last supper. In the midst of arguing over who was the greatest (something that I have never heard adults with intellectual disabilities do, but have heard from state university professors), Jesus strips to his underwear and washes his disciples' feet. Upon finishing, he says that if your Master would do that for you, what should you do for each other? That is the interesting thing about true service, it is fully inclusive and not at all exclusive. I don't need to set up a separate room for washing the feet of the disabled people because their presence bothers those currently not experiencing disability. If we are all trying to be modeling the behavior of our master, we would be vigilant to look for ways in which those who might be served are getting access to being served, and/or serving them ourselves. The last thing we would do would be to construct obstacles to people finding their way to the Lord, and our having the opportunity to serve. **I think we**

have gotten to the point that we think service is about being served, not about serving. If the church truly believed in service, there would be more people needing service there. The presence of persons with disabilities would be one great evidence that that particular church was one that fought exclusion and worked at serving.

Sunday, May 21, 2006

"Points of insubordination"

I have been reading some Michel Foucault (which may worry some of you). Actually, I am reading the writings of others who are translating Foucault for me, and I am not just talking about the French. One of the most interesting ideas shared is that of "bio-power." I quote an article from Tremain's book, *Foucault and the government of disability* where Martin Sullivan quotes Foucault,

In short, rehabilitative medicine fits Foucault's description of subjecting power insofar as rehabilitation is "a form of power...which categorizes the individual...attaches him to his own identity, imposes a law of truth on him which he must recognize and which others must recognize in him. It is a form of power which makes individuals subjects" (1982, 212).

Later in that same article, Sullivan mentions Foucault's idea of rebelling against subjecting power through acts which are called "points of insubordination...which are a means of escape." by virtue of their birth, individuals with various congenital disabilities fall under subjecting power which identifies them, ascribes an identity to them, imposes a "law of truth" on them which he and those around him must submit to. The problem with most of the evidences, the "behaviors, objects and language" (Berger & Luckman, *The Social Construction of Reality*, 1966) of this subjecting power is that unfortunately, they are untrue. The only way to break out is through points of insubordination, by not going along with the program. The people with disability, particularly intellectual disability, haven't the ability to recognize their subjugation, and wouldn't know what to do if they did.

Burton Blatt wrote an interesting book many years back called "Revolt of the idiots" about a group of residents of an institution who revolted against those in charge of the institution. It was of course pure fiction but it resonated with me. In terms of changing things in their lives, persons with intellectual disabilities are rarely going to be able to be their own advocates. I recognize there are many excellent self-advocates in the disability movement, but such advocates are rare.

It is we who are not intellectually disabled who are the ones who must recognize the subjecting power being applied inappropriately to persons with disability and we who must engage in "acts of insubordination" on their behalf. Let me give you two examples of what I mean.

One happened many years ago. I approached a pastor at my church and told him that I wanted to begin a ministry to adults with disabilities. His response was that it is not a priority. In some ways, he was using subjecting power on both me (in my desire to do ministry) and persons with disability in categorizing them as not a priority. My response to this subjecting power was to engage in a point of insubordination. As Kathi and I left the meeting, I remarked to her, "It will become a priority when I start bringing adults with disabilities down here." Kathi didn't punch the pastor in the nose, but our attitude and ultimately behavior was insubordinate. I don't vilify that pastor anywhere, in fact he is a friend of mine, but I was not going to go along with the subjecting power that was wielded.

Then recently, I had the opportunity to speak in a chapel at a local Christian school. The focus of the week was on calling, so I was to tell them how I came upon the calling I believe I have. I briefly shared how I felt God had led me to the calling of including persons with disabilities in the Church and its agents. I then went off on how a person with disability could never attend that school. That although that school sets itself up as one which represents Jesus Christ to that community, in reality it doesn't because of its exclusion of persons with disability. Once again, an example of insubordination. I didn't burn the school down, I just wasn't totally obedient.

I believe we need to engage in these types of behaviors on occasion in order to get people's attention. As Christians, we can sometimes be so nice that no change will come. I would encourage you to be insubordinate if it opens your church to persons with disabilities. However, remember that as with the message of Christ, the message might be offensive but we are not to be. I confront, but not to ridicule or embarrass. My attitude has to be one that calls the Church to obedience.

Friday, March 31, 2006

A "replacement narrative"

Arthur Seale and I have been in discussion about the notion of a replacement narrative. That is, a story, a narrative to replace the one which guides people socially in their day to day lives. For the Christian, the replacement narrative is what she/he learns from the Bible. The teachings of the Bible are prescriptive social constructions which in many ways replace the social constructions we were raised to believe by our society. For example, we might have been taught as a child that if someone hits you you hit him back. The biblical replacement narrative would perhaps say you should turn the other cheek.

This notion of a replacement narrative really came home to me this past weekend as our pastor discussed Romans 12. The passage says,

"Do not conform any longer to the pattern of this world, but be transformed by the renewing of your mind" (Romans 12:2).

I wondered about this in terms of the narrative the church is currently working under relative to persons with disabilities. I hate to say it, but in many ways, the society reflects more of a biblical construction of disability than the church does. However, generally we do have a lot to offer the world, and we must not conform to the patterns of this world but renew our minds.

To what extent does the church reflect or contribute to negative social constructions of persons with disabilities, and, I would argue move away from a truly biblical narrative about who people with disabilities are and Christians and the Christian church's responsibility towards them? I even wonder at times whether the church knows what the biblical replacement narrative about disability is.

Anyway, that is what Arthur and I are chewing on.

Monday, February 06, 2006

Nicholas Wolterstorff on Matthew 25

Dr. Nicholas Wolterstorff provided the Alan Keith Lucas lecture at the recent NACSW (North American Association of Christians in Social Work). He spent a significant amount of the lecture discussing the Matthew 25 scripture regarding judgment: the separation of the sheep and the goats. He made the point that the translations which have predominated over the years may be in error in translating the word **dikaios** as "the righteous" rather than as "the just" or "the just ones". No doubt this distinction will be dealt with in depth in the book on justice which he has sent off for publication. However, it is an interesting distinction. So to fail to do justice to the "least of these" is to fail to do justice to Jesus himself.

One of the primary points I think he made was that justice implies the worth in another. I strive to facilitate justice for another for reasons unrelated to myself (my righteousness) and more related to the desire for all people to live under just conditions. I go beyond just aiding victims to attacking victimizers.

He also made the comment that in the Beatitudes, that the translation should not be "Blessed are those who are persecuted for the sake of righteousness" but rather "Blessed are those who are persecuted for the sake of justice" or doing justice. He commented that those who are righteous aren't typically persecuted for doing righteous things. Rather those who do justice or are constantly advocating for justice can be quite annoying i.e. the recipients of persecution.

He also talked about how the Bible uses the word "downtrodden," the implication being that they are being actively trodden down.

In summary, he said, attentiveness to justice means attentiveness to the worth of another. This is a fascinating take on a section of scripture often used in relation to persons with disabilities or intellectual disability. The least of these deserve justice because of their worth. Their worth comes from their humanity, not their intellectual or other ability levels. Disability does not decrease worth and therefore does not diminish one's right to justice.

Saturday, November 05, 2005

Church's protective function

I recently had the opportunity to attend a training on the sanctity of life put on by the Training Institute for Human Service Planning, Leadership and Change Agency at Syracuse University. The training was outstanding and was very eye opening on a variety of levels, however, one of the lessons to me was that I came away with an insight into the potential protective function of the Church in a variety of areas.

First in terms of advocating and looking out for the safety of persons with disabilities, whether it be from bad people in the community, or human services, or even a stay in the hospital. The presence of the a community member in those settings works wonders in terms of changing the perceptions of those around a person with disabilities.

Second in terms of the unborn. If people with disabilities were really enfolded into the local church, people would not be able to make the arguments they make to justify the killing of unborn babies. Quality of life (although it is largely a spurious argument) is believed as an argument by many. If it could be demonstrated that people who are involved in churches are happy and enfolded, it would go a long way to protect their lives before they were born. It would also go a long way in assisting parents to want to have a child with a disability if they are considering terminating the life of an unborn child. They would see an environment where they were supported which would translate to support for their own child.

Other areas might be envisioned as well. But to the degree that we as the Church are not including and supporting persons with disabilities is the degree to which we expose them to devaluing and even death. Go back and look at Ezekiel 34 again. Because we have not brought them in, we place them at risk.

255

Wednesday, October 26, 2005

A movement of lay professionals

The desire to facilitate a movement of lay professionals is not necessarily an effort to indict the church, but rather for disability professionals to lead by example. In contrast to the way that individuals with disability are not represented in churches in a manner which reflects their numbers in the community, Christian special educators, Christian social workers, Christian rehabilitation counselors, are represented in the Church.

It is we who are in the know about persons with disabilities. Arguably, it is we who have dropped the ball, and not lived up to our responsibilities. As the Bible says, "From everyone who has been given much, much will be demanded; and from the one who has been entrusted with much, much more will be asked" (Luke 12:48). We who have been given much knowledge and significant experience with the disenfranchised in society, hold a special responsibility to recognize their absence in the Church and rectify that situation. We need to be doing the work of inviting them in, introducing them to our congregations, and as appropriate, developing programs for them. In the same manner as we might be critical of a person with financial abilities not coming to the aid of her church should it need financial guidance, we as human service workers should be held accountable. The Church is disobedient, but then it has been disobedient in this area for a long time. There have been pockets of incredible insight and programs that must delight the Heart of the Lord, but there is also incredible ignorance, uncaring and a lack of concern. The Church is disobedient because we have been disobedient.

Church leaders speak of all people being created in the image of God, of all souls being equal, of the value of every human life, but as we look around our congregations, we don't see the diversity typical of the community represented in our congregations. Where are the nearly 20% of persons nationwide who are disabled? Where are the 10% of persons with "severe" disabilities? Where are the people with intellectual disability? "These people honor me with their lips, but their hearts are far from me" (Matthew 15:8) might be a fair characterization of the church in reference to persons with disabilities.

Those of us who are attempting to change the Church face barriers from our pastors, barriers from our denominations, barriers from those who sit next to us in the congregation. But rather than trying to overcome barriers, we dismiss ourselves from our responsibility in the name of church/state separation, or the rules of our organizations relative to clients, or the ignorance of our congregational brothers and sisters or our pastor. Or we say that our training and our work with persons with disabilities is our job and our church life is our church life. Personally, I need to see the chapter and verse on that one. This cannot be something that our Lord would condone. Can we as believers say that we are unwilling to serve in a particular area, especially when that area is our area of strength, the area we are devoting our working life to? Can we as believers say that we are unwilling to serve, when partially due to our lack of service, the Church lives in disobedience?

We hear pastors, or children's program leaders, or Christian school administrators tell us that programs are too expensive, or too time intensive, or require persons having a lot of training. How do we respond to these excuses for living in disobedience? The last question is the easiest to dispel for the disability professional. Simply say, "I have a lot of training and I will run your program." However, the types of things that are required to open the Church really don't take a tremendous amount of training. Are church programs for persons with disabilities too expensive? A survey of pastors of churches running such programs says they aren't (Sanchez & McNair in preparation). A survey of people who attend Christian churches say they are not. As a professional in the field of special education, I would agree with both of these groups and say that such programs are not expensive. Well aren't programs too time intensive? Well, service is time intensive, but programs for persons with disabilities aren't any more or less intensive than other programs.

However, the toughest protestation to the initiation of a program for persons with disabilities is that "Its just not a priority right now." So ala Matthew 25, church leaders indict themselves. That will be my response in the future should I ever hear that excuse again.

We, the experts, need to act like the experts we are. Imagine going to your pastor to correct his interpretation of the Greek on a particular biblical passage. My pastor wouldn't take too kindly to my attempted correction, and he would be right to not listen to me as I have never studied Greek or Hebrew, or systematic theology. But he has never studied the education of persons with intellectual disability, or behavior management or best practices in the delivery of human services. I am the one who needs to take the lead in this discussion. I should know enough about my Bible to tell her/him where to get off should she/he talk about such a ministry not being a priority (I don't need Greek or Hebrew to do that). But I have to be the one to go forward on these issues.

I had a discussion with a pastor and a couple of his staff members once. At one point in the discussion, one of the people in attendance said, "Nobody stays up at night wondering how to teach people with intellectual disability about the Bible." I responded, "I do," which was the absolute truth.

257

Special education professionals live disability, particularly special education classroom teachers. They do, because if they don't, they will be eaten alive by their students, or the student's parents, or their administrators among others. But that preoccupation with persons with disabilities and the types of services they require, needs to be carried over to the church setting so as described in Matthew 25, they can be obedient to God's command there and elsewhere to minister to the least of these.

Pastors, you need to confront disability professionals with their responsibilities in the church. You need to bring people with disability into the Church and support the efforts of those who do the same. As leaders in the Church, you are disobedient yourselves, and are allowing those within your purview to be disobedient as well.

Did Christ see people with disability? Very often these people are also poor. Did Christ have any interest in the poor? We read the stories of the extent to which Jesus went to minister without considering the context or the effort on his part to get with these people. Jesus' interactions with persons with disabilities are breath-taking, and they were intentional on his part. We trivialize these interactions when we use them simply as illustrations or metaphors of spiritual principles. These were real people confronted by a real God, and these confrontations with real people by a real God are ubiquitous in the New Testament.

So don't miss the priority Christ gives to these people as an example for you as a church leader in terms of the priority you should give to these same individuals who are living in your midst today. If you say that these people are not a priority, you indict yourself and diminish the service of those who do work with the disenfranchised.

And professionals in disability, don't miss your responsibility to help a disobedient church to become obedient. If you, if we do not facilitate the inclusion of persons with disability into the church, who do we expect will? We are the experts.

Monday, October 03, 2005

Leadership in prayer

Last night we had a meeting of the leadership of our "Light and Power Co." program which seeks to integrate persons with disabilities into our local church. In the midst of the discussion of future activities, we got the idea of having L&P sponsor an all church evening of prayer. At the time it sounded like a good idea: give back to the church by praying for the needs of the church, opportunities for integration between persons with and without disability, good stuff. But the more I think through this idea, the better it seems to me.

One thing that persons with disability, particularly intellectual disability can do is pray. Their prayers are often short and to the point (John is going into the hospital for cancer surgery . . . "Oh Lord, please guide the hands of the surgeons and help them to be a blessing-blah-blah-blah" versus "God, please help John get better, Amen.") which can be a good example. Their prayers are heartfelt. We have one member of our group who cannot keep himself from crying nearly every time he prays. They oftentimes have big time faith. But the bottom line, is that their prayers are EQUAL to my or anyone else's prayers. SWEET! You don't need to be highly intelligent or have any special skills to be able to say a prayer. So their service is equal in every way to that of those in the church who do not experience disability.

Man do I love the level playing field we have before the Lord. As I have mentioned elsewhere in this blog,

BUT- God chose the foolish things of the world to shame the wise . . . He chose the lowly things of this world and the despised things - and the things that are not - to nullify the things that are, **so that no one may boast before him**. (1 Corinthians 1: 27-29)

We can set the standard for a life of prayer through the example of persons with intellectual disabilities. We for sure can raise the standard for the church through the prayer life of persons with disability. This is truly exciting.

So start this at your own church. The disabled community has all the skill required to be the leaders of the church in prayer. Let's raise the bar and set the standard.

Wednesday, September 28, 2005

Lay professionals should lead the way

This past week I had the opportunity to meet a woman who was applying for a position at the university where I work. I asked her how she as a school psychologist at a large school district was able to integrate her faith with her professional position. She related a variety of things she was doing, but then spoke of how she started a support group for parents of persons with disabilities at her church. The group met about once a month and discussed successes and failures, resources and battles with various human service agencies. She also related that her church had begun to infuse special education best practices into the Sunday school classes for students with disabilities.

I walked away from that conversation feeling that what she is doing is **exactly** what professionals need to be doing at their local churches. We need to bring our expertise to the church, but not for the reason you might think. You see, I believe that...

259

it **does not** take special training to be involved in disability ministry
it does not take **special training** to be involved in disability ministry
it does not take special training **to be involved** in disability ministry
it does not take special training to be involved in **disability** ministry

Now don't get me wrong. The training professionals receive is important and contributes a great deal to their understanding of persons with disability. I am a trainer of professionals for goodness sake. But, what the church needs more than anything else is to have professionals model how one is to act, how one is to include, how one is to love persons with disabilities. The key attribute that we bring to the church setting is not our special training, but our experience. We have learned to see past the minor social skill deficits. Just about anything a person with a intellectual disability could do, we have probably seen before and have learned to take in stride. It is this experience of being accepting to persons with disabilities that we bring to the situation. You see, we have learned that people with disabilities are just people, and because we understand that truth, we treat them like we would treat anyone else.

But that experience is huge. People will say that they can't do something because they don't have training, but what they really need is experience, because experience will ally their fears better than any training ever would. And how are they to get this experience? Well, if we as professionals would be proactive in bringing persons with various disabilities to church they would get the experience. They would also have the opportunity to see appropriate interactions with persons living on the fringes of society modeled for them. Perhaps through our example, those on the fringe wouldn't be on the fringe anymore because our example would break down the stigma which put them on the fringes in the first place.

It is interesting that in churches we hear that God loves all people and that God sees all people the same, that God values all people the same and that we are created in the image of God. We hear that, but we don't always see it acted out in our midst. We as professionals who love and work with persons with disability can provide the example of what it looks like to act on the notion that God loves all people the same. We can provide the example of what it looks like to act on the principle that we are all created in the image of God. We can provide the example of what it looks like that God sees all people the same. We can provide the example of what it looks like that God values all people the same. We hear such statements made in church, but how often do we see such statements acted out within our midst. You know it is funny that when we do see the act of kindness toward a persons with intellectual disability, or the pastor who takes social skill deficits in stride, we are like, taken aback. It is like for an instant we are not seeing through the glass darkly. The question is why are such interactions rare? Perhaps it is because the opportunities to do real acts of kindness towards people who are in need cannot occur if the people in need are not in the church.

WE ARE THE PROFESSIONALS!

It is we who need to make the church reflect the community. If you are a professional in aspects of disability and there are few if any persons with disability at your church, it is YOUR FAULT! You are not doing, not being all you should be in your church. When I see a lack of acceptance at my church, I immediately look at myself. How am I providing the example of how the church should be towards persons who have been traditionally excluded. I cannot expect a church which has literally centuries of exclusion to suddenly lead the way in change. To put it kindly, the "lack of priority" of disability ministry is an inbred part of the structures of the church it would seem. The excuses for a lack of involvement which are typically provided by those in leadership have worked for decades if not centuries.

BUT WE ARE THE PROFESSIONALS!

We are the ones who need to change the church. It is time for a lay movement of professionals to bring the church into obedience on issues related to reaching out to all its members with disability.

Wednesday, July 13, 2005

A theology of disability

In 1965, Robert Perske presented a paper to a conference entitled "The Church and the Mentally Retarded." The title of his paper was, "An attempt to find an adequate theological view of intellectual disability." He discusses "a history of how we have dealt with intellectual disability in America" as a kind of a backdrop to the theology which might have been developing at the same time. He discusses periods of "total rejection . . . found early in American society" followed by attitudes about "bad blood and sins of the fathers." From there we proceeded to the feeling of "God's special children with the publication of the books "Angel Unaware" and "Retarded Children: God's Children."

He then says we came to the point where we sought a "special theology." He says, "This is probably the first period in American history that pastors have sincerely sought an adequate theology for the mentally

retarded." Ultimately he says, "A special theology may not be adequate...
the theological view we seek cannot be a special view." He suggests,
"Therefore our task should be to enlarge the existing general theological
views so that they include the intellectually disabled. If we sincerely see
the intellectually disabled as human beings, we should struggle to
broaden and strengthen our general theological views to encompass
people with other deficits as well."

I am unsure that we have actually passed the point of wanting a
"special theology." If normalization means treating people as normally as
possible, perhaps a once size fits all theology would be sufficient. But one
size never fits all, and although we are all humans our experiences are
different.

Answers.com defines *social construction* in the following manner

A social construction, or social construct, according to the school of
social constructionism, is an idea which may appear to be natural and
obvious to those who accept it, but in reality is an invention or artifact of
a particular culture or society. The implication is that social constructs are
human choices rather than laws of God or nature.

If a theology of intellectual disability would in some way flesh out a
God perspective on disability, then perhaps we do need such a theology
in order to counter the "invention or artifact" of nearly all cultures about
who persons with intellectual disability are. These perceptions are built
into us, and become as close to us as intuition or conscience. Clearly
cultures see people with disability as something different. The church
appears to see them as something different. So although we say we are all
the same in God's eyes, it seems we have adopted a cultural perspective
on disability, as a church, rather than what might be called a theological
perspective on disability.

One of my quests has been to try to understand disability from God's
perspective to the extent I am able. The main reason is to be able to
somehow take off the social constructions which are like blinders on my
eyes, making me look in a particular direction, and instead see the truth,
the truth about "disability" from a God, or theological perspective.

Thursday, June 23, 2005

Patronizing Good Will

Oftentimes when describing work with persons with disabilities, or
even in introducing persons with intellectual disability to those without
disability, I have the feeling that I am the recipient of a kind of
patronizing good will. Whether it is based on some notion of political
correctness in relation to the particular environment one is in, or a
reflection of some general social etiquette of how one is to act or speak

262

when the question of intellectual disability arises, people move into this sentimental seriousness about persons with disability. Their speech belies good will of language on their part, but there is also a laziness about it. It's like they reverence the challenges of the families of those persons and what they suspect is the experience of the persons with disabilities themselves, however, they speak out of ignorance; a kind of lazy ignorance at that. it's like the response many special educators joke about that they receive when they say they are special educators. Without fail, others will respond, "You must have a lot of patience." Ask any special educator and he will report that he has heard that response.

It seems when confronted with disability, the general public is often so unfamiliar with persons with disability and their experiences that they respond with the pat answers, the patronizing replies which have been used over and over again. It is good will, but it is patronizing and unreflective of knowledge. But apparently they have heard others use those mindless replies and they appeared to sound heartfelt, kind and maybe even intelligent. So they repeat them as well. And so on and so on. In the end, we have social constructions reflected in the trite language used in response to the unknown of disability.

Now it is obviously better that the mindless responses of the general public should be patronizing good will over something negative, however, oftentimes the pat answers convey negativity which is just below the surface. I use positive speak in public environments about persons with disability, however, in private speak or when challenged to put the positive into practice (drop a group home in the neighborhood, for example) the positive is quickly replaced because the "due diligence" has not been done to actually support the positive.

So when confronted with trite, good speech about persons with disability, ask the questions that will cause the speaker to either back up the speech with actions, or at least go a bit deeper in his understanding of disability.

Monday, March 14, 2005

Make disability ministry a priority

I am aware of a ministry to adults with developmental disabilities that has been in existence for nearly 40 years. My wife, Kathi, and I were involved in the ministry for 5 years ourselves, nearly 20 years ago. Housed in a large church in Pasadena, California, the forward thinking woman who started the ministry is retiring from it, and as a result, it is at risk of no longer being in existence as no one, including the church leadership, has stepped forward to take her place.

At what point in the life of a ministry will a church embrace and adopt that ministry to the point of investing in it with resources, a pastoral position, etc.?

I wonder whether the ministry at my own church would survive if Kathi and I were no longer involved in it? This question about ministry survival goes to the heart of the church, the priorities of the church and what it is willing to invest in. Nearly any church will have singles ministry, and children's (non disabled children's) ministry, and ministries to singles and seniors. Very often there will also be pastoral positions linked to these ministries. The hiring of a pastor is a statement on behalf of the church that this area of ministry is a given, a priority. Such churches don't expect or depend exclusively on lay volunteers to make such ministries go. They don't wait for a lay person to step forward to make a commitment to the ministry before they will start it. The church leadership (pastors, elders, etc.) have decided that the particular area of ministry is a priority to them and they make it happen.

For example, my own church recently made the decision to commit resources to beginning a "Spanish language" ministry to persons living in the town who are largely Spanish speakers. They invested in buildings, hired staff, including a pastor, and have devoted significant energy to the project.

My question is not to doubt that the "Spanish language" project is worthy, but rather to ask why disability ministry is so often dependent upon lay people, and so infrequently an idea of the church leaders to be pursued as an important area for ministry development to the point of hiring staff to ensure it happens?

Can it actually be that after nearly 40 years of ministry, the Pasadena church will now refuse to support the ministry and ensure that it will continue? I can recall that there were many Sunday mornings where 60 or more developmentally disabled adults would participate in the church's activities. They lived in the apartments and group homes from all around Pasadena. Some folks we picked up, some rode the bus, and some were brought by their care providers. Very few were brought by church members, other than those working in the ministry.

Sometimes I think about going to a church other than the one I have attended for the past 14 years. Not that I am in some way dissatisfied with my church. But more I wonder whether the 14 years that Kathi and I have invested in disability ministry there have made any difference in terms of the priority such ministry would have at the church if we were no longer there.

"Its too bad Kathi and Jeff left. We had a pretty good program going on there for 14 years. Oh well . . ."

Church leaders, YOU should be taking the lead in ministries to persons with disability. YOU should ensure that such ministries are occurring at your church. Maybe put off your building program and hire a pastor to persons with disability instead. Make a statement to the community about the degree to which you are willing to go to serve others, rather than making another edifice to comfortable worship.

Elsewhere in this blog we discuss the Catholic Bishop statements. Statement number 9 (January 9)says,

"Our pastoral response is to become informed about disabilities and to offer ongoing support to the family and welcome to the child."

At least the Bishops see the role of their clergy is the development of ministry, if only becoming knowledgeable about disability in order to offer support. It is a good starting point.

Sunday, March 13, 2005

"Disabled" by design

"And Jehovah said to him, Who has made man's mouth? Or who makes the dumb, or the deaf, or the seeing, or the blind? Is it not I Jehovah?" (Leviticus 4:11).

Moses tells God that he didn't do the greatest job on his mouth. He says he is "heavy of mouth" and "heavy of tongue." Good description. However, in spite of his qualms, God doesn't relent. God responds with a kind of a rhetorical question put down. God knows Moses' mouth. The reply, however, is much broader when it says "who made man's mouth." To me the implication is that God knows about mouths (being the inventor) not just Moses' mouth, and also knows about the variations within and between mouths. "Who makes the dumb" God goes on to say, implying 1) that he knows of the variation between mouths, and 2) that he made the variations between mouths. That is, God even made the mouths of the dumb, those who cannot speak for whatever reason.

These observations on God's part are not restricted to the mouth, however. He goes on to say, "or the deaf" (i.e. variations in the ear) or the "seeing or the blind" (i.e. variations in the eye). Once again, the implication is that God created the variations we see in human beings, down to what are called disabilities; being unable to speak, unable to hear, or unable to see. One would assume that these variations could also include other types of "disability" including physical and mental differences. After all, sensorineural deafness and blindness imply nerve tissue insults or changes which could include intellectual disability.

Taking this type of thinking to its final conclusion, these individuals we call persons with disability, are in reality part of the normal variation within human functioning. To think that God created a person who is unable to speak as a person who is unable to speak changes 1) the way I think about that person, 2) the language I choose to describe the abilities of that person, 3) the notion of who God is.

Tuesday, February 15, 2005

More on "disabled" by design

I appreciated the thoughtful comments posted in reference to the last blog. It is interesting and I also think important to ask whether differences which our society has categorized as "disability" are examples of human variation or the result of "the fall." I will freely admit that I do not entirely understand what the answer is to that question. Observations I have made include those in the previous blog as well as others made at other times in months past in the blog. For example, is aging, and the degradation of the body the result of the fall? Are accidents like the one that caused me to blow out my ACL (anterior cruciate ligament) resulting in the bad knee I continue to have the result of the fall, or was there the possibility that someone could injure themselves to the point of having a bad knee pre fall?

As I said, I really am unsure, however, I am beginning to move in the direction of understanding differences called disabilities as a part of simple variations in the human race. When God says that his creation was "very good" does that mean that all of the human members of the creation were entirely equal in every way? At the very least, we know there were differences between men and women. At what point does a difference become a "disability?" History tells us that the number of persons labeled as disabled increased dramatically with the industrial revolution. That is, people who were within the "normal" range when all they had to do was have a strong back were now thought of as disabled in light of the demands of urban society. So one might ask, to what extent is "disability" a characteristic of an individual and to what extent is "disability" a reflection of the environment.

I recently saw the movie Ray about the life of Ray Charles. As I look at that movie, as I consider all that Mr. Charles achieved, I wonder at his "disability." In the range of visual ability, he was on the dark end of the scale, having lost his vision. So he had a severely diminished ability to perceive light. It is also true that he relied on persons in his environment to assist him throughout his life (as do I). But I kind of agree with his mother (as portrayed in the film) when she says something to the effect that "you cannot see, but don't become a cripple." Is the limited ability to see the result of the fall? I would think becoming a "cripple" is definitely a result of the fall as it appears to reflect a lack of reliance on God, on oneself, and people. A person who is a "cripple" in the way that Ray

266

Charles' mother implied is reflecting a negativity, a buying of the notion that one is less than created in the image of God. This notion is taught to a person, is pounded into a person by society and it is society at its worst.

It has always struck me as ironic that people like me, who are largely within the normal range of ability levels, can look at our sin scarred selves with all the foibles and proclaim that we are created in God's image.

It also haunts me to come back to God's comment "who makes the dumb, or the deaf, or the seeing, or the blind." Does God purposely create "imperfection" or do I need to change my definitions?"

. . . don't know, still working through it.

Wednesday, February 16, 2005

Acknowledge God loves them

I was reading Watchman Nee today, and he makes this comment in relation to Revelation 3:7-10.

"The church needs leaders, but it also needs brothers. I believe in authority, but I believe also in brotherly love. In Philadelphia they respected authority, for they kept the Lord's word and did not deny his name. But philadelphia in Greek means 'brotherly kindness.' It was to these caring brothers and sisters that the door was opened. Let them set out to serve him together and not wait for the specialists; then we shall begin to see what the Church's service really is."

After the excuse of no money, the next most common excuse for a lack of involvement with persons with disability is "I don't have any training." But as Nee says, "serve him together and not wait for the specialists." This is not to demean specialists. I have dedicated my life to the training of special education specialists and there is much that such specialists can learn. However, don't confuse being a specialist with being a willing servant. No one is asking the average church member to develop behavior intervention plans, or teach adults with intellectual disabilities to read, or how to develop language in those who have no language. But it is reasonable to expect them to carry on a conversation, to take someone out to lunch, etc.

In that passage in Revelation it also says, "I will make those of the synagogue of Satan, who claim to be Jews though they are not, but are liars - I will make them come and fall down at your feet and acknowledge that I have loved you" (Rev 3:9). Now I am not saying that the church is the house of Satan or that people with disabilities are the ones about whom the Lord earlier says, "I know that you have little strength," however, something about the statement "I will make them come and fall

267

down at your feet and acknowledge that I have loved you" really resonates with me.

I met a man today who along with his wife is convinced that his church refused to put a birth announcement about his disabled child in the church bulletin because the child was disabled. Elsewhere in this blog I have spoken of other situations whereby persons with disabilities or their families were ostracized by churches or church members or pastors. Too often we treat persons with disability as if we believe God does not love them. By our words or actions we say to them, "God does not love you." But before the Lord has to put me in a position where I am made to fall at their feet and acknowledge that God loves them, I want to do it of my own accord as I believe that is the heart of God.

Tuesday, November 16, 2004

U.S. Catholic Bishops

The following is from the "Doctrine and Pastoral Practices" website sponsored by the United States Conference of Catholic Bishops http://www.nccbuscc.org/doctrine/disabilities.htm   I became aware of this thanks to a student of mine at Cal Baptist.
The document is titled,
> "Welcome and Justice for Persons with Disabilities
> A Framework of Access and Inclusion
> A Statement of the U.S. Bishops"
The following quote begins after a brief introductory paragraph.

"This moral framework is based upon Catholic documents and serves as a guide for contemplation and action. We hope that the reaffirmation of the following principles will assist the faithful in bringing the principles of justice and inclusion to the many new and evolving challenges confronted by persons with disabilities today.
1. We are a single flock under the care of a single shepherd. There can be no separate Church for persons with disabilities.
2. Each person is created in God's image, yet there are variations in individual abilities. Positive recognition of these differences discourages discrimination and enhances the unity of the Body of Christ.
3. Our defense of life and rejection of the culture of death requires that we acknowledge the dignity and positive contributions of our brothers and sisters with disabilities. We unequivocally oppose negative attitudes toward disability which often lead to abortion, medical rationing, and euthanasia.
4. Defense of the right to life implies the defense of all other rights which enable the individual with the disability to achieve the fullest measure of

personal development of which he or she is capable. These include the right to equal opportunity in education, in employment, in housing, and in health care, as well as the right to free access to public accommodations, facilities and services.

5. Parish liturgical celebrations and catechetical programs should be accessible to persons with disabilities and open to their full, active and conscious participation, according to their capacity.

6. Since the parish is the door to participation in the Christian experience, it is the responsibility of both pastors and laity to assure that those doors are always open. Costs must never be the controlling consideration limiting the welcome offered to those among us with disabilities, since provision of access to religious functions is a pastoral duty.

7. We must recognize and appreciate the contribution persons with disabilities can make to the Church's spiritual life, and encourage them to do the Lord's work in the world according to their God-given talents and capacity.

8. We welcome qualified individuals with disabilities to ordination, to consecrated life, and to full-time, professional service in the Church.

9. Often families are not prepared for the birth of a child with a disability or the development of impairments. Our pastoral response is to become informed about disabilities and to offer ongoing support to the family and welcome to the child.

10. Evangelization efforts are most effective when promoted by diocesan staff and parish committees which include persons with disabilities. Where no such evangelization efforts exist, we urge that they be developed.

We join the Holy Father in calling for actions which "ensure that the power of salvation may be shared by all" (John Paul II, Tertio Millennio Adveniente, n. 16). Furthermore, we encourage all Catholics to study the original U.S. bishops and Vatican documents from which these principles were drawn."

I found this a wonderful statement overall so I provided it here (with the weblink), but I will also go through the many points raised by this statement in future blogs. The U.S. Conference of Catholic Bishops website is searchable, and has much good information.

Tuesday, November 16, 2004

U.S. Catholic Bishops Statement 1

1. We are a single flock under the care of a single shepherd. There can be no separate Church for persons with disabilities.

269

Sometimes when someone writes something such as the above, they are either responding to what they have observed, or are firing a preemptive strike. The above seems to be a bit of both. The latter following from the former.

A single flock under the care of a single shepherd implies we are all the same animal, all the same type. The single shepherd is Jesus. Now can you as a shepherd imagine hearing one of your sheep saying, "Fluffy is not like the rest of us and so we don't want him in our herd." As a shepherd you would probably say, "Wow, I didn't know sheep could talk." You would then say, "Shut up and get back with the rest of them, and I won't hear anything else about who is or who isn't a part of my herd." Interestingly, when an animal is rejected by its mother, like in the case of a litter of pups, the caretaker suddenly takes a special interest in the one rejected. The pups look at each other and see differences. The caretaker perhaps sees differences in appearances, but sees the pups as basically all the same. They are each a part of the litter.

The latter part of the statement says there can be no separate church for persons with disabilities. If there were a separate church for persons with disabilities, the question would be why would there be one, why would it be needed? I know of separate churches in the United States, and I honestly believe that those in leadership of those churches have a tremendous heart for persons with disability, and want to both meet their needs in a "culturally" relevant manner, and perhaps protect them from those who are not disabled. There are many problems with this perspective, however.

First of all persons with disability, particularly intellectual disability, aren't of a different culture, they are the same culturally as the rest of us. If they have developed any different form of experience, it is an experience of rejection, they are those who have been rejected. It is totally against Christian principles to say to a group of rejected people, "Hey all you rejected people, let's get together and form a church of the rejected people," at least as it relates to disability. Yes there are those who have done such things among groups like the untouchable class in India, however, that is an entirely different matter. Those people have developed to the point of having a distinct culture. You are born into that caste and as a result experience the same culture as your family etc. Now this doesn't dismiss the fact that such discrimination is wrong and should be fought, however, the situation is different.

People with disabilities are born into virtually any culture and experience some degree of rejection from that culture. So they don't really form a separate sub culture, they have experiences similar to others also experiencing disability. They group with these others not through

270

any cultural affinity (perhaps like the deaf who have a different language in common) but because they have been relegated to the same stations in society, the same communities or parts of communities due to their near or actual poverty existence, the same agencies who provide various forms of assistance. These individuals were not necessarily born into these aspects they have come to experience in their lives, they have spiraled or gravitated toward these ends as a result of society and its constructions of disability.

Now if the church were some country club or golf membership, one might expect that there would be clubs for those who can afford them, clubs for those of importance, clubs for those with less money or influence and public clubs for those who for some reason are not able to attain the status of the higher clubs. The starting of separate churches for persons with disability is analogous to the "selective" clubs. If I can't get into the club I want to join, I will have to form my own club. Or if I cannot facilitate the integration of persons with disabilities into regular community churches, I will start a church for them. People of rejected status will generally not argue with a situation where they feel acceptance. Persons with intellectual disability will probably not recognize the philosophical issues of a separate church. But those of us who understand how things should be, who see the discrimination, must advocate for those who don't recognize the problems.

I know of a young man with Down's syndrome, about 14, who is still in the first grade Sunday school class. Now he is portrayed as being a "helper," however, he is much more like another first grade student. As a newcomer to that church, if I saw that young man in the first grade class, my response would be "What is wrong with him that he isn't with the other fourteen year olds?" My response would not be, "He is a good colorer." He doesn't belong in that class because it is not age appropriate for him. He belongs with his peers.

If I visit a church for persons with disability, my response is not, "Isn't it great that they have their own church!" My response is "Why aren't they with their peers?" If I attended a church local to that church, I would be ashamed that those persons with disability were so rejected, or felt so rejected that they had to start their own church. I would not tacitly accept that they were somehow different from me, of a different flock, ostensibly a different shepherd, such that they needed a different church.

You might respond, "Well what about denominationalism?" I would respond that persons with disability are born within denominations. They, at least by birth, are members of those denominations. If all the retarded people, by example, were Congregationalists, I would still argue that they should not be put in a separate Congregational church for the disabled people. But the fact that they aren't, that they represent all denominations,

271

and that they need to form their own disabled church, indicts all of the denominations. They pat the people with disabilities on the back and say, "See you later" perhaps relieved that they no longer have to address the "problem" of disability.

But because we are one flock with one Shepherd, and should believe that we should all be one church, we need to do the required work to find persons with disability, bring them into our congregations, fight the rejection. Let the discriminators form the "Our Lady of those who Reject disabled People" church and they can deal with the Lord on the final day. Rather than rejecting those with disability, we should root out those who discriminate and reject them, find those who are unable to soften themselves and the environment to persons with disability and reject them.

My students have been interviewing their pastors about programs for persons with disability within their home churches. It has been interesting. A typical comment is, "We would welcome them if they came. We have elevators and are wheelchair accessible. We have disabled parking!" (Many of these things, by the way, were not there until required by law). But what they don't realize is, why would a group of people who have been rejected in the past suddenly go to a place which has rejected them? It would be like an all White church in the South in the 1960's saying, "We would welcome all the Black people if they came here." Well if you really wanted those people to come, you would need to go out and find them. You would need to try and convince them that they really were wanted there. To sit back and say "We would accept them, but none have come" is truly foolish in an age of discrimination. The fact that there are churches populated by persons with disability almost exclusively is a testimony to our failure.

Tuesday, November 16, 2004

U.S. Catholic Bishops part 2

2. Each person is created in God's image, yet there are variations in individual abilities. Positive recognition of these differences discourages discrimination and enhances the unity of the Body of Christ.

The notion of being created in God's image is an interesting one. It must imply something of a positive nature, I would assume. I never paid much attention to the notion when most of the people I interacted with were like me: healthy, apparently happy, got along with others, etc. But then I worked for a year in an institution for persons with profound

272

disabilities. As I walked the halls of that institution, I passed people who literally were so physically disabled, they appeared to fluid lumps of humanity thrown to the ground that solidified to form something resembling a deflated ball. Many of them had accompanying severe intellectual disability to go along with their physical disabilities. I was involved in sensory stimulation training, which I ultimately stopped doing as I felt I was more of an annoyance than a help (I mean imagine not being able to move or communicate, and then having someone rubbing ice on your hand, or a prickly brush across your skin, with the best intentions of course, in the name of stimulating you). Anyway, I looked on those individuals and tried to reconcile the notion that they were created in the image of God with any past ideas I might have had about the concept. It was obvious to me that the image of God is not intellect, it is not physical health, or even as I once thought, social interactivity as none of these were present in these individuals. At this point in my life, it occurs that it might be that all people have a spirit. In the end it is more important from a leveling the field kind of perspective to note that we are all created in God's image. Such a perspective to my biased eyes raises the importance of those with profound disabilities and convicts my own vanity (it is easy for those without disability to see that we were created in God's image, I mean, c'mon, just look at us!).

Yes, it is also true that there are variations in our abilities. I am confident that the Bishops meant the best by this part of the statement, however, it can come off a bit patronizing. I suspect to them, it was simply the other shoe falling in relation to the image of God statement. It is true that we all have different abilities, but I really resist the "looking for the abilities in others" trap as abilities are linked often to worth. I say people have abilities because I am trying to assign them worth. Well I honestly have met people that I don't think have any abilities. And please don't tell me that their severe disability is actually the ability to bring out something in those around them. Variations in our abilities, sure, fine, however, worth is from God in being created in His image, and being loved by him. People get hung up on abilities and variations in abilities.

Positive recognition of ability differences may actually discourage discrimination and enhance the unity of the Body of Christ, but it can also be so much "whistling in the dark." I might actually have something to fear in the dark and whistling does little in light of that fact. Once again, positive recognition of ability differences benefits those with abilities. Recognition of differences in abilities if fine but it really isn't about abilities or the lack thereof. No, God says I have value so I have value. My ability to write a sentence or kick a ball, or smile in a friendly manner must be treated as irrelevancies in terms of worth. This is, I believe, where the Church is in a morass of confusion. It is not about what you can do for me, it is what can I do for you.

And whoever desires to be first among you, let him be your servant;

Even as the Son of Man did not come to be served, but to serve and give his life a ransom for many (Matthew 20:25)

Discrimination will go away when we stop having "peeing contests" over abilities and recognize that we are to serve one another. . . when we quit looking at appearances, when we quit feeling the need to affirm abilities because we are so darn fragile. The more needy, the more opportunity for service. You want to enhance unity? Let's serve one another and spend our lives for each other, for many.

Tuesday, November 23, 2004

U.S. Catholic Bishops part 3

3. Our defense of life and rejection of the culture of death requires that we acknowledge the dignity and positive contributions of our brothers and sisters with disabilities. We unequivocally oppose negative attitudes toward disability which often lead to abortion, medical rationing, and euthanasia.

The notion of a culture of death has been well described by Dr. Wolf Wolfensberger. He uses the term "deathmaking" to refer to a wide variety of programs, positions, laws which would in total contribute to the Bishops' notion of a culture of death. I will go into Wolfensberger's notion of deathmaking at another time. The defense against the culture of death, I believe, does begin with recognizing that there is such a culture in our society. The culture of death can be related to actual physical death, or perhaps more commonly more of a "social death" in which a person with disability is relegated to life situations different from the mainstream but common to many of those with disability. Perhaps a defense of life is made when we acknowledge the dignity and positive contributions of persons with disabilities, however, I always wonder about who those to whom such a defense must be made, are. Are they even convincible? On what basis would they see persons with disabilities as anything other than worthy of dignity? There is an evil here which must be labeled for what it is.

The notion of positive contributions once again gets back to my last entry about this statement. Somehow, we need to see positive contributions, abilities, in persons with disability in order to make the case for their lives. We need to see abilities, apparently on some scale of worth, which will move the balance of the scale toward the defense of life and the rejection of the culture of death. Honestly, I refuse to play that game because of the evil behind it which requires one to prove someone's worth. I will not argue about someone's worth. I am given a glimpse into the soul of the person I am speaking to, when I hear that they feel worth must somehow be proven. Of course those who would challenge the worth of another assume they themselves have worth.

I too, unequivocally oppose negative attitudes toward persons with disability, in particular those which lead to abortion and other forms of death making (I do share the negativity persons with disability often have toward their own disability: I would prefer that persons with cerebral palsy, for example, not have cerebral palsy). However, there are other forms of negative attitudes which don't directly lead to death which should also be condemned.

I never cease to be amazed at the negativity I see in church people. An instance arose in my own church a couple of weekends ago. Someone who is a wonderful man of God made a decision affecting adults with disability in a very discriminatory fashion, and probably never even saw what he did as being discriminatory. Somehow, he feared the impression of others in the church, in terms of turning them away, or limiting the spiritual experience he was attempting to develop. I would respond by asking, "How can you have an experience with God, when you begin the experience by excluding persons whom God loves on the basis of their disability?" Yet somehow, this seemed logical to him.

I appreciate the Bishops' strong statement in defense of life, however, we must be careful to avoid situations where even our participation in the discussion somehow provides support for those who would detract from the humanity of persons with disability.

Monday, November 29, 2004

U.S. Catholic Bishops part 4

4. Defense of the right to life implies the defense of all other rights which enable the individual with the disability to achieve the fullest measure of personal development of which he or she is capable. These include the right to equal opportunity in education, in employment, in housing, and in health care, as well as the right to free access to public accommodations, facilities and services.

Once the right to life is secured (and it is arguable that it has not yet been secured, as evidenced by the Bishops' third statement) our hope would be to expand rights to include those which facilitate the fullest measure of personal development. This is one of the reasons this blog spends so much time on opening the church to persons with disability as churches do indeed facilitate a fuller measure of personal development, and not just in the spiritual arena. The notion of personal development of persons with disabilities is not one that the church necessarily knows how to do. The comment was once made to me that disabled persons don't improve, so why devote so much time to them? The fact of the matter is that even the most severe of disabled persons do evidence improvement although perhaps not to the degree of those without disability. However, as with all church members, it should interest the church whether its members are achieving the fullest development possible, as least as much as they are able to impact development.

Then there should be equal opportunity in
education
employment
housing
health care
Education is improving, although equal opportunity doesn't necessarily mean access to the core curriculum being used for students without disability. It should mean access to the type of curriculum which would best serve each student (would facilitate personal growth as above). However, sadly many disability advocates have fought for access to the core curriculum, which is a curriculum built upon a social efficiency model (having the greatest impact for the greatest number of people) not a critical/functional skills model. So students have gained the right to a curriculum which is not necessarily even relevant for them. People have confused access to the core curriculum with integration and so even though children are being educated next to each other, it is arguable as to whether they are receiving the instruction each individually (both those with and without disability) needs to be the most successful.

Employment access has improved somewhat through both the requirements of the Americans with Disability Act, and the increasing recognition among employers that persons with disabilities make good employees. In particular, persons with intellectual disability make great long term workers in entry level jobs. Increasingly, employers are learning that they can save money on hiring a person with intellectual disability to fill positions that have a high turnover rate when persons without disability hold those positions. Actual equal opportunity, well, not quite. The bias against persons with disability is evident in the workplace as employers are simply a subgroup of a larger population who hold the same biases. However, employers go to church and if the church were to involve persons with disability, there would be a greater opportunity for employers to know persons with disabilities and potentially employ them. The gains from network membership are also great in terms of increasing employer tolerance for minor social skill "deficits." More on this aspect of network development is provided at the following website http://www.jeffmcnair.com/CSRD/networks.htm

Access to housing, well, they have access to what they may be able to afford. There used to be a program whereby persons with disability were able to receive supplements such that their rent would be no more than a third of their income, however, for whatever reason new applications are not being taken. As a result, I have one friend who is an adult with intellectual disability who pays over 700$ for his apartment and another friend who pays about 260$ for the exact same apartment. The second got into the program when they were still taking applications. Now imagine getting a little over 700$ per month in Social Security, and then having a part time job on the side (part time as you don't want to loose your Social Security benefits) and trying to pay 700$ in rent. As he has stated, he hasn't had the **luxury** of eating out at McDonald's in the last 6 months because he can't afford it. So access to housing? Access to housing in the worst areas of town.

Health care is better than I might have thought if I hadn't had contact with many of the people I know. I have one friend who has received two kidney transplants, and has been in the hospital on numerous occasions. I have another friend who is dealing with depression who has received great medical support both in terms of long term hospital care, outpatient services and even assistance with medication. Both of these persons have developmental disabilities. Perfect, no, however, I would say it is better by comparison than say housing opportunities by far.

The folks I know also have access to public accommodations (including travel assistance) and various facilities and services. Of course I am not privy to every aspect of their lives, however, I hear few complaints about busses, etc.

So the right to life in terms of other rights is a mixed bag. The church holds huge potential in improving access to other right simply through their inclusion of persons with disability.

Wednesday, December 01, 2004

U.S. Catholic Bishops part 5

5. Parish liturgical celebrations and catechetical programs should be accessible to persons with disabilities and open to their full, active and conscious participation, according to their capacity.

Accessibility and participation.

277

Accessibility is much more than wheelchair access or handicapped parking spots. Today, virtually any new, public, building will have many accessibility aspects nailed down because it is the law. However, accessibility is much more than that. If I have chairs in my auditorium, does that mean I am willing to accept any person who sits in those chairs? Hardly.

Accessibility should imply a certain desire to have people involved, it implies that I have done a bit more of something, something out of the ordinary perhaps, to facilitate access. So in my church, for example, we not only say we invite children with autism to be involved in the children's classes, we have people who are available to serve as "buddies" to help the child feel a part of the group. It is a small thing, but it allows one to say, "Not only are you and your child welcome here, but we have buddies to help your child to be successful in the children's program here." It implies we have thought about people like you, with your life situation before. It implies that we value you, so, we have come up with a way to make access to our church easier for you.

The Bishops' statement says access to "liturgical celebrations" and "catechetical programs." Although not a Catholic myself, I recognize the importance of liturgy to the Catholic tradition. If one is to be a full fledged Catholic, she must have access to liturgical celebrations, which include much of the public meetings of the faithful. The catechetical programs are the educational programs leading to catechism as well as other benchmarks of church membership/participation (I would assume). Persons with disability should have access to these educational programs so that they can participate fully, "according to their capacity."

On the basis of experience with persons with intellectual disabilities in church situations, it would be easy to dismiss someone as not having the capacity to benefit from a variety of programs the church has to offer, if you don't provide time and opportunity for those individuals to participate in the programs. Yet, there are people who are prayed for on a weekly basis, simply because friends of mine who are adults with intellectual disability ask our group to pray for them during a time of prayer requests. I have prayed for the bus driver of several men who make the request each week, for years. If you honestly believe in the power of prayer, you must believe that the desires on the part of those men to have their bus driver prayed for has somehow made a difference. They also always ask me to pray for their teacher. Another man who lives in a senior center (arguably not the most appropriate placement for that man, although I think he has a ministry there as he brightens the lives of many of the residents through his knowledge of sports and unabashed ability to start a conversation with anyone) asks me to pray for his mother and a nurse who helps him each week. I can't help but wonder how many of the other residents are not prayed for each week. One staff member always asks him to pray for her as well and we make a point to remember to pray for that person. I guarantee to you that were those men not involved in the program at our church, for sure the people for whom they ask for prayer might not be the topic of prayer, at least not by me and others in the group. Will these men remember that Paul and Barnabus split up and Paul went with Silas and Barnabus with Mark (our current lessons are from Acts)? Does it even matter? They are participating to the extent to which they are capable and they are making a difference in their own lives as well as the lives of those for whom they are praying or facilitating prayer through their request for prayer.

The Bishops touch on a notion which I suspect has a great deal behind it, that of "conscious participation." I suspect this term implies a notion of understanding. My son recently took a class in Philosophy as a part of his college curriculum. At the end of the class, students could ask the professor any question they wanted. He asked, "Do you believe in God?" He replied "No," but followed up the statement with the analogy of him being like a flea on a dog, trying to understand what a dog was (as an aside, that is why God-the dog, became a flea-in the form of Jesus, so we would get some understanding of who He is). Anyway, we understand a lot less than we think we do. We compare ourselves to others who know less than we and congratulate ourselves, or segregate ourselves on the basis of our knowledge. As I have stated elsewhere in this blog, however, such comparisons are silly. They are particularly silly when we think about what we know about God in relation to what might be known about him, and then we segregate our selves on the basis of what we supposedly know.

"He chose the lowly things of this world and the despised things - and the things that are not - to nullify the things that are, so that no one may boast before him. It is because of him that you are in Christ Jesus, who has become for us wisdom from God - that is our righteousness, holiness and redemption. (1 Corinthians 1: 26-29)"

You know, sometimes the above sounds like a warning to me. It makes me wonder about the things that I choose in comparison to the things God chooses. My choices are evidenced by to whom I give access and for whom I facilitate participation.

Tuesday, December 07, 2004

U.S. Catholic Bishops part 6

6. Since the parish is the door to participation in the Christian experience, it is the responsibility of both pastors and laity to assure

279

that those doors are always open. Costs must never be the controlling consideration limiting the welcome offered to those among us with disabilities, since provision of access to religious functions is a pastoral duty.

The parish (aka the local church) is indeed the door to participation in Christian experience. It also is the responsibility of both the pastors *and the laity* to keep the doors open. I have been in situations where the pastors kept the doors open to persons with disability in spite of the laity and the laity kept the doors open in spite of the pastors. The latter seems more difficult to me. But a larger question is what is meant by keeping the doors open.

In one of the courses I teach, students are required to interview their pastors about ministry to persons with disability. Perhaps the most common answer they receive is that the church is 1) wheelchair accessible and 2) has handicapped parking spots. Somehow, these legal requirements for public buildings have been confused with the Bishops' notion of the churches' doors being "open." Obviously, openness must mean something more than simply physical access. The fact that I can go somewhere doesn't mean that I am welcomed there. There is a qualitative difference that distinguishes open in terms of access from open in terms of wanting or desiring someone's presence. The latter form of openness implies that those who are open have done something to be more than just physically accessible.

The Bishops imply openness is participation in the Christian experience. For some that implies a facilitation of participation as participation will not occur on its own. It's like the catalyst in a chemical experiment.

catalyst - A substance usually present in small amounts relative to the reactants, that modifies, especially increases, the rate of a chemical reaction without being consumed in the process. (American Heritage Dictionary, 1976)

Interesting definition.
Small amounts, yes.
Especially increases the rate of reaction, yes.
Without being consumed in the process, yes.

Costs are at times given as the reason for a lack of programs for persons with disability. The point I find interesting about this excuse, is that we accept it. Perhaps it has just been used for so long, that we assume it is a justifiable response. But I would say, that the next time someone tells you they cannot afford something relative to serving

280

persons with disability, ask them to share with you what the specific costs are, and how they came to determine those costs. I am quite confident they do not know of what they speak.

".. . since provision of access to religious functions is a pastoral duty."

I do not claim to be a Bible expert, however, I cannot remember a time in the New Testament when people were excused from ministry on the basis of finances. It is almost as if finances are somewhat irrelevant. Please do not get me wrong, I understand that things cost money, however, there is much that can be done without money. A major focus of the Bible is both ministry to the poor, and the responsibility of the poor in ministry. God would not call us to only expensive forms of ministry as not all would be able to participate then. It is just as God would not make walking, or vision, or hearing, or cognition a prerequisite to ministry. We are all called to serve independent of our abilities. To whom much is given, much is expected, however, there are very few to whom nothing is given and nothing is expected. We cannot use the excuse of no money for nonparticipation in ministry. That is the cool thing about God's call. Pretty much all of us have what is required for some level of service, we have the ability to be servants independent of our salaries.

The Catholic Bishops are all about access, facilitating access, and removing barriers. This statement (statement 6 above) would not be relevant if the Bishops had not seen a lack of access or the placement of barriers somewhere.

Tuesday, December 14, 2004

U.S. Catholic Bishops part 7

7. We must recognize and appreciate the contribution persons with disabilities can make to the Church's spiritual life, and encourage them to do the Lord's work in the world according to their God-given talents and capacity.

You know, I honestly don't think we do recognize and appreciate the potential contribution persons with disabilities can make. We have an idea of what it might be like if persons with disability were integrated into the church, but really, we don't know.

I remember back in 1985 when I bought my first computer, a Mac (it was amazing). Although I had a notion of what I might be able to use a computer for, part of me felt like I was buying a Cadillac to go the grocery store when I already had a perfectly good electric typewriter. Now, I can hardly imagine life or work without a computer.

Perhaps if persons with disability were truly integrated into the church we would begin to recognize the contributions they have always been available and able to make but never had the opportunity to make because they were not fully included.

The Bishops also chide us that we must "encourage them to do the Lord's work." As I have stated elsewhere in this blog, a friend of mine named Jack is an adult with developmental disabilities who lives at a healthcare center for seniors. Jack lives there because of a medical problem he has, however, he is far and away the youngest man at that place. Many of the other residents are in advanced stages of senility, Alzheimer's, whatever you might want to call their gradual mental regression. But Jack knows all their names, says hello as he walks through the facility, talks about the Lakers (his favorite subject), reads the newspaper with them among many other things I am sure I am just not aware of. Jack is a minister of friendship and encouragement to the people living in that place. He also facilitates prayer for people in that place, staff and residents at times, through mentioning their names at times when we pray at church.

In my mind there is also something special about the prayer of a person with intellectual disability. Now don't get me wrong. The specialness has nothing to do with some idea that they have a special soul, or any other theological goofiness. The Bible says that the prayer of a righteous person avails much. Other notions of prayer are linked to faith. I find that persons with intellectual disability often have great deal of faith (as Jesus recommends, the faith of a little child). I really don't think God looks on us and says, "Your faith isn't as good as someone else's faith because you are intellectually impaired. Or your faith is greater because you are a professor." It is more about what we do with what we have. If I am to have the faith of a little child, then there might be something that I need to loose in order to gain that innocence. I need to loose my overly analytical mind, my need for proof. We are saved by faith. I see some of my intellectually disabled friends much ahead of me in terms of basic faith in God. I also find they are righteous. No they are not perfect. But their unrighteousness is often different from my unrighteousness.

People with unquestioning faith are definitely in need in the church. I could give many examples of such faith in persons with intellectual disability. Times where they encouraged children and adults with their "take Him at his word" approach to God.

So although I appreciate the Bishops' statement, and agree with it, I really don't think we know of what we speak, as the saying goes. Are there blessings to be had if the church is more open to and inclusive of persons with disability? What would we see if the congregation represented the community?

Let's find out...

Thursday, December 16, 2004

U.S. Catholic Bishops part 8

8. We welcome qualified individuals with disabilities to ordination, to consecrated life, and to full-time, professional service in the Church.

Although the primary focus of this blog has been integration of persons with disability, particularly intellectual disability, into the church we have at times touched on other areas of disability. Although I do not understand all aspects of "consecrated life" as mentioned by the Bishops, I suspect there could be vocations which might be filled by persons with some form of intellectual disability. Particularly those which might not require a great deal of study or theological understanding. Those which would not require the supervision of those without intellectual disability or some of the more demanding aspects of teaching. However, I want to move away from intellectual disability for a moment.

There is no doubt that persons with various forms of disability (physical disability, blindness, deafness, etc.) have been ordained and served in full-time professional service to the church. If they did not have these disabilities when they began service, they certainly have developed them over time. As we are using a Catholic document as a point of departure for this discussion, one need only consider the Pope who with advanced age has found himself increasingly facing apparent physical disabilities. Although these disabilities have impacted his ministry, they have in no way limited the impact of his ministry. I suspect there are many who upon seeing his disability are actually encouraged by the fact that he can relate to the physical issues they are facing in their lives.

There are also those who have been disabled by others in the service of God. The Bible speaks of horrific tortures people have faced over time because they refused to either denounce a belief in God, or refused to stop telling others about God. I cannot imagine we would now disqualify those who endured such trials from working in ministry.

I have known a variety of people who have served as ministers who also experienced disability. One of the most powerful sermons I ever saw was delivered by Rev. Steve Chance. He is an ordained minister who also has cerebral palsy. I remember Steve would sit in the front row of the church waiting to be introduced. Upon his introduction, he would slowly go up the steps leading to the stage so that he could deliver his message. You struggled with him as he made his way up the steps. Just the act of him climbing those steps drew you in, gave you some small bit of empathy toward the challenge moving around the community might be for him. As he would reach the platform and move toward the lectern, you were relieved. Steve, somewhat haltingly, would then turn and rivet the audience with a brief pause. "Is God fair?" he began, and you knew that he had a good notion of whether on not God was based upon his personal experience. Contrast that presentation with the good looking well built pastor who bounds up on stage and asks the same question. Steve had and has a vital ministry because of the experiences God has placed in his life. Experiences you and I and probably Steve would chose not to have, but the end result is a powerful witness for God in a way that others could not emulate.

I was in a meeting the other day where several deaf leaders in their church spoke about the incredible benefit of having a pastor/priest who was able to sign. It was not shared whether or not the person they spoke of was deaf himself. If he was, what a great investment on the part of the church to train up and place him among others who spoke the same language and had similar experiences (I am reminded of God coming to the Earth in the form of man). But even if he wasn't deaf, what an obvious thing to do to minister to a community. Can you imagine going to a church where you not only don't speak the language they speak, you can hardly even perceive it.

Involvement of persons with disability in church leadership is not a mandatory thing that must be done, but it does send a message to the congregation about what the church thinks about persons having that characteristic. If I see persons with my same racial flavor in leadership, it implies to me that people like me are valued. If I never see anyone who looks like me in leadership it implies that people like me cannot rise to leadership at worst, or at best that the church is too lazy to find someone like me.

I remember that at the university where I used to teach, a new building was built with a large lecture hall. The stage of the lecture hall had no wheelchair access to it. I can imagine the discussion between those who planned that stage . . . "Do you think we need to have wheelchair access to the stage?" "Naw, nobody in a wheelchair would be speaking to this group. Besides, if the university thinks it's important, they can add a lift or something later." The ultimately did.

If the church wants to engage the community, to bring the community in, to minister to the community, then the congregation must reflect the community AND the leadership must reflect the community as well. If I don't see myself there, then I won't come.

Tuesday, December 21, 2004

U.S. Catholic Bishops part 9

9. Often families are not prepared for the birth of a child with a disability or the development of impairments. Our pastoral response is to become informed about disabilities and to offer ongoing support to the family and welcome to the child.

It is interesting the Bishops in response to a family being unprepared for a child with disability, say that it is the pastor's own responsibility, the pastoral response to become informed about disability. Wow, what an incredible response! The point is that although the family may be unprepared, the Bishops and their representatives within the church are not. Priests have received training and developed experience to assist families. Pastors and leaders in any type of a pastoral position recognize that in order to have a pastoral response, they must become informed about disabilities in order to offer ongoing support. The goal is to 1) support the family and 2) welcome the child.

As I have interacted with the Bishops' statements, it has become increasingly clear that these statements are a vision the Bishops are describing, not the reality of the situation "on the ground." I am reminded of a presentation I did a while back at Wright State University's Religion and Disability Issues Symposium. I built the presentation around comments made by Scrooge in A Christmas Carol, and the response of those requesting charity. Dickens dialogue goes like this. . .

"Are there no prisons? . . .And the Union workhouses?" demanded Scrooge . . ."Are they still in operation? . . .The Treadmill and the Poor Law are in full vigor, then?". . . "Oh! I was afraid, from what you said at first, that something had occurred to stop them in their useful course," . . ."I wish to be left alone" . . . "since you asked me what I wish, gentlemen, that is my answer" . . . "I help support the establishments I have mentioned – they cost enough: and those who are badly off must go there."

"Many can't go there; and many would rather die."

"If they would rather die," said Scrooge, "they had better do it, and decrease the surplus population. Besides – excuse me – I don't know that."

"But you might know it," observed the gentleman.

I sometimes feel like those requesting money in the Scrooge vignette. There is sometimes a bluster which comes from the pulpit which reminds me of Scrooges response. People in positions of leadership make decisions to exclude and in so many words are saying that they didn't know they were making the decision to exclude, implying that those around them are in error to confront them on such issues. The response by the "gentleman" is wonderful in simply saying that although you do not recognize the contribution you are making to exclusion, to in some ways worsening the problem, ". . . you might know it." The information shared on this weblog, for example, is not something that is hidden from people, or is the result of significant training on my part. One needs only dig a bit into the response of the church to persons with disability to quickly recognize that there is significant failure at nearly every turn. The Bishops recognize that the knowledge required to be pastoral towards persons with disability and their families is knowable. How people can be supported is not only knowable, it is as a rule pretty easy.

Finally the Bishops speak of welcome to the child. Pastors have told me of a church member having a child with Down's syndrome, and not knowing what to say, or commiserating in the horror of it all. This is not an informed response to disability. As I have said elsewhere, persons with Down's syndrome are some of the nicest people in the world, and the problems they face typically have less to do with them than they have to do with the society around them. If I were to grieve at the birth of a child with Down's syndrome, I would grieve more for the inappropriate manner in which society will often treat the child than I will grieve for the child himself or for his disability. This comes from knowledge and experience. ". . . becoming informed about disabilities" through interactions with persons with Down's syndrome and their families.

The fact that pastoral leaders are not informed is indicative of the lack of persons with disabilities and their families within their churches.

Thursday, January 06, 2005

U.S. Catholic Bishops part 10

10. Evangelization efforts are most effective when promoted by diocesan staff and parish committees which include persons with disabilities. Where no such evangelization efforts exist, we urge that they be developed.

It is true that for many forms of disability (blindness, hearing impairment particularly deafness, and physical disability) the inclusion of persons with disability on "diocesan staff" would be helpful. These folks might be perceived as more accessible to others having similar disability.

But it might also be felt that the role of the disabled staff member is to work with the congregational members that were disabled. Using that rationale, we need a white guy for the white people, a black gal for the black people, a bald guy for the bald people and so on. I wonder at the phrase that "evangelization efforts are most effective . . . committees which includes persons with disabilities." Please don't get me wrong, I am in favor of inclusive practices. I understand the need to relate to the community, to identify with the community, to have the community identify with those in any form of leadership. But we must not fall into the trap of patronizing people or seeing them as a Hispanic person or a tall person or a disabled person. We first see them as people. Should there be an evangelist amongst them who wants to serve on the committee, great. But, the person in the chair is on the committee because she is the best person for the committee. She is an evangelist (in this case) who moves about in a wheelchair.

Persons with various disabilities should feel that they have access to the same whatever, the same everything that those without disability have access to. But being in a wheelchair doesn't make a person an evangelist to others in wheelchairs. Placing a person with blindness doesn't not mean we now have a blind ministry. It does mean, however, that we see people for the gifts they bring to the table, and blindness is not a disqualifying factor.

Are there some disabilities which would disqualify a person with that disability from some aspects of Christian service? Absolutely. A person with intellectual disability should probably not be the leader of the Bible study. Particularly if he can't read the Bible, or understand the subtleties of the scripture, his intellectual impairment makes difficult for him. Should such a person serve on the evangelization committee? Maybe. Is he an evangelist?

Can you imagine if someone asked you to serve on a committee because they didn't have anyone who looked like you on the committee. Say it was a committee discussing particle physics, or some other obscure matter that you would have little knowledge of, and probably little to contribute. I for one would last about 10 minutes before I would say,

"You know, I'm sorry, but I really don't have a lot to contribute here. I mean science is great and particles, sure, I'm in favor of particles, but you are not taking advantage of my gifts, and frankly, I just don't understand what you are talking about."

"But we want someone who looks like you on our committee so we can be diverse."

"You know, that's great. I am all in favor of diversity. But I would rather have the best people possible, whatever they look like. It sure is nice to know that people who look like me are welcome on your committee, but there must be someone else who looks like me who could participate. If not, then I am happy to support your work, because the main thing is that you have people who can do the work, not people who look like me."

Now the flip side, however, is that if I am a great candidate for the committee and you don't choose me because of what I look like, well, that's another issue. That's called discrimination. But like section 504 of the Rehabilitation act of 1973 says, "No otherwise qualified handicapped person should be denied access. . . " The key is the otherwise qualified qualifier in the statement.

I must admit, however, that the notion of having persons with various disabilities on the evangelization committee could have its upside. Perhaps this is an effort on the part of the church to begin ministry to persons who they have ignored in the past. Perhaps this is an effort on the part of the church to say,

"Hey, we have gotten our act together and are doing better on this issue. We will prove it to you by placing a person with disability in a position of leadership. Look, there she is on the evangelization committee. In the past we would discriminate against persons such as her, but look at us now! We are doing much better than we did in the past!"

Now that I like. It's like allowing the intellectually disabled man to be an usher, or to serve communion. It's like hiring a staff member who is being PAID to develop ministries to persons with disability (whether or not the person is disabled herself). It's like having support staff available to support a child with autism who happens to show up some Sunday morning. From this perspective, it represents a change on the part of the church, an effort to reach out by correcting past wrongs.

Tuesday, January 11, 2005

U.S. Catholic Bishops: Final Statement

May God Bless the U.S. Catholic Bishops for the vision they describe in the "moral framework" communicated through their 10 statements. These folks are no fools; they recognize that they are describing a vision for the Christian church which we are not currently experiencing. Their statement also empowers those who would work within the church (particularly the Catholic church) to make changes which would result in their statement being a reality. I know this is the case as I have used it myself for that very purpose.

You can say they are unrealistic, but doesn't God often call us to be unrealistic? Is our unrealism a reflection of our vision for the church which in some ways reflects God's vision for the church, or is it a lack of faith on our part to believe that the church could be all that God would want it to be.

You see, in any discussions, when you talk about including all God's children in the church, you have God's heart. I know that when I say that the church needs to be more caring toward persons with disability I am not just Jeff McNair speaking. I have full confidence that I am reflecting the God of the Bible. People will say that we need to be realistic, but I honestly don't know what they mean by that.

I often think people who say those kinds of things assume that I know as little as they about the issue and so they can therefore give me a snow job about costs, or time commitment, or some other reason for why we do not need to include persons with disabilities. It is not just me that they try to convince, it has become the standard response to just about anyone who attempts to call them into account for a heartless approach to persons with disability. The problem is, however, that those responses (cost too much, no facilities, etc.) have been used so successfully in the past, they HAVE become the reason for limited programs (in reality, a lack of caring).

But it's not just me who knows better. The leadership of the Catholic church in America knows better, and it is my hope that they will educate members of their church and the Christian church generally so that the pat answers for a lack of caring which have been so successful in the past will be regarded for what they are.

TASH, The Association for Persons with Severe Handicaps used to have a button that said something like, "When someone says, let's be realistic, it means that someone is about to get screwed." I am tired of the church being realistic. I want the church to be faithful.

Tuesday, January 11, 2005

Wolfensberger on social integration

One of my favorite books on social integration, is "*Normalization, social integration, and community services*" edited by Robert Flynn and Kathleen Nitsch (1980). In an article by Wolfensberger (*The definition of normalization: Update, problems, disagreements, and misunderstandings*), he makes the following comments.

" . . . in the long run, no good can come of any program, including normalization, that is not based on intimate, positive one-to-one relationships between ordinary (unpaid) citizens and those who are handicapped and who would otherwise be devalued."

One on one contact is reminiscent of the idea of matching families in churches with persons with disability within churches in a life partner kind of arrangement.

"Indeed, there is little within the implication of the Wolfensberger definition of normalization that is not empirically supportable, and one would almost have to go to metaphysical systems for more broadly applicable concepts. One such system might be radical Christianity, which would subsume much of normalization, but which would also reject some (not many) of its implications."

Interesting that Wolfensberger suggests "radical Christianity." I am unsure what he means by the term *radical*, but I suspect the implication is something other than what is typically observed in churches.

In a second article in the same book (*Research, empiricism, and the principle of normalization*), Wolfensberger states

"Thus, when devalued people are served in valued settings, where familiar and valued methods are used, and together with other valued people (i.e., associated with positive images), their social desirability in the eyes of others (i.e., the potential assimilators) will be increased.

The findings also imply that the development of highly valued personal traits, such as courtesy, friendliness, generosity, hospitality, sociability, and attractive appearance, in devalued persons is extremely important in moving them toward acceptance by members of society and therefore toward the integration onto the community."

This is similar to Berger and Neuhaus' 1977 article, "*To empower people: The role of mediating structures in public policy*" who define the concept "mediating structures." Mediating structures being people who help a devalued group by introducing them to those who can help them, or by helping them themselves. This is the track the church should be on. By our involvement, our service, our work, we validate the lives of persons with disability and in some ways make it "cool" to serve them. The more we embrace this notion as the church, the better for persons with disability and the church.

Monday, September 20, 2004

How would things be different? People with disability

For the next few blogs, I want to look at how things might be different if the church around the world were more responsive to persons with disability, particularly intellectual disability. Let's next look at how things might be different for persons with disability.

These differences can be considered according to several general headings.
1-how persons with disability would perceive the church
2-how persons with disability would perceive God
3-how persons with disability would perceive themselves
4-what persons with disability would do

Let's look at each of these areas briefly.

An interesting study would be to determine how persons with disability currently perceive the church. It is always tricky asking persons with intellectual disability what they think about anything as they will try to tell you what they think you want to hear, not necessarily what they think. But I do wonder what they say to each other about the church. I suspect it is mostly related to the people they know at the church and less related to "the church" per se.

But wouldn't it be incredible if the community of persons with disability (persons with disabilities and their families) thought of the church as their "go to guy" in virtually any situation. That the words which would come out the mouth of any person either directly or indirectly interacting with a person with disability would be, "Where do you go to church?" Or even "You should go to a church because they will definitely take care of you there." Or "If you want to meet some really friendly, helpful people, you ought to go to the church." I can almost imagine a world where the church would be the best, first place for a family or a person with a disability to get connected. If the church was being obedient, it would quickly gain that reputation. The connection between the church and persons with disability would be as natural as bringing a new baby home to a family, or going to the hospital if you are sick. It would be the obvious thing to do because of the results others who did the same thing experienced. Word of mouth would quickly spread and even state agencies would be caught up in the natural supports being provided by churches.

Persons with disability and their families would then perceive God as someone who cares. Someone who reaches out to those in need. Someone who sees value in all people. Someone who is willing to be inconvenienced in order to include everyone. Isn't that who God is? Christians are quick to speak of how God in the form of Jesus was willing to die for them so He could have fellowship with them and they could be a part of His kingdom. Are Christians willing to take people with disabilities out to lunch, or call them on the phone so they can be a part of the church? Are they willing to be "inconvenienced" in any way so that people with disability can feel the value they have in God's eyes? Interestingly there is research which indicates that parents of children with disabilities feel supported personally by their religious faith, but do not feel supported corporately by the church. Sad.

That the church does not do what it should, impacts how persons with disability perceive themselves. We have outreach programs for a variety of groups, but not necessarily for persons with disability. One might counter, "But we don't exclude them from our outreach?" Perhaps true, however, you won't recruit poor people if you exclusively go to Starbucks. You won't recruit older people if you go exclusively to the YMCA. Unfortunately due to a variety of factors which influence the life experience of persons with intellectual disability, they are often do not have access to the same avenues for recruitment that typically might bring in other groups. They often can't read, they have limited transportation abilities because they typically can't drive, they often have financial problems. No, in order to recruit members of that group, you must specifically go after them, find and reach out to them. The fact that specific efforts are not being made to bring these individuals in says to them that they are not of particular interest to the church. The fact that there aren't more persons with intellectual disability attending the church is particularly damning, because if invited, probably the majority would come. That they are not there indicates that no one is inviting them. It is not difficult to make the jump between the fact that because the church doesn't want me that probably is because God doesn't want me.

What persons with disability would do is come to church to access the friendship and supports they would receive (their motivation then, would be no different from persons without disability who attend church).

Saturday, July 31, 2004

How would things be different? The church

For the next few blogs, I want to look at how things might be different if the church around the world were more responsive to persons with disability, particularly intellectual disability. We will first look at how the church might be different.

If the church were more accepting of persons with disability, there are several ways in which things would be different. Let's consider these differences according to several general headings.

1-congregational make-up
2-congregational attitudes
3-community perceptions
4-God's blessings

If all congregations were accepting of persons with intellectual disability, the make-up of the congregation would be different. Instead of

292

the hundreds of individuals with disability remaining at home on Sunday mornings, they would be at church, in the congregation. It would not be unusual for you to come to church and sit down next to a person who had a intellectual disability. There would also be a greater likelihood that families of these persons would be in attendance which would further increase the percentage of individuals directly affected by disability. At least initially, until the practice became more commonplace, there would be those who would come to see whether the church was really open to these individuals. They would hear about the unpredictability of the congregation at times, and might want to come to see if something unusual would happen, and how those in the congregation would react.

By having a steady diet of persons with intellectual disability in the congregation, people would either come to accept those members, or seek to find another church where they can worship undistracted (I wonder where the practice of undistracted worship first came into place in the church? We are to at times pray in a private place, however, there is no indication that I can see that worship ALWAYS needs to be so predictable and regular, to the point where a baby crying is cause for my consternation). If all churches were open to persons with intellectual disability then there would be nowhere you could go to get away from them! I like that idea. The presence of these kinds of disabled persons also broadens your definition of normal. You break out of a situation where everyone is just like you who attends your church. I come to learn that there are variations in the manner in which a person can act and still be a Christian. I come to learn that there are variations in ability level in persons who are Christians. I confront my own hard, brittle attitudes towards acceptable differences in persons, and am hopefully softened with the rest of the environment. I am confronted by Christian brothers and sisters who wisely tell me that I am the one who needs to change, not necessarily the persons with disability.

Community perceptions will change as well. Christians are criticized for being intolerant. Trust me I know after 15 years at a state university campus. It is difficult to be accused of intolerance when you are leading the way in including disenfranchised persons in your fellowship, taking them into your home, meeting their needs. Not only do you serve those who come to you, you scour the community to find others whose needs you might meet. The church becomes preoccupied with meeting the needs of hurting, in this case disabled, persons in the community. Quickly the community will know, that if you have a problem, go to the church as they will do whatever they can to help you and include you. I remember hearing speeches by politicians who held diametrically opposed views on issues like abortion or programs to the poor, to those of Mother Theresa. However, whenever she was with them, they could not argue with her life

293

as she spent it with the poorest of the poor in India. I remember her even upbraiding a president about his position on abortion, and all he could do is listen. It is that kind of life the church needs to evidence in the community. A life of caring and service which silences the voices of many deriders, and becomes a place where people are drawn to see what it is that motivates these people to do what they are doing.

Finally, there are the blessings we will receive from God for being obedient in this area. Who knows what God might do in our midst if we were obedient in this area? I personally would like to find out what He might do. I think He would expand the numbers of the church exponentially. I think he would bless us beyond belief for reaching out to the types of people that Jesus himself reached out to.

I once attended a conference on the church and disability where Dr. John Stott was the keynote presenter. After his presentation, I followed him and was able to get off a brief question. "Why is it do you think, Dr. Stott, that the church has been so unresponsive towards persons with disability?" His response was basically, because the church is simply being disobedient. Wow. I have never forgotten that brief interchange. It is true, that the church is disobedient. Yet we mask our disobedience under a variety of excuses.

Imagine meeting the Lord and saying,
"You know, we would have fulfilled the great commission, but it was just too expensive.
Or, we would have fulfilled the great commission, but it just wasn't a priority.
Or, we would have fulfilled the great commission, but if we did, lots of the members of our congregation would have left.
Or, we would have fulfilled the great commission, but we didn't know where the people were.
Or, we would have fulfilled the great commission, but nobody in our church wanted to provide leadership.
Or, we would have fulfilled the great commission, but we didn't have any training.
Or, we would have fulfilled the great commission, but we thought that because we pay taxes that the needs of those people were being taken care of.
Or, we would have fulfilled the great commission, but we were worried about our children if we brought those people in.
Or, we would have fulfilled the great commission, but those people disrupt the worship service, by clapping wrong, or not whispering, or having social skill deficits.
Or, we would have fulfilled the great commission, but when we ask for prayer requests, they always air their dirty laundry.

Or, we would have fulfilled the great commission, but if those people come we can't cover the same material in our Bible classes that we typically would.

Or, we would have fulfilled the great commission, but those people are a black hole for service.

Or, we would have fulfilled the great commission, but those people never get better anyway.

Or, we would have fulfilled the great commission, but I could never do that, it takes a lot of patience to work with those kinds of people.

It takes more patience to work with a disobedient worldwide church. Each of the above are real excuses I have heard for why churches/people are not working with persons with intellectual disability. It is easy to see why Dr. Stott portrayed the church as disobedient.

Thursday, July 29, 2004

How would things be different? The community

For the last part of this discussion, I wanted to briefly discuss how the community would be different if the church truly was obedient in the area of disability ministry. First of all, the church would be "the church," not separate churches. It is true that it is easier to talk ecumenically than it is to live it because each denomination has a slightly different perception of what is the truth. We often find ourselves distancing from each other over arguably lesser matters of theology even though we agree on the kernel of the truth; that is who Jesus is and was. Perhaps this will always be an insurmountable hurdle in community collaboration among "the church" for ministry purposes. In my mind, however, this is an important first step.

If you take the city where I live, for example, the City of Redlands, California, Christian churches are a pervasive presence. If the churches in Redlands could somehow become "the church" in Redlands, the impact would be incredible. But as Tolkien has one of his characters in the Lord of the Rings comment, the power of the enemy is seen in the disarray of those who oppose him. If "the church" in Redlands made ministry to persons with disability a peculiar focus (it would be peculiar in comparison to the church worldwide) families of persons with disabilities would flock to Redlands to receive the support and compassion of "the church" there. Secular community agencies would speak of the powerful impact of "the church" in the community and the lives of persons with disabilities and their families. Even the most radically secular of individuals would have to admit, "I'm no Christian, but 'the church' in Redlands surely would make me give Christianity a good look." The churches in Redlands truly being "the church" would be a model for the entire world.

Monday, August 02, 2004

Ideals for church ministry

I sometimes wonder whether I really know what specifically I am after when I think of the ideal for involvement of persons with intellectual disabilities in the church.

I know I want the church to be accepting. I think there is an institution wide problem of perception. A misunderstanding about who people with disabilities are. In its best form it is simply paternalistic and condescending. People with intellectual disabilities are treated as if they are children. In its worst form, it is theologically incorrect and even evil. People with disability are seen as the result of evil, or lacking faith. The response might even be, "But they are the result of evil. Disability is the result of the Fall" which illustrates the point. As true as that statement might be, I have compassion on the child of the alcoholic, I don't blame the child for the sins of the parent. If disability is indeed the result of sin (from the Fall or parents) the victim should not be the one blamed. The sin should have little or no impact on interactions (other than perhaps increasing compassion), as those interacting with the person with intellectual disability carry the same burden of inherited sin that I experience.

I want people, Christians overall to be more patient and more accepting. I know of a situation where a woman with moderate disability was excluded from a Bible study. As it turned out, the people in the Bible study basically just didn't want her there. There wasn't anything in particular that she was doing "wrong." How can this happen in a Christian church? If the reason I go to church is for me, then it can easily happen. I want comfort, sameness, no confrontation, music I like, and my donut to be fresh. If I go to church to meet with God, I want accessibility and acceptance for those around me so that they can have a positive worship experience. I want to be in a place where people are serious about taking the Gospel to the world, to all people and welcoming those people when they come to the church.

I want the church to be willing to adapt what it does in order to include persons with disability. Rather than saying "we have no place for you" the church should be saying, "we will change so there is a place for you." We shouldn't say things like, "that is not a priority for ministry" or "we haven't the funds to start that" or "we haven't the training to do that" all of which are just excuses for a lack of interest. We should be saying, "We don't have anything today for your child with autism, but can you give us 2 weeks and we will be ready. Please give us 2 weeks so we can have the opportunity to serve you, your child and your family."

I want people to see their responsibility toward others in the church as a 24/7 kind of thing. I am speaking to myself when I say that we need to care more about all the people in the church. In regards to persons with disability, phone calls, an occasional lunch out would be great, and so appreciated. Many persons with intellectual disability, particularly in the town where I live, consider a lunch at a burger place a big deal as such extravagances are often not within their budgets.

I want families to teach their children about persons with disabilities. I want children to have experiences with persons with disabilities. To know people with intellectual disabilities by name so they can understand who they are and develop relationships with them. It is through this kind of understanding that fear and discomfort goes away.

I want people in the church to be prepared to live in the world. Obviously instruction in the Bible is critical. Instruction in other areas of life is also important. Using our subject, instruction might be provided in interacting with persons with disability; how does one interact, what would you say, what might you do. This instruction is perhaps necessary not because there is some secret about it, or some special knowledge that is needed, but just to break down the intellectual walls which cause people to believe that there are special secrets or special knowledge that is needed.

I will never forget the first time I was given instruction in what to do if someone has a seizure. I expected complicated instructions about, well I don't know what, but I expected complicated instructions. When a person has a seizure, the best thing you can do is to help them to the ground, if they haven't already fallen down, and just allow them to go through the seizure. You might keep track of how long the seizure lasts or keep their head from banging against something hard and you want to help the person once they come out of the seizure, be sure they are ok, don't need anything, etc. but otherwise you basically do nothing.

I want people within the church to understand that the way you interact with persons with intellectual disability is no different than those without intellectual disability.

Wednesday, July 07, 2004

Confession of faith

In efforts to make a determination of whether an individual is or is not a Christian, people will attempt to determine whether or not an individual has made a "confession of faith." Ostensibly, this confession of faith implies that the individual in question has made statements to the effect that, "Jesus is Lord," or "I believe in Jesus," or something to the effect that "Jesus died for my sins." Each of these affirmations are good and proper. One might indeed infer that those who make such claims are Christians. However, one must also be careful about considering this form of confession as the exclusive manner in which a confession might be made, or even the most appropriate form of confession.

When someone makes a verbal confession, the underlying assumption on the part of those "receiving" the confession is that the requisite understanding of the principles underlying the confession are present. However, unless described specifically, the hearer has little idea of what has been the thought process which has led the confessor to his statement.

For example one might say "Jesus is Lord" in the same manner as someone might say "Dachshund is dog." That is, a dachshund is a kind of a dog, or that although a dachshund is a dog, I don't want a dog. One might also say, "I believe in Jesus" in the same manner as one would sway, "I believe in gravity." In this case, Jesus is some individual in the background of history that I believe existed and was by all accounts a good man. One might even say "Jesus died for my sins" without an understanding of what Jesus did, or what my sins are or mean. The point is that verbal confession although useful, should not be considered the exclusive confessional form.

Might one evidence a faith commitment without the typical outward evidences of a reasonably described understanding of faith and the accompanying verbal confession? Obviously, if one was unable to speak, she could not tell her story, although perhaps she might be able to tell in written form. Yet, what if one could not relate one's confession in verbal or written form, due to disability, or other circumstantial reasons?

Imagine one having made the "battlefield confession" and then dying as a result of the enemies skill in marksmanship. A confession would have been made, ostensibly to God, to whom it most importantly must be made, but there was no opportunity for others, other people to have heard the confession.

I know an individual who all her life has been somewhat wishy washy in regards to where she stands in relation to Jesus. Neither I or anyone around her have heard her make the basic confession of faith one might consider essential to being a Christian. That is, no one has heard her say, "Jesus is Lord," or "I believe in Jesus." As she approaches the close of her life she is experiencing compounded disability. In addition to the typical pains of old age (particularly of being in one's late nineties) she has had a broken arm, a broken hip and a broken leg, each separate instances over a two year period. Additionally, she woke one morning to find she was completely blind. Because of these disabilities, she is now

298

experiencing the ignominy of limited freedom in a very controlled environment arranged by her care providers. My most recent memories of her include entering her room, with largely blank walls. Only the hospital type of curtains provide some semblance of privacy. Additionally, only the clothes on her back and a tin of peppermints reflect a life which until recently was filled with typical possessions. Interactions with her range from borderline hysteria and paranoia, "You are all trying to make me out to be crazy. No matter what I say, you will turn it around," to clear, intelligent and engaging discussion, to crawling around on the floor of her room in search of her cane (which due to her disability she couldn't use should she find it).

In the midst of these interactions there are times when she lies on her bed and sobs saying, "God, why are you doing this to me? What have I done that was so wrong that you are doing this to me?"

The question that might be asked, is whether these pleas are a reasoned affirmation of faith? Also, what is a more reasoned affirmation of faith? That of the "reasoned" thinker who says the correct words, or that of the desperate person in their last days of life, calling out to "God," if only with questions. The question of which is the more reasoned is perhaps the wrong question. Perhaps it is better to ask what are indications of a real faith in God? I am glad I am able to leave it in his hands.

Thursday, June 24, 2004

Responsibilities versus rights

In our current society, groups are clamoring for various rights. The disabled community is no different. Obviously some rights, such as the right to a public school education, should have been available much before 1979. However, as discussed in Phillip K. Howard's *The Death of Common Sense*, rights can get out of hand. My friend Dr. Rick Langer says that if you want to empower someone give them responsibilities not rights. As soon as I become dependent upon you everything changes. I will expect more of you, I will value you, I will actually need you to fulfill whatever it is that you are doing.

People with disabilities have long been in the position of being reliant upon those without disability to help them. It is those in the not-yet-disabled community who need a little dose of reality when it comes to dependence. I will admit that one of my biggest problems is recognizing my that my "strength" is an illusion in so many ways, particularly in relation to God. As DC Talk says, "the physical world creates a spiritual haze." It takes an effort on my part to see past myself to my utter dependence upon others.

I am also extremely dependent upon my wife Kathi, my children Josh and Amy, and so many others.

One looks upon someone with disability, particularly a severe physical disability and feels sorry for that person, at times because of their dependence upon others. I should look at such a person as I would look at a reflection in a mirror as that is who that person is. She is a physical example of a physical and spiritual reality. I do well to understand that reality.

But I also do well to empower such people by using their gifts within the church. One of the greatest things I can do as a Christian is to pray. People with severe physical disability, for example, have a tremendous opportunity to serve the church in this way (and others) if we will only value them, and also recognize in our dependent situation that our strength is an illusion, and celebrate and practice, our dependence on prayer.

Thursday, June 10, 2004

Using "limited" gifts

"As he looked up, Jesus saw the rich putting their gifts into the temple treasury. He also saw a poor widow put in two very small copper coins. 'I tell you the truth,' he said, 'this poor widow has put in more than all the others. All these people gave their gifts out of their wealth; but she out of her poverty put in all she had to live on.'" (Luke 21:2, NIV)

The obvious analogy here is that persons on fixed incomes, like individuals with disability living on social security are similar to the widow who gave a small amount which was by comparison was a large amount. I have sat in church when persons with severe intellectual disability put a dollar in the offering and saved fifty cents for a donut after church, recognizing that these were probably their two financial splurges for the week. You might say that this is less than the 10% tithe the church has adopted, however, it is the heart of these people which impresses me, not the amount of their gift.

But this verse struck me in another way as I read it this morning. "All these people gave their gifts out of their wealth" caused me to think of other gifts that people without disability have. Gifts like intellect, health, physical strength, social skill, community mobility, understanding of things of the Lord. We often hear that 90% of the work of a church is done by 10% of the people. I honestly think that I have yet to ask a person with a intellectual disability to do something for me and for them to refuse. They are quickly willing to spend their "limited resources" due to disability to do just about anything for the church, for others, whatever might be asked. They are certainly not limited in their desire to serve.

300

Perhaps that is why persons with intellectual disability are beginning to gain the reputation of being such good workers.

Through programs such as supported employment, employers are beginning to see that once the worker understands what she is to do, she will be reliable and dependable. As stated elsewhere they will treat an entry level job as a career. There is a movie I once saw about a woman with cerebral palsy and mild intellectual disability. After years of training she was finally able to get a job as a ticket taker in a movie theater. Her comment upon receiving the job, and being able to hold it for several years was, "To you this might seem like a small thing but to me this is my life."

In Jesus' example of the widow, I think there are at least three take home lessons. One is to celebrate the gifts of those who aren't as gifted. The second is apply her example of sacrifice to ourselves in the way we use all that we have been given. The third is to provide opportunities for those who perhaps aren't as gifted to express their gifts. If your standard for participation is always and only excellence, then only a few will be able to participate. Imagine if the minimal standard for giving in Jesus' time had been a silver coin rather than any gift. The copper coins the widow sacrificed to give would never have been given and therefore never have been used. Her desire to give to God might have gone ignored.

However, if your standard is meeting the desire to give or to serve then all can potentially be involved. If people with intellectual disabilities in my church have the desire to serve but no opportunities are available, then it is my fault, the church's fault, not theirs.

Wednesday, June 09, 2004

Expectations of the rank and file

One of the things I have wondered about over the years, is what is the rank and file Christian's responsibility toward persons with disability in the church? There are people like myself who have chosen this area of ministry (or have been guided to this area of ministry) but what of people who have not taken this on as their focus of ministry?

A friend of mine has given his life to cross cultural missions particularly in foreign countries. He once said that if people were truly serious about their faith they would give themselves to this area of ministry. I responded that from my perspective if people were truly serious about their faith they would give themselves to ministry to persons with disability. Obviously we were both wrong. God calls each of us to different areas of ministry. Our role is to find that area and spend ourselves in that area.

However, the idea of the responsibility we each have in foreign missions might help to understand our roles in other areas of ministry. I am by no means the role model for service to the local church, but it helps me to consider what I might expect of others by thinking what God might expect of me, what others expect of me and what I expect of myself relative to ministries developed by the church.

1. I should recognize that the people involved in ministry have somehow experienced a call to that area of ministry. It is therefore a priority for them and I should respect them for responding to that area.

2. I should support their efforts through prayer, financial support as I am able, and perhaps even occasional service.

3. I should take the time to understand their mission, their goals and how I might support them in some way by what I do.

But I also think there is a larger question in disability ministry as the focus of the ministry is present at the church. People go somewhere to do foreign missions. People with disability are regular members within my midst, at my church. What are the rank and file's responsibilities toward these individuals in their midst? It is interesting how passionate people suddenly become about disability when disability visits their family. Obviously one cannot be passionate about everything, and of course I will take a greater interest in diabetes if my father has it, or in India if my daughter is serving in ministry there. But is there some middle ground of interest, support, service that I might engage in even if disability ministry is not the focus of my life?

I have been coming to a growing realization that when I set foot on my church's campus on Sunday mornings, that I am not there for me. Well I am there for me but it is all not about me. Of course there is the worship service which should focus on God, but there are also other interactions with people, and I am not the focus of those interactions. I guess when I buy my donut and coffee I focus on myself (I have become so predictable that the donut lady has my favorite one waiting for me each Sunday!). But when people talk to me, I try to listen. I try to make other's smile with my silliness. I try to teach people with disabilities about the Lord. I try to make others with severe intellectual disabilities feel welcome as they go through their personal church rituals (see May 22). I try to be accepting and encouraging. At times I will take someone out to lunch later in the week or give them a phone call.

I guess these are the kinds of things I should expect of regular church members. As a rule, at least at my church, they are doing a pretty good job.

Tuesday, June 08, 2004

The memory of disability

John Hull, in his article "A spirituality of disability: The Christian heritage as both problem and potential" states,

". . . Only the disabled seem incapable of inclusion within this universal realm of accepting love. We see the force of this if we ask the naive question why there were not disabled people among the group of close disciples to Jesus. There were none, and it would have been impossible that there should have been any, for the simple reason that Jesus would have restored such people to full health. Indeed, such restoration becomes in itself symbolic of the experience of becoming a disciple."

This is an interesting perspective. However, it is also interesting to note how many of the followers of Jesus during the time he walked the earth would have been people who had been healed of disability, persons who had a memory of disability. The metaphor of becoming a disciple was not lost on me. Later in the article Hull describes how individuals with disability may have a greater experience with the range of human experience. I believe this is particularly true for persons with acquired disability, as for persons with congenital disability, as that experience would be their sole experience. Anyway, how interesting to think that the church was born amongst a significant proportion of people who were once literally disabled, and were healed out of that experience. One wonders what effect that perspective had on the foundation of the church. Although Paul was healed from the metaphoric disability of unbelief, his personal disability remained.

Hull at times wonders at the Bible's metaphorical use of disability in connection with sin, which in my mind seems to be the idea which blossomed in the church. Metaphorical disability was equated with actual disability, and metaphorical healing of disability through belief was equated with actual physical healing. The result being the condemnation of persons with disability as either being sinful or faithless (see April 24 posting).

Thursday, April 29, 2004

Understanding People With Disabilities

The regular life

A friend of mine contacted me this week. She is a someone with a disability who told me about her feelings of loneliness and being stressed about other aspects of her life that she is currently going through. Hopefully, I can try to do better in terms of calling or visiting, but it is difficult. I work full time, I have a family. These responsibilities force choices on my time that I often don't like to make but I must make nonetheless.

An aspect of the empowerment of people with disabilities whereby they take on typical lives are the consequences of living typical lives. My friend was living in a group home where there were other adults living. She was unhappy there because of many of the restrictions that go along with living with others, particularly in a group home setting. She made the decision to move out on her own. She is now living independently, and largely doing very well. However, when you live by yourself in an apartment, a natural consequence is that your friendships must be developed by you. If you want people to come to your house, you need to invite them. A natural consequence of living by yourself, is that if you do not make efforts to get out, to meet other people, to invite people to your home, you will be lonely.

This illustrates a critical principle in our efforts to facilitate regular lives for people who have been denied regular lives. That is, regular lives are not perfect lives. My presence in the community, living independently, does not mean that my life is suddenly filled with things that I necessarily would not have if I had less independence. A critical aspect of a regular life is that I am largely left alone. I find this in my own life. I have many friends, however, unless I invite them to do something with me, I spend a lot of time alone. Now I have the benefit of being married, but a regular life is a life of independence and aloneness if I rely exclusively on others to just come by on a whim. Those living regular lives who don't experience a disability don't typically expect such a thing, so what does it imply about the "regularness" of the life of a person with a disability if they expect to be catered to in a way different from those not experiencing a disability?

I am acutely aware of the restrictions on the lives of those who experience less independence. They have neither the ability nor the understanding of how to facilitate friendships with people outside of the facility in which they live. I therefore make an effort to come to them to bring the regularness of a friend stopping by for a conversation. I go, for example, to a group home for adults with intellectual disabilities and have a coke and some ice cream while we just talk about what is going on in their lives. If someone didn't do that, then their lives would largely be filled with people paid to be with them or people with equally regulated lives experiencing similar disabilities. My presence brings a wild, off the reservation, kind of regularness. When I visit, they stay up later, they eat foods that are fun (and not necessarily "good" for them or on the diet plan developed by a nutritionist) in larger quantities that they wouldn't typically eat, they may travel with me to someplace in the community they wouldn't otherwise be able to visit, they meet new people who are interested in them but not paid to be with them, have experiences typical to the average person, but not to people with regulated lives and so on and so on.

The person with disabilities living independently may live in poverty, but they are independent and pretty much have the opportunities to move about the community that anyone has. But I find an expectation in a subset of people with this experience that I don't see in those who live in more restricted settings and I admit that I am not sure what to make of it. I am confident that some do not know how to make their own lives less lonely. I also try to do what I can to enrich their lives and when someone tells me they are lonely, I feel a responsibility to reach out to them.

I guess I just also want to tell them "welcome to the regular life." Regular life is often loneliness. It is often making what you can of your own life. It is maximizing your opportunities and not relying exclusively on others to make your life for you. Obviously, there are people who have such significant disabilities that they have to have people in their lives, volunteer or paid, to do the simplest of things. However, if I have achieved a "regular life" and I simply wait at home for other people to make my life into something when I have the ability to do most everything for myself, I may be proclaiming that I do not want a regular life.

Friday, December 12, 2008

"Us" becoming like "Them"

I have had a bit of a revelation in the last few weeks. I finished writing an article that has a great title. It is called, "The indispensable nature of persons with intellectual disabilities to the church." It should be coming out in the next few months in the *Journal of Religion, Disability and Health.* Anyway, as often happens when you submit an article, it was sent back to me with some questions, and suggestions for changes both of which need to be addressed if the article is to be published.

As I was working through the revisions, an idea hit me. In an integrated setting where people with and without intellectual disabilities are together, you obviously have two different groups in interaction with each other: those with intellectual disabilities and those without intellectual disabilities. Now those without intellectual disabilities have the ability to learn social skills, and to pretty much reflect what might be called nondisabled society. In contrast, those with intellectual disabilities may not understand social skills and therefore do not reflect nondisabled society. So for example, research indicates that people with disabilities loose their jobs most frequently because of minor social skill deficits. But I also note that my friends with ID have a very different perspective on disability. They may not see themselves as disabled, and may not regard others with disabilities like their own or even more severe, as disabled. I find that they typically just see others as people.

I have one friend with ID who says that a person with a disability is someone who can't get along with other people and gets into fights. So when I ask him whether he knows someone who has a disability, even though I know that he knows people who use wheelchairs or walkers and have severe ID to the point of being nonverbal, he comes back to his definition and tries to think of someone who is difficult to get along with.

But getting back to my point, as I am spending time with friends with intellectual disability, I find that I have the ability to change in a variety of ways while they don't always have the ability to change. So, in order for there to be social interactions with them, I have to change. Actually (and this was my revelation), I think that I become more like them, I become more like my intellectually disabled friends. Specifically,

I don't worry so much about social skills and there are few things someone might do, socially, that would shock or alarm me. I become like them in that way.

I begin to see people as people whether or not they have a disability. They are not characterized in my mind as my friends and my disabled friends. I become like them in that way.

They are very forgiving of others who are unkind to them. Hopefully I become like them in that way.

I will also say, unapologetically, that they are more loving toward others than I often am. Hopefully I become like them in that way.

These and other changes are not forced on me in any kind of willful acts on their part. It just kind of becomes the rules of the game if I am going to be able to interact with them. So they change me/I become more like them. In order for the environment to soften to include them, there is a level at which the environment becomes like them.

In the words of the title of my article, the indispensable nature is at least partly the positive ways that I become like them as a result of being with them.

Wednesday, September 24, 2008

Typical experiences

In his discussion of the wounding experienced by persons with disabilities, Dr. Wolf Wolfensberger relates that often, particularly people with intellectual disabilities do not have the experiences typical of people in their culture. So in the US, for example, I have known adults with intellectual disabilities who had never been to a restaurant before. I actually had the delight of taking a few friends to their first restaurant when I found they had never been to one. Being in Southern California, we have found that many people have never been to the beach, or up in the snow when the mountains are white in the Winter. But recently in our group at church, I have discovered a few other examples.

People enjoy hearing about other people's trips to exotic places. Most persons with intellectual disabilities don't get to hear about people living or traveling to Africa, for example, because they do not have people who are making such travels in their social networks. Therefore the simple experience of someone going on a trip, coming home, and then sharing pictures is something that may have never experienced.

This past week, the women of our group sponsored a wedding shower for another woman who participates in our group. I wonder how many wedding showers the typical adult with intellectual disabilities participates in her lifetime? Kathi told me that it was a delightful time where gifts were carefully selected and presented with pride and anticipation, and received with sincere thanks. What a wonderful memory for the future bride and all those who participated in her shower. The men of the group also teased about the shower as a "chick" occasion as men do which is actually a part of the fun of whole experience.

How wonderful to be able to enrich lives of people who through no fault of their own miss out on typical things that are part of the lives of those who do not have an intellectual disability.

Tuesday, September 16, 2008

"Forgiveness"

At the IASSID conference in South Africa, I attended a session by a researcher from the UK. The woman was doing research on attitudes towards children with disabilities, and particularly toward their mothers in some of the more remote, tribal areas of Africa. Among the tribe she studied, there is the perception that a woman has a child with a disability because of something wrong she has done. She has "sinned" in some way and the result is that the spirits have given her a child with a disability as a punishment. The researchers, recognizing how important the relationship is between mother and child in the development of children with intellectual disabilities, wondered whether there could be a way within the tribal system that the perceived "sin" of the mother could be "forgiven" such that a better relationship might be fostered with the child and with the community for that matter. They facilitated mothers going through rituals with the tribal leaders/healers that cost lots of money and took many months, but in the end, the mothers were "forgiven" of their supposed "sin" that led to the birth of their child. This ritual resulted, according to the researchers, in better relationships between mother and child as the mother no longer felt the disdain of the society (she was "forgiven") nor her own guilt for something that she had been taught that she must have done (but probably had little idea of what it might be).

Lest you laugh off this account as you look at it through your western eyes, women, families in the West, in the US for goodness sakes often face the same kinds of perceptions as was evidenced in tribal Africa. Research indicates that families, in particular mothers, will question God at the birth of a child with a disability wondering "What did I do to deserve this?" The fact that this question is even typically in their mindset illustrates that it is a part of how our society thinks about disability and the birth of a child with a disability. Somehow this social construction seems somewhat universal. Unfortunately, it has at times also been reinforced by various societal groups, including to a greater or lesser extant, Christian churches. Because this notion is such a basic part of our psyche, and because the Bible does not support such a notion, we as Christians must go out of our way to fight such an understanding of disability

There is a ministry of mercy that the church and Christians can play in the lives of families, particularly mothers and fathers of children with disabilities. That is, that as the opportunity arises we refute claims about a parent's sin being the reason for a disability. We don't provide some silly, syrupy notion of God looking down and choosing families to have a disabled child, however, we do support that disability is in some way a part of God's plan for human beings. The child with Down's syndrome is not someone who somehow escaped God's notice and was born with an

311

extra chromosome. In many ways, such children are part of God's plan for people.

Now obviously there are things a parent, particularly a mother can do, like drink excessively during pregnancy, that can lead to a disability in their child. What I am talking about, however, is the birth of a child with Down's syndrome, for example and other similar disabilities. Not that we should criticize the mother of a child with fetal alcohol syndrome, but rather that the healing process in that mother's life is very different from that of a mother of a child with Down's syndrome, for example.

Because disability is or has taken on such a negative perception, people assume there must be some form of evil behind it, and wrongly and unfortunately, the evil is usually placed at the feet of the mother. It is interesting to note, for example, that when autism was first described, its cause was said to be due to "icebox parents." Once again, it was believed that it was unloving parents who had children with autism. Nothing could be further from the truth, however, because of the notion once again of sin linked with disability, even 1940's researchers would make the connection between the two.

Another of the researchers at the IASSID conference was from Iceland. Interestingly, she noted that in Iceland the divorce rate among parents of children with disabilities was LESS than that of couples who did not have a disabled child. This is quite a statistic. With supports, parents can see the birth of a child with a disability in a totally different manner. Supports can be provided that may actually make the family unit stronger rather than weaker. I suspect a lot of this strength is related to the manner in which disability is perceived, or people are taught over time to perceive the birth of a child with a disability.

That is my prayer for the Christian church. I pray for the day that parents of children with disabilities are drawn to the church because of the support they will feel there. That the response to the birth of a child with a disability is not "I must have sinned" but "I need to go to a church where they will love, understand and support me." **That people, Christian or otherwise, would intrinsically link disability and church.** If we were really supporting people with disabilities and their families, the community witness would be irrefutable. It would also go a long way in refuting the socially constructed link between disability and sin.

Wednesday, September 10, 2008

On the death of a friend

A friend of mine, a woman who lived her life with severe intellectual disabilities died this week. She wasn't particularly old, maybe in her 40's. She lived in a group home with other adults with similar disabilities. Her roommate is a wonderful gal, who saw her relationship with her roommate as a ministry. You see, she herself was cared for by a woman with Down's syndrome in the institution in which she lived as a child, and now feels it is her responsibility to care for people with Down's syndrome. She has now had two roommates over the last 16 years who were women with Down's syndrome, very similar in personality that she has cared for and has ministered to.

Anyway, the woman who died, wasn't particularly ill, she had had the cough that has been going around Southern California this year, but otherwise was not sickly. The men who also lived at her group home told me as I walked in the door last night, "Pray for Sally. She in hospital. Pray for Sally." They then went on to tell me how a fire truck had come and took her away to the hospital on a bed. I knew that she had died, but they didn't as of yet.

But Sally (not her real name) was a sweet woman. I think I will always remember her as being the gentlest person I have ever met. When she would touch your hand, or touch your face, her touch was so caring, so gentle. She used few words, and was at times distracted by things around her. She would interact with you somewhat when you got her attention. She would respond "yes" at times to questions with a kind of up swinging inflection to her voice. She would attempt to communicate at times, and we were always delighted when we understood what she was trying to communicate. When I would visit the group home, I would bring Coke and ice cream cones. She enjoyed both, and although she would occasionally need encouragement to eat her dinner, she never needed encouragement to eat her ice cream cone. As I was thinking about her passing, it gave me great joy to think that I had the privilege of doing something for her that she really enjoyed. I may have given her more ice cream cones than any one else in the waning years of her life, and may have given her her last ice cream cone. It makes me smile to think of that. She had the ability to bring out the best in people around her. As I have already said, her gentleness caused others around her to be gentle with her and to be patient with her. Her gentle voice caused people around her to be kind and gentle with their own voices. I wish I had the ability to recruit that kind of response from people.

Her "working life" was spent going to a day program, largely adult day care, but that type of program maximized her abilities vocationally. I think it took much to get her to move from place to place.

313

She was loved by her roommate, by the group home caretakers, who both cried at her passing and by the men at the group home who were so intent on her being prayed for while she was in the hospital. I too will remember her the rest of my life.

Because her group home parents are limited in their ability to speak English, they asked me if I would tell the men in the group home about the fact that she died. I must say that I have never had the experience of sharing the death of a person with a group of intellectually disabled adults before. I asked them to all sit down together on a couple of couches and I sat on the floor in front of them.

"Do you remember that you told me that the fire truck came, and they took Sally to the hospital on the bed?"

"Yes" they all replied and recanted the excitement of the fire men and the fire trucks, and said once again, "You need to pray for Sally, she in hospital."

"Well, Sally was very sick when she went to the hospital and while she was in the hospital, she died."

"She died?"

"Yes, Sally died in the hospital. That means that we won't ever see Sally again and that makes me sad. But we know that Sally is in heaven with Jesus."

There was silence for a moment.

"So we will be sad for a while, but we can be happy because we know that Sally is in heaven with Jesus."

"Sally is in heaven" several of the men repeated.

One of the men said, "Will I die?"

"Yes, you will die, and I will die, and Kathi (my wife who they know) will die, and Fred (the group home dad) will die. We will all die someday."

"I no die" said one of men. "I no die, Jeff."

"Well you will die someday, and you will be with Jesus in heaven."

"I no die, Jeff."

I then led them in a prayer for Sally's family, and they stopped asking me to pray for Sally in the hospital. It seemed they understood.

One last comment on this. My wife Kathi noted to me today that in at least two recent situations where a close friend of one of our friends who are Christians with intellectual disabilities died, that there is immediate acceptance. Sure they are sad, but very briefly, and they are quick to talk about their friend being with Jesus, being in heaven. It is as if their faith is so strong, that they immediately accept the truth of what they have been told about what happens to someone who dies "in the

Lord." As 1 Thessalonians 4:13 says, "But we do not want you to be uninformed, brethren, about those who are asleep, so that you will not grieve as do the rest of those who have no hope." My friends with intellectual disabilities appear to grieve as people with hope.

Upon hearing about Sally's passing, her roommate commented, "She doesn't have Down's syndrome anymore." I don't know if that is true, but I know what she meant and what she meant is true. Her future is one that is entirely unimpaired in her vision and her understanding of God.

Tuesday, February 26, 2008

Sally's memorial service

To follow up on my last entry, we held a memorial service for Sally at our Light and Power class. Circumstances prohibited us from doing this on the two occasions over the past 15 years when two other members of our class died. The first had left the class, had been very ill, and lived at home. We literally didn't know until several months after her death that she had died as for some reason her family cut off contact with us. Then the second person was a man and his family requested that we not tell the group that he had died, but that he had moved. So we honored their requests for a while, but then the other men that he had lived with started reporting that he had died, but once again that was about 6 months later. So Sally was the first person in our group for whom we had the privilege of having a memorial service.

The memorial service went very well, I thought. There was singing and tears, as there should be when a life is remembered. There was discussion of the hope of our salvation, and that Sally was now in heaven with the Lord. But the most poignant moment, to me, was when her room mate read the 23rd Psalm to the class. I was blessed to be able to stand with her as she read, and help her with unfamiliar words. She had the Psalm largely memorized which can become confusing when you are trying to read something. Anyway, she did beautifully. She also closed the meeting with a prayer.

One of the most interesting things, however, was that the group home owners were there. They are a wonderful Christian couple, who are very loving towards the residents. The gal owner, related a story of how there had been many licensing people around, obviously checking to make sure there was nothing wrong about the death. They noticed that there were flowers and a nice sympathy card that had been sent to the home. In fact there was a bouquet for the home, and a bouquet for Sally's room mate. The licensing people were surprised and shocked that someone from the community had not only noticed Sally's death, but that they had responded so kindly by sending flowers. I must tell you that I had nothing

315

to do with the sending of the flowers, but was very proud of my church for sending them. What a great example, a great witness to those licensing people. But it also made me sad to think of how many people like Sally live in group homes where they have no community interaction with others. The group home owner made the comment about how important our group was to Sally because we were here friends, and everyone should have friends in their lives. Such a small thing, but such a huge thing in terms of the quality of a person's life. People in group homes are so isolated. But they are people who would love to have friends as much as anyone loves to have friends. Too often, however, the church has ignored those people.

You know the average person in a group home is someone who would come to church if invited. They would be responsive to the Gospel message. With simple acts of kindness, we could literally change their lives. But we don't do it. We don't try to reach out to people in group homes as the Christian church. As a result they live segregated lives with few friends and limited opportunities for social integration. In the end they die and no one other than licensing even notices. It was such a blessing today to know that the passing of a woman with severe intellectual disabilities was noted by a room full of perhaps 80 people who largely gathered to remember a life. They were also genuinely sad to see her go. It is a small thing, but once again it is an important thing.

Sunday, March 02, 2008

"I used to have Down's syndrome"

I frequently teach a class called "The Exceptional Child" class. The class is also referred to as the intro to special ed class. In the early stages of the course, I like to bring friends of mine with intellectual disabilities to class to be both interviewed by me and also interviewed by the students. For example, this past week I brought four folks, divided the class into four groups, and cycled the class through a time of spending a half hour with each person. Typically students tell me they really enjoy the activity and also learn a lot.

In the course of my interviews of my friends, I always ask the question, "Do you have a disability?" Their response is often "No" or "I don't think so." Which is instructive to students demonstrating to them that disability is not necessarily the defining characteristic of a person's life. This past week, I received a very interesting response to that question from one of the women I brought. I asked a woman who has Down's syndrome...

"Do you have a disability?"

316

"My friend has a disability" she replied. "My friend has Down's syndrome."

"Really" I answered. "I was wondering if you have a disability." She paused.

"I used to have Down's syndrome" she replied.

"What was that like?"

"Well I don't remember too well."

I have known this woman for many years and she often says things that are very profound. I don't think she was trying to make some kind of a point but as I thought about her response it seemed very powerful to me. I can be treated like I am a particular way or I cannot be treated like I am a particular way. If I don't know someone with Down's syndrome, I can treat them like they are strange, or different, or other. To them that might come to mean that they have Down's syndrome. That is, if I have Down's syndrome, people treat me like I am strange or different or other. However, if I am just a friend, I am treated as a known friend, and the same as everyone else. In that way it is kind of like I don't have Down's syndrome anymore.

I am not saying that we pretend that people do not face challenges from their disabilities, or that they sometimes need some deferential treatment. This is not about denying a person has a disability. It is about treating a person like a person in the 95% of areas of life in which the disability is largely irrelevant. My woman friend with Down's syndrome likes conversation and coffee, and working and going to church and dogs, and is concerned about her aged father and so on and so on. And she also has Down's syndrome. This is not the greatest comparison, but I have bad knees. However, I can be in situations where my bad knees are always front and center or my bad knees are pretty much forgotten. In most of my daily life, you needn't remind me of them because they are irrelevant. There are aspects of disability that are like that, things about Down's syndrome that are like that. I don't have to bring someone's Down's syndrome front and center all the time. There are times when I might, but not very frequently in most of my interactions with people.

So my friends words were very encouraging to me. Perhaps her Down's syndrome is not the focus of her life that it was when she was in school, or trying to get eligible for some services. At this point in her life, to her, she "used to have Down's syndrome." Now she is just "a normal human adult" as she would say.

Saturday, January 19, 2008

"Christmas" "Comer" "Bible"

There is a man in the group at our church named Eddie. He is a person affected by significant intellectual disabilities. Because of this disability, he has limited language, although based upon his language you would easily tell that Christmas is his favorite time of year. He uses words like, "Christmas tree" and "Santa Claus" and "presents" among a few others. Recently, however, Eddie added the word "Bible" to his cadre of words. When he would approach me he would now not only say "comer" or words associated with Christmas, he would also now say "Bible." I would respond, "Would you like a Bible?" and he would shake his head yes. Well, I finally got with it and found a Bible for him. I am actually in the process of reviewing picture Bibles to determine what one I would recommend as being the most appropriate for adults with intellectual disabilities. Most of them are very childish in their presentation (they are largely designed for children) or include stories that are not very applicable to adults (or even kids for that matter...one depicts Absalom being yanked from his horse, by the hair, by a tree branch, and another Mary and Joseph on the way to Bethlehem being surrounded by lions).

Anyway, I arrived at one that seemed the most appropriate in the short term, removed some of the childish aspects of it and wrapped it up for Eddie as a Christmas present. He opened it up last week and literally sat for most of the half hour we met just looking through the pages. As I watched him, I wondered what the meaning of all of this was? His requesting a Bible, then receiving one, and then enjoying it.

I can recall at past Christmas parties Eddie would want a book as a Christmas present so perhaps there is an interest in books overall. It could also be that because many others in our group do bring Bibles perhaps he noticed them as well. When we are sitting at tables for the Bible study part of our group, others around him also would open up books as I was talking. So somewhere that interest developed and grew. I am unsure of how he learned the word "Bible" although the fact that he did is a good sign, I think. It is indicative of the environments that he finds himself in. People around him be they those of us at church, or those in his home where he lives have used the word sufficiently enough that it has appeared on his radar screen and now is a part of his vocabulary. He knows what a Bible is (I suspect his understanding is that it is a book that people look at) and he wanted one based upon the request he made to me. Interesting from a special education perspective that he has learned to come to church, come to me and say "comer" and I would give him a donut or something. He then comes to me saying "Bible" with the assumption that I would also give him a Bible. I wonder what the next new request will be?

There is also a membership component of wanting a Bible. The people around him and he himself are all a part of this group. It is a group that he gets into his van, and travels for 15 minutes to go to. They are friendly to him, they interact with him, they listen to him, they seem to like him and they give him good food to eat. But perhaps he noticed that they all had something that he didn't have, a book called a Bible. So in order to be a full member of this group, he needed to have one of these Bibles as well. It is like the initiation into the group.

On a deeper spiritual level, I am unsure what this is all about. Isaiah 55:11 says,

"So will My word be which goes forth from My mouth; It will not return to Me empty, Without accomplishing what I desire, And without succeeding in the matter for which I sent it."

That is something that we know. So God's word in the form of a picture Bible is accomplishing something, I would hope. I trust in that promise, however, I also use what I know about pedagogy to facilitate spiritual development in people who have the characteristic of an intellectual disability. I use the knowledge that people have gained to provide the best Christian education I can without exclusively relying on miracles for someone to learn something. God can use our efforts whatever they may be. However, we should not ignore the knowledge we have about how people learn and rely exclusively on miracles as the way people learning anything about God. Our credo should not be, "Come to our church...it will be a miracle if you learn anything!"

Finally, it is interesting how Eddie, arguably the person who experiences the most significant disability of our group is in some ways providing leadership in this area. I have already heard from at least one other person, "I want a Bible like Eddie's." It is my plan to work through the various picture Bibles as I have said above and provide the best of the group to anyone who would want one, but I may have to speed up that process because of Eddie's example of relishing in his new Bible

It was also funny how once he had it, he would not share it with anyone, even to look at it. I don't know how he will be in the future, but he really valued his Bible, and kept it close like a prized possession even though he probably didn't understand what all the pictures meant, or what the Bible even stands for. It is my prayer that I, as someone who does know what the Bible says, and who can read it to understand it even more, that I may value it like Eddie does; a man with limited understanding.

Thursday, December 13, 2007

Sitting at the feet of people with Down's syndrome

I have been writing about and wrestling with and reading articles on the topic of inclusive Christian religious education. As I have thought through issues, obviously one lesson we should be teaching in any form of religious education is love. People need to learn how to love. The Bible is largely a book about the love of God for people. In religious education circles, we do learn things about love and we do study love. But it feels to me like we study and learn about love like we would learn and study about baseball. I can know a whole lot about baseball and still be a lousy baseball player. To become a good baseball player, or good at anything for that matter, requires practice at that thing. For the Christian, the idea is not to simply learn about love, it is to practice love and become good at love. To sit at the feet of people who really do love their neighbors.

It also struck me recently, what the well known passage in 1 Corinthians 13:2 says, "If I have the gift of prophecy and can fathom all mysteries and all knowledge, and if I have a faith that can move mountains, but have not love, I am nothing."

Isn't it interesting that Paul would juxtapose knowledge with love? He puts two things together which I can only assume have the potential of being confused. That is, I can have all knowledge, but without love I am nothing. So people can become confused thinking that knowledge is more important than love, that the development of knowledge is more important than the development of love. Note also that the opposite is **not** true, "If I have all love, without knowledge I am nothing." In the church, particularly as it relates to religious education, I think we have gotten this one wrong.

I once had the honor to meet Jean Vanier. I asked him, "How is it that the church has missed people with disabilities in terms of ministry and inclusion?" He responded something to the effect, "The church has been focused on the rectitude of doctrine when it should have been focused on the rectitude of love." He too saw he church's confusion about the focus of their efforts. What are the greatest commandments? Jesus said to love God with all your heart mind and strength, and love your neighbor as yourself. Once again it is important to note that he didn't say, memorize 100 Bible verses, and read the complete works of the Niebuhr brothers. That is not to say that those things are not important things. It is just that they are far and away **not** the **most** important things.

So where might I go to learn love, to see it acted out? I would honestly say to go to a place where there will be people with Down's syndrome. I should "sit at the feet of a person with Down's syndrome" because it is there that I would learn about loving other people. I wish I had the love of most of the people with Down's syndrome that I have

320

known in my life. They may not entirely understand love but they sure do love well. We criticize their love saying that they are disabled, that is why they aren't as discriminating as we who are not intellectually disabled. So we put ourselves in the position of criticizing someone who loves his neighbor by saying he should discriminate more. That makes a lot of sense.

If I have all knowledge and not love, I am nothing...

If I could have the knowledge of a theologian or the love of a person with Down's syndrome, what would I choose? Wrong answer again, Church and Christians and world. In our world today, we not only choose to not learn love, we choose to kill those who might teach love to us by their example. We go so far as to prevent them from even being born. We have such a rabid desire to not change that we will even prevent the birth of those who might change us. In our lives, knowledge trumps love and that is a mistake.

Tuesday, December 11, 2007

Elf

Our group periodically has a "movie night" where we rent a film, get a bunch of pizzas and bottles of coke, sit in chairs or lay on the floor and watch the movie. We have found that the more slapstick, the better. Well we had a movie night last night, and with the Christmas season here, we decided to watch *Elf*. It was a big hit and everyone enjoyed it.

It is funny, though, because a lot of the comedy revolved around Buddy (the elf) who although he is pure and loving and kind, struggles because he doesn't understand the social behavior of life in New York. He is friendly and open and loving, but that doesn't always work in New York City. He finds his father (who is on the naughty list) and becomes his "redemption" (I assume he now moved to the nice list). So all the slick sophisticated people move through their lives in a kind of funk while Buddy sees beauty, sees excitement in all that is around him. He is also brutally honest with himself and others about his environment. In the end, the environment changes, his brother likes him, his girlfriend believes him, his father takes a greater interest in his family. It is obvious the connection with adults with intellectual disabilities who are often very similar in their honesty and their loving nature.

The family is also confronted with the choice of changing to adapt to Buddy, or rejecting him. This is the choice I see for the church, change and adapt to persons with various disabilities or reject them. The mother in the family advocates for the family to change while the father advocates for rejection. Ultimately, the father confronts Buddy and does reject him. Once again, this is a perfect illustration of the two options the church has before it. Acceptance or rejection. As an outsider you understand the father's frustration, but you resonate with the mother's and the brother's acceptance. Only a Scrooge would side with the father in the rejection of Buddy in spite of the difficulties he brings to the family because of his differences. But all too often, we as the church have sided with the rejecters (those on the naughty list I might add) rather than going through the changes necessary to accept a person who is different in some way.

At one critical point in the movie, the son, Buddy's brother says to his father, "Buddy loves everybody. You only love yourself." I see that sometimes in the church. The person with intellectual disability loves pretty much everybody. We as the "non-disabled" love mostly ourselves and our own comforts.

At the climax of the movie, people sing *Santa Claus is Coming to Town* as an indication of their Christmas spirit (which could be another complete blog entry) and Santa's sleigh is lifted into the sky. As we rode home in the van, the men in the car one by one, broke out in a mostly unintelligible (as far as the words go) version of *Santa Claus is Coming to Town*. One of the men, Tom, didn't know all of the words. He just sang over and over

You better watch out
You better watch out
You better watch out
You better watch out

Good words for any Christian, any Christian church to remember.

Saturday, December 01, 2007

99 Balloons

My wife Kathi, turned me on to a wonderful video entitled *99 Balloons* which you can view on the internet. In a nutshell, it is the story of a young couple who via prenatal diagnosis discover that they are carrying a child with trisomy 18, a chromosomal difference that causes children to have severe intellectual disabilities, and who typically die within their first year of life. This couple, the Mooney's, however, do not take the route of abortion, thereby "preventing" the birth of the child. They have the child and take you on a journey with them through Eliot's short life. It is a wonderful video, very life affirming.

It reminded me of a book I read a while back called *Defiant Birth* which I wrote about in this blog on 8/11/06. In that posting I wrote the following:

In the book *Defiant birth: Women who resist medical eugenics* the author Melinda Tankard Reist takes on the notion of prenatal diagnosis leading to abortion through the stories of women who having received the diagnosis that the child they were carrying was determined to be disabled, chose to have the child anyway. Of course she relates stories of those who were misdiagnosed, however, the thrust of the story is the experience of women who gave birth to children who were born with various disabilities. These disabilities include anencephaly (a disability which typically takes the life of the newborn within hours or days) and of course Down's syndrome. There are many amazing lessons to be gained. One, for instance relates to carrying a baby with anencephaly to term.

Overwhelmingly, doctors would advocate for abortion of such children as they will die soon after birth anyway. Tankard Reist, however, says that if you knew your child would die in an hour or a day, would you choose to kill your child or would you enjoy the hour or day you had remaining with your child? Mothers spoke of their child living his entire life in their arms, of celebrating the 1 day birthday, or the trip home from the hospital. They also spoke of the impact for good the birth of the child had on their lives.

These types of stories are an affront to too many in the medical profession who advocate prenatal diagnosis and abortion. In an Animal Farm kind of way, they describe this procedure with words like "prevention" but we are talking about the killing of an infant. It is particularly insidious to me that people, particularly women who are in a very stressful, very unsure position are not given all the information in order to make their "decision." Even the notion of a "decision" as to whether someone should live or die reflects a position in favor of death. I don't get to make decisions about the people I work with because that is immoral, and should I make a "decision" to take someone's life, there is a good chance that justice would prevail and I would loose my own. Yet in the case of a newborn with severe disabilities, we have engaged killing by couching it as a decision. I have had many interactions with the medical profession which supports my feeling that they are morally and ethically lost.

I once worked with one of the top physicians in disability in the country. This doctor is known for his work on behalf of children with disabilities. However, I often accompanied him when he would tell parents or teach students to just tell the family who have received a prenatal diagnosis of disability to "abort and try again." That is all that life is...abort and try again. Could I cheapen the value of a life any more than to dismiss it by saying, "kill it and have another baby." This is wisdom in the eyes of many in the world, and many in the medical profession.

In another instance I was a medical student taking a class in Genetics. After you have watched the *99 Balloons* video, consider this. The professor speaking specifically about trisomy 18, what Eliot had, told the medical students, "You can reassure the parents that the child will die in the first year of life." Once again, I am struck by the perception of the lives of people with disabilities as perceived by the medical profession. It is portrayed that their deaths are a blessing for themselves and all those around them. We can relax, and be comforted by the knowledge that they will soon be dead.

Videos like *99 Balloons* and books like *Defiant Birth* are critical strikes in the war for life. They are an attack on the supposedly conventional wisdom about disability and we need many more of them. We also need people with severe disabilities to have a presence in the church.

I remember in the whole Terry Schaivo incident, whenever reporters were filmed at the scene, in the background, there were many protesters holding signs which often had a Christian message. Christians are quick to condemn the taking of innocent life as they should be. But I also wondered how many innocent lives of persons with severe disabilities were present in the churches of those protesters. You know, it is one thing to talk about fighting home invasion and quite another to invade my home. I will fight to protect the life of children, but I will go much further when it comes to my own children. If people with severe disabilities are in our churches, our fight for their lives will become more heated, more urgent. As it is, we are fighting for an ideal, not for our friend who sits in the pew next to us (imagine if persons with severe disabilities were actually in the pew next to you...I pray that God will make it happen).

May God bless this little family who had the courage to bring their severely disabled child to life, to love him for 99 days, and to have the wisdom to film their experience such that we can all be edified by it.

Wednesday, November 21, 2007

More on social skills

I was doing some more thinking on social skills today (see Tuesday August 21). So last night I went with a friend to see the California Angels play. He had been wanting to go for a long time and once we got there, he almost immediately wanted to go home. I convinced him to stay till midway through the 5th inning, and of course after we left, the Angels exploded and scored 9 runs...oh well. At least he got the free blanket, an Angels baseball, and other free paraphernalia.

My point, however, was this friend of mine, a man with severe intellectual disability, walked around greeting people the whole time we were at the game. In his somewhat difficult to understand speech, he would say, "Hello, how are you?" to just about everyone he passed. I must admit that I found that kinda refreshing, and most of the people he addressed were very kind to him as well, responding to his greetings.

By all accounts, he was evidencing a social skill problem, to use technical terminology, to darn much greeting. Obviously when you go somewhere, especially at a pro sporting event, you get in and get to your seat. You don't take the time to greet everyone you pass in the arena, it takes too long. Besides no one else is greeting everyone else that they pass. So my friend's friendliness was an example of poor social skills, according to societal standards, not mine, on his part. Instead of greeting and being friendly, he should have kept to himself and shut up. But his friendliness brought a smile to nearly everyone that he came into contact with. Sure they gave him the benefit of the doubt because he has a intellectual disability, but nevertheless, he didn't follow the rules with the result being that he softened those around him.

Friday, September 07, 2007

Disabled man / Christian man

As I have mentioned before, I have a friend, a man who uses a wheelchair who challenges me to think about many issues related to disability and Christianity. As he works through various issues in his personal life, he asks me what I might suggest, how I might counsel him regarding the various issues he is grappling with. On several occasions, he has asked me, "Why is it that the disabled person has to change and not the nondisabled person?" My response typically is "I am not speaking to you as a disabled man, I am speaking to you as a Christian man." I hope that is encouraging to him.

But I have been wondering lately, how does being a disabled man impact being a Christian man? Does being a disabled man change one's expectations regarding what that person might be able to be as a Christian man? Clearly if a person has a intellectual disability, has intellectual disability, there will be some limits in terms of knowledge, or specific ability levels. However, I have known people with intellectual disability who although limited in some areas, were very gifted in areas of faith, forgiveness, loyalty, and love among other things. So on the one hand, to limit a person with a disability is wrong. I limit others at my peril, in terms of not being Christ-like in my interactions with them. Because there is more to disability than just the outward signs of physical or mental disabilities, I must see those people as I see myself. I too have strengths and weaknesses, some related to differences in my abilities, some related to my sinful condition. But overall, we are the same.

Now clearly, I cannot expect self-control from a person who is mentally ill, or emotionally disturbed. They may have the desire to be self controlled, but they lack the ability to be so. It is no different in a person with intellectual disability wanting to read the Bible, but lacking the ability to learn to read. But I wonder whether there are other aspects of being a disabled man which may limit a person's particular abilities. Jean Vanier speaks of the wounds of persons with disabilities. Wounds which Wolf Wolfensberger expands upon, breaking them out into specific types of wounds. If I were to have a stab wound in the arm, you would hardly expect me to throw a baseball, or use a hammer. I might desire to do so, but I am unable because my wound has incapacitated me.

So thinking about the particular wounds faced by a person with a particular disability, I might find that that person would face limits due to his wounding. Wolfensberger talks about diminishing wounds, attempting to limit them to the degree possible. His goal generally is largely to simply limit the wounds a person has to face, out of caring, out of concern out of love. I, however, would also argue that as we work to diminish the wounds of our disabled brothers and sisters we empower them to grow in various aspects of their Christian faith. We enable them to forgive, we enable them to love, we enable them to do a myriad of things they would desire to do in order to be Christ-like, but are unable to do because of the wounding they face.

In summary, we must work to diminish, to attend to, to love those who are wounded. In doing so, we literally heal the wounds that prohibit them from being all they can be as Christians.

Thursday, July 26, 2007

Divorce and children with Down's syndrome

In the recent *American Journal on Intellectual disability*, there is an article entitled, "Divorce in families of children with Down's syndrome: A population-based study" by Urbano and Hodapp (vol. 112, number 4, 261-274, July 2007). The abstract states the following...

"In this study we examined the nature, timing and correlates of divorce in families or children with Down's syndrome (647), other birth defects (10,283) and no identified disability (361,154). Divorce rates among families of children with Down's syndrome were lower than the other groups. When divorce did occur in the Down's syndrome group, however, a higher proportion occurred within the first 2 years after the child's birth."

The article goes on to mention the "Down's syndrome advantage" that being that "families of children with Down's syndrome cope better than do parents and families of children with other disabilities." Over the 12 year period studied (1990-2002) the divorce rate was 7.6% in families with children with Down's syndrome, 10.8% in the comparison group (not identified disability) and 11.2% in the other birth defects group. The one caveat finding relative to Down's syndrome, was, "Of families who divorce after the birth of the index child, families of children with Down's syndrome were almost twice as likely to divorce during the first two years of the child's life."

Finally, the authors make the following statement in the discussion section of the article.

"Taken together, the results of this study have important practical and theoretical implications. Practically, parents of newborns can be counseled about the risks and timing of possible marital discord. For many families, especially those steeped in the still commonly heard notion that "divorce is rampant" among families of children with disabilities, it may be comforting to know that divorce is neither a necessary nor a common outcome of having a child with Down's syndrome."

They go on to say,

"...social workers and early interventionists can educate parents about common stresses that arise during the earliest years. Those parents with less education can be especially targeted, as can those parents-especially fathers-who are both less educated and who live in rural areas...neither of the United States' two main parent groups in Down's syndrome currently feature special programs designed for outreach to rural families."

What wonderful opportunities for the church. Counseling early on in the life of a family with a child with Down's syndrome and outreach to rural families in particular. There are a lot of Christian churches in rural settings. How about stepping up to the challenge.

Wednesday, July 11, 2007

A confession

I have a friend named Thom who is a person who has a intellectual disability. You might even say it is a severe disability. I have known Thom for probably 8 years. He comes to my church and I visit his group home. Our interactions have largely revolved around him saying things like,

327

"I got paid this week. A hundred dollars!"
or
"You know that man on the radio? He sings good!"
or
"I was good this week, will you give me a hundred dollars?" (he means
one dollar)

These phrases are repeated over and over and over. My interactions
with him over the past years have revolved around him approaching me
and repeating one of the above statements. I would respond, hopefully, in
a friendly affirming manner, but no doubt distracted manner.

But a couple of weeks ago, I had him visit my university campus
with me. He had my undivided attention for several hours. The result was
that I realized how I had never given this friend of mine sufficient time to
express himself to me because he never had my undivided attention. I
was impressed once again by this last evening when I visited him at his
group home. We shared a bag of jelly belly jellybeans and discussed
everything from changes in his room, to his friends at work, to clothing
he liked to wear, to baseball, to the jellybean flavors we were sampling
together. I left the group home in repentance over the fact that I had never
given this person whom I referred to as my friend, the time I would have
given other friends of mine. I am now committed to working on our
friendship, by being the friend to him that he was trying to be to me. His
repetitive statements were efforts for me to see him as a person, as a
person who wanted to be my friend. However, with his limited intellect
he could do little more than repeat phrases that he probably had learned
would get a response from me. I enjoyed his statements about his
paycheck or the music he listened to, and I often gave him a dollar.

A student of mine shared with me something I had shared with her
and my class on many occasions. That is, that the more time you spend
with people with intellectual disability, the more "normal" they seem to
you. The fact of the matter is that they ARE normal, just different than
most everyone else who are all the same. It is true that I at times enjoy
my friends with intellectual disability more than my friends without. It is
true that I am growing more impatient with people without disabilities as
I grow in friendship with people with intellectual disabilities (probably
not a good thing, but reality nonetheless). It is true that Thom seems more
"normal" to me because I have been taking the time to talk with him and
be with him and really get to know him. Until I did that, he was always a
little crazy. Now I recognize that I am too busy, he is not crazy.

Another friend of mine wondered about when we could get together.
I responded I would love to (I really would) but at this particular moment
in my life, I am very busy. His response, probably out of frustration with

me and others like me was "Busy, busy, busy. Everybody is too busy."
He cut me to the quick. I communicate to him how important I think he is
by the amount of time I spend with him. It is almost like he is telling me,
"I am a person worth getting to know, worth being your friend, worth
your time. You are missing out on my friendship."

It is true that I am.

I have danced with the idea of buying a different home with many
rooms so that people would be in more of a community together. But I
have got to understand that I cannot do it all as much as I might want to.
That is why there is a church. In the same manner that my church cannot
meet the needs of all the people with disabilities in my region of the
country, I cannot meet the needs for friendship of all the people in my
community. The church needs to step up and do the simple thing of
taking the time to make friends.

May God help us to do so.

Tuesday, April 17, 2007

What is the standard?

I had an interesting interaction with a friend the other day. He is a
man who uses a wheelchair who attends an adult Bible class I teach at my
church. He was sharing some challenges he faces in his life with
relationships with various people. In response I would tell him what I
understood the Bible to prescribe. So if he is interacting with a person
who is impatient, the Bible would say that as Christians we should be
patient...we are the Christians in the situation. If another person who is a
Christian acts in a non-Christian manner, we are responsible to still act as
a Christians. Independent of what the other person does in a relationship,
we are still responsible to act as Christians.

A couple of days later, we were having lunch when he asked, "Why
is it always the disabled person who has to act like a Christian and not the
non-disabled person?"

I thought it was an interesting question on a variety of levels. My
immediate response was, "I am not speaking to you as a disabled person
or as a disabled Christian, I am speaking to you as a Christian." I think
that was enlightening to him (although disheartening to me in that I must
project to him that I see him as a disabled person). But it is true that we
expect more and better from people with disabilities I think. It is true in
special education. When we write objectives we either pull criterion
percentages out of the air, or we have too high or too low expectations for

a person we are hoping to educate. I have always tried to tell the teachers I am working with to look at the environment that the person you are working with is going into. If it is time on task at work, how much time does the average worker spend on task. If it is accuracy, how accurate is the average worker at the task. There is also discrimination which must be taken into account, however.

There is the research study about the man with intellectual disability who was about to loose his job. People from the agency facilitating employment asked why. The response was that he repeated topics at break too much (which is an indication of the discrimination of the workplace, not the skill deficits of the man). Anyway, the researchers determined how often the man's coworkers repeated topics, and worked with the man till he did not repeat topics any more than any of the coworkers. When he was repeating topics at the same level as coworkers, they asked the boss how he was doing. To their dismay, the boss said there had not been any significant change. You see it was a problem with the environment. The environment needed to be changed.

I think that is what my friend was getting at. It didn't matter how good he would get at being a Christian, he would always be expected to be better, and would be vilified for the smallest of infractions because of the difference he brought to any interaction, because he uses a wheelchair. So there is a sensitivity there that relates to the previous post about wounding. A sensitive individual who has acquired a disability will become even more sensitive because of the other wounds which are piled on the functional impairment. I compare how I would respond to a situation with how my friend who uses a wheelchair responds, and I say to him, "Lighten up!" A much better response would be for me to address the environment to soften it, to help it become more sensitive to devalued, wounded people. It would also be good to encourage the person experiencing the disability.

I think my words to my friend were encouraging to him. He was quiet for a minute after I told him how I see him, what I was thinking as I counseled him. But sentiments like, "I am not speaking to you as a disabled person or as a disabled Christian, I am speaking to you as a Christian" need to be repeated sufficiently often that both the person with the disability and I myself will come to believe and practice that sentiment.

Wednesday, March 28, 2007

An example of a servant

I received word last night that a woman who had been attending our group died suddenly. She was a person who used a wheel chair, and had been surviving breast cancer although it seemed her condition suddenly worsened. I remember the day that a friend of mine, a man who experiences an intellectual disability decided to move in with her and out of town. They made the decision with guidance from a community supports agency, although I felt the agency handled the situation very poorly (facilitating his move away from his entire support network which continues to be a problem for him as he has to take the bus about 1 1/2 hours each way to get to church). He and I used to have coffee together once a week and enjoyed a friendship which was made more difficult when he moved. Of course there were the questions of the two of them living together from a Christian standpoint as well, which I also felt the agency stepped all over through their recommendations. The whole situation could have handled much better, which I communicated to the agency. My hope is that with her passing, my friend will be moving back into town again so we can enjoy coffee together again.

However, if it hadn't been for my friend and his selfless service to his girlfriend, I don't know what her life would have been like. When he first met her, she was living in a group home, only because she lacked the ability to take care of her basic needs. The physical nature of her disability constrained her. By my friend coming along side of her, her world was opened. She could now have an apartment with significant independence in the community. She had someone who could help her to move about the community, pushing her wheelchair from place to place. Her significant hygienic needs were handled well. I cannot remember my friend ever offering so much as a complaint although he had to get up most nights to change her when she soiled herself in bed, or wet the bed. He would transfer her to the bathroom, clean her up, clean up the bed and then go back to sleep. What dedication! What love for her! In many ways, he literally sacrificed himself in service to her with the result being a much more normalized life for her.

Towards the end of her life, she became impatient with those around her, no doubt because of the discomfort and pain she was feeling. I would at times get upset with her, I must admit. He, however, was nearly always friendly, always compassionate, always caring. Like any other relationship, they would at times get upset with each other, but the kindness and compassion always shined through the clouds.

I am unsure that he realizes all he did for his friend. But I plan to make sure that I express to him for her, the tremendous difference he made in her life. He was an example to me of what a servant is. I pray I will be as caring and compassionate with the people in my life as he was to his friend.

Wednesday, November 08, 2006

"It was easy to see us as people that Jesus loved then and loves now"

I have a good friend who is a man who has significant physical disabilities as a result of being attacked several years ago. He sends emails to a group of people several times a week which are very encouraging, and reflect his thinking about God, Christianity, disability, among other issues. Yesterday he sent out the following email, which I have reproduced here with his permission.

Monday, October 9, 2006

"I think my desire for friends and people that I can identify with has come to a wonderful end. Yesterday, with my Sunday school class of handicapped adults, we got together and went to Huntington Beach and spent the WHOLE DAY at the beach. None of us is perfect, in the normal human sense, but each of us was good company.

I simply cannot understand what people are saying, so I often sit quietly for hours at a time but that's OK. I don't even notice when a long period goes by.

There were a number of other adults there who could do other things like get my food for me, get my pills, take me to the restroom, barbecue hot dogs, make smores, put sun block on me, etc.. I watched them and none of them seemed to think less of us. So it was easy to see us as people that Jesus loved then and loves now.

So you bet your life, I felt at HOME. "

This is the face the church needs to have towards all people, including persons with disabilities. My friend states, "It was easy to see us as people that Jesus loved then and loves now." One might conclude it was easy for him to see, but hopefully it was also easy for those around he and his friends at the beach to see as well. Matthew 9:2 says, "And seeing **their** faith..." he then goes heal the paralytic on the mat.

Is it easy to see that Jesus loved all people then and loves all people now at your church, at my church? What would it take for that to characterize the church?

Tuesday, October 10, 2006

Reflecting their surroundings

I was in a classroom this morning visiting a student teacher of 10 year old children with moderate to severe disabilities. Some of the children had autism, others intellectual disabilities. As I sat in the back of the room, there was suddenly a lot of screaming from the next room. Ultimately a student was placed in the little office which connected the two rooms. For the next 10 minutes you would hear a calm woman's voice followed with screams of "Shut up b**ch." Over and over again.

In another setting of children with severe disabilities of kindergarten age, there was a boy who didn't communicate other than to say "Hi" on occasion. However, as he moved through his day, he constantly repeated, "F***ing sh*t." That was his complete language repertoire. Knowing the number of times something has to be repeated in order to find its way into such a student's language repertoire, I couldn't help but wonder about the environment these students were living in.

Maybe people around them thought them cute in their nonsensical swearing. However, that kind of language is not thought of as funny in many, maybe most social settings. People who talk that way will never be able to have any job in which they work with customers. You need only tell your boss "Shut up b**ch" once before you will be fired (in case you didn't know).

We, however, in the church need have patience and acceptance for people who use such language while also trying to teach those individuals that such language is not appropriate. However, we must take the position that the swearing cannot be a reason for exclusion from a church setting.

I used to work with kids with serious emotional disturbance. I have been called many memorable things as has my mother, my wife, my dog and anyone else they thought might cause me to get angry. In every case, I have had to repeat to myself, "This is the disability talking. This is the disability talking." Had I rejected them, I would have supported what they were trying to prove to me. That is, basically that they are worthless and that I would ultimately reject them. It is tough when you faced with such a barrage, however, in these cases it truly is the disability speaking.

In the case of the severely disabled children above, it isn't really the disability talking as in the second case, he was doing little more than making sounds that he had heard and had discovered would get a reaction positively or negatively from his environment. In the first case, he learned that that is how you interact with your environment by examples that had been provided to him. His particular choice of language he probably also discovered got the maximum reaction from his environment.

Is the church prepared to include people such as these or are we only willing to take those who act in a particular socially circumscribed manner? If these types of children and adults are in the congregation, how do we prepare congregational members for the things they might say or do? I think it begins by having those people present to begin the conversation. I think people have not been forced to come to grips with their faith in terms of having demands made on them in areas of acceptance and understanding of others. The church environment has in many ways become too sterile.

I need to begin with acceptance and then move to change. I don't begin with change and then move to acceptance.

Tuesday, August 08, 2006

Choosing disability

I met a woman yesterday for whom I have a lot of respect. She is a friend of my Mother-in-law whom I met at a party. She related the following story.

She and her husband had two young boys, one 10 and one 12. She had had some experience volunteering to work with at risk children, but thought that she would like to do more. She decided to be a foster parent for a couple of the children. However, there wasn't a need at the particular time that she was interested, for the type of children she had been working with. Undeterred, she decided to adopt two children with developmental disabilities. One had Down's syndrome, and the other some very rare syndrome that she related had hardly been described at the time. It is powerful to note that she had never known a person with Down's syndrome before. The two girls lived with her family for about 11 years. Ultimately, one of the girl's father moved out of state, and the regulations stated that a family member needed to live in state for a child to remain in the foster care situation. The other girl moved out of the home to a group home. Apparently and sadly, one of the conditions of her foster care arrangement was that she could not contact them once they left her. It has been nearly 20 years now and she hasn't heard from either of them. She suspects one of the girls probably has died because she had severe medical problems at the time she was their parent.

Upon hearing her story, my only response was, "God bless you for taking those girls into your home!" She related that she had received tremendous benefits to her family as a result of having the girls. Effects, positive effects, on her and her husband as well as on her two boys were lifelong.

Thursday, July 13, 2006

Bruce and Cam (aka Martha and Mary)

I had the privilege of presenting to a group of Christian medical students at a meeting on the University of Redlands (Ca) campus last night. What a great group of future doctors they were. Our program was comprised of myself talking about impairment vs. disability, Kathi (my wife) interviewing 3 adult friends with intellectual disabilities, Alice a friend and medical student and her son Josh sharing about their experiences with the medical world and another friend and university

334

colleague, Bruce sharing about his experience as a parent of a child with a disability.

I got a bit choked up at one point, when Joyce, one of my friends experiencing disability shouted to me, "Spit it out" which shook me right out of it! Kathi asked great questions and Alice provided wonderful pointers, mostly about treating people with even the most severe disabilities as people, with respect. This seems so obvious, however, if you have any experience with persons with severe intellectual disabilities, you know that it is not at all obvious.

In the midst of the evening, Bruce shared the story of how he was keeping an eye on his son, Cam a preteen with autism while he was doing yard work. As he was working, trying not to be distracted by his son, an older gentleman walked on the sidewalk past them. His son ran up and positioned himself in front of the older man and began a conversation. "What do you have in the McDonalds bag you are carrying" it started after name introductions. The man stood there and kindly interacted with the boy for several minutes. Finally the man said it was time for him to leave. As Bruce stood there, he kind of shook his head to himself, wishing that his son would leave the man alone as he got back to his pruning. The man began to walk away when his son called out to him again. "George!" he said. "Do you know Jesus as your savior?" the autistic boy called out. Bruce said he was moved and really convicted. He was the Martha to his son's Mary (to use the Biblical story). At that moment Bruce said that he learned a great deal about himself in relation to his son, and also about his son.

It was a wonderful evening. I was very impressed by the students and the program (put on by Campus Crusade).

Wednesday, July 12, 2006

Swearing at the people

About a year ago, I was just coming out of a Mexican restaurant with my family when I heard this guy standing by the restaurant's dumpster, swearing loudly at people passing by. His language was such that you could tell that he was someone with mental illness. I went over to him and asked him gently, "What's the matter?" Through a lot of gibberish sprinkled with references to me as "Officer" he related that he could really use a pack of cigarettes. I told him to wait there a minute as I went across the parking lot to a convenience store where I bought the cigarettes and came back to him with them. He was very grateful, saying over and over, "Thank you officer!" I left him by saying, "Please don't swear at the people. Please say after me, 'I won't swear at the people.'" After several more "Thank you officer" I left him sadly.

I have often thought about that interaction. The fact that he was standing by the dumpster like so much human garbage. That he called me "Officer" perhaps because most of the people he interacted with in the community were police officers responding to a complaint. The fact that he interacted with people by swearing at them, perhaps out of frustration with people. Interestingly, he placed himself where there would be people as he obviously wanted some human contact if only to be told to stop swearing or to get the cigarettes he ultimately got for me. What a difficult life he appeared to be living. And as I always ask myself in these types of situations, I wondered "Where is the church?"

Why did I not feel uncomfortable with the man when many others might? True I am a large man, but I think my lack of fear is more related to the fact that I have spoken to many people like that man before. I have experience with people like him. I definitely did not get that experience at church which is a problem. I mean Jesus went out of his way to talk to people like that man (see the Gereseen demoniac story). But I don't see people like him at my church, or pretty much any church for that matter. From a strictly humanistic perspective, imagine the good it would do for a man like the one I met to find himself in a church where people loved him and talked to him and listened to him.

One of my favorite people in my life was my wife's grandfather. He was a kind gentle man who loved God deeply, and had a great wit. Toward the end of his life, however, he developed Alzheimer's disease. I think it would embarrass his wife that I would sit and talk with him whenever we were together. He would repeat things over and over and over and over. He would talk about nonsensical things. I enjoyed being with him because I knew I was learning about people like him; I had a professional interest. But I also knew that I was in a very small way contributing to his self esteem, his feeling that someone loved and cared for him. That was very important to me. That is the kind of ministry that the church should be about. If I am present with people like him, I protect him from those who would do evil to him. By spending my "valuable time" I say that I think he has value to me and ultimately value as a human being. I choose to be with him. I want to be with him.

It seems the church doesn't want to be with people with mental illness unless a person's mental illness is under control to the point that it is hardly recognizable. It doesn't want to be with intellectually disabled people, and I am not sure why. If we spent time with them, they wouldn't be the crazy person outside of Walgreen's, they would be a person who has been rejected by society but who God says he loves as much as he loves you or me.

When will we as individuals and the church reflect this aspect of the character of God?

336

Monday, June 26, 2006

Secret Girl

I read a recent article in the January/February issue of the AARP newsletter (no cracks about my age please, my in laws graciously provided the article to me). Anyway, the magazine has an excerpt from a book entitled *Secret Girl* by Molly Bruce Jacobs, which is scheduled for release in March of this year (2006). I have not read the book, but would for the moment recommend the article. The book is about the placement of a girl in an institution by her family and her ultimate reuniting with her family through her sister, Molly. Here is a quote from the article/book.

"The notion I'd conjured in my imagination decades ago-that Anne was my dark antithesis-faded rapidly. Instead I began to see her as my counterpart, one I'd lost touch with long ago. She had what the world I grew up in had suppressed in me, what drinking had numbed. In spite of her disabilities, she was everything I wasn't, or what I'd imagined I wasn't allowed to be. She exuded the joie de vivre that dries up in you when you're raised to believe that the trophies and rewards you accumulate will make you happy, and that the pursuit of truth and beauty is only for dreamers and fools. Blue blooded manners had not made her self-conscious. The light in her eyes had not dimmed with complacency. Formality had not put a lid on her howls of laughter. If she felt like dancing, she danced-wherever she was. If she wanted to sing, she sang-whatever song happened to drift into her head. When she had an urge to smell your hair, your cheek, or a magazine, she leaned over and sniffed. She was in every sense of the term a free spirit."

You know that freedom that free spiritedness is something that persons with intellectual disabilities can bring to the church. The joy of life. The freedom of being unconcerned about the judgment of others.

In *Becoming Human* (2008), Jean Vanier has a chapter called "The Path to Freedom." In it he writes,

"We set out on the road to freedom when we no longer let our compulsions or passions govern us. We are freed when we begin to put justice, heartfelt relationships, and the service of others and the truth over and above our own needs for love and success or our fears of failure and of relationships."

The Church could learn these things if persons with intellectual disabilities were regularly in their midst. But in the same manner as *Secret Girl*, we have sent them away, at least in terms of not having them in our midst.

Molly Bruce Jacobs talks about how her sister asked her, "How was your vacation" because that is what her sister had been told as the reason no one had ever come to visit her. Your family is on vacation...for 30 years. Her response upon seeing her sister was not an angry "Where have you been for 30 years." It was a loving, and Jacobs argues, forgiving, "How was your vacation."

How was your vacation, Church?

Tuesday, March 21, 2006

Proverbs and Jeremiah

Proverbs 3:5

Trust in the Lord with all your heart, don't lean on your own understanding. In all your ways acknowledge him and he'll make your paths straight.

Jeremiah 29:11

For I know the plans I have for you, declares the LORD, plans to prosper you and not to harm you, plans to give you hope and a future.

Oliver (1990) states,

They also see themselves as pitiful because they are socialized into accepting disability as a tragedy personal to themselves.

There is a disconnect between the ideas presented above, at least there is for the Christian.

In all our life circumstances we are encouraged to trust in the Lord, because He can be trusted. He loves us and has a plan for our futures. However, disability seems to totally throw us into a tizzy. We loose our balance. We, due to our socialization, accept disability as a tragedy. Now clearly tragedy enters the lives of people. I just wonder sometimes about disability, as tragedy. Does tragedy happen which causes disability? Of course. There are car accidents, and violence against people. But for the moment, let's consider congenital disability. That is disability that people are born with. I am not naive enough to say that life with a child with a disability is always easy or even mostly easy. I just wonder about how I think about disability when the Bible which I claim to base my life upon tells me things like the above. I also wonder to what degree the socialization of disability as tragedy is reflected in the life of the Church which claims to be built upon those same verses listed above?

Disability brings challenges. We have translated challenges into tragedy. Because we have done that, they truly do become tragedy. Because the Church has not stepped forward to support all members, including persons experiencing disability and their families, the likelihood that disability will become tragedy is increased. If I can trust the Lord, and if my Church will support me as I move through the challenges of having a family member experiencing disability, then the works of God will be made manifest (in family members, the person experiencing disability, and the larger Church community). However, if I interpret disability as tragedy, what is there to do but mourn and try to make the best of things. Somehow I don't think that is our calling. It definitely has become our behavior, our experience, but I don't think it is our calling.

There was this totally spurious method of working with persons with severe disabilities several years back. I don't want to give you the name of those who advocated it or the name of the procedure as I don't want to give it any support whatsoever. However, the upside of the approach was that it brought the community together to help the family to help the child with severe disability. That aspect of the program was truly inspiring and remarkable. Imagine a group of people coming together to support a family in the same manner, only their support was not based on some false approach to working with people with disability, it was based on God's word. The results would be amazing.

Once again, we need to not be conformed to the world, but be transformed by the renewing of our minds. Interesting, isn't it, how what has become the "obvious" might fall away in the light of the truth of the Bible, if acted upon by the Church.

Monday, March 20, 2006

"Yes Virginia, there is a Santa Clause"

I was recently talking with some colleagues about how there are many apocryphal stories floating around, and have been for years, which embrace an unjustifiable spirituality about who people with disabilities are or are not. By unjustifiable, I mean from a Christian perspective based upon the Biblical narrative. I focus my comments on Christians, who claim to believe the message and narrative of Christianity, and then cling to unjustifiable spiritual claims. In being critical of these stories, a friend disagreed saying that the stories were comforting and encouraging to he and his family at the birth of their family member with disability.

No doubt, that those who create such stories are probably motivated by the thought of being encouraging to the parents and families of persons with disabilities, but I would rather hear the truth. Please don't tell me that there is an Easter Bunny no matter how good it makes me feel, if there really isn't one (there isn't is there?). Also, don't tell someone that their child with Down's syndrome is an angel, because I know that he is just a person like me. Don't tell me that he has something special to do, unless you are telling all the other children the same thing, because we all are unique and all therefore have special things that we alone can do. But those with disability are not any more special than anyone else. They are just people. They are not heroes, or angels, or devils, or object lessons for the nondisabled. They are not demons, or sub-human animals, or to be considered objects of dread or pity, or holy innocents (see Normalization by Wolfensberger), or any other notion you might come up with other than that they are people.

Now, some may do heroic things or angelic kinds of things or even evil kinds of things, but that is because they are people like you and me and we sometimes do heroic things and angelic things and evil things.

So it may make you feel nice to think that there is a Santa Clause, but there is no Santa Clause. We jokingly tell our children that they will get nothing from Santa Clause this year, nor have they gotten anything from Santa Clause ever. To say otherwise, particularly to a child, is an untruth...an untruth perhaps shared out of kindness, but an untruth nonetheless.

But we are not dealing with children when we are attempting to answer the questions of parents, adults, who have had a child with disability born into their family. Yet we must also clearly understand what the truth is so we can share it accurately. That is where church leaders need to step up to the plate so that Christians are not misinformed. But then, I wonder what percentage of church leaders know the truth in this area? I wonder how many churches will advertise that next week's sermon topic is, "Yes Virginia, there is a Santa Clause?"

Wednesday, February 08, 2006

Moses and his mouth

One of my students provided me with an interesting perspective on the passage in Exodus 4:10 (LITV). The passage states,

And Moses said to Jehovah, O Lord, I am not a man of words, either from yesterday or the third day, nor since You have been speaking to Your bond slave. For I am heavy of mouth and heavy of tongue. And Jehovah said to him, "Who has made man's mouth? Or who makes the dumb, or the deaf, or the seeing, or the blind? Is it not I, Jehovah?"

There are many conclusions which might be drawn about who people with disability are, not the least of which is that they are made by Jehovah. However, I found it interesting that God comes to Moses, a man who it appears both Moses and God agreed had some form of a speech impediment, and asks him (Moses) to speak for Him (Jehovah). God goes to a person with a disability and challenges him in the area of his disability. Later in verse 15 the passage says,

And you shall speak to him, and you shall put the words in his mouth. And I will be with your mouth, and with his mouth, and I will teach you what you shall do.

Other than noting that God is a special educator, He is consistent in providing people to come alongside of persons with disabilities so that they can move beyond themselves. No doubt in addition to looking for an excuse to not do what God wanted him to do, Moses had defined himself as this person with a speech problem. He was probably teased as a child, felt uncomfortable around women, and all the other things which accompany such a disability. But God didn't see him in that way.

Moses also must have either known that God made him the way he was, or perhaps he wasn't sure and was wondering how God would respond to his complaint about his disability. God, however, leaves him no doubt. "Who has made man's mouth?" Now apparently, God didn't make just one mouth, but a variety of mouths, as he recognizes that Aaron's mouth does not face the same issues as Moses' mouth. It appears that Moses' mouth and Aaron's mouth are simply within the range of mouths God made.

However, the point I wanted to make here is to those who might read this blog who experience a disability. God may choose to challenge you in the area of your disability. This doesn't surprise me as it is a scriptural principle that God works through weakness such that His glory might be seen. Perhaps disability is an opportunity for the Christian who experiences disability. It is a chance to show God's glory through weakness. It is also an opportunity for those around that person with disability to also demonstrate God's glory by "working the works of Him who sent me.

Thursday, January 12, 2006

A moving prayer

This past week, a friend and hard worker who attends our Light and Power class at Trinity Church was honored for her last week in the class. She is moving across the country. Anyway, at one point we gathered around her, and as is our custom laid hands on her and prayed for God's blessing and direction. Amy, a member of our class contributed to the blessing by offering a beautiful prayer. After speaking of how we will miss Lella in a voice broken with emotion, she said ". . .and I pray that God will give you peace in your life at your new home." It was a lovely prayer with a heartfelt sentiment.

Lella had devoted a significant amount of time assisting Amy and her family over the past few months. In spite of her intellectual disability,

Amy wanted to give back to Lella in some way and did through her beautiful prayer.

It made me once again wonder how many people would not be prayed for if persons with intellectual disability didn't pray for them. I am impressed with the steadfastness of these individuals in remembering to pray for people known to them. Remembering their parents and families and friends. Their righteous indignation over injustice when they become aware of it.

I will never forget a man named James who was an elderly adult with intellectual disability. James was feisty and let you know what he thought. At one point in a lesson I was giving in class, I mentioned that several children had been abused by their parents. They had been locked in a closet for months fed through a slit in the door. Angrily but tentatively James rose to his feet and said, "I will not stand for that. I will not let that happen." Although powerless to do most things about the abuse of children, James used what he had, impressing those there that day with the absolute evil of the situation. He also used his voice to pray that such abuse would stop.

Do we really believe that all people are equal in the sight of God? Do we really believe that God hears our prayers, ALL of our prayers by ALL of us?

By the way, Amy has Down's syndrome. In a perfect world (see July 7th entry) her voice and therefore her prayers would not be heard as she would have been aborted to protect HER from a poor life quality.

"I will not stand for that. I will not let that happen."

Monday, August 01, 2005

More on Down's syndrome

I have been thinking more about the Down's syndrome discussion in the last blog. Here are a few more thoughts.

With some forms of disability, the disability occurs after the person has lived without the disability for a period of time. So a person who has lived a normal life becomes injured in some way and as a result experiences disability. First of all, I think this form of disability needs to be separated from a disability like Down's syndrome, one that a person is born with.

With Down's syndrome, the life experience that the person has is not influenced by life without the disability in the same manner. That is, their experience is all they have known. Now society would approach a person with Down's syndrome saying,

"I am sorry you have a poor quality of life" or
"I am sorry that you are not as smart as I am" or

"I am sorry that things will be more difficult for you, in terms of learning" or
"I am sorry that society is discriminatory against you."

However, a person with Down's syndrome would potentially reply, "Poor quality of life in comparison to what? This is the only life I know."
"I didn't realize you were smarter than me," or "aren't there people smarter than you?"
"This is the way I learn, are things more difficult for me?"
"Sometimes people are just mean, but sometimes they are nice."

However, the problem is that on the basis of the statements I made about quality of life, etc., I then make the decision that the life of a person with Down's syndrome is not worthy of living. Our society has convinced many that the best, the wisest thing to do when you are pregnant and meet certain criteria (advanced maternal age, elevated levels of a particular protein, etc.), is to have a prenatal diagnosis done so the presence of an extra #21 chromosome (the cause of Down's syndrome) can be detected, and the unborn baby aborted. I am pretty sure that it is considered malpractice for a doctor **NOT** to suggest prenatal diagnosis should the criteria for a higher chance of Down's syndrome be present.

Now for years, I have been aware of these procedures, and although my wife and I chose not to do prenatal diagnosis because abortion of any form was not an option for us, it suddenly struck me that **the end desire for these procedures would be the eradication of persons with Down's syndrome from the world**. In the same way we might say, "Thank goodness we have done away with polio in the United States" there are those who would say, "Thank goodness we have done away with Down's syndrome in the United States." That must be the goal of prenatal diagnosis and abortion of these individuals. In order to prevent this from happening, you as a pregnant woman/family must actually tell the doctor "No" in terms of doing prenatal diagnosis and potentially abortion. The assumptions in these interactions are you meet the criteria, you do the test, you have the abortion. That is the assumption.

But let's think about what Down's syndrome is. It is not something you get, like a disease or something. It is not something you experience as a result of some injury, or lack of oxygen during birth, or something. It is genetically who you are. Just like I am white and others are black or brown, it is genetically who you are. I cannot hope to be cured of my white skin color. The only way to prevent my birth as a person with white skin color is to abort me, as that skin color is a part of who I am. Down's syndrome is a genetic part of who those persons are. So through abortion, I am not preventing intellectual disability, I am wiping out people who have a particular genetic trait that is a part of who they are, simply because they have that trait and I think it is bad.

Now I have probably known over a hundred persons with Down's syndrome over the years. I have come to believe that their Down's syndrome is a characteristic of theirs much like my skin color is a characteristic of mine. My skin color impacts much which will happen to me throughout my life. In the United States, it may mean that I have an advantage over those with a different skin color. It affects how much sun I am able to take before I get burned. It has cultural repercussions to me. But when you boil it down, it is only culturally that my skin color really has any relevance to me. The society around me will decide on the basis of somewhat random social constructions whether or not it is good or bad to have white skin. But outside of social constructions, my skin color is largely an irrelevant characteristic. Should society decide it is bad to have white skin, I will have trouble in my life for that reason. But in reality the decision that white skin is bad or good is not based on anything rational.

I believe the same thing about Down's syndrome. I know people with Down's syndrome who live at home with their families are loved by them. I know others who have apartments or are supported to live in the community. I know others who have jobs. I know some who are in adult day care, or do not work. But for most, when you distill their life experience it is the same as mine. They have friends, they have a job, they live in a home or apartment, they are just people. Now because they will not go to college, or take longer to learn some things, or look different, society has stigmatized them, convincing many that they are something different, something other than human even, that there is rationality in the decision to prenatally diagnose and abort them. To me Down's syndrome is somewhat of an irrelevant characteristic. It is particularly irrelevant when one is making determinations of human worth.

For the millionth time, I heard someone at church say that we are all the same in God's eyes, we are all equal in God's eyes. You know I am sure the woman who said that yesterday meant it when she said it and I really believe it as well. But if it really true that we are all equal in God's eyes, why are we looking for unborn babies with Down's syndrome so we can abort them? They think they have a pretty good quality of life. God forbid that we put ourselves in the position of taking the lives of others because they don't meet our criteria for a good quality of life, particularly when most who are making that determination don't even know what their quality of life is.

Wednesday, July 13, 2005

The Phantom of the Opera

This past weekend, my daughter Amy and I went to see "The Phantom of the Opera." We both loved it. I recognize that it is just a story, but there were many aspect of the story which made me think.

The loving character of Christine, the Phantom's love interest, toward him is really interesting. At one point she speaks of how his exterior is not what alarms her, but rather the way his soul has become. We learn from the movie that his soul is what it is largely because of the treatment he received as a child, being put on display and abused. On one level, he is able to overcome the abuse he faced and develops a relationship with her, originally as her "angel of music" and later he attempts to become her lover. She has fallen in love with someone else, and at a critical point in the movie, the Phantom tells her he will kill her love interest if she doesn't abandon him and love him (the Phantom) instead. She chooses to go with the Phantom to save her lover, but prays that God will give her the ability to love him (the Phantom) if she makes the commitment to him. After a kiss from her, the Phantom realizes that he loves her, and releases her from the bargain so that she can go with the man she loves. In a remarkable show of love toward the Phantom, she goes back to him and places a ring in his hand, given to her by the man she loves.

This interaction between Christine and the Phantom was a wonderful example of understanding someone who has been devastated by the cruelty of society over a disability. Through her kindness, his love for her grows although he must ultimately let her go. With that in mind, the final scene is particularly poignant.

I have run across persons with disability in my life, who literally hated the church because of the interactions they have had with Christians. Sometimes the church can be even more hurtful than the world, particularly toward those who have a desire to belong to the church. But true love on the part of the church toward those with disability can at times heal the pain of the past. Like the Phantom stewed as he observed the interactions at the opera house, there are those with disability, or family or friends of persons with disability who stew as they stand on the outside. The Phantom wanted to be involved, wanted to be a part of the opera. Ultimately he wrote his own opera, which was a ploy on his part to not only become a part of the opera itself, but to become close to someone on the inside who captured his heart.

I want to be one who captures the heart of persons with disability and causes them to want to come back to the church, or come to it for the first time. I want to be the one who shows the love that softens the heart of the aggrieved; those who have actually experienced cruelty from people like me, Christian or otherwise.

345

Monday, February 07, 2005

Big Fish

I must admit that I am intrigued by Tim Burton's films. They all have an edge and seem to me at least to have many lessons. In "Big Fish" there is a comment made by Edward Bloom which resonated with me. Before I share it with you, I must tell you that I don't agree with the statement, although there is an aspect of the statement that I very much agree with. Bloom says,

"It was that night I discovered that most things you considered evil or wicked are simply lonely and lacking in social niceties."

They are "simply lonely and lacking in social niceties." There are some things which are perceived, maybe not as evil, but as deviant or devalued which fit that description. To be deviant is often to be lonely. To lack in social niceties is to be perceived as different in a negative sense. The tolerance by society of minor social skill deficits is limited. In fact, research in special education in the 1980's indicated that the reason most persons with disabilities lose their jobs is due to minor social skill deficits. Persons who are lonely and lack social skills are devalued by society. Persons with intellectual disability are often lonely and are characterized as a group as lacking in social niceties, social skills. They also find themselves devalued.

A question that might be asked, however, is whether loneliness is the result of poor social skills, or are poor social skills the result of loneliness? Persons with intellectual disability have been characterized as having minor social skill deficits. Could it be that these deficits are partially the result of limited contact with the general public? Could it be that these deficits are partially the result of loneliness? I know of no research supporting either of these notions, however, it is definitely arguable that contributions to the social deficits of persons with intellectual disability might be made by loneliness.

But the other part of the statement is that the speaker says that things he considered evil or wicked were the result of loneliness and social niceties. People have perceived persons with disability as evil or wicked because they didn't understand them and didn't take the time to understand them. We also have very little tolerance for anything outside of the expected socially.

I need to deal with this notion in further depth at a later time, however, the environment, society needs to change. Not all of the tolerance blather that is currently advocated is worth listening to. However, tolerance to minor social skill deficits on the part of society should be something that most can champion. If you give people a little latitude, you will often find that they are great people, much more like you than different from you. However, we as members of the environment need to change. We need to broaden the definition of normal to include those with minor social skill deficits.

We may not be able to completely address the social niceties part of the equation, but we can definitely do something about the loneliness.

Tuesday, January 18, 2005

Why so accepting?

I wonder why persons with intellectual disability (in particular) are so accepting of others, almost an unconditional acceptance.

You might say, that because of the state of need they find themselves in, they have somehow learned to be accepting in order to get what they need from others. I think there is some truth to the fact that acting politely has been pounded into them by parents and others. I remember a woman who had Down's syndrome who was a friend of mine who would precede literally anything she would say with, "Now, I want to say this in a nice way . . ." Obviously those around her had constantly reminded her to say things in a nice way, and it became a part of her vocabulary. However, people who can help them and people who cannot help them are both treated with the same general level of acceptance. So the notion of being nice in order to "get something" is really pretty much foreign to these individuals.

You might say they are accepting in order to get friends, because they lack friends. I am sure there are those who are lonely for whatever reason (parents won't let them out of the house, aspects of their disability, etc.) but although they may lack friends within the nondisabled community, they are often rich with friends within the community of persons with disabilities. In interviews I have done with adults with disabilities, they pretty much equate their friends with and without disabilities. I have also noticed that the network amongst persons with disabilities in the community can be pretty extensive.

But there are characteristics of persons with disabilities which endear you to them, make you feel accepted. It's funny that in interviews with adults with disabilities, if I ask who their best friend is, they always say me, and if my son Josh is in the room, they also say Josh or whoever else is with me. Now as with other people there are some with disabilities who I am very close to and others with whom I am just friends. But they characteristically, will take the person close to them at the moment, in the room, and refer to him as their best friend. I know caseworkers who have been confused by this. Because they hear such affirmations from disabled adults they believe that that is the case, but it is not. This is not a put

347

down of the caseworkers and perhaps they are the best friend of some of their clients, but rather it is a statement about persons with disabilities. As in the old Crosby, Stills and Nash song, they truly do love the one they are with.

Because of characteristic difficulties with social skills, the manner in which this acceptance is shown is not always understood by those without disabilities which causes some of the distancing. A fellow I know, whenever he sees me, will steal my keys, or tickle me (I haven't been tickled in many years, except by him), or grab my hand and refuse to let go. All these are expressions of affection by him. But he did these things the first time we met. If people aren't in an accepting mindset I think they probably will reject these kinds of advances even though they are innocent and friendly on the part of the individual with disability.

Another reason persons with intellectual disability are so accepting is that they don't always understand the subtle social cues indicating rejection. These minor social skill deficits will at times get them into trouble in the workplace. These same inabilities to recognize social cues will cause them to be undaunted in social relationships. They themselves are different. If for some reason they don't like you, they will say so; you pretty much always know where you stand. Whereas we in our socially appropriate manner will give you subtle cues of rejection becoming increasingly more overt in our rejection. There is something refreshing in someone honestly saying to you, "I don't like you because you use bad language," or "I don't like you because you hit other people" as compared to speaking about others behind their backs or simply avoiding them.

By way of example, we recently had a new member come to our church program for adults with disabilities. The new guy, a big fellow with Down's syndrome, came in. I immediately plopped myself down by him and started to make conversation. "Where are you from?" "Do you have any brothers and sisters?" "What do you like to do for fun?" "What kinds of things bother you?" After answering all the questions preceding, he answered the last question, "I don't like people asking me a bunch of questions." Great answer, great honest answer. We have continued to grow in friendship, and I know I can count on him to be honest with me.

One can never take a whole group and characterize them in one particular way. That is called stereotyping. However, just a person with Down's syndrome look like they are all from the same family, I think there is a characteristic of persons with intellectual disability, with intellectual disability, which makes them similar in the ways in which they interact with others. In the midst of their intellectual disability, God gives them in some ways, a social advantage. It is a strange combination of honesty, a lack of defensiveness, gregariousness, and social ineptitude. There is also an ability to be forgiving which I think is beyond that of the

348

rank and file nondisabled person.

Wednesday, July 14, 2004

Models of acceptance

A few weeks back, I went to pick up a man with disabilities who lives at a retirement home, mostly for seniors. Typically when I go to pick him up, he is asleep in his chair, and has to go through a variety of varying routines before we can leave (which is why I am pretty much always late for church). Anyway, as I waited for him, his room mate was awake, sitting in a chair. Before him sat his breakfast which he was largely unaware of. He is a man of about 70, obviously in later stages of Alzheimer's disease. As he sat there, he had a running diatribe with someone who wasn't there, but was very real to him. The conversation went something like this. " You (deleted) I'm going to kill you. I am going to (deleted). You (deleted)." I think you get the idea. Violent language littered generously with various profanities and racial slurs. On the wall there were pictures of the man with family members, with children, so obviously he was definitely not what his language now makes him appear to be. (I shudder to think what might come out of my mouth were I in his same condition).

Anyway, as we were walking out to the car, I asked my friend if he liked his room mate. "Yes" he replied. He told me his name and said he liked him although "he doesn't talk much to me." I was surprised at his response.

But then I thought of other people with developmental disabilities I have known. I know a guy, good looking, athletic, muscular build who also has intellectual disability who would always introduce me to his latest girlfriend. I found it interesting that such a good looking guy would choose girlfriends who were very severely disabled. Sometimes not, but it was obvious that appearance had very little to do with how he chose his girlfriends. I doubt that he consciously had rejected the standard that secular society places on good looks, etc., however, he had. When I would ask him about a girlfriend, he would talk about how she worked hard at the workshop, or was very friendly, or had a nice smile.

It is this type of acceptance which originally amazed me about persons with intellectual disability and drew me in to the point that I wanted to spend my life with them. They accepted me with a full acceptance independent of who I was. They loved me openly, without the kinds of walls that we put up between ourselves in relationships even between friends. Acceptance is a wonderful thing.

How can people who are so accepting of others be often so rejected by them? Hmmm. I see the image of God in the manner in which people

349

with intellectual disability love others for who they are, independent of the things which would typically cause people to be stand offish (appearance, social skills, hygiene, disability, etc.). They show acceptance and simply hope for acceptance back. Oftentimes, even if it is not reciprocated, they press on with love and acceptance. If you give them a chance you will find them a model for you as to how to accept others.

Tuesday, July 13, 2004

Ga-way

As I have related elsewhere in this blog, I used to work at an intermediate care facility for adults (over age 18 at that time) with severe intellectual disability among other developmental disabilities. There are two stories I thought I would relate today. One about Bert and the other about Shaquanda.

Bert was a man with severe intellectual disability who was confined to a wheelchair as a paraplegic. His upper body was pretty much fine, and he was well able to move around in his chair. He had dark hair and a bit of a long face. I think I connected to him because other than a difference of an hour or so, we were exactly the same age. I sometimes wondered if he might have been born in the same hospital as I. Yet there I was in the budding stages of a career in special education, he in a place he would probably remain for the rest of his days. He had no language to speak of other than saying "Ga-way" all the time.

I met Shaquanda quite by accident. As I roamed the halls of the facility, I would walk past people who appeared to be little more than piles of humanity. They were balled up and contractured. Their disabilities were so severe, they were literally moved from their beds to a mat, then the mat was moved, perhaps, and then back to their beds. They were nonverbal, unable to feed themselves or take care of any other personal needs, largely unable to move. Anyway, one day as I was going about my business at the facility, one of these little blobs of flesh said "Hi!" to me with all the personality she could muster. I immediately stopped. I learned from **her** that her name was Shaquanda, and from that day forward we spent many hours together having the largely one sided conversations you will often have with persons with severe intellectual disability.

Shaquanda was always there looking for someone to take the time to interact with her. She saw the activity around her, but it took a mighty "Hi" from her to gain the attention of those around her. I must admit that although I then tried to interact with others like her, there was no response. I think at times I was probably more of an irritant to those people who had become used to being ignored (assuming they were able to even make that determination).

It took months for me to finally figure out what that one thing was that Bert was constantly repeating. It was literally his only language. His phrase was the words he heard most often in the place he lived to the point that he as a non verbal man was able to repeat them. Sadly, "Ga-way" was "Go away." What words would a person with intellectual disability learn from the congregation at your church?

Wednesday, June 30, 2004

Aunt Peg

My Aunt Peg died last night. She had lived a long life, much of it alone as her husband died relatively early on in their marriage and she never had any children. She grew up as a tough kid on the streets of Philadelphia. An orphan, she was taken in by a woman everyone in the family, at least the older ones, spoke of respectfully as Aunt Hattie. She must have been quite a woman herself. A big heart to take in these girls (my grandmother lived with her as well)and the toughness to raise them to become the women they became.

The last few years of my aunt's life were particularly difficult. The loss of independence coming with moving into a Christian retirement home was a severe assault. Her faith was never really something that the family was entirely sure of. I often offered to sneak in a Brandy Alexander (her favorite drink, and I think I was only half joking) but she was worried she would get thrown out if she was found out. But she was a tough pragmatist and realized it was for the best. Ultimately she embraced her new home. Things appeared to be going about as well as they might, when she awoke one morning, at about age 91, totally blind. I don't think functionally she ever really recovered from that. But then, how would one? A younger person would think of the years ahead. A 91 year old thinks of the years remaining, and trying to live them out with some degree of comfort.

I remember visiting her (I live in California, she in New Jersey) several months after the onset of the blindness. She spent a great deal of time crying over the difficulties she was facing. She just kept saying, "What did I do for these things to happen to me?", and "I just wish the Lord would take me," although I am not entirely sure she knew what he would do with her once he had her. During my visit, however, I remember having a discussion with her which I think helped her, and certainly has caused me to stop and think over the intervening months and years. She spoke about how discouraged she was and that there was no purpose anymore to her life. I asked her what her purpose was before she

351

became blind and she went silent. "It seems to me your purpose before you were blind was to try to do what's right, and to acknowledge the Lord in everything. So even though you are now blind, your purpose in life is still the same." I think I helped her a bit because she didn't cry as much during the rest of our visit.

You know the requirements of the Lord for us are pretty much the same independent of who we are mentally, physically, etc. Micah 6:8 says "And what does Jehovah require of you, but to do justice, and to love mercy and to walk humbly with your God?" People with intellectual disabilities are well able to do what Jehovah requires of them. I, however, see them as disabled, devalued, damaged. Yet I myself also struggle to walk humbly.

Tuesday, June 29, 2004

Unschooled and ordinary but had been with Jesus

In the book of Acts, the story is told of Peter and John healing a man who was lame. After healing him, they were arrested and went before the various Jewish leaders. The comment is made in Acts, "When they saw the courage of Peter and John and realized that they were unschooled, ordinary men, they were astonished and they took note that these men had been with Jesus." Acts 4:13 (NIV)

Wow, they were unschooled and ordinary men. As I shared this verse yesterday with the group of adults with mental handicaps with whom I work at my church, I was struck with how that verse applied to those in the room. They are all pretty much unschooled and ordinary. At the same time I can say to you that they are mostly very courageous. One fellow, Mark, often tells of the teasing or hassles he receives at work or in the community because of his disability, or because he is a Christian. Typically his response is "You need the Lord" which is followed by further ridicule from his detractor. But I look at Mark and see his courage while recognizing that he is an unschooled and ordinary man . . . or is he?

The verse goes on to say that they "took note that these men had been with Jesus." I see that in many of the Christian adults with developmental disabilities that I interact with. You hang around with them and you realize that many of them have been with Jesus. Not in a physical sense as with Peter or John, but in a sense of being with Jesus through faith.

Call it a lack of social skills leading to the ability to not know better, but the honesty of persons with intellectual disabilities seems courageous to me, and they may not understand many things, but they understand their basic faith, and are unabashed in speaking it.

Sunday, June 27, 2004

The unfulfilled desire to serve

If people in my church have the desire to serve but no opportunities are available, then it is my fault, not theirs. This is too often the case for persons with intellectual disabilities. At times a service niche is found and they serve famously. In an earlier blog I mentioned the man who served communion for many years who worked as a pot scrubber professionally. I have known of people who have served in the nursery, or worked with children of the church. Another man was simply present in a resource room to help when he could, but to also keep an eye on the food and materials there to keep scavengers out.

In most of these cases, the terms of service were suddenly stopped. In the case of the pot scrubber, there was a change over in the leadership and he was determined to be no longer mentally competent to provide the service (although he had for many years prior to the change over). In the case of the nursery worker, his goofy interactions with parents about what he thought Jesus' favorite color was, or some other fabrication he came up with caused him to be no longer able to rock babies to sleep in his perfect grandfather lap. Another person left due to the depression he was facing and has not been able to regain his status as an assistant with the children. Another was replaced with a person without disability.

In filling spots where service is needed in local churches, those who fill the spots and those who supervise the filling both have to be aware of the human resources within a church and be more surgical, more judicious in filling those spots. I will use myself as an example.

I have been contacted on many occasions to serve in a variety of capacities within my church. These opportunities have ranged from drama, to movement, to ushering, to ministry leadership. With each of these opportunities I have to ask myself whether 1) this is the best use of my gifts and 2) are there others who might do this thing whose place I am taking. Now my assumption here is that I am looking for opportunities to serve, not simply providing the above as reasons not to serve. For example I have often turned down opportunities because I recognize that without my service to persons with disabilities at my church, the ministry might be limited and might not grow. So I turn down opportunities at drama and take up opportunities to work with persons with disability. I do that both because my gifts are in the area of disability ministry, and there are others who are able to fill the spots in the other ministries.

All that to say, that there are opportunities for ministry, say taking the offering for example, which persons with intellectual disabilities can do just as well as those without disability. Perhaps those spots should be reserved for individuals with disability. Can you imagine if a team of 8 people with Down's syndrome came forward to take the offering at a church! Pretty cool. Those individuals without disability who are engaged in service, like taking the offering, might stretch themselves to use more of their talents by perhaps assisting in a ministry like children's' Sunday school, leading a Bible study, or some other form of ministry. This is not to disdain those who serve via the taking of offering, etc., however, in the economy of opportunities for service, the economy of people willing to serve, human resources must be used judiciously so that as many as possible can have the opportunity to serve. We also must be careful to keep people from "copping out" by only serving in an unchallenging manner.

Of course service is important independent of what it is. If it is really true that in churches 10% of the people do 90% of the work, then that is a symptom of a larger problem. The point here is not to dismiss myself from doing the menial service of a church. Rather it is to do the challenging service of the church and the menial service of the church, but to also look to others to do what they can, to do what is within their ability level in service as well.

The Bible talks about David and his desire to build the temple. God "credited" David for his desire to build the temple even though he didn't permit him to actually build it. Will people with intellectual disability only be "credited" by God for their desire to serve, or will we work to provide actual opportunities for them to serve. It may require our speaking up when an opportunity comes to us, saying "I am willing to do this, but have you considered a person with disability for this position? Why don't you ask one of them first, and then I will help if no one is available." It will also require our stretching ourselves to take on the more challenging aspects of service.

Tuesday, June 22, 2004

354

A Conclusion.

Description of a nightmare

A friend of mine is a man who attends my church. He is a big guy, about 6'1" and wide as well. He likes to work out. He is also a man with an intellectual disability. He has been attending the church for about 7 years. Yesterday at church he pulled me aside (true story).

"I had this terrible dream last night...it was a nightmare!" he said.
"What happened?" I asked.
"Well I dreamed that nobody in the church loved me anymore."
"Well, you know that isn't true" I quickly replied.
"Oh sure, I know that. Everybody loves me down here. It was just a dream. It was just a nightmare."

I have had that nightmare, most often when I am awake, and it doesn't have to do with me personally per se. I am glad that for my friend it is only a dream and when he awakes he knows that it was just a dream. For too many people, however, the dream is that they have a place in church and are loved. The nightmare is when they are awake, when the reality of their situation where they are isolated and in need of love and companionship visits them again.

Monday, August 06, 2007

Dr. Jeff McNair is a Professor of Special Education and advocate for persons with intellectual disabilities. He has spent his career working to open Christian churches to include individuals with disabilities. He maintains a web page at http://jeffmcnair.com and a weblog on the topic at http://www.disabledchristianity.blogspot.com

If you would like to contact Dr. McNair, you can email him at mail@jeffmcnair.com, or at his post office box,

Jeff McNair
P.O. Box 7415
Redlands, CA 92375